Assessment in Student Affairs

Assessment in Student Affairs

A Guide for Practitioners

M. Lee Upcraft

John H. Schuh

With contributions from Theodore K. Miller,
Patrick T. Terenzini, and Elizabeth J. Whitt

Jossey-Bass Publishers • San Francisco

Published by Jossey-Bass
A Wiley Imprint
989 Market Street, San Francisco, CA 94103-1741   www.josseybass.com

Jossey-Bass books and products are available through most bookstores. To contact Jossey-Bass directly call our Customer Care Department within the U.S. at (800) 956-7739, outside the U.S. at (317) 572-3986 or fax (317) 572-4002.

Jossey-Bass also publishes its books in a variety of electronic formats. Some content that appears in print may not be available in electronic books.

Library of Congress Cataloging-in-Publication Data

Upcraft, M. Lee.
    Assessment in student affairs : a guide for practitioners / M. Lee Upcraft, John H. Schuh.
        p. cm.—(The Jossey-Bass higher and adult education series)
    Includes bibliographical references (p.) and index.
    ISBN 0-7879-0212-8
    1. Student affairs services—United States—Evaluation—Handbooks, manuals, etc.
    2. Education, Higher—United States—Evaluation—Handbooks, manuals, etc.
    I. Schuh, John H. II. Title. III. Series.
    LB2342.9.U63   1996
    378.1'98'06—dc20   95-46016

Printed in the United States of America
FIRST EDITION
HB Printing 10 9 8 7

The Jossey-Bass
Higher and Adult Education Series

Contents

Preface   xi

Authors and Contributors   xvii

Part One: The Context for Assessment in Student Affairs

1 Why Student Affairs Needs a Comprehensive
   Approach to Assessment   3
2 Key Questions to Ask in Assessment   32
3 Using Qualitative Methods   52
4 Using Quantitative Methods   84
   Patrick T. Terenzini and M. Lee Upcraft

Part Two: Dimensions of Assessment in Student Affairs

5 Tracking Clients' Use of Services, Programs,
   and Facilities   113
6 Assessing Student Needs   126
7 Assessing Student Satisfaction   148
8 Assessing Campus Environments   166
9 Assessing Student Cultures   189
   Elizabeth J. Whitt
10 Assessing Program and Service Outcomes   217
   Patrick T. Terenzini and M. Lee Upcraft
11 Benchmarking: Comparing Performance Across
   Organizations   240
12 Measuring Effectiveness Against Professional
   Standards   252
   Theodore K. Miller

Part Three: Assessment Challenges for Practitioners

13   Reporting and Using Assessment Results   275
14   Maintaining High Standards of Ethics and Integrity   290
15   Making Assessment Work: Guiding Principles and
      Recommendations   315

      Appendix   325
      References   345
      Index   363

Preface

At the time of this writing, one of us had recently attended a meeting in the office of his institution's governing board. The discussion among a group of senior student affairs officers turned to the board's concern about eroding public confidence in higher education. The participants agreed that an assessment should be conducted for the board so that the quality of higher education could be demonstrated to the state legislature and to the citizens of the state. We can only assume that a similar discussion is occurring ever more frequently all over the country.

In the past several years, the assessment movement in higher education has grown dramatically. Colleges and universities have come under increasing pressure from their various constituencies to demonstrate their effectiveness in measurable terms. The federal government, state legislatures, state boards of education, accrediting associations, boards of control, parents and families, students, and the general public are demanding better results and greater accountability from higher education. Unacceptable dropout rates; increased attendance costs; scarce resources; lack of equitable access; graduates who are underprepared, underemployed, or unemployed; faculty who seem to teach less and less; and employers who believe today's graduates are not prepared for the world of work are just some of the many reasons why the citizenry are demanding the reform of higher education. Demands for this reform are not exclusively the result of public pressure. Institutions must respond to internal pressure to improve the quality of students' education, both inside and outside the classroom.

The myriad pressures for reform have a huge impact on student affairs. As resources become more scarce, the question "Why student affairs?" is asked more frequently, and by persons or constituencies with considerable power. Faculty ask why student affairs should be funded when resources for academic programs are scarce. Students and their families demand accountability for fees spent for student services and programs; they insist that funds are spent in accordance with their wishes.

Student affairs practitioners must have some basis upon which to answer these external and internal demands for reform, and we believe a comprehensive assessment program can be an effective means not only of answering external critics but also of improving the quality of student services, programs, and facilities.

As student affairs practitioners with some combined fifty-five years of experience, we have struggled to find a single resource to guide the development of a comprehensive student affairs assessment program. It was toward that end that this book was written. We wanted to write a book that would prepare the practitioner to answer such questions as why to assess, what to assess, and how to assess. Perhaps most important, we wanted to show practitioners how to use assessment results to influence policy and practice as well as to communicate to both internal and external constituencies the worth, importance, and effectiveness of student affairs.

But let us move back to the board office for a moment. Although there was general agreement that an assessment should be conducted, no one was quite sure what kind. Should it be an outcomes assessment, where the impact of higher education on student achievement across the state is measured? Perhaps it should be a satisfaction assessment, where students are asked to rate their satisfaction with their educational experiences? Or should it be an assessment comparing the educational offerings of the state with those of other states? No conclusions were reached, but the more cogent fact is that these questions represented a very limited and somewhat simplistic view of assessment.

Audience

Assessment in Student Affairs is directed to student affairs practitioners from the most senior student affairs officer to all staff levels. Senior staff will want to use this book's comprehensive assessment model to help deal with issues such as accountability, quality, accessibility, accreditation, and affordability, among others. It can also be used as an important tool in strategic planning, policy development, decision making, problem solving, and other administrative issues. But perhaps most important of all, this book can help address the basic issue of justifying the existence of student affairs, helping to communicate our worth and effectiveness to faculty, students, other administrators, and important external constituencies. Student affairs staff addressing more practical concerns will use this book as they attempt to assess student needs, student satisfaction, campus environments, campus cultures, and student outcomes.

One of our dilemmas in writing this book was how to keep it practitioner-focused. On the one hand, by drawing upon the wealth of information available in the social science and educational research and evaluation literature, we wanted to give the practitioner a context within which to view assessment. On the other hand, we wanted to produce a book which practitioners would actually read and which would give them the ability to understand and conduct assessment studies. In other words, we were aiming for something between a research text and an assessment cookbook. In an effort to find this middle ground, we cover some topics in a somewhat cursory manner, while others are covered in greater detail. Our middle ground, then, consists of a presentation of key assessment concepts—using specific assessment studies as examples—as well as specifics about such student affairs functional areas as residence life, counseling, and career placement.

Because of our "middle ground" perspective, students, faculty, and graduate students in professional preparation programs may find this book helpful, both as an overview of student affairs assessment and as a guide to their own assessment efforts.

Overview of the Contents

This book was written under the assumption that it would seldom be read from cover to cover by busy practitioners. However, we recommend that all readers review the first two chapters, which provide an overview of assessment and establish a framework for the rest of the book. In addition, everyone should read Chapter Thirteen, on reporting and using assessment results; Chapter Fourteen, on the ethics of assessment; and Chapter Fifteen, which summarizes the book. Readers can then go to the chapters that match their interests and needs. Also, it will be helpful to note that we have tried to develop Chapters Three through Twelve as stand-alone chapters.

Although this structure will be convenient for the busy practitioner, the resulting redundancy may frustrate people reading the book from beginning to end.

Part One provides the reader with a context for the rest of the book. Chapter One reviews the reasons why both higher education and student affairs should take assessment seriously, offers a basic vocabulary within which to discuss assessment, reviews the assessment process, discusses some basic principles of good assessment practice, and describes a comprehensive model for student affairs assessment upon which the rest of the book is based.

Chapter Two attempts to answer some frequently asked questions about how to conduct assessment studies, while providing readers with enough information to ensure that quality and useful assessment studies are conducted. Chapters Three and Four discuss qualitative and quantitative methodologies—two quite different but complementary approaches to assessment—in a way that we hope the nontechnical reader will understand. (Chapter Three was coauthored by Patrick T. Terenzini.)

Part Two provides the reader with eight specific types of assessment included in the comprehensive assessment model presented in Chapter One. Chapter Five discusses how to track clientele use of services, programs, and facilities, both as an assessment method and as a way of providing baseline data for other forms of assessment. Assessing student needs is the focus of Chapter Six, which emphasizes that our services, programs, and facilities should be based on systematic approaches to student needs rather than on intuition or anecdotal impressions.

Chapter Seven explains how to assess student satisfaction, stressing the importance of delivering services and programs in ways that students see as beneficial. Environmental assessment is discussed in Chapter Eight, where we broaden our vision of assessment to include the aggregate as well as the individual. In Chapter Nine, guest author Elizabeth J. Whitt discusses how to assess student cultures, focusing on the fact that peer groups are very powerful influences on students. Assessing outcomes is the topic of Chapter Ten (coauthored by Patrick T. Terenzini). This chapter stresses the importance of demonstrating to our various constituencies that what we do has some measurable impact on those we serve. Chapter Eleven focuses on the importance of assessing what we do in relation to other comparable institutions, organizations, and student affairs divisions and departments. Chapter Twelve, by guest author Theodore K. Miller, discusses the use of standards as a means of assessment, focusing on those developed for student affairs by the Council for the Advancement of Standards in Higher Education and by accrediting agencies.

Part Three offers three concluding chapters, which are important to those conducting assessments. Throughout this book we stress the importance of reporting and communicating assessment results in ways that influence policy and practice. Chapter Thirteen provides readers with a blueprint for ensuring that assessment results will have an impact. Of course, assessment must be approached within a context that ensures rigorous adherence to ethical principles, and Chapter Fourteen discusses ethical issues related to assessment. The final chapter integrates and summarizes the book, offering some guiding principles for assessment and reemphasizing the importance of assessment for student affairs.

To reinforce our concern with the needs of the practitioner, throughout the book we have offered several examples of assessment studies. These examples include needs assessment studies, satisfaction studies, environmental and student culture studies, outcomes studies, and others within the overall context of student affairs, as well as studies of specific functional units such as counseling centers, health centers, residence halls, student activities, career placement offices, and others.

Acknowledgments

As the saying goes, when you see a turtle sitting on a fencepost, you know it had some help getting there. We "turtles" must first thank our office staff, including Joan Sherman and Rebecca Murphy at Wichita State University, and Sally Kelley, Suzanne Worth, and Regina Shaw Biddle at Penn State University. These folks were extremely helpful in preparing the manuscript and we are very grateful to them.

No one was more helpful to us in writing this book than our colleague Patrick T. Terenzini, Senior Research Scientist at Penn State's Center for the Study of Higher Education. He provided especially valuable assistance in coauthoring two chapters and consulting on several others. We also owe a great debt to Elizabeth Whitt and Ted Miller for agreeing to contribute chapters to this book and producing very high quality work.

We also wish to acknowledge the advice and support of Gale Erlandson at Jossey-Bass Publishers, who first suggested this topic to us, as well as other support staff at Jossey-Bass. Of course, none of this work could have been accomplished without the patient support of our family and friends. Thanks to all of them. Finally, when we started this project, we were valued professional colleagues and friends. We still are!

January 1996

M. Lee Upcraft
State College, Pennsylvania

John H. Schuh
Wichita, Kansas

Authors and Contributors

Authors

M. Lee Upcraft is a research associate at the Center for the Study of Higher Education, assistant vice president emeritus for student affairs, and affiliate professor emeritus of higher education at the Pennsylvania State University. He received his B.A. degree (1960) in history and his M.A. degree (1961) in guidance and counseling, both from the State University of New York, Albany, and his Ph.D. degree (1967) in personnel administration from Michigan State University.

During his more than thirty years in higher education, Upcraft has served in various student affairs administrative and faculty positions. His published works include *Residence Hall Assistants in College* (1982, with G. T. Pilato), *Learning to Be a Resident Assistant* (1982, with G. T. Pilato and D. J. Peterman), *Orienting Students to College* (1984), *The Freshman-Year Experience* (1989, with J. N. Gardner and Associates), *Managing Student Affairs Effectively* (1988, with M. J. Barr), *New Futures for Student Affairs* (1990, with M. J. Barr and Associates), *Designing Successful Transitions: A Guide for Orienting Students to College* (1993, with R. Mullendore, B. Barefoot, D. Fidler, and Associates), and *Academic Advising for First-Year Students* (1995, with G. Kramer and Associates). In addition, he is associate editor of *New Directions for Student Services*. He has received the Outstanding Contribution to the Profession awards from the college personnel associations of New York and Pennsylvania, the Outstanding Contributions to the Orientation Profession award from the National Orientation Directors Association (NODA), and the Contribution to Literature or Research award from the National Association of Student Personnel Administrators (NASPA). In 1993 he was elected a senior scholar of the American College Personnel Association (ACPA).

John H. Schuh is associate vice president of student affairs at Wichita State University, where he is also a professor in the Counseling and School Psychology department. Previously he held administrative and faculty appointments at Arizona State University and Indiana University. He earned his B.A. degree (1969) in history from the University of Wisconsin, Oshkosh, his Master of Counseling degree (1972) from Arizona State University, and his Ph.D. degree (1974) in higher education from Arizona State University.

The author, coauthor, or editor of over 125 publications, including ten books and monographs, Schuh has served on the executive boards of the National Association of Student Personnel Administrators (NASPA), the American College Personnel Association (ACPA), and the ACUHO-I. He was joint principal investigator (with G. D. Kuh) of the College Experiences Study, which led to the books *Involving Colleges* (1991, with G. D. Kuh, E. J. Whitt, and Associates) and *The Role of Contributions of Study Affairs in Involving Colleges* (1991, coedited with G. D. Kuh). He has been the publications coordinator for ACUHO-I, the media editor and chair for ACPA, and the associate editor of the *Journal of College Student Development*. He has also served on the editorial boards of the NASPA monograph series, ACPA Media, the *Journal of College and University Student Housing*, and the *Journal of College Student Development*.

Schuh has received the Contribution to Knowledge award from ACPA, the Leadership and Service award from ACUHO-I, and the Contribution to Literature or Research award from NASPA. He has also been elected a senior scholar of ACPA and received the Annuit Coeptis award from that organization. In 1994, Schuh received a Fulbright to study higher education in Germany.

Contributors

Theodore K. Miller is a professor of counseling and human development services at the University of Georgia, where he also heads the Department of Counseling and Human Development Services and is coordinator of student development in the Hager Education Preparation Program within the College of Education's School of Professional Studies. He earned his B.S. degree (1954) in business and English and his M.A. degree (1957) in counseling and guidance, both from Ball State University. His Ed.D. degree (1962) in counseling and student personnel services is from the University of Florida.

Over the past thirty years, Miller has gained extensive experience as a practitioner and scholar in student affairs. He has coauthored or edited numerous books, including *Using Professional Standards in Student Affairs* (1991). He served as president (1979–1989) of the Council for the Advancement of Standards in Higher Education and was coeditor of the *CAS Standards and Guidelines for Student Services/Development Programs* (1986) and the *CAS Standards for Self-Assessment Guides* (1988, 1989, 1991). He has directed nearly fifty doctoral dissertations and has been a consultant to more than eighty-five colleges and universities. In 1992, Miller was awarded NASPA's Robert H. Shaffer Award for Excellence as a graduate faculty member.

Patrick T. Terenzini is a professor of higher education and a senior scientist in the Center for the Study of Higher Education at the Pennsylvania State University. He is the associate director of the U.S. Department of Education's National Center for Postsecondary Testing, Learning, and Assessment. He received his A.B. degree (1964) in English from Dartmouth College, his M.A.T. degree (1965) in English education from Harvard University, and his Ph.D. degree (1972) in higher education from Syracuse University.

Terenzini has written numerous journal articles and book chapters, but he is best known for his collaboration with Ernest T. Pascarella in the landmark publication, *How College Affects Students* (1991). He is the editor in chief of *New Directions for Institutional Research,* associate editor of *Higher Education: Handbook of Theory and Research,* and a consulting editor for *Research in Higher Education.* He has received research awards from the college personnel associations of the states of New York and Pennsylvania, the Association for Institutional Research, the Association for the Study of Higher Education, the American College Personnel Association, and the National Association of Student Personnel Administrators. In 1994, he was elected a senior scholar of the ACPA.

Elizabeth J. Whitt is an associate professor in the College of Education at the University of Illinois at Chicago (UIC). She received her B.A. degree (1973) in history from Drake University, her M.A.

degree (1977) in college student personnel administration from Michigan State University, and her Ph.D. degree (1988) in higher education and sociology from Indiana University.

Prior to moving to UIC, Whitt served on the faculties at Oklahoma State University and Iowa State University, and she worked in residence life and student affairs administration at Michigan State; the University of Nebraska, Lincoln; and Doane College. She currently serves on the board of directors of the National Association of Student Personnel Administrators and the editorial boards of the *Review of Higher Education, ASHE/ERIC Higher Education Reports,* and the *NASPA Journal.* Her research interests include college student learning experiences, students in women's colleges, qualitative research methods, and college and university cultures.

Assessment in Student Affairs

Part One

The Context for Assessment in Student Affairs

Why Student Affairs Needs a Comprehensive Approach to Assessment

Those of us who have been involved in the assessment of student affairs services, programs, and facilities over the past few years often get calls from colleagues which go something like this: "Hey, you've been doing assessment stuff for a while. I need some help. We just had a very bad racial incident on our campus and things are very tense. My boss believes we need some data about race relations on our campus, in part because we don't have anything, and in part because we need to do something positive instead of just reacting. Do you have any surveys you might recommend? You know, something 'quick and dirty' we could do to take some of the pressure off."

A second version of this conversation: "We're really on the spot just now. There's a faculty 'Futures Committee' which is asking some tough but very naive questions about certain student services, because our college is going through some rough financial times, and clearly there will be substantial cutbacks. The faculty, of course, has their sights on reducing 'nonessential' student services first. Many services have been targeted for reduction or elimination by the faculty. For example, they ask, 'Why do we need psychological counseling? If students are troubled, let them pay for those services themselves, or get help off campus. After all, we're an educational institution, not a rehabilitation agency.' Do you have a needs assessment survey which would help us convince the faculty that students need psychological services?"

All too often it is the case that, while these problems are real, the solutions are not. Responding to a crisis with a survey is not assessment; it is crisis management. Assessment is a very complex process of which the selection and use of an instrument may be only a part, or no part at all. In reality, the mindless surveying of students in a crisis situation will probably do much more harm than good. Not only will it not solve the problem, but it will destroy the credibility of assessment as an important tool for gathering information about student programs, services, and facilities. Assessment in a crisis situation will also destroy the assessment's potential for determining the worth of such services, programs, and facilities, and communicating this worth to important political constituencies.

For many reasons—which are discussed in more detail later in this chapter—student affairs needs high-quality and comprehensive assessment programs. Unfortunately, among many staff in student affairs, assessment is an unknown quantity at best, or, at the worst, it is misunderstood and misused. It has been our experience that while everyone in student affairs would agree that assessment is important, too often it is considered a low priority and never conducted in any systematic, comprehensive way. And even if it is done, it is often done poorly; as a result, it simply gathers dust on someone's shelf, with little or no impact.

One of the reasons for this situation is the fact that many of us fail to understand why assessment is important in the first place. This lack of understanding is compounded by confusion over what we mean by assessment and the assessment process, and how to conduct assessment in ways that are consistent with good practice. Even if all these issues are clear, we may not have a framework within which to develop a comprehensive assessment program.

In this chapter, we discuss the first step in implementing an assessment program: establishing an assessment rationale that all our constituencies will understand—including students, student affairs staff, administrators, faculty, and boards of control, as well as legislators, accreditation agencies, graduates, funding agencies, and the general public. We also (1) review several reasons why assessment is important, for both higher education and student affairs, (2) develop a vocabulary within which to discuss assessment, (3) review the assessment process, (4) discuss some basic principles of good assessment practice, and (5) describe a comprehensive model for assessment in student affairs upon which the rest of the book is based.

Why Assessment in Higher Education?

There are plenty of reasons why higher education should take assessment seriously. Since the 1970s, assessment has become a growing and necessary part of higher education. At first, the assessment "movement" was considered by some to be just another fad that would quickly fade from the scene. They were wrong. In the mid 1980s, several national reports within higher education called for a greater emphasis on assessment in higher education, including the National Institute of Education (NIE) report, *Involvement in Learning* (1984), and Ernest Boyer's Carnegie Foundation report, *College: The Undergraduate Experience in America* (1987).

External pressure also mounted. In 1986, at their annual meeting, the governors from all fifty states declared that they wanted to hold higher education institutions more accountable for the performance of their students. Since that time, forty states have mandated one type of assessment or another, and all regional accreditation associations have adopted criteria for assessment-oriented outcomes (Marchese, 1990).

Tough questions are being asked. What is your college's contribution to student learning? Do your graduates know what you think they know and can they do what your degrees imply? How do you assure that? What do you intend that your students learn? At what level are students learning what you are teaching? Is that the level you intend? What combination of institutional and student effort would it take to get to a higher level of student learning? (Marchese, 1990). What *does* one get out of a college education? What *should* one get out of a college education? What *should* one get out of an education at this institution? How do we know? (Terenzini, 1989).

Just why all the fuss about accountability? For about 350 years, our citizenry accepted as a matter of faith that education was good and that our system of higher education was doing its job, and doing it well. The tremendous rise in enrollment since World War II was testimony to the country's unquestioned faith in the educational, if not economic, benefits of higher education. What happened? What caused the public—and many in higher education—to lose faith?

Many factors have contributed to the current environment. First, there are too many examples of people with college degrees who do not appear to be educated, even in the most basic sense of that term: graduates who are unable to read, write, compute, reason, or do anything else indicative of an educated person. Other graduates come out of college seemingly ill-prepared for the world of work, as evidenced by the increasing amount of time spent by employers in training and retraining new college graduates (Wingspread Group, 1993). In other words, the public is gaining the impression that higher education is not producing what it promised: educated persons prepared for the world of work. Thus, accountability becomes an issue.

Second, the public is increasingly dissatisfied because of the rising cost of higher education. For example, from 1973 to 1988, college costs rose more than 200 percent, a pace well ahead of inflation rates for that same period (*Parade,* Mar. 19, 1989). The cost of four years at an Ivy League school is now well over $100,000, and the question being asked is, "Is it worth it?" Even more distressing to students and their families is the declining availability and sufficiency of federal and state grant and loan programs (Astin and others, 1991; Schuh, 1993a). As a result, more students are relying on their families, their savings, and part-time jobs to finance their educations. For example, in 1990, about 80 percent of students said they were getting financial help from their families, compared to 66 percent in 1980 (Astin and others, 1991). So, cost has become a big issue.

Third, there is increasing dissatisfaction with the quality of instruction at many institutions. This dissatisfaction includes large classes, fewer faculty who actually teach, poor academic advising, an emphasis on research at the expense of teaching, failure to do anything about poor teaching, and so forth. In the opinion of many educators at many of our large, public research universities, the learning experience—particularly at the freshman and sophomore levels—is largely passive, delivered through lectures and focusing on the memorization of information that is verified through multiple-choice examinations (Upcraft, 1996).

This external dissatisfaction about the quality of higher education has revitalized ongoing efforts within the institution to improve and renewed internal commitment to quality. Signs of this change are the "total quality" efforts cropping up at many institutions. These are based on the principles of total quality management developed by Edwards Deming (1986) and applied to higher education by several others (Teeter and Lozier, 1993; Sherr and Teeter, 1991; Cornesky, McCool, Byrnes, and Weber, 1991). So, quality is an issue.

Fourth, and no less important, are the issues of access and equity in higher education. While higher education has made considerable strides toward becoming more inclusive and diverse by race, ethnicity, gender, disability, sexual orientation, age, socioeconomic status, and other factors, many groups are still underrepresented. Even more alarming is the discrepancy between the success rates of traditionally underrepresented groups and those of the majority. For many underrepresented groups, dropout rates are higher and graduation rates lower. The public, particularly those from underrepresented groups, wants to know why. So, access and equity are issues.

And finally, assessment is now a part of the accreditation of higher education institutions. According to the Commission on Higher Education's *Standards for Accreditation* (1982), one of the criteria for accreditation is outcomes or institutional effectiveness. "The deciding factor in assessing the effectiveness of any institution is evidence of the extent to which it achieves its goals and objectives. The necessity of seeking such evidence continually is inescapable; one of the primary hallmarks of faculty, administration, and governing boards is the skill with which they raise questions about institutional effectiveness, seek answers, and significantly improve procedures in the light of their findings" (pp. 17–18). This moves assessment from the "nice to have if you can afford it" category to the "you had better have it if you want to get accredited" category. So, accreditation is an issue.

Why Assessment in Student Affairs?

A Matter of Survival

As questions of accountability, cost, quality, access, equity, and accreditation combine to make assessment a necessity in higher education, they also make assessment a fundamental necessity in student affairs as well. Are we delivering what we promised, and are we doing so in a cost-effective, high-quality way? Do our services and programs provide access to underrepresented groups, and are our campus environments free of bigotry, discrimination, and prejudice? Do our services, programs, and facilities contribute to student learning? These and other questions place an enormous responsibility on student affairs to develop assessment programs which measure the extent to which these overarching institutional goals are being met.

For student affairs, variations on these questions are being asked and new ones posed, both from outside and inside of student affairs. Perhaps the most important of all is this basic question: In an era of declining resources, are student services and programs really necessary? As resources decline and pressures for accountability increase, there is a natural tendency for institutions to reallocate resources to its academic priorities, allocations which are most often narrowly interpreted as support for the faculty, the classroom, the formal curriculum, and those support services that are *clearly* academically related, such as learning support centers and academic advising.

Unfortunately, this narrow academic focus ignores the substantial evidence that the out-of-class environment is an important factor in learning, development, academic achievement, and retention. Also ignored is the substantial evidence that student use of student services, programs, and facilities enhances such outcomes, which are usually interpreted as strictly academic. In short, the fact of student learning and development outside the classroom is not understood among decision makers and seldom taken into account when decisions are made to reallocate resources to narrowly defined academic priorities.

For example, when reviewing the many studies that identify the factors required for persistence and degree completion, Pascarella and Terenzini (1991) concluded that one's level of integration into an institution's social system has significant implications for educational attainment. For example, both involvement in extracurricular activities and the extent and quality of one's social interaction with student peers and faculty have a positive influence on degree attainment, educational aspirations, and graduate school attendance. Living on campus rather than commuting has a strong positive effect on persistence and degree completion, particularly in living-and-learning residence halls, where students' academic and social life are programmatically linked. Participation in orientation programs and freshman seminars have also been positively linked to persistence and degree completion.

Upcraft (1985) reviewed other studies which showed that belonging to student organizations, involvement in social and cultural activities, attending lectures, using campus facilities, and general participation in extracurricular activities are all activities which enhance retention. There is also evidence that the availability and use of student personnel and counseling services is positively related to graduation rates (Hedlund and Jones, 1970).

In spite of this very conclusive evidence, there are strong indications that "student services have borne the brunt of budget cuts. . . . For college administrators, it was a Hobson's choice: to shield academic programs from severe cuts, all other budget categories had to suffer a disproportionate share of reductions" (Cage, 1992, p. A25). Examples include substantial cuts in student activities and support for student government, reduction in career and psychological counseling staff, and outright elimination of programs and services considered less essential, such as legal counseling. In addition, some student services have survived only by initiating fees for such services as placement, health services, student activities, and counseling (Cage, 1992). Another trend is to eliminate selected services and programs, on the assumption that student needs can be met by off-campus and community services. In other words, substantial evidence underscores the contribution of student services and programs to persistence and degree attainment, but that evidence, to date, appears to have had little impact on resource allocations.

As a result, student affairs must respond not only to the more global pressures of accountability, cost, quality, access, and equity but also to internal pressure to justify allocation of resources to programs and services that appear to be "nonacademic" and therefore "less essential" to the educational enterprise. Student affairs needs to demonstrate its central role in the academic success of students, and the potentially detrimental effect if student services and programs are curtailed, eliminated, offered differentially depending upon one's ability to pay, or handed off to community agencies which may or may not be prepared to handle students' demands.

Thus, demonstrating the importance of student affairs to the educational enterprise starts with the rationale for our existence. Unfortunately, student affairs is somewhat divided on this point. One view is probably best represented by the National Association of Student Personnel Administrators (NASPA)'s *Perspective on Student Affairs* (1987), in which the first assumption identified is that the academic mission of an institution is preeminent: "Colleges and universities organize their primary activities around the academic experience: the curriculum, the library, the classroom, and the laboratory. The work of student affairs should not compete with and cannot substitute for that academic enterprise. As a partner in the educational enterprise, student affairs enhances and supports the academic mission" (pp. 9–10). In other words, everything we do must somehow contribute to the academic mission of the institution, most often defined as students' academic achievement and retention.

A second perspective is best described as promoting student development. That is, there are certain developmental goals (such as psychosocial development, attitudes and values formation, moral development, and career choice and development) which are related to, but somewhat apart from, academic goals (such as verbal, quantitative, and subject matter competence, and cognitive and intellectual growth). In this view, student affairs assumes the primary responsibility for the achievement of developmental goals, while faculty assume the primary responsibility for the achievement of academic goals. Thus, everything we do in this scenario must somehow contribute to students' development.

The debate over the basic purposes of student affairs has been reignited recently by two very important publications. The first, a position paper developed by the American College Personnel Association titled *The Student Learning Imperative* (1994) argues for a refocusing of the basic mission of student affairs toward the concept of "student learning." We must be concerned not only about affective development and the out-of-class environment but also about cognitive development, both in and out of class. According to this document, "Student Affairs professionals must seize the present moment by affirming student learning and personal development as the primary goals of undergraduate education" (p. 4).

A recent publication goes even further. Bloland, Stamatakos, and Rogers (1994) argue that the uncritical adoption of "student development" in the 1970s is too narrowly focused on psychosocial development, shifting the role of student affairs away from educating the "whole student." They argue that the mission of higher education consists of learning "not only substantive facts but also values, ethics, an informed way of life and occupational identity, personal and occupational skills—the list goes on—but the focus [should be] on what is learned, not what is developed" (p. 101). On the other hand, the recommended role of student affairs should be more than simply the support of the *academic* mission of the institution; it should support its *educational* mission as well.

To complicate matters even further, a third perspective holds that although academic and developmental outcomes are important, other equally important institutional and societal expectations must be addressed first. Providing basic services such as housing and financial aid is absolutely vital to the institution, as opposed to any educational or developmental outcome for which a student affairs office may aim. Students need a place to live, and we assume varying degrees of responsibility in helping them do that, not necessarily because of their educational or developmental interests, but because students will not be able to attend the institution if they do not have affordable, accessible, and livable housing.

Of course, in reality, we do all three: our services and programs contribute to both academic and developmental goals of students and provide basic services to students and other clientele. But it is also true that in an era of declining resources, it is much easier to defend student affairs' contributions to the academic mission of our institutions, or to students' and others' basic physical and financial needs, than to justify our existence strictly on the basis of our contribution to students' developmental goals. Put another way, faculty and upper-level management are more likely to support student affairs services and programs which contribute to academic outcomes such as academic achievement, cognitive development, and retention or provide effective basic services such as financial aid and housing than any contributions they might offer toward meeting developmental goals for students, goals which are somewhat "softer," perhaps less valued, and certainly more difficult to define, achieve, and assess.

By now, our bias should be clear. We believe the primary purpose of student affairs is to contribute to the academic enterprise and to meet the institution's need for basic services. We see student development as a legitimate but less important purpose of student affairs, viable only to the extent that it contributes to students' academic goals. And we see assessment as a way of making the connection between what we do, and how we contribute to the academic mission of our institutions and other institutional expectations. For example, through an assessment study we may find that students increase their interpersonal skills as a result of living in residence halls. That outcome may be important, but it will not do much to justify resource allocation for residence halls. Rather, we should attempt to show that there is a relationship between living in residence halls and such outcome variables as students' academic achievement and retention, or student decisions to select the institution in the first place, live in residence halls in the second place, and return to residence halls in subsequent years. Both of these outcomes (academic success and decisions to live in residence halls) may well be a function of how well students develop interpersonal skills, as well as creating interpersonally supportive residential environments, but it would not be effective to justify residence halls solely on the basis of the development of interpersonal skills; it is more feasible to encourage funding of residence halls on the evidence that the residence hall experience contributes positively to the academic success of students, or to their decision to attend an institution, live in residence halls once they enroll, or return to them in subsequent years.

Without assessment, student affairs is left only to logic, intuition, moral imperatives, goodwill, or serendipity in justifying its existence. To be sure, even the most comprehensive and highest-quality assessment is no guarantee that student affairs will survive, but it will go a long way toward making the argument of the importance of student affairs to students and to the institution.

A Matter of Quality

There are many other reasons, besides our survival, why we should have a commitment in student affairs to do assessment. Let's assume that the basic question of the value of student affairs to the institution has been answered affirmatively. There remain many other questions to consider. Even if it is demonstrated that student services, programs, and facilities are essential and needed, a second question is, are they of high quality? To be sure, quality is a somewhat illusive concept, subject to many definitions, depending on who is doing the defining. Generally speaking, high quality requires one to compare one's work against some predetermined standard, which may be absolutely defined (comparing oneself to the Council for the Advancement of Standards in Higher Education or other professional standards—see Chapter Twelve) or normatively defined (comparing oneself to comparable organizations—see Chapter Eleven).

But regardless of the definitions, questions of quality must be asked: Do we have high-quality programs, services, and facilities? How do we define quality, particularly when these definitions will vary from institution to institution, and even among departments within student affairs? What evidence do we have of quality, once properly defined, and what criteria are used to measure it? How do we know if we have improved quality? Assessment is a very important way of linking goals to outcomes, helping define quality, and determining if quality exists in student affairs. It is a fundamental responsibility of student affairs to provide services, programs, and facilities that are of high quality, however quality might be defined and for whomever.

A Matter of Affordability

Another reason for assessment in student affairs is to gauge affordability and cost-effectiveness. The question to be faced goes something like this: "Sure, this program or that service is needed, and there is evidence of their quality, but in an era of declining resources, can we afford them? Can we continue to fund them at current levels?" For example, let's assume that, based on an assessment of student needs, there is abundant evidence that someone should be available to give students legal advice. Let's further assume that, based on a customer satisfaction survey, there is also abundant evidence that legal clients are being very well served by the legal counselor. But let's also say that because this service is offered free of charge to students, it is exorbitantly expensive to the institution, particularly when compared to other student services and the number of students served. What then? A cost-benefit study may well help us decide what to do. It may be that the service is too costly, resulting in a discussion of ways to maintain the service at reduced levels, keep it alive using other resources (such as charging students fees for visits), or eliminate it altogether.

A Matter of Strategic Planning

A fourth reason for developing a comprehensive assessment program is for strategic planning. According to Baldridge (1983), "Strategic planning examines the big issues—the organization's purpose, its mission, its relationship to its environment, its share of the market, its interactions with other organizations. Strategic planning is not concerned with nuts-and-bolts issues. . . . [It] asks the basic questions of institutional health and survival" (p. 175). Assessment contributes to strategic planning by helping define goals and objectives, pointing to critical issues or problems that must be resolved successfully if the organization is to achieve its goals, providing baseline data so that student programs and policies can respond appropriately to students' needs, providing essential feedback about the effectiveness of long-range plans, and pointing to areas where plans must be modified to achieve goals. Assessment is especially important in the early phases of strategic planning, to identify strengths, weaknesses, and opportunities for the future; it is also important in the later stages of planning, when evaluation is important (Jacobi, Astin, and Ayala, 1987).

Assessment, then, can help us decide what we do, as well as how well we do it. For example, let's return to the issue of determining whether or not to continue to offer legal counseling to students. There are several ways assessment can help us make that decision. Is there evidence that legal counseling is a high-priority need for students? Is there evidence that sufficient numbers of students, representing the spectrum of students, use the legal counseling service? Is there evidence that legal counseling is done in a high-quality way? Is there evidence that students who use this service are satisfied with it? What would be the cost of improving this service? All these questions are best answered through systematic assessment, rather than sporadic anecdotal accounts, intuition, piecemeal bits of unrelated information, or no information at all.

A Matter of Policy Development and Decision Making

A fifth question, indirectly related to student services, programs, and facilities, is likewise very important: Do we have evidence to support this decision or policy? For example, on what basis did we decide to include sexual orientation in the institution's nondiscrimination clause? What evidence did we cite in the establishment of a center for women students on the campus? Was the decision to rescind our "hate speech" policy based on solid evidence? How do we decide who shall live in on-campus residence halls? And perhaps most important, on what basis do we decide to allocate resources? Thus, policies and decisions, if they are to be developed in a systematic and cogent way, must be driven at least in part by assessment results.

A Matter of Politics

A sixth reason for doing assessment is a practical one, sometimes not related to any of the other questions asked. We do it because someone or some institution of importance wants some information, which makes it politically important to produce. It is part of the "political evaluation" defined later in this chapter. For example, a state legislator, in response to a constituent who thinks residence hall fees are too high, may want to know how many RAs we have, what they do, what they are paid, and how we know they are doing a good job. While this information may be important for a variety of other reasons, we may not have chosen to assess this issue because it was less important than others. So we have to run off and get this information to satisfy a person who might well be very important to the funding or even survival of student affairs.

So there are many reasons why assessment is important for student affairs, including helping to develop a rationale for student affairs, determining and improving the quality of student affairs, analyzing and determining affordability, developing strategic plans, assisting in policy development and decision making, and dealing with political pressures and realities. The questions we are being asked are best answered when we can base them on a comprehensive assessment program. We in student affairs can no longer presume that our jobs are important and effective simply because we think they are or because we've always done them or even because we're doing the right thing. There must be evidence gathered from a comprehensive assessment program to answer these questions.

One more very important issue needs to be addressed at this point. Even if nationally based studies show the importance or effectiveness of student affairs, these studies may not be that important if they are not campus-specific. Tip O'Neill, the late speaker of the House of Representatives, once was reported to have said, "All politics is local." To paraphrase Tip, we believe that "all assessment is local." If our residence halls are unruly and do not contribute to the educational mission of our institution, then all the evidence of the general positive effect of residence halls will not make a difference if we don't have the evidence that good things are happening in *our* residence halls. If our counseling center has no evidence of its effectiveness, even if it is effective, then protecting our counseling centers from resource reductions, or elimination altogether, will be very difficult. If our campus alcohol prevention programs have no evidence of their impact on student knowledge, attitudes, and behaviors, even though there may be some studies reported in the literature which demonstrate such effects, then questions should and will be raised as to whether or not these programs should be continued.

Some Basic Definitions

Before we get too far into the assessment issue, we must provide a common language, because one of the causes of confusion about assessment is terminology. Some terms are used interchangeably ("assessment" and "evaluation"), some phrases are used incorrectly ("statistics show . . ."), and some terms are so vague as to strip them of any commonly accepted meaning ("quality" or "excellence"). So our discussion of assessment in student affairs must be prefaced by developing a common vocabulary.

Let's start with defining the term *assessment*. There are many definitions in the assessment and evaluation literature. One reason for this confusion is whether assessment involves simply gathering data, or if it also includes interpretation and analysis. For example, Astin (1991) defines assessment as "the gathering of information concerning the functioning of students, staff, and institutions of higher education" (p. 2). Others, notably Lenning (1988), would disagree, asserting that assessment involves more than just gathering information. "Assessment refers to gathering *evidence:* gathering data, transforming data so that they can be interpreted, applying analytical techniques, and analyzing data in terms of alternative hypotheses and explanations" (p. 328).

Another conflict regarding assessment is the purpose of assessment. Most would agree one purpose of assessment is the improvement of something, although there is wide disagreement over what it might improve. For example, mainstream academic assessment experts would restrict the term assessment to refer to only those efforts which demonstrate improvement in student learning (Hutchings and others, 1993; Terenzini, 1989). Others consider this definition too restrictive. For example, Banta (1988) defines assessment as "collecting evidence of (1) student performance on specified measures of development, (2) program strengths and weaknesses, and (3) institutional effectiveness" (p. 1). She argues that we should assess not only what students and graduates know, but what they are able to do with their knowledge, as well as their perceptions of the quality of institutional programs and services. Ewell (1988) agrees, for example, that student survey information can be particularly helpful in gaining broad insights into student perceptions.

But restricting assessment exclusively to student learning and perceptions is also debatable. Institutions of higher education have clientele other than students, and the perceptions of those people are also important. Astin (1991) believes the basic motive for assessment is the functioning of students, staff, and institutions not only for the purposes of student learning, but also for higher education's contribution to knowledge and to the greater society it serves. We prefer an approach which consciously adopts a broad definition of assessment, one that includes and also reaches beyond the collection and analysis of evidence about effectiveness to include *all* parts of the institution. Thus, although evidence for the quality of student learning is a major concern—in general education, for example, and in one's major or professional training—so, too, is evidence of the institution's success in such areas as the cocurricular program and an ethnically diverse campus community.

So what do we make of all these conflicting expert opinions? We can only make an admittedly arbitrary but, we hope, reasoned judgment. Therefore, for the purpose of this book, *assessment is any effort to gather, analyze, and interpret evidence which describes institutional, departmental, divisional, or agency effectiveness.* Effectiveness includes not only assessing student learning outcomes, but assessing other important outcomes as well (cost-effectiveness, clientele satisfaction, meeting clientele needs) for other constituents within the institution (the faculty, administration, governing boards) and outside the institution (alumni, legislators, funding agencies, accreditation agencies).

One further clarification: for the purposes of this book we are not particularly interested in assessing an individual student or other individual clientele outcomes. For example, this book will not cover how to assess an individual for the purposes of deciding his or her admission to an institution, or how to conduct a psychological screening of a potential client in a counseling center. We are interested in these assessments *in the aggregate*. That is, while we may not want information about how an individual prospective student is assessed, we may want to know if, in the aggregate, the students we assess actually persist and graduate. In the context of this book, we may not want information about an individual counseling client, but we may want to know if, in the aggregate, the information gathered in the screening process is actually helpful, on average, in the subsequent therapeutic process.

This definition of assessment is very broad. As will be seen in subsequent chapters, assessment by this definition ranges all the way from keeping track of who uses our services, programs, and facilities to whether or not such offerings have any impact, or the desired impact, on our clientele. It includes student needs assessments, environmental assessments, comparisons to accepted standards or other institutions, and clientele satisfaction with what we offer.

Assessment, however, must be contrasted with but also linked to *evaluation*. Here there is much greater agreement among the experts. Astin (1991) defines evaluation as the utilization of information for institutional and individual improvement. He believes that "there is a fundamental distinction . . . between the information we gather and the uses to which it is put, and that we often forget this distinction when we talk about assessment in higher education. Evaluation . . . has to do with motivation and the rendering of value judgments" (p. 2). Others agree. Ewell (1988) argues that assessment results should be used to make appropriate changes in instruction and support services, and to set the context for an entire range of decisions, from academic advising to the structure of student housing units. He also believes assessment information can be useful in selling a decision once it has been made.

Here again, for the purposes of this book, our arbitrary but reasoned judgment is that *evaluation is any effort to use assessment evidence to improve institutional, departmental, divisional, or agency effectiveness.* While assessment describes effectiveness, evaluation uses these descriptions in order to improve effectiveness, however that might be defined by an institution, department, division, or agency. For example, determining whether or not our admissions criteria predict subsequent persistence and degree completion is assessment. Using that assessment as a rationale for changing admissions criteria is evaluation. Likewise, determining whether or not the information gathered in psychological screening of clients is useful in subsequent therapy is assessment. Using that assessment as a rationale for changing the screening process, or eliminating it altogether, is evaluation.

Having defined evaluation in a general sense leads us to more precise definitions of various types of evaluation. Scriven (1967) was the first to distinguish between *formative* evaluation and *summative* evaluation. Simply put, formative evaluations are those used to improve organizational or institutional effectiveness. Formative evaluations typically focus on improving the processes which potentially lead to increased effectiveness. The admissions and counseling examples used above were clearly formative evaluations, because assessment results were used to improve effectiveness through the improvement of processes. Formative evaluations may also be used to help solve problems and to enhance decision making directed toward improvement.

Summative evaluations are used to determine if a particular organizational activity or function should be continued, enhanced, curtailed, or eliminated. In other words, summative evaluations are conducted for purposes of accountability and strategic planning. In the psychological counseling example, let's suppose that the improvement of the psychological screening process requires more funding because it involves hiring more qualified staff, developing more sophisticated psychometric techniques, and purchasing more computer hardware. Someone may decide that additional resources will be allocated, and the program enhanced. This would be a summative evaluation. On the other hand, someone may decide that such improvements are prohibitively expensive, and that if we can't do screening in a quality and cost-effective way, we shouldn't do it at all. Either we connect prospective clients to therapists without any screening, or eliminate counseling altogether. These evaluations are also summative, but with quite different outcomes.

To these two forms of evaluation Brown and Podolske (1993a) add a third: *political* evaluation, which they define as evaluation that is used to communicate and defend student affairs to potential stakeholders, including professional staff, office staff, faculty, administrators, parents, taxpayers, and funders. To these stakeholders we would add boards of control, state legislators and the general public (in the instance of public institutions), graduates, foundations, and, of course, the ever-present federal government with its vast array of legislation and regulations. Again, using the admissions example above, a state legislature concerned about admissions standards may require minimum scores on standardized admissions tests for the funding of certain institutions. In this instance, a cutoff score would be established for political rather than summative or formative reasons.

Two other terms also need to be defined: quantitative and qualitative methodologies. *Quantitative methodology* is the assignment of numbers to objects, events, or observations according to some rule (Rossman and El-Khawas, 1987). According to Borg and Gall (1989), "Quantitative researchers attempt to keep themselves from influencing the collection of data. Instruments with established psychometric properties . . . are used to collect data. Statistical methods are used to analyze data and draw conclusions. In other words, quantitative researchers attempt to be objective, meaning that they wish to develop an understanding of the world as it is 'out there,' independent of their personal biases, values, and idiosyncratic notions" (p. 23). Again, using the admissions example, the ability to predict college success might involve gathering all the quantifiable data about those variables that are thought to influence persistence and degree completion, such as high school grades, scores on standardized aptitude tests, involvement in high school activities, parents' education and income, etc. These data might then be correlated with subsequent student behavior (dropping out or persisting) to determine which ones, and in which combination, best predict college success. (For a more complete discussion of quantitative methods, see Chapter Four.)

On the other hand, *qualitative methodology* is the detailed description of situations, events, people, interactions, and observed behaviors; the use of direct quotations from people about their experiences, attitudes, beliefs, and thoughts; and the analysis of excerpts or entire passages from documents, correspondence, records, and case histories (Patton, 1990). According to Borg and Gall (1989), "Qualitative researchers view themselves as a primary instrument for collecting data. They rely partly or entirely on their feelings, impressions, and judgments in collecting data . . . and using their own interpretations in understanding the meaning of data" (p. 23). Using the admissions example, instead of (or in addition to) analyzing some numerical data, admissions personnel might want to interview students who persisted and those who dropped out to determine the extent to which their backgrounds and experiences might have contributed to their success or lack thereof. Variables that seem to predict college success but are difficult to measure (motivation), might be better understood through qualitative rather than quantitative measurements. (For a more complete discussion of qualitative methods, see Chapter Three.)

Another definition is worth mentioning, although it will not be a focus of this book. The term is *research*. In the 1960s and 1970s, it was fashionable to use the term "student affairs research" to refer to assessment and evaluation efforts. The term proved to be confusing, particularly to faculty, who had a much narrower definition of research. When comparing research and assessment, Erwin (1991) argues that although they share many processes in common, they differ at least in two respects. First, assessment guides good practice, while research guides theory and conceptual foundations. Second, assessment typically has implications for a single institution, while research typically has broader implications for student affairs and higher education.

Definitions of other important terms will be introduced as necessary in subsequent chapters. To review, assessment is the gathering, interpreting, and analyzing of evidence of effectiveness, while evaluation is how assessment results are used to improve effectiveness, however that may be defined. We can gather information through qualitative or quantitative methodologies, and we can use assessment results to evaluate student affairs by providing a rationale for our existence, improving quality, determining affordability, and guiding policy development and decision making. Assessment can also be used for strategic planning, helping administrators decide, for example, whether or not a particular student service, program, or facility should be enhanced, curtailed, or eliminated. And finally, assessment can meet the demands of those persons and institutions that have influence over what we do.

Principles of Good Practice for Assessment

Before we move to the more specific issues of the assessment process and a model of student affairs assessment, we should consider some general principles of good practice for assessment. In 1992, the American Association of Higher Education Assessment Forum invited twelve practitioners and students of assessment to develop common principles behind good practice for assessing student learning (Hutchings and others, 1993). Although these principles were developed with a focus on assessing student learning, with some adaptation they apply equally well to the assessment of student affairs.

1. *The assessment of student affairs begins with educational values.* Assessment is not an end in itself but a vehicle for organizational effectiveness. Its effective practice, then, begins with and enacts a vision of student affairs we most value. These values should drive not only *what* we choose to assess, but also *how* we do so. When questions about the organizational mission and values are skipped over, assessment threatens to be an exercise in measuring what's easy rather than what is needed.

2. *Assessment is most effective when it reflects an understanding of organizational outcomes as multidimensional, integrated, and revealed in performance over time.* Assessing student affairs is a complex process. It entails supporting the rationale for student affairs, developing evidence of quality and affordability, informing policy development and decision making, guiding strategic planning, and dealing with political realities. Assessment should employ a diverse array of methods, including both quantitative and qualitative approaches.

Such an approach aims for a more complete and accurate picture of the effectiveness of student affairs.

3.   *Assessment works best when it has clear, explicitly stated goals.* Assessment is a goal-oriented process. It entails comparing intended purposes and expectations derived from the institution's mission, and from the stated purposes and goals of the student affairs. Where student affairs lacks specificity of agreement, assessment as a process pushes student affairs toward clarity about where to aim and which standards to apply; it also prompts attention to where and how organizational goals will be offered and implemented. Clear, shared, implementable goals are the cornerstone for assessment that is focused and useful.

4.   *Assessment requires attention to outcomes but also, and just as important, to the processes that lead to them.* Information about outcomes is of high importance, but to improve outcomes, we need to know about the processes that lead to particular outcomes— counseling, advising, educational programming, budgeting, etc. Assessment can help us understand what processes work best under what conditions, with such knowledge comes the capacity to improve the whole organization.

5.   *Assessment works best when it is ongoing, not episodic.* Assessment is a process whose power is cumulative. Although an isolated, "one shot" assessment can be better than none, student affairs is best served when assessment entails a linked series of activities undertaken over time. This means tracking the progress of student affairs units or the whole student affairs organization; it may mean collecting some examples of assessment studies or using the same methods year after year. The point is to monitor progress toward intended goals with the intention of enhancing organizational effectiveness. Along the way, the assessment process itself should be evaluated and refined in light of emerging insights.

6.   *Assessment is most effective when representatives from across student affairs and the institution are involved.* Assessment is a way of enacting the many responsibilities of student affairs and the institution. Thus, while assessment efforts may start on a small scale, the aim over time is to involve all people whose interests may be affected by assessment. Student affairs staff play an especially important role, but assessment's questions cannot be fully addressed without participation by students, student affairs leadership, and others in the educational community. Assessment may also involve

individuals from the institution as well as those outside it (graduates, trustees, employers), whose experience can enrich the sense of appropriate aims and standards for organizational effectiveness. Thus understood, assessment is not a task for small groups of experts, but rather a collaborative activity; its aim is wiser, better-informed attention to organizational effectiveness by all parties who have a stake in the organization.

7.   *Assessment makes a difference when it begins with issues of use and illuminates questions that people really care about.* Assessment recognizes the value of information in the process of improving student affairs. But to be useful, the information must be connected to issues or questions that people really care about. This implies assessment approaches that produce evidence that the relevant parties will find credible, suggestive, and applicable to the decisions they must make. It means thinking in advance about how the information will be used, and by whom. The point of assessment is not to gather data and return "results"; it is a *process* that starts with the questions of decision makers, that involves them in gathering and interpreting data, and that informs and helps steer the decision makers toward organizational effectiveness.

8.   *Assessment should be part of a larger set of conditions that promote change.* By itself, assessment changes little. Its greatest contribution comes on campuses where student affairs is visibly valued and worked at. On such campuses, the push to improve student affairs is a visible and primary goal of leadership; improving student affairs is central to establishing the rationale for student affairs, as well as its quality, affordability, strategic planning, and policy development and decision making.

9.   *Through assessment, student affairs professionals meet responsibilities of students, the institution, and the public.* There is a compelling student, institutional, and public stake in assessment. As student affairs professionals, we have responsibilities to the stakeholders who support or depend upon us to provide information about the ways in which our organization meets its goals and expectations. But that responsibility goes beyond reporting such information; our deeper obligation—to ourselves, our students, our institution, and our society—is to provide a high-quality student affairs program. Those to whom educators are accountable have a corresponding obligation to support such attempts at quality enhancement.

The Assessment Process: Some Important Questions

If, as pointed out in the beginning of this chapter, the assessment process does not begin with selecting an instrument, where does it begin? And where does it end? Drawing on the writings of Terenzini (1989), Hanson (1982), Brown and Podolske (1993a), Erwin (1991), and others, we have formulated six basic questions which help define the assessment process, and should be asked *before* the assessment is begun.

1.   *Why are we doing this assessment?* What is its basic purpose? Why do we need information in the first place? Are we looking to improve a service? Are we trying to justify the existence of a program? Do we need information to help us make a decision or formulate a policy? Do we need information to satisfy one or more of our clientele? Are we in a crisis where we need some information, and need it fast? Do we need information to determine budget priorities? Or the answer to why we are doing this assessment may be some or all of the above. Answering this "why" question determines in large part the answers to all of the subsequent questions.

2.   *What will we assess?* With the "why" question answered, the "what" question must be posed. What information is to be gathered? We may need information about who uses our services, programs, and facilities. We may need information which describes the quality of services, programs, and facilities, or assesses affordability, or guides policy development, decision making, or strategic planning. (The "what" question is discussed in greater detail in Chapter Two.)

3.   *How will we assess?* With the "why" and "what" questions answered, the "how" question arises. What methodologies will we use to gather the information we need? Qualitative, quantitative, or both? What will be the source(s) of information? Institutional records? Data collected directly from clientele? Unobtrusive measures? What designs are appropriate to our purposes and what we need to know? (Chapters Two and Three discuss in much greater detail methodological issues in assessment.)

4.   *Who will assess?* Here there is always a lot of controversy. Some would argue that those closest to the situation should conduct the assessments and determine their meaning. Others would suggest that assessment, to be objective, should be done by those

outside the particular service, program, or facility, but inside student affairs. Still others would suggest that, for complete objectivity, assessment should be done by those outside student affairs, or even outside the institution. All would agree, however, that those who conduct the assessment should be qualified to do so, regardless of their place inside or outside the institution.

5. *How will be results be analyzed?* In other words, how will the information gathered be analyzed and interpreted? Information, in and of itself, tells us very little. The interpretation and analysis of data, however, does tell us something, and we need to give careful consideration to this process. What does a specific piece of information mean? How do specific pieces of information fit together? What is the context within which the information is being interpreted? (Chapters Three, Four, and Ten discuss data analysis in much greater detail.)

6. *How will the results be communicated and to whom?* These two questions are very much interrelated, because the plan for communicating assessment results will be determined, in part, by the target audiences for whom the assessment is intended. As discussed in greater detail in Chapter Thirteen, we recommend multiple formats for various internal and external audiences when reporting results, rather than one comprehensive report for all intended readers. A typical report, regardless of the length and intended audience, should include an executive summary, the purpose, design, and results of the study, and any recommendations the investigators have to offer. The timing of communicating results is also very important and must be considered.

To summarize, it is important to ask these questions for every assessment study *before* it is done, and the answers must be communicated to all those who may be involved in or influenced by the assessment. To do anything less compromises the assessment process, not to mention the ethics of assessment, which will be discussed in Chapter Fourteen.

Using Assessment Results: Evaluation

So the vice president for student affairs has just received an assessment report on how participants assessed the educational programs conducted by the health education office. It was a very good assessment, taking into account all of the components identified in the previous section. The conclusion reached was that while students know about these programs, they attend them very sparingly, and those who do attend are mostly white females. What now? How will this report be used? What is the process by which the results are applied to the organization? Who will determine how these results will be used? In other words, are these results to be used for *formative* reasons, *summative* reasons, *political* reasons, or one or more of the above?

These are very important questions because how the results will be used (how these educational programs are evaluated) may be critical in gaining the cooperation of those who might be affected. Nothing creates more resistance from students and staff than the suspicion that assessment results will be used to "get" an individual, program, or service. *How assessment results will be used is very important and must be clearly stated before an assessment study is begun.* It is also very important to involve those who will be affected from the very beginning of the assessment process.

There is, however, a very perplexing problem with regard to the use of assessment studies. Sometimes it is difficult to limit a particular assessment to its original purpose(s). That is, while we may gather certain data for the expressed purpose of quality improvement (formative evaluation), once the information is out, it may be used by "unfriendly critics" as ammunition to reduce or eliminate a program, service, or facility (summative evaluation). Likewise, one never knows when formative evaluations will be used by other important clientele for political purposes. In this sense, in spite of good intentions, one can never really be sure that a particular assessment will be used exclusively for formative evaluations. Chapter Fourteen will elaborate on these and other issues involved in ensuring that assessment studies be used in ways consistent with their purposes.

A Comprehensive Assessment Model

So, all of these issues must be addressed. But how? What are the components of a comprehensive model of assessment, how are they defined, and why are they important? The reader will find elements of this model in virtually all the examples presented in this book, though at times packaged slightly differently!

The first component of a comprehensive student affairs assessment is *keeping track of who uses student services, programs, and facilities*. How many clients use services, programs, and facilities, and how are they described by gender, race, ethnicity, age, class standing, residence, and other demographic variables? Are there clients other than students who must be counted and described?

This component is very important because if our intended clientele do not use our services, programs, or facilities, then our intended purposes cannot be achieved. The first thing to consider is numbers; if too few of our intended clientele use our services, programs, and facilities, then we have a problem. For example, if very few students attend our alcohol education programs, we must reassess what we are doing and why. If we have a problem filling our residence halls, we must reassess what we are doing and why. (Chapter Five discusses this issue in greater detail.)

However, sheer numbers do not tell us the whole story. Even if programs, services, and facilities are well used in terms of critical numbers, the users or participants must be representative of our student population. For example, a few years ago a health center at a major university discovered that while the total number of patients seen was reasonable, a closer analysis revealed that virtually no African American students were using the health service, in spite of the fact that African American students represented 6 percent of the student population. This assessment result was then used as a basis for reassessing the services and programs offered, and marketing them specifically to African American students. Within two years, African American students were not only using health services in proportion to their representation in the student population, but in some instances their use of the facility exceeded that proportion. Similar analyses might be made by gender, class standing, place of residence, age, and other demographic variables. (Chapter Five describes in greater detail how to keep track of our clientele.)

The second component of this model is *the assessment of student and other clientele needs*. The basic principle that we should meet the needs of our clientele is a good one, and well supported in the literature. For example, much of the thrust of various "total quality" efforts focus on "customer" needs as the main ingredient in quality improvement (Deming, 1986). While describing students and other users of our services as "customers" is offensive to some educators, it is a good idea to abide by the basic principle that whatever services, programs, and facilities we offer must meet the needs of our clientele.

Assessing the needs of student and other clientele is not easy, and there are many questions to be answered. What kinds of services, programs, and facilities do students and other clientele need, based on student and staff perceptions, institutional expectations, and research on student needs? How do we distinguish between clientele "wants" and "needs." What are the ways of determining if the services, programs, and facilities we offer "fit" with our clientele? Are some of our offerings obsolete? Are additional or different kinds of services, programs, and facilities needed? (Chapter Six discusses these and other questions in greater detail, and offers some strategies for assessing needs.)

The third component of this assessment model is *clientele satisfaction*. Of those persons who use student services, programs, and facilities, what is their level of satisfaction? What strengths, weaknesses, and suggestions for improvement do they identify? Would they come back? Would they recommend us to a friend? Clientele satisfaction is important for obvious reasons: if they are not satisfied, they won't use the service, program, or facility again, and they will not recommend them to friends and colleagues. Getting clientele to use what we offer is the first step; providing what we offer in ways that satisfy our clientele is the second step, and we must be able to assess their level of satisfaction. (Chapter Seven describes the many ways in which clientele satisfaction can be assessed.)

The fourth component is *assessing campus environments and student cultures*. While assessing individual use, needs, and satisfaction is important, it is also important to take a look at their collective perceptions of campus environments and student cultures within which they conduct their day-to-day lives. (Chapter Eight offers ways in which to assess campus environments, and Chapter Nine provides guidance for assessing student cultures.)

The fifth component of this comprehensive assessment model is *assessing outcomes*. Of those persons who use our services, programs, and facilities, is there any effect on their learning, development, academic success, or other intended outcomes, particularly when compared with nonusers? Can programmatic interventions be isolated from other variables which may influence outcomes, such as background, characteristics, and other experiences? These kinds of studies are very difficult to design, implement, and interpret, but in some ways they attempt to answer the most fundamental question of all: Is what you are doing having any effect, and is that effect the intended one? (In Chapter Ten, we discuss outcomes assessment in greater detail, as well as the problems and pitfalls of such studies and the caution that should be used in interpreting and using the results.)

The sixth component is *comparable institutions assessment:* How does the quality of services, programs, and facilities compare with "best in class" comparable institutions? Again, the "total quality" literature (Deming, 1986) would support the notion that one important way of assessing quality is to compare oneself to other institutions which appear to be doing a better job with a particular service, program, or facility. One purpose would be to discover how others achieve their results, and then to translate their processes to one's own environment. The key to this assessment component is to select comparable institutions which have good assessment programs, rather than going by anecdotal or reputational evidence. Also, one must select comparable institutions with great care, because institutions vary greatly, and selecting the wrong institutions could result in "apples and oranges" comparisons. (In Chapter Eleven, we discuss in greater detail how to make valid comparisons to other institutions.)

The final component of this model is *using nationally accepted standards to assess.* How do our services, programs, and facilities compare to accepted national standards, such as those developed by the Council for the Advancement of Standards for Student Services/Development Programs, various national and regional accrediting agencies, and professional organizations? (In Chapter Twelve, Ted Miller discusses the use of such standards in assessing student affairs.)

Conclusion

There are many reasons why assessment is important to both higher education and to student affairs. Institutions must respond to both internal and external pressures to improve what we are doing, and to demonstrate that what we do is what we say we do.

External pressures from legislatures, funding agencies, accreditation agencies, and the general public, among others, have moved assessment from an option to a necessity. It is clear that higher education must be more accountable for its accessibility, cost-effectiveness, quality, and results.

As part of the educational enterprise, student affairs must also respond to these pressures and others. Internally, questions about whether or not student affairs should exist or not are being raised, along with questions about affordability, quality, and effectiveness. Assessment can provide some of the answers to these questions, as well as support strategic planning and policy development and decision making. Assessment can also provide some of the answers in dealing with political realities and institutional expectations.

It is our contention that we do this by following good assessment practices, asking the right questions before we do assessment, and using a comprehensive assessment model that includes keeping track of who uses what we offer, determining how satisfied they are with what we offer, determining if what we offer meets their needs and has an impact, gathering their collective perceptions of their environments and cultures, and comparing how well we do with other comparable institutions and accepted national standards. The rest of the book is devoted to providing practitioners the means to implement this model.

Chapter Two

Key Questions to Ask in Assessment

Since this book is written primarily for student affairs practitioners with varying degrees of assessment expertise, it is necessary to review several basic assessment issues in order to "level the playing field" among readers. While this book is not intended to create assessment experts out of practitioners, it is our intention to provide practitioners enough basic information to ensure that high-quality and useful assessment studies are conducted. This chapter, then, will attempt to answer some of the basic questions frequently asked about how to conduct assessment studies, illustrated by a problem faced by a student affairs unit and how an assessment study helped solve that problem. In many instances, the reader will be referred to other chapters in this book for more specific information about the issues raised.

What's the Problem?

We assert throughout this book that all assessment activity flows from some problem, so establishing a clear and precise definition of the problem facing the student affairs practitioner is the first step in the assessment process. Our example presents the following problem: at a predominately white institution, African American students complained that they did not feel comfortable seeking counseling services from the counseling center. The counseling center was able to confirm, through institutional and counseling records, that it was true that, while African Americans represented 12 percent of the total student population, they represented only 2 percent of students receiving counseling services. On the other hand, majority students, while making up 75 percent of the student population, represented 88 percent of those served. The use of counseling services by other underrepresented groups, including Asians and Hispanics, was approximately equal to their proportion of the total student population. (The reader will note the importance of tracking student usage, the first component of our comprehensive assessment model, as a way of confirming a problem.)

Underuse of counseling services by African American students was a problem for at least three reasons. First, the counseling center's mission included meeting the needs of underrepresented groups, and obviously this element of the mission was not being fulfilled for this group. Second, the institution was very concerned about an excessively high attrition rate among undergraduate African Americans, and saw counseling services as a very critical part of a comprehensive program to increase African American retention. Third, the African American Student Association got wind of the issue and charged that African American students did not seek counseling at the center because the counseling center was "insensitive" to the needs of this group; this charge was particularly problematic considering that other underrepresented groups didn't seem to have this problem.

So, the institution needed to solve this problem, and solve it quickly.

What's the Purpose of the Assessment?

Once the problem has been identified and clarified, the next step is to design a study which gives some insight into how to solve the problem. All research designs begin by asking the question, what's the purpose of the study? In this example, it is obvious that, if the problem is to be solved, the counseling center must gain some insight into the problem. Therefore the purposes of this study were to (1) determine *why* counseling services were underused by African American students, and (2) identify *what* steps must be taken to increase use.

Who Should Be Studied?

The population to be studied is the next question that must be answered. It may seem obvious, but defining the population precisely is important because the conclusions drawn from a particular inquiry apply only to those studied in the first place. However, too often assessment studies of "college students" are often conducted using populations (or samples of populations) which do not reflect the demography of the college students currently enrolled. For example, according to the *Chronicle of Higher Education Almanac* (Sept. 1, 1994), 40 percent of students in higher education are over twenty-five years of age, 43 percent are enrolled part time, and 38 percent study at two-year institutions. Yet most studies of college students concentrate on students who are eighteen to twenty-four years of age, studying full time, and attending four-year institutions. Thus, defining the population is very important, and qualifying conclusions, accordingly, is even more important.

The simplest (and probably most misleading) definition of the population for our study might be all African American students at the institution. But it must be remembered that the problem was defined, in part, as an undergraduate retention problem, so perhaps only undergraduate African American students should be included. On the other hand, the mission of the counseling center was to serve all students from underrepresented groups, not just undergraduates. Further, while most African Americans at the institution study full time, some are enrolled less than full time. To complicate matters even further, part-time students range from students taking one course to students taking three courses.

But should the population examined be limited to students? What about others who might have insights into this problem? What about the counseling center staff? Might it have some insights based on the few African American students they have seen? What about African American faculty? Based on their relationship with African American students, might they have some insights into the problem? How about African American leaders in the greater community, or African American graduates? Might they also have some insights?

So, one can see that defining the population to study is not as simple as it may seem. While the ideal definition might be to include all of the people and groups mentioned above, in spite of how important this is, in most instances there is not enough time or money to include them all. In this example, for several reasons it was decided to limit the population to all African American students currently enrolled full time. First, while others may have some insight into why African American students underused counseling services, the students themselves probably have the most insight. Second, the cost of studying all the other groups was prohibitive, not to mention the problem of collecting data from less accessible groups. Third, while undergraduate retention was a motivation for this inquiry, it was not the only one; the problem of underuse extended to graduate students as well as undergraduates, so both were included. Finally, since the part-time enrollment of all students at this institution was less than 1 percent, they were excluded from the study.

What's the Best Assessment Method?

Of course, the best assessment method depends on the purpose of the study. Basically, we have three choices: quantitative methods, qualitative methods, or a combination of both. According to Patton (1990), "Qualitative methods permit the evaluator to study selected issues in depth and detail. Approaching fieldwork without being constrained by predetermined categories of analysis contributes to the depth, openness, and detail of qualitative inquiry" (p. 12). Qualitative methods include gathering data from interviews, observations, and documents, and they require much smaller samples than quantitative methods.

"Quantitative methods, on the other hand, require the use of standardized measures so that the varying perspectives and experiences of people can be fit into a limited number of predetermined response categories to which numbers are assigned" (Patton, 1990, pp. 13–14). Quantitative methods include gathering data from a survey or other instrument, and require much larger samples than qualitative methods. As a result, one can generalize from the sample to the population studied.

The advantage of the quantitative approach, according to Patton (1990), "is that it's possible to measure the reactions of a great many people to a limited set of questions, thus facilitating comparison and statistical aggregation of the data. This gives a broad, generalizable set of findings presented succinctly and parsimoniously. By contrast, qualitative methods typically produce a wealth of detailed information about a much smaller number of people and cases. This increases understanding of the cases and situations studied but reduces generalizability" (p. 14). (For a more detailed discussion of both methodologies, see Chapters Three and Four.)

So, which methods are appropriate for this study? The answer, in the end, was both. On the one hand, the institution needed to be confident that the information collected did, in fact, represent the views of the population of African American students enrolled full time, yielding a broad, generalizable set of findings. So, the quantitative part of the solution was to conduct a survey of African American students which asked a series of "objective" type questions about why African American students underused counseling services and what they felt must be done to solve the problem.

On the other hand, the institution also needed to more fully and completely understand why African American students were not using counseling services, so a more in-depth analysis was required. The qualitative solution was to invite a small number of African American students to participate in focus groups using an open-ended interview protocol about why African Americans underused counseling services, and what might be done to change this.

How Do We Decide Whom to Study?

Having decided upon the population to be studied, it is rarely possible to include the whole population in a study, regardless of the type of study chosen. Sometimes, if the population is very narrowly defined, it is possible. For example, if we were concerned in this study only about African American undergraduate females, studying part time, living on campus, and majoring in anthropology, including the whole population might be feasible. But in most assessment studies, the population is much more broadly defined, so a sample of the whole population must be selected in a way that ensures that those chosen are *representative* of that population according to some criteria. The most typical criteria are the demographic characteristics of the population, such as gender, age, race or ethnicity, and others. In the collegiate setting, such factors as class standing, grades, place of residence, full-time or part-time enrollment, major field, and others may also be important. If the sample is, in fact, representative, then one can *generalize* with much more confidence to the whole population from the findings of the sample (Shulman, 1988).

There are very different sampling issues, however, depending upon whether qualitative or quantitative methods are chosen. In this example, since both were chosen, a brief overview of the sampling issues for both will be discussed.

Quantitative Study

There are several different quantitative sampling techniques (discussed in greater detail in Chapter Four). For the quantitative study of African American students, the first question is, how do we select a sample in ways that ensure that it is representative of the whole population of full-time African American students at our institution? Given the purposes of this study, it was decided to do a computer-generated simple random sample of all African American students enrolled full time from institutional records, based on the last four digits of students' identification numbers. This allowed for analysis not only by the total sample, but also by gender, graduate or undergraduate status, and (within the undergraduate portion of the population) class standing.

The second sampling question for a quantitative study is, how many students should we sample? The answer is at once methodological, political, and financial. The methodological answer depends on three factors. First and most practical is the question, what is your expected rate of return? If one needs five hundred usable responses (based on other factors described below), then one has to estimate how large the sample must be to yield five hundred responses. So, for a return rate of 25 percent, you would need a sample of at least two thousand subjects.

Second, the number of people sampled depends on the amount of "sample error" we can tolerate. According to Suskie (1992), sample error "describes the possible difference between your findings and the true results if you were able to obtain valid responses from everyone" (p. 8). For example, if a 4 percent sample error is tolerable, then a usable sample of six hundred is required. (For a more detailed discussion of sampling error, and how it is calculated, see Chapter Four.)

Third, the number sampled may depend upon what units of analysis the study requires. In this example, let's assume that it's important to analyze the data by gender and class standing. The sample should be large enough to provide enough responses for each variable in a multivariate analysis. A standard and somewhat conservative rule of thumb in most multivariate analyses is to be sure you have at least thirty-five subjects for each variable. In this example, then, we would need to obtain at least 240 usable responses to make sure that there were at least thirty-five responses in each gender or class standing category.

At this point, the reader may ask, doesn't the size of the population become a factor in determining sample size? Doesn't it make a difference if we're sampling from one hundred students or twenty-five thousand students? Suskie (1992) argues that it does not, except for the case of very small populations, because the representativeness of the sample is much more important than the percentage of the population in the sample. While lay audiences probably consider sample size the most important sampling criteria, from a methodological standpoint, size is not as important as representativeness. That is, a smaller sample that is representative of the population is probably more generalizable than a larger sample that is not representative.

Fourth, cost is often a practical consideration in determining the size of the sample. Sample size is often influenced by how much money one has available for expenses such as printing, postage, data entry, follow-up of nonrespondents, statistical consultation, staff time for interviewing, and other expenses associated with conducting assessment studies.

So, what must we do? Based on expected rate of return of approximately 25 percent, we need two thousand respondents. Based on sampling error, we need about a thousand. Based on the analysis chosen, we need at least 240. But before answering this question, yet another factor must be taken into account: the credibility of the sample size with the audience to be informed. Regardless of the defensibility of the number chosen—even when using the three criteria identified above—the number must have some "face credibility" with the audience to be informed. Based on our experience as student affairs investigators, anything less than three hundred usable responses in a quantitative study lacks credibility with typical collegiate audiences. Even if we can justify a smaller usable sample based on analytical rules (for example, 240 usable returns), the study likely will be questioned by the lay audience as too small to generalize to the larger population. There doesn't seem to be any particular reason for this range, other than some unexplained "common sense" of various collegiate audiences.

So, we return to the original question: How many should be included in this sample? Two thousand? A thousand? 240? The best answer, of course, is "the more, the better." However, please remember that at the beginning of this book, we note that institutional assessment is always a series of compromises leading away from the "perfect" research design. One of these compromises must be made when determining sample size, and the decision is not always easy. So, we return to the practical and decide on a sample of one thousand, anticipating a 60 percent response rate using a telephone survey (see below). This would yield approximately six hundred usable responses, which gives us enough responses for (1) a sampling error of 4 percent, (2) a multivariate analysis by gender, graduate or undergraduate enrollment, and, within undergraduates, class standing, and (3) establishing credibility with the intended collegiate audiences. This sample size is also within funding parameters.

Qualitative Study

The sampling issues for qualitative methodologies are in some ways the same as quantitative methodologies, but in other ways they are very different. According to Patton (1990), quantitative methods typically depend on larger samples selected randomly. The logic and power of such sampling depends upon selecting a truly random and statistically representative sample that will permit confident generalization from the sample to a larger population. The purpose, in short, is credible generalization.

Qualitative methods, on the other hand, typically aim for an in-depth focus on relatively small samples—even single cases (as in the case study, for example)—selected *purposefully*. Purposeful sampling, according to Patton (1990), is the selection of *information-rich cases* for in-depth study. "Information-rich cases are those from which one can learn a great deal about issues of central importance" (p. 169).

In this example, you will remember, the purpose of assessment was to determine why African American students were underusing the counseling center. By focusing in-depth on the reasons behind the opinions and recommendations of a smaller number of carefully selected African American students, we may learn a great deal more than by gathering standardized data from a large, statistically representative sample of African American students (Patton, 1990). (For discussion of several different sampling strategies for purposefully selecting information-rich cases, see Chapter Three.)

Intensity sampling was selected for this study. This qualitative, more in-depth sampling method consists of information-rich cases that can provide insight into the problem being studied (Patton, 1990). In this study, it was decided to sample a small number of groups of African American students who had not used counseling services. So, a small number of graduate students, undergraduate underclass students, and undergraduate upperclass students were randomly selected to participate in the qualitative part of the study.

Again, the question arises, how many should be sampled? According to Patton (1990), "*There are no rules for sample size in qualitative inquiry*. Sample size depends on what you want to know, the purpose of the inquiry, what's at stake, what will be useful, what will have credibility, and what can be done with available time and resources" (p. 184). More specifically, Patton (1990) also recommends specifying *minimum* samples based on expected reasonable coverage of the problem, given the purpose of the study. Taking all these factors into consideration, it was decided to select a minimum sample of approximately thirty persons, (ten graduate students, ten underclass undergraduates, and ten upperclass students, equally divided between men and women). Again, based on our experience in conducting qualitative studies, this number seems to have "face credibility" with collegiate audiences.

How Should the Data Be Collected?

The reader will remember that for the quantitative part of the study, the size of the sample and the projected rate were based upon the assumption that 60 percent of those sampled would respond. Since mailed questionnaires rarely if ever reach that return rate, a telephone survey was chosen over a mailed questionnaire. Even in the best of circumstances, mailed questionnaires rarely yield more than a 50 percent response, with 25 percent to 30 percent being more typical. However, telephone surveys almost always yield a much higher response rate (Suskie, 1992). In addition, telephone surveys are often cheaper and faster, and the interviewer can deal with unanticipated problems or questions. Of course, telephone interviewers must be trained, and "user-friendly" ways of recording responses must be developed. Still, mailed questionnaires are more expensive, especially if one is also paying the postage for the returned questionnaire and doing another mailed follow-up for non-respondents, both of which are strongly recommended.

If, however, given the particular purposes of a study and other more practical factors, it turns out that a mailed questionnaire is the best answer, here is some advice based on our own experience as well as that offered by Suskie (1992):

1. Include a cover letter which explains the purpose of and importance of the study, and its relevance to the respondent.
2. Write the cover letter on letterhead stationery and signed by someone in a position of authority who is thought to have credibility with the participants.
3. Personalize the cover letter, unless the subject of the study is so sensitive that the anonymity of the respondent must be respected.
4. Offer to send a copy of the results of the study.
5. Identify the measures you intend to take to ensure the confidentiality of the information provided by the respondent.
6. Offer an incentive, such as a free ticket to a college event, a bookstore certificate, a charitable contribution, participation in a drawing for a prize, or other items of value.
7. Estimate the amount of time it will take for the respondent to complete the instrument (the shorter, the better). Anything more than ten minutes will probably reduce the response rate considerably.
8. Include a self-addressed, stamped (or metered) envelope to return the instrument. If the cost is prohibitive, ask the respondent to deliver the instrument to a large box located in an administrative office not associated with the unit being studied.
9. Identify the name and telephone number of someone who can be contacted if the respondent has a question.
10. Mail the instrument at a "user-friendly" time for students. Hitting students with a questionnaire just before mid-semester or

final exams will almost guarantee a reduced response rate. Likewise, questionnaires received during the week are more likely to be returned than those received on a weekend.

But returning to our study of African American usage of the counseling center, as discussed earlier, we decided to use a telephone survey. How may we conduct such a survey to maximize the response rate? Probably the best known and most effective program of telephone surveys is Project Pulse at the University of Massachusetts, Amherst. Topics are selected based on the needs of the institution. Every Wednesday evening from 4:45 to 10:00 P.M., approximately thirty-five work-study students (known as "Pulsers") conduct a telephone survey of a random sample of approximately one thousand undergraduate students. The usual response rate is from 50 percent to 60 percent of those called, so the sample from which results are drawn is between five hundred and six hundred undergraduates. Approximately twenty surveys per year are conducted, requested by clients which may include the vice-chancellor for student affairs, student affairs units, student governments, colleges, academic departments, and other university administrative offices.

Project Pulse operates from an interview protocol developed by the Student Affairs Research, Information, and Systems office, always in consultation with the office or client that requested the survey. The protocol is first piloted on the student interviewers and is revised accordingly. It is then recorded on a computer disk, using a software package which is loaded into the computers of several different student affairs offices. The student interviewers make the call, introduce themselves, and describe the purpose of the survey. The questions are typically multiple choice, and the responses are recorded on the computer as they proceed through the interview protocol. One interviewer typically conducts between fifteen and twenty interviews per night. This data collection procedure was applied to our study.

We strongly recommend pilot testing both mailed questionnaires and telephone surveys. According to Suskie (1992), there are always a few items which are perfectly clear to the investigator, but confusing or misleading to respondents. The simplest pilot test is to hand out the questionnaire to a few people similar to those in your sample and ask them not only to complete it, but to tell you about any questions or directions that were unclear, confusing, or ambiguous, as well as how long it took to complete the questionnaire.

For the qualitative part of the study, it was decided to conduct focus groups rather than individual interviews. There are advantages and disadvantages to both (discussed in Chapter Three). In this study it was decided to use focus groups, because this took less time than individual interviews, and respondents were not asked to disclose extremely confidential information. Three focus groups of ten students each were conducted, using the interview protocol discussed below. One focus group consisted of African American graduate students, another consisted of African American underclass undergraduates, and the third consisted of upperclass undergraduates. Each group contained an equal number of males and females. Homogeneous groups were selected to enhance peer group interaction and make the analysis of the information collected easier to process.

What Instrument Should We Use?

The answer to this question rests upon several factors, depending upon the methodologies chosen. For quantitative methodologies, an instrument must be chosen that yields results which can be statistically analyzed. If we are fortunate, there is an instrument already developed that meets our needs. There are many advantages to using such instruments. First, we may not have the time or the expertise to develop a good instrument on our own. Second, we may assume that the instrument has been constructed and tested to establish its validity (does it measure what it says it measures?), its reliability (is it consistent internally as well as across groups?), and other important characteristics of a good instrument. Third, often the instrument may be scored and analyzed by its publisher, saving the time and expertise needed for this task. Finally, a nationally recognized instrument likely will have more "face credibility" with audiences, compared to a locally constructed instrument.

One important caveat must be mentioned about another supposed advantage of using an existing instrument: the availability of nationally established norms against which local results may be compared. When norms are available, one must be certain that these norms are, in fact, representative of the population studied, and not just simple accumulated databases which may or may not be representative. Probably the best example of this dilemma is Astin's Cooperative Institute Research Project (Astin, Korn, and Berz, 1991), which publishes annually a profile of entering freshmen, along with selected attitudes and behaviors. Unless your institution fits the profile of those surveyed (primarily enrolling traditional aged, full-time, majority students), comparing local results to these national norms will be very misleading. On the other hand, when the norms are representative, and comparable to your institution, they can be extremely valuable in assessing how your institution compares.

Previously developed instruments have other disadvantages. First, often it is very difficult to find an instrument that entirely meets local needs. Almost always, there are tradeoffs: the instrument yields information that is not needed and lacks information that is needed. Second, already developed instruments can be expensive to buy, score, and analyze. After all, the publishers of these instruments are in the business of making money, and instrument developers deserve to be compensated for their efforts. Third, such instruments frequently become out of date very soon, thus moving even further away from current, local needs. Fourth, while most good instruments are developed and tested properly, some are not and thus may be no better than a good, locally constructed instrument.

In our example, there were no existing instruments that could determine why African Americans underused counseling services, so an instrument had to be developed locally. It is not the intention of this chapter to teach the reader how to develop an instrument (see Suskie, 1992, for an excellent discussion of this issue), but there are some general guidelines drawn from Suskie's (1992) work that you can use. She argues that an instrument should be developed which:

1. *Is considerate of respondents.* This includes length (the shorter, the better), clarity, sequencing of items, and ease of completion and return.
2. *Appears professional to the respondents.* This includes asking interesting and important-sounding questions, reproducing the

instrument on quality paper with readable print, and avoiding grammatical and spelling errors.

3. *Has clearly stated and understood items.* This includes keeping the items short, readable, interesting, and specific. Each item should ask only one question, and making all assumptions, definitions, and qualifiers clearly understood. Perhaps most important, items should not be loaded, leading, or biased.

4. *Elicits consistent responses (has reliability).* This usually means that responses to similar questions within an instrument should be similar. To determine reliability one should ask at least two questions on the same subject. To keep the instrument short, however, this may not be possible.

5. *Measures what it says it measures (has validity).* Ideally, each respondent should interpret each question in the same way, which in turn means questions must be consistently clear. Also, items should have an intuitive relationship to the purpose of the study; this relationship can be tested by a pilot test.

6. *Has properly ordered items.* The first items should be chosen with care. They should be intriguing, easy to answer, general, and impersonal. This means demographic inquiries such as gender age and major should *not* go first. Remaining items should follow a natural flow, both logically and psychologically. Contingency questions (those where if you check "yes" to one question, then you "go to" another set of questions) should be avoided because they are confusing and frustrating. If you have several questions you want only a small group to answer, put them at the end of the instrument, and tell everyone else to stop before reaching them. Even better, send this select group a separate instrument.

Of course, there are many different types of quantitative items, including yes/no items, multiple-choice items, rankings, Likert rating scales (usually five items along a continuum ranging from "strongly agree" to "strongly disagree," "excellent" to "poor," or "never" to "very frequently"), semantic differential rating scales (antonyms with several spaces in between), self-made rating scales (asking the respondent to rate a topic excellent, good, fair, poor; frequently, sometimes, never; or approved, undecided, disapprove), and open-ended questions (respondents write their own answer to a question). Usually, open-ended questions are more appropriate for qualitative methodologies, since they are not coded and quantified easily.

Returning to our study of African American student underuse of counseling services, it was decided to use a self-made rating scale, asking respondents to react to a list of reasons for not using counseling services by agreeing, disagreeing, or having no basis for a response. There were several reasons for this choice. The fact that it was a telephone survey made many other item types cumbersome and confusing. On the other hand, it was simpler, easier, and less confusing to ask respondents to agree or disagree with, or have no basis for responding to the statements such as "African Americans do not use the counseling center because there are no African American counselors" or "African Americans do not use the counseling center because we have heard negative comments from other African American students." Likewise, respondents were asked to agree or disagree with statements suggesting solutions to the problem, such as "The counseling center should add more African American counselors" or "The counseling center should do a better job of making African American students aware of services."

The reader will recall that for this study, we decided to use a qualitative approach as well. For qualitative methodologies, an interview protocol must be developed, consisting of standardized, open-ended questions. According to Patton (1990), an item is standardized when it is written out in advance *exactly* the way it is to be asked during the interview. Clarifications or elaborations should be included, as well as any probing questions. Variations among interviewers can be minimized, and comparisons across interviews can be made if the interview protocol is standardized. Open-ended means there are no prescribed answers (such as yes/no); respondents are free to provide any answer they choose. (For a further discussion of this issue, see Chapter Three.)

In the study under discussion, there were three basic interview questions asked of African American students:

1. Our records indicate that counseling services are underused by African American students. Why do you believe this is so?
2. What, if anything, could be done to increase use of the counseling center by African American students?
3. Do you have any other comments on this issue?

From among the types of questions identified in Chapter Three as appropriate to qualitative interview questions, opinion questions were chosen because they best reflected the purposes of the study. There was also a logic to the sequences of these questions. First, the questions parallel the purposes of the study. Second, the first question asks participants to discuss African American students in general, without disclosing their own reasons, which would be much more threatening. If we had wanted participants to disclose their own reasons, an individual interview probably would have been more appropriate. The second question seeks their advice about how to solve the problem, and the third gives students an opportunity to bring up issues not stimulated by the first two questions. (For further discussion about how to conduct focus groups, see Chapter Three.)

Who Should Collect the Data?

At first glance, this question may not seem to matter much. Obviously, data should be collected by people who are competent to do so. But often the most qualified people are also those who have a vested interest in the outcome. This is less of a problem with quantitative methodologies, where bias—if there is any—is more likely to have occurred in the selection or development of the instrument. In qualitative methodologies, however, where the data collected and filtered by those who conduct and record the data, bias becomes a much larger issue. (For further discussion of this issue, see Chapter Three.)

Also, there is the lingering problem of the "face credibility" of the study, depending on who collected the data. For example, in this study, how much credibility would the results have had with African Americans if only white Americans had collected and analyzed the data? Based on our experience, probably not much, if any. So, in the instance of the quantitative part of this study, all the telephone interviewers were African American students who received proper training. In the instance of the qualitative part of this study, the focus group leaders were African Americans from the counseling psychology department, who had a background in counseling but no vested interest in the outcome of the study, and who were trained in how to conduct focus group sessions.

How Should We Record the Data?

The data collected from the quantitative study, as discussed above, were recorded on a computer program by the telephone interviewers, so the data file was established directly. If the instrument was answered by a computer scored answer sheet (even more useful if created in-house for a specific survey), then the answer sheets must be scanned and organized into a data file.

With today's computer technology, respondents should never be asked to record their answers on a nonscannable form, which then must be converted to a scannable form by hand. This procedure requires more time and expense, and increases the likelihood of data recording errors. Scannable forms, however, do have limitations, from the failure of respondents to follow directions in answering items to the failure of scanning equipment.

The data collected from the qualitative study presents a very different problem, as discussed in Chapter Three. In this study, the focus group conversations were tape-recorded, and the focus group leaders were asked to summarize participants' responses. Since three questions framed the inquiry, the summaries were organized around these questions. For example, the reasons for underuse mentioned most frequently were identified and discussed, followed by all the other reasons, even if they were given by only one respondent. The same was done for the most frequently mentioned recommendations for solving the problem, and for other issues.

How Do We Analyze the Data?

Analysis of the quantitative data again depends on the purpose of the study (see Chapter Four for the options available). Probably the most important first step is to determine if the respondents are, in fact, representative of the population to be studied (details on how to address this issue are also discussed in Chapter Four). If we wanted to know only the reasons, we could simply record the percentage of responses of the instrument items, and draw conclusions accordingly. If we wanted to know if differences existed by gender, we could conduct a bivariate analysis to determine if there were any significant differences between men and women. The same analysis could be done on the basis of graduate or undergraduate status, part-time and full-time status, or class standing (freshmen and sophomores as compared to juniors and seniors). If, however, we wanted to analyze reasons by combinations of student demographic characteristics, a multivariate analysis would be more appropriate.

In this instance, a multivariate analysis was selected because it was important to find out not only why African American students were underusing the counseling center, but if this underuse was affected by demographic characteristics such as class standing, gender, graduate or undergraduate status, and (within undergraduates) class standing. A statistical consultant did the analyses, presented the findings, and interpreted their meaning for the purposes of the final report. (For a more detailed discussion of quantitative analyses, see Chapters Four and Eleven.)

For the qualitative part of this study, the results were summarized as described above. In this study, the interviewers met with the counseling center staff to enlist their help in interpreting the responses. From this discussion, an elaboration of the reasons and recommendations were written by the interviewers.

How Do We Report the Results?

There are two issues here. First, how are the results of the quantitative study integrated with those of the qualitative study? One would hope that there will be some consistency between the two studies where they overlap, but each will provide valuable information not provided by the other. In this instance, the reasons overlapped both studies. The quantitative analysis yielded results by the demographic characteristics of respondents, while the qualitative results yielded much more in-depth information on the reasons for underuse and what should be done about it. Hence, the beauty of using both methodologies, with each approach contributing both confirming and unique information.

The second issue concerns the fact that the results should be reported on the basis of who will read the report, why they will read it, and what they will do about it. The reader will remember that in this instance, there were three interested groups: the counseling center staff (because underuse by African American students was inconsistent with the counseling center's mission), African

American students (because they felt their needs were not being met), and the institution's administration (because it was concerned about counseling services as a means of increasing African American retention). The report was written in ways that spoke to each of these audiences and their concerns. (See Chapter Thirteen for more discussion of the guidelines for the format for reporting results.)

How Do We Use the Results? The Evaluation Process

The importance and intricacies of using assessment results cannot be underestimated. That is, as defined in Chapter One, how do assessment results become a part of the evaluation process? Too often, even the best-designed and most carefully reported studies end up collecting dust on someone's shelf because the institution failed to take advantage of the results, for whatever reasons: lack of resources, lack of courage to implement the recommendations, indecisiveness. Managing the use of assessment results is very important and is discussed in greater detail in Chapter Thirteen.

In this study, there was a happy ending. The counseling center, based on the result indicating that a greater African American presence was needed, sought resources to create more diversity among its counselors. The administration, based on this same result, provided the resources as a way of promoting African American retention. Based on the result that efforts to promote counseling services among African American students should be strengthened, the counseling center enlisted the support of key leaders in the African American student community to make counseling services better known and more accessible.

Of course, not all studies are used effectively in the evaluation process. The counseling center could have dismissed the results as unattainable, given the scarcity of resources. The same could have been decided by the institution's administration. And we all know that students come and go, so it would have been tempting to await a turnover among the African American student leadership, hoping that the issue would not be as important to the next generation of leaders—a too cynical view, perhaps, but too often the realistic one.

Conclusion

This chapter provides answers to some of the basic questions about how to conduct assessment studies: defining the problem, identifying the purpose, deciding the best assessment methodology, defining the population to be studied, defining the sample to be studied, deciding how to collect the data, selecting the proper instruments, selecting the data collectors, recording and analyzing the data, reporting the results, and using the results. As pointed out in the introduction to this chapter, it is not our intent to make assessment experts out of practitioners. It is our intention, however, to provide the practitioner with enough information to make informed decisions about assessment issues. These issues must be addressed in order to develop a high-quality and credible assessment study.

| Using Qualitative Methods

In a 1992 publication, Fran Stage argued for greater flexibility in conducting research and assessment of college students. She concluded that "those who study college students have discovered that many of their most burning questions could not be answered through simple quantitative approaches to data collection and analysis" (p. 4). Qualitative approaches to assessment are discussed in this chapter to complement the material on quantitative methods introduced in Chapter Four. Qualitative methods will be defined and discussed in detail, and, when appropriate, compared with quantitative methods. This chapter will provide the reader with a background on qualitative methods as well as some practical information about how to conduct qualitative studies. A great deal has been written about qualitative methods in recent years. Many excellent sources are cited in the reference list and the investigator is encouraged to seek these additional readings to develop a robust understanding of qualitative methods.

The reader who is unfamiliar with qualitative methods should not assume that qualitative methods are not rigorous. In collegiate environments where qualitative methods may be unknown or misunderstood or, even worse, rejected as inferior compared to quantitative methods, this misperception needs to be corrected. As Schuh (1992) points out, "These methods, when applied with precision, take more time, greater resources, and certainly as much conceptual ability as qualitative measures. Making precise meaning of language, for example, is not easy because language for the purposes of understanding college and university students cannot be reduced by use of statistical formulas. Qualitative methods require every bit as much skill as quantitative methods" (pp. xii–xiii).

Defining Qualitative Methods

It is not a simple task to define what qualitative methodology is. In fact, Eisner and Peshkin (1990) observed, "there is no general agreement about the use of this term [*qualitative methodology*]. It has rivals, such as *naturalistic, case study,* and *ethnographic.* There is, moreover, no general agreement about the conduct of any of the types of qualitative inquiry; perhaps there never can be consensus of the sort that is embodied in the standardized procedures of quantitative research, for example in path analysis or single subject design" (p. 1).

These observations underscore the healthy debate about what might fit under the tent of qualitative approaches. For the purpose of this book, the definition offered by Patton (cited in Chapter One) is useful. Patton (1990) defines qualitative methods as the detailed descriptions of situations, events, people, interactions, and observed behaviors; use of direct quotations from people about their experiences, attitudes, beliefs, and thoughts; and analysis of excerpts or entire passages from documents, correspondence, records, and case histories. Others, such as Stage (1992) and Wolcott (1990) agree with this definition. It will serve this chapter well, especially when compared with Stage's (1992) definition of quantitative methods, "measures requiring that a numerical or other evaluative symbol be assigned to the construct of interest" (p. 7).

To build on Patton's definition, it is useful to review five features of qualitative research suggested by Bogdan and Biklen (1992). First, qualitative research is conducted in a natural setting, where people work and play, rather than in a laboratory. In the natural setting the researcher serves as the key data-gathering instrument. Qualitative researchers are less concerned about standardized instruments or controlling intervening variables. Second, the research tends to be descriptive in nature. That is, the data are collected in words or pictures rather than numbers. When asked judiciously, the question "Why?" has the potential of providing a rich description of how people make meaning out of their behavior and experiences. Third, qualitative research is concerned with process as much as it is with outcomes and products. Data collection and analysis are conducted simultaneously, and as the researcher learns more about the topic under consideration, additional avenues of inquiry are opened. Fourth, inductive analysis is a strategy that is employed in making meaning. As information is collected, suppositions are developed. Hypotheses are not developed on an a priori basis. Fifth, how students make meaning of their experiences is of essential concern to the researchers; the participants' perspectives are of primary importance. Quite commonly, drafts of reports are shared with the participants so that the researchers may verify that they have interpreted the participants' reports accurately and completely.

These five features challenge many of the assumptions of those trained in graduate school in quantitative methods, particularly those trained in the fields of science and engineering. These features, as well as other aspects of qualitative research that will be discussed later in this chapter, require a different kind of thinking about research, evaluation, and assessment.

Comparing Qualitative and Quantitative Methods

Debates have raged in the research literature about these two methods. Layder (1993) provides an interesting commentary about this debate in sociological research by observing that "favouring of quantitative data has often been coupled with the view that macro analysis is primary in sociology. Conversely, those who advocate qualitative analysis have often been hostile to the use of quantitative data on the grounds that the data 'impose a fixity on social life that it does not have,' and thus they have emphasized the primacy of micro analysis" (pp. 109–110).

This debate, however, is too often posed as an either/or proposition. In reality, the most cogent answers to some of the problems confronting student affairs may best be answered through a combination of both methodologies, as discussed in Chapter Two. Moreover, while distinctions are drawn between the two methods in this section, the reader should not infer that these two methods necessarily represent polar opposites. They do have distinctive features, but both are rigorous methodological approaches used to determine the truth.

Key Concepts

Unless otherwise noted, the following observations on the differences between qualitative and quantitative methods are drawn from Bogdan and Biklen (1992), and Worthen and Sanders (1987).

Making meaning of what respondents have to report is a key concept in qualitative methods. Quantitative methods, on the other hand, tend to be concerned with identifying statistical relationships. In a qualitative study, understanding how the respondents make meaning of their circumstances—that is, how they respond to questions—is of great interest to the researcher. Quantitative studies are focused on the *relationships* between numbers rather than the numbers themselves, showing correlations, identifying significant differences, and so on.

Patton (1990) argues that "qualitative methods permit the evaluator to study selected issues in depth and detail. Approaching fieldwork without being constrained by predetermined categories of analysis contributes to the depth, openness, and detail of qualitative inquiry. . . . Quantitative methods, on the other hand, require the use of standardized measures so that varying perspectives and experiences of people can be fit into a limited number of predetermined response categories to which numbers are assigned" (pp. 12–14). In very simplistic terms, on the whole quantitative methods are well suited to answer the "what" questions, while qualitative methods are best at answering the "why" questions.

Data

Substantial differences exist between the data collected in each methodology. In a qualitative study, the data are the words of the respondents, the field notes of the researchers, documents, and, in some cases, pictures, film, or videotape. Quantitative studies include data such as numbers, measures, and counts, typically drawn from predetermined instruments that produce such data. On the surface, quantitative data may seem to be more precise than qualitative data, but when collected carefully and completely, qualitative data can be every bit as precise as quantitative data.

Sampling

Not surprisingly, sampling assumptions and techniques are different in the two methodologies as well. In quantitative research, samples are drawn from populations in ways that ensure that those chosen are representative of the population according to some criteria. The most typical criteria are the demographic characteristics of the population, such as gender, age, race, or ethnicity. If the sample is, in fact, representative, then one can generalize the findings with much more confidence from the sample to the whole population (Shulman, 1988). Quantitative methods typically depend on larger, randomly selected samples. Quantitative researchers also must worry about sampling error, rate of return, and a host of other problems discussed in greater detail in Chapter Four.

Qualitative sampling methods, on the other hand, according to Patton (1990), typically focus in depth on a relatively small sample—sometimes even single cases—selected purposefully. "The logic and power of purposeful sampling lies in the selection of information rich cases for studying in depth. Information rich cases are those from which one can learn a great deal about issues of central importance to the research, thus the term purposeful sampling" (p. 169).

Patton (1990) identifies fifteen different sampling approaches for qualitative studies (pp. 169–181):

1. *Extreme or deviant case sampling* focuses on cases that are rich in information because they are unusual or special in some way.
2. *Intensity sampling* consists of information-rich cases that manifest the phenomenon of interest (but not extremity); one seeks excellent or rich examples, but not unusual cases.
3. *Maximum variation sampling* attempts to minimize problems associated with small samples, in which there is a great deal of heterogeneity; the question becomes how to maximize variation in a small sample. First, identify the diverse characteristics or criteria for constructing the sample, and then select the sample accordingly. The goal of this technique is not to attempt to generalize findings to all people or all groups, but rather to look for information that elucidates programmatic variation and significant common patterns within that variation.
4. *Homogeneous samples* requires that you pick a small, homogeneous sample and describe it in depth. Focus group interviews are typically based on homogeneous groups.
5. *Typical case sampling* provides a profile of one or more "typical" cases, selected with the cooperation of key informants who have knowledge of potential subjects.
6. *Stratified purposeful sampling* consists of taking a sample of above average, average, and below average cases.

7. *Critical case sampling* involves looking for critical cases that can allow researchers to make a point quite dramatically or that are, for some reason, particularly important in the scheme of things. This method is based on the notion that "if it happens there, it will happen anywhere."

8. *Snowball or chain sampling* allows the researcher to locate information-rich key informants or critical cases. Ask well-situated people: "Who knows a lot about . . . ? Whom should I talk to?"

9. *Criterion sampling* involves reviewing and studying all cases that meet some predetermined criteria of importance. Critical incidents can also be a source of criteria sampling.

10. *Theory-based or operational construct sampling* requires that the researcher sample incidents, slices of life, time periods, or people on the basis of their potential manifestation or representation of important theoretical constructs.

11. *Confirming or disconfirming cases* involves searching for and sampling confirming cases (those that fit already emergent patterns) as well as disconfirming cases (those that don't fit already emergent patterns).

12. *Opportunistic sampling* requires that the researcher include in the sample some unexpected case that arises during the data collection procedure.

13. *Purposeful random sampling* selects cases in advance of the knowledge of how outcomes would appear. A small, purposeful random sample aims to reduce suspicion about why certain cases were selected.

14. *Sampling politically important cases* builds the sample on the basis of political sensitivity.

15. *Convenience sampling* aims for sampling what's fast, cost effective, and convenient. Convenience sampling, however, is neither purposeful not strategic. While convenience and cost are real considerations, they should be the last factors considered and only after strategically deliberating on how to get the most information.

Which sample procedure to select will depend upon the nature of the problem under consideration, and the purpose of the study. However, having selected a certain sampling type in advance of the study does not mean that one necessarily has to stick with it once the study is underway. One of the unique advantages of qualitative methodologies is that the researchers may change the sampling type in response to field conditions. For example, one may start with purposeful random sampling (selecting cases in advance of knowledge of how outcomes would appear), but through interviewing persons selected under this type, uncover other persons who might be rich sources of information, thus moving to a snowball or chain sampling technique. The only caveat is to note this shift when reporting the findings.

Role of Researcher

Perhaps in no instance do quantitative and qualitative methods differ more than in the role of the researcher. According to Patton (1990), critics charge that qualitative approaches are too subjective because the researcher is the instrument of both data collection and data interpretation. They also charge that qualitative approaches include personal contact between the researcher and the people and situations under study, allowing an intimacy that may compromise the researcher's objectivity. From the critics' perspective, subjectivity is the very antithesis of scientific inquiry.

On the other hand, objectivity has been considered the strength of the scientific method, usually interpreted as independent of human skill, perception, or even the presence of human beings. Yet it is clear that while the researcher may be an objective collector of data, his or her subjectivity and bias always affect the tests and questionnaires developed as well as the design of the study, including issues such as sampling and data analysis. Hence, the subjectivity-verses-objectivity argument is phony because subjectivity exists in all research methodologies (Patton, 1990).

Nevertheless, Patton (1990) argues that any credible research requires the investigator to adopt a stance of neutrality with regard to the phenomena under study. In other words, the investigator must not set out to prove a particular perspective or manipulate the data to arrive at predisposed truths. The neutral investigator has no axe to grind, no theory to prove, and no predetermined results to support. Neutrality is not easily attained, and because the human being is the instrument of data collection, qualitative inquiry "requires that the investigator carefully reflect on, deal with, and report potential sources of bias and error" (p. 56). On the other hand, according to Patton, "neutrality does not mean detachment. . . . Qualitative inquiry depends on, uses, and enhances the researcher's direct experience in the world and insights about those experiences" (p. 56).

Relationship with Respondents

It follows, then, that the qualitative investigator establishes a much different relationship with respondents than does the quantitative researcher. While quantitative research requires the investigator to limit or eliminate relationships with their subjects, qualitative research requires that the investigator establish personal contact with respondents, toward the goal of establishing a trust that will yield honest and insightful information. Techniques will be described later in this chapter for conducting interviews and asking questions, all designed to establish a rapport with subjects.

Instruments

The most important instrument in a qualitative study is the researcher, because the researcher plays an absolutely pivotal role in the research process. For example, it is the researcher who conducts the in-depth, open-ended interview, or directly observes a phenomena in the field, or reviews written documents. It is the researcher who very much determines what is seen, often participating in ways that influence the outcome of a study. In quantitative studies, the researcher uses inventories and questionnaires as the instruments, never intervening in ways that influence the outcomes. While the concept of "researcher as instrument" is often very difficult for a person steeped exclusively in quantitative methods to accept, it nevertheless exists in properly run qualitative studies, and, as discussed above, it is appropriate and credible.

Data Analysis

The quantitative researcher uses a deductive approach after data has been collected, applying statistical methods to analyze the quantifiable information collected, inferring conclusions from these analyses, and generalizing these conclusions to the larger population. The qualitative researcher, however, uses an inductive approach, often organizing, interpreting, codifying, and categorizing information both during and after data is collected, drawing conclusions from both the data and the researcher's experience.

Some Advantages

The advantages of qualitative over quantitative methodology should be thought of as relative, not absolute. In discussing the advantage of qualitative methods, it is important to emphasize that both require logic, rigor, and hard work on the part of the investigator. Our view is that the advantages (and disadvantages) hold true for the majority of cases, but certainly not for all. Three advantages stand out: Qualitative studies are very flexible, which allows the researcher to follow promising lines of inquiry as they emerge. Another benefit of qualitative studies is their emphasis on understanding how people make meaning of their circumstances. Finally, the fact that qualitative researchers can become advocates of the object of the assessment is a great advantage, particularly if the object pool consists of faculty who are being exposed to something unfamiliar.

On the other hand, quantitative studies have several prominent advantages as well. They can be easier to conduct, and conclusions drawn appear to have more certainty. Partly as a result of this, quantitative studies tend to have a higher degree of acceptance. It is not difficult to persuade audiences that good quantitative studies are rigorous and objective. As pointed out earlier, qualitative studies also require rigor, but it may require a bit more effort to persuade an audience of the precision and objectivity needed to conduct a good qualitative assessment.

Some Disadvantages

As one might imagine, problems are associated with each of these methods. In quantitative studies, controlling for intervening variables can be difficult. For example, a survey on campus safety could be influenced by a violent crime occurring two days before questionnaires are mailed to the respondents. Defining the population can also be a bit of a challenge. For example, the student body of a campus changes virtually every day as students withdraw from the college or enroll through correspondence courses. Furthermore, unless a quantitative study is reviewed carefully, readers can over-simplify the results. Merely because the numbers can be shown to have certain relationships, they do not necessarily dictate certain changes or administrative behaviors. (For a more thorough discussion of the limitations of quantitative research, see Chapter Four.)

Qualitative studies also have some disadvantages. For example, it can take a great deal of time to conduct a qualitative study. One does not conduct such a study in a few days, or even a few weeks. Conducting interviews and observing student behaviors can be time-consuming, as are the challenging processes of organizing, codifying, analyzing, and interpreting data. Making meaning of words and experiences is also quite difficult. Equally difficult is conducting a qualitative study of large groups of students. Think for a moment what it would be like to study the quality of student life at a university which enrolls first-year undergraduates as well as graduate and professional students. This very complex task may require shifting the definition of the research (such as studying the quality of life for first year students, liberal arts students, graduating seniors, and so on) in order to make the project more possible. Another problem with qualitative studies may be resistance by members of an institution on the grounds that such studies are not legitimate methods of inquiry. According to Patton (1990), one way of dealing with this problem is to combine methodologies (see Chapter Two, where both methodologies are used in a research design). Finally, anomalies in qualitative studies can be difficult to explain. Negative case analysis can be used, which means that anomalies are eliminated from the final report, but that does not mean that the anomalies were not part of certain students' experiences.

While the discussion of differences between qualitative and quantitative methods is not complete, some of the major differences have been identified. Many of these differences are quite dramatic and require a different kind of thinking on the part of those conducting the inquiry. Nevertheless, Borg, Gall, and Gall (1993) conclude that "both qualitative and quantitative research have much to offer education if they are used with sensitivity and discipline" (p. 201). A summary of these differences is presented in Table 3.1.

Table 3.1. A Brief Comparison of Qualitative and Quantitative Methods.

Qualitative	Quantitative
Key Concept	
Meaning	Statistical relationships
Design	
Emerging, flexible	Structured, predetermined
Data	
Field notes, people's own words, documents, behavior	Measures, counts, numbers
Sampling	
Nonrepresentative, small, snowball	Large, stratified, random
Methods	
Observations, reviewing documents, interviewing	Experiments, survey instruments, data sets
Relationships with Subjects	
Personal contact, emphasis on trust	Short term, distant
Instruments	
Researcher, tape recorder, cameras	Inventories, questionnaires, computer
Data Analysis	
Ongoing, inductive	Deductive, statistical
Advantages	
Flexibility, emphasis on understanding	Ease of use, high acceptance
Disadvantages	
Time, hard to reduce data, hard to study large groups, hard to explain anomalies	Controlling other variables, defining universe, oversimplification

Source: Adapted from Bogdan and Biklen, *Qualitative Research for Education* (1992) and Worthen and Sanders, *Educational Evaluation: Alternative Approaches and Practical Guidelines* (1987).

Data Collection Techniques

As mentioned previously in this chapter, the three methods of collecting data in qualitative studies include interviewing respondents, reviewing documents, and observing people in natural settings. In this section, we will review each of these methods and provide practical advice on how to do each.

Interviews

In qualitative research, interviews are the central data collection technique. They involve personal engagement with subjects, an opportunity for the researcher to explore topics in depth (Manning, 1992), and the immediate testing of hypotheses (Carnaghi, 1992). We would add that interviews require interviewers with exceptional interpersonal skills, because, as Patton (1990) pointed out, "the quality of information obtained during an interview is largely dependent on the interviewer" (p. 279). Several decisions must be made about interviews, including the type of interview to be used, the types of questions to be asked, the sequencing of the questions, the wording of questions, probes and follow-up questions, the preparation, role, and skill of the interviewer, and the interview format (individual interview or focus group).

Types of Interviews

Patton (1990) identifies three basic types of interviews: the informal conversational interview, the general interview guide, and the standardized open-ended interview. Each type requires a different kind of preparation, conceptualization, and instrumentation.

1. The informal conversational interview relies entirely on the spontaneous generation of questions in the natural flow of an interaction. It typically occurs as part of ongoing participant-observation field work. In some instances, the person with whom the interview is talking may not even realize they are being interviewed.
2. According to Patton (1990), the general interview guide approach "involves outlining a set of issues that are to be explored with each respondent before interviewing begins. The

issues in the outline need not be taken in any particular order and the actual wording of questions to elicit responses about those issues is not determined in advance. . . . The interviewer is thus required to adapt both his wording and the sequence of questions to specific respondents in the context of the actual interview" (p. 280).

3. According to Patton (1990), the standardized open-ended interview "consists of a set of questions carefully worded and arranged with the intention of taking each respondent through the same sequence and asking each respondent the same questions with essentially the same words" (p. 280). This type of interview is most appropriately used when it is important to minimize variation in the questions posed to respondents, especially when a large number of interviewers are used. (For a more thorough discussion of each of these techniques, see Patton, 1990.)

It has been our experience that when using the interview for assessment purposes, the standardized, open-ended interview is the most appropriate, and the most credible with various audiences. Respondents answer the same questions, thus increasing comparability of responses, and data are complete for each person on the topics addressed in the interview. As suggested above, this type of interview reduces the effects and bias of the interviewer when several are used. It also permits the users of the evaluation to review the instrumentation used before the study is actually carried out. Finally, the organization and analysis of the data are much easier to accomplish when the exact same questions are asked of all those interviewed (Patton, 1990). That is not to say that the informal conversation or interview guide approaches are never to be used, only that in our experience, their usefulness is very limited in student affairs assessment studies.

Kinds of Questions

Several different kinds of questions may be asked in an interview, depending upon the purpose of the study. Patton (1990) identifies six:

1. *Experience and behavior questions* probe what a person does or has done, with the aim of eliciting descriptions of experiences, behaviors, actions, and activities that are observable—for example,

"If I had followed you as you tried to get an appointment in our placement service, what would I see you doing?"

2. *Opinion and values questions* are aimed at understanding the cognitive and interpretive processes of respondents. These questions tell us what people think about certain issues, including their goals, intentions, desires, and values—for example, "In your opinion, how might career counseling be improved?"

3. *Feeling questions* try to elicit the emotional responses people have to their experiences and thoughts. In asking feeling questions, we are looking for adjectives such as anxious, confident, angry, happy, frustrated, elated, etc. Unfortunately, feeling and opinions are often confused. For example, in response to the above question about career counseling, the student may say, "I feel career counseling services should be better advertised." This is an opinion, not a feeling (in this context, *feel* means "believe" or "think"), and the interviewer must make that distinction. A properly expressed feeling question might go like this: "How do you feel when you try to get an appointment in the career center?" An appropriate feeling response might be, "I get very frustrated when I can't get an appointment to see a counselor."

4. *Knowledge questions* help the investigator find out what factual information the respondent has. These types of questions are very important to student affairs, because we worry a lot about whether or not students know about our services, programs, and facilities, and whether that knowledge is accurate. For example, we might ask, "How much is a student charged for one visit with a physician at the health service?" or "What are the weekend hours of the student union?"

5. *Sensory questions* are about what is seen, heard, touched, tasted, and smelled. The purpose of these questions is to explore the respondent's sensory apparatus. Examples might be "When you walk into the student union, what do you see?" or "What did you hear when you first met with your substance abuse counselor?" Technically, sensory data are a type of behavioral data, but they are sufficiently different to merit a separate category.

6. *Background and demographic questions* identify the characteristics of the person being interviewed and help locate the respondent in relation to other people. Student demographic characteristics might include age, education, major, class standing, place of residence, and so on. In instances where the students

who are interviewed have been selected from an institutional database, it may not be necessary to collect this information in the actual interview, thus saving valuable interview time.

Sequencing of Questions

According to Patton (1990), there are no fixed rules of sequence when organizing an interview, particularly when using the informal conversational interview or the general interview guide approach. However, when using the standardized open-ended interview, a fixed sequencing of questions is very important. It has been our experience that opening the interview with some "icebreakers" allows participants to disclose relatively "safe" information, and starts the process of making students more comfortable with the interview situation. It is very important for the interviewer to participate in this process, both to model the behavior and to establish the notion of the "researcher as instrument." As mentioned above, valuable interview time can be saved if background questions are kept to a minimum. And when they are necessary, they should be asked at the beginning of the interview, particularly in a heterogeneous focus group where the perspective of the participant may be crucial to the interviewer's interpretation of the data collected.

Then, according to Patton (1990), it is probably best to begin with questions about noncontroversial behaviors, activities, and experiences, because they are easy to answer and pose very little threat to the participant. The next set of questions should be focused on opinions, interpretations, and feelings. Save knowledge questions for last; they can often be quite threatening. Consider how the student union board chair would feel if he or she did not know the weekend hours of the student union.

Wording of Questions

Patton (1990) argues that interviewing is an art, that good questions should be open-ended, neutral, singular, and clear, and that "why" questions should be asked with great care. Constructing truly open-ended questions that do not bias responses is a very delicate task. For example, at first blush, the question, "How satisfied are you with our alcohol education programs?" may seem to be a perfectly appropriate open-ended question. It is not appropriate because it presumes that the person is, in fact, satisfied to some degree, and thus limits the possible responses. A better question might be, "What is your opinion of our alcohol education programs?" Or "What do you think of our alcohol education programs?" Questions that are closed-ended ("Are you satisfied with our alcohol education programs?") are even worse, because they require only a "yes" or "no" answer, which hardly encourages participants to provide an elaborate discussion.

Neutral questions are preferable to questions where the interviewer appears to have concluded that a problem exists. For example, "How does the noise in residence halls prevent you from studying?" Here the interviewer has a made a clear supposition (noise has a negative affect on studying) which may or may not be true. A more appropriate question might be, "Tell me how, if at all, noise in residence halls affects your studying?" In this question, the bias is eliminated because the question does not assume any relationship between noise and studying, and if there is one, its effect has not been identified.

Singular questions (asking only one question at a time) is also very important. For example, "I'd like to know more about your experiences with our women's center. How did you find out about the center? What did you think when you first entered the office? Who was most helpful?" This is probably a well-intended effort on the part of the interviewer to offer participants some examples of their responses. But it kills the whole idea of qualitative interviewing (because it structures the responses), and it is very confusing to the participants. Any one of these questions is appropriate, however, when asked one at a time. Lumping several questions together also creates unnecessary confusion when the interviewer begins to organize and codify responses.

Clarity of the questions is critical. According to Patton (1990), it is the responsibility of the interviewer to find out, in advance of the interview, what terms are familiar to the participants, and to make sure any unfamiliar or ambiguous terms are defined. For example, the question "How might CDPC be improved?" assumes that the student knows that CDPC stands for the Career Development and Placement Center. It is difficult to restrict oneself to language that is understandable and part of the frame of reference of the person being interviewed. For example, on any given campus the language students use when they talk with each other may be quite unique.

Depending on the campus, or even on different groups on the same campus, the pairing off of persons in a romantic sense may be "dating," "hooking up," "connecting," or some other colloquial expression. It is important for the interviewer to have some awareness of local student language when preparing interview questions. Lack of clarity will also haunt the interviewer if he or she does not understand the terms used by those interviewed, in which case the interviewer must ask participants meanings of words he or she does not understand, even if it is awkward to do so.

"Why" questions are always problematical because they assume a cause-and-effect relationship, presupposing that there are reasons things occur and that those reasons are knowable (Patton, 1990). Such questions may also threaten participants, making them feel they have to justify their behavior (for example, "Why did you illegally consume alcohol in your residence hall?"). Most "why" questions can be asked in ways that avoid these pitfalls. For example, instead of asking the question, "Why did you join a fraternity?" we might ask, "What was it about the fraternity that attracted you to it?"

But wait a minute. In Chapter Two, we constructed a study that probed *why* African American students underused the counseling center. It is a perfectly appropriate purpose of a study to explore the "why" question, but the reader will remember that while the purpose was to explore the "why" question, the actual questions asked were: "Our records indicate counseling services are underused by African American students. Why do you believe this is so? What, if anything, should be done to increase usage of the counseling center by African American students?" These questions are better than asking "Why don't you use our counseling center?" because they are not personal and they clearly put the responsibility for nonuse on the center, not the participant.

Probes and Follow-Up Questions

According to Patton (1990), a probe is a follow-up question used to go deeper into the interviewee's responses. There are detail-oriented probes (asking the when, who, where, what, and how questions) and elaboration probes. From our experience, "Tell me more about . . ." or "Help me better understand . . ." are good elaboration probes, because they put the focus of the elaboration on the interviewer rather than the participant. A probe should never go beyond what the person said, or beyond the scope of the original question. For example, if the participant is asked to offer an opinion about an AIDS program, and the participant says, "I believe one of the strengths of the AIDS program was good visual aids," it may be appropriate to encourage elaboration by asking, "Help me understand better what impressed you about the visual aids."

A temptation to be avoided in probes is to suggest a response you believe a participant may have overlooked. For example, the presenters of the AIDS program may have spent a great deal of time and effort developing high-tech and interactive visual aids. Let's further assume that the interview protocol was very broad and simply asked the question, "What is your opinion about the AIDS program?" and the respondent makes no mention of the visual aids. It may be tempting to follow up by asking, "What did you think of the visual aids?" But in this instance, we may learn as much from what participants didn't say as what they did say. If all respondents failed to mention the visual aids, then that tells you a lot about their impact on participants. On the other hand, if you really want to know about visual aids, then ask the question separately rather than as a probe. In short, a probe should never suggest an answer that was not first mentioned by the participant.

Document Review

Document review is the second data collection technique that is commonly found in the portfolio of the qualitative researcher. Whitt (1992a) observes that document reviews tend to be ignored in favor of more active or interactive techniques of collecting data, such as interviews or observations. Nonetheless, the researcher concludes that "documents are a potentially fruitful source of both primary and secondary data, and as such, demand attention in any study of college student experiences" (p. 89).

Bogdan and Biklen (1992) indicate that materials such as personal documents (including diaries, letters, and autobiographies) and official documents (internal documents, external communications, and records and files) can provide useful data. In addition, many large-scale databases have been constructed in considerable detail by government and private agencies (Bowering, 1984). Documents have advantages and disadvantages as Whitt (1992a) points out. Documents are readily available, provide a stable source of data, and are grounded in the setting in which they are found. On the other hand, they may be incomplete, reflect author bias, and be nonreactive, meaning that the researcher may not be able to sit down with the author and raise questions about those items that are unclear. Nonetheless, documents provide a rich source of information and should not be ignored by the person contemplating assessing some aspect of student life.

Observations

Observations may take the form of simply watching how people behave in the setting, or they may involve actually being a participant observer—that is, joining the subjects in their setting and interacting with them. However it is performed, the method of observation provides the investigator with an opportunity to see how people behave in a natural setting. A notable example of participant observation is Moffatt's study at Rutgers University (1988), where he lived with students in a residence hall over an extended period of time.

The investigator must consider a variety of issues when conducting observations. For example, do the students who are being observed need to be informed that they are being observed? Is the length of time that the observation is being conducted long enough? (Russell, 1992). Do participant observers reveal their purpose in participating with the group? Is the investigator able to observe all the relevant behavior in a particularly active setting? For example, at a speech, does the observer watch the speaker, the audience, or both? These issues and others provide challenges for the investigator who is engaged in observing student behavior as part of an assessment project. Nonetheless, potentially useful information can be gleaned from simply observing students on campus, and this technique should be considered when developing a qualitative assessment project.

Responsibility and Role of the Investigator

Most qualitative investigators would agree that success of the interview depends on the preparation, role, and skill of the interviewer, even if everything else is well planned and implemented. The first task of the interviewer, of course, is to establish rapport with those being questioned. Patton (1990) believes rapport must be established in such a way that it does not undermine the interviewer's neutrality. Neutrality means the person being interviewed is free to discuss anything without feeling judged by the interviewer. As an interviewer,

> I cannot be shocked, I cannot be angered, I cannot be embarrassed, I cannot be saddened—indeed, nothing the person tells me will make me think more or less of them. At the same time that I am neutral with regard to the content of what is being said to me, I care very much that the person is willing to share with me what they are saying. Rapport is a stance vis-à-vis the person being interviewed. Neutrality is a stance vis-à-vis the content of what that person says. Rapport means that I respect the people being interviewed, so what they say is important because of who is saying it. I want to convey to them that their knowledge, experiences, attitudes, and feelings are important. Yet, I will not judge them for the content of what they are saying to me [p. 317].

Other important ways of facilitating a free and open discussion, according to Patton (1990), include giving the person reinforcement and feedback. This means letting the person know from time to time that the purpose of the interview is being fulfilled. Words of thanks, support, and praise are especially important. It has been our experience that one must make sure that the reinforcement is directed toward the person, not what the person is saying. It is important, for example, for the interviewer to occasionally reflect back and summarize what the person has said, to make sure that both the interviewer and the person interviewed agree on what was said. It is inappropriate, however, to reinforce what was said by agreeing with the opinions and attitudes expressed. Also, during the interview, the interviewer should be "tuned into" the reactions of the person interviewed, sensing when he or she may be uncomfortable, confused, or rambling, and react accordingly.

Since the primary audience of this book is student affairs professionals, there is no further need to elaborate on this point, because the concepts of rapport, neutrality, reinforcement, feedback, and sensitivity to the interaction are among the guiding principles of counseling. The good news for student affairs professionals is that by training and experience, we are already very well prepared to conduct interviews in ways that allow those interviewed to speak freely and comfortably. All the skills and behaviors that go into a good counseling intake interview apply to the qualitative interview as well.

However, student affairs professionals are educators as well as counselors, and the educator part of our skills may present a problem. In the interview situation, we must resist the temptation to "educate" as well as "investigate." When we conduct educational programs or teach courses, we have an educational responsibility to correct incomplete or wrong answers. It is very tempting, then, to do the same in a qualitative interview. For example, let's say you're the director of residence halls and someone says, "I'd love to live in the residence halls next year, but I prefer a single room and there are no single rooms in residence halls." As director of residence halls, you know that, in fact, there are single rooms in residence halls, and you will be very tempted to step out of your interview role and clear up this misconception. But you must resist this temptation, because it will seriously jeopardize your role as a neutral and impartial interviewer.

Second, the interviewer has a responsibility to develop an opening statement which informs those interviewed of (1) the purpose of the study, (2) who is conducting the study, (3) why they were selected, (4) what questions will be asked, (5) the conditions of confidentiality, (6) the importance of full participation, (7) how long the interview will take, (8) how the results will be used, and (8) any incentives for participating. If the study requires written, informed consent as determined through the Institutional Review Board/Human Subjects Committee (see Chapter Fourteen), it should be explained in the opening statement and signed by the person interviewed. The opening statement should be clear and concise, taking up no more than a minute or two.

Third, it is important for the interviewer to maintain control of the interview. This includes making sure that the person answers the questions asked, and does not go far afield from the purpose of the interview. It also means keeping track of time so that all the questions can be covered in the time allotted. In the instance of the focus group interview, it means making sure that all persons get a chance to speak, that no one person dominates the interview, and that the group dynamics assure open and free communication.

Fourth, the interviewer is responsible for making an accurate record of what was said, because if the interview fails to capture the essence and meaning of what was said, the whole methodology fails. The best and most effective way of doing this is to audiotape or videotape (if appropriate to the purposes of the study). While some would argue that the presence of a tape recorder may inhibit the person's responses, it has been our experience that (1) a person seldom questions the use of an audiotape recorder, and (2) within a few seconds after the interview has begun, the presence of the tape recorder is quickly forgotten. And if the tape recorder is functioning properly, the use of tape leaves no doubt as to what was said. (The interviewer should always test the equipment before the interview, no matter how often it has been used successfully in the past.)

Other methods of recording interviews in no way measure up to actual taping. For example, if the interviewer tries to take notes during the interview, the person interviewed may get distracted and think, "She's writing down what I just said; it must have been important" or "She hasn't written anything lately. I must not be saying anything important." It is also difficult for the interviewer to give full attention to what is being said while writing down responses. And there is the problem of missing important comments. Using another investigator (and nonparticipant) to take notes allows the interviewer to concentrate fully on what is being said, but still suffers from the other limitations of this method. Recording nothing during the interview and attempting to reconstruct what was said after the interview is also strongly discouraged, for many of the same reasons.

Finally, the interviewer has the responsibility of closing the interview. This process includes expressing appreciation to the person for participating in the interview. Closure may also involve asking the person to comment upon the interview experience, the questions, and the interviewer, especially if it was a pilot interview. Other matters might include making arrangements to send the results to the person or providing an incentive such as movie tickets, a discount coupon redeemable at the bookstore, or a free meal at the student union. It has also been our experience that giving the person an opportunity to come back or call back with additional information or clarification is helpful to the closure process and may increase the validity of the responses.

Individual Interviews or Focus Groups?

How to decide which interview technique to use depends on several factors. An individual interview is probably most appropriate when the topic discussed may require subjects to disclose information they might not be comfortable disclosing in a group. Individual interviews allow the person to express thoughts, feelings, and opinions without competing for "air time" with others, or feeling intimidated by the group. It is also easier for the interviewer to establish rapport quickly with one person than with an entire group, and keeping track of one-to-one interaction dynamics is much easier than keeping track of group interaction dynamics. And when the individual interview is taped, there is no question who made the comments. In a focus group, it is often difficult to distinguish who said what from a tape.

On the other hand, a focus group is a highly efficient data collection procedure. In an hour or two, an interviewer can gather information from a small group of people (no more than ten) instead of just one person, thus increasing sample size. Perhaps the most important advantage of a focus group is that participants can "feed off each other" as they respond; a response that may not occur to a person in an individual interview may be stimulated by something someone else said in the focus group. Focus group members can support or disagree with one another, creating more energy and thus more data.

Disadvantages of Focus Groups

First of all, interview options are reduced. Conversational interviews or even outline interviews do not work well with focus groups, so the open-ended structured interview format must be used. Focus groups are also more difficult to manage. Not only does the interviewer have to do all the things required in an individual interview, he or she must also keep track of what's going on in the group. Unexpected conflicts, power struggles, and other group dynamics may inhibit discussion. Shy persons may be intimidated by more assertive persons. One person may dominate to the exclusion of others. And as mentioned above, if the group is taped, it is often difficult to distinguish who said what. This may be a problem when the demographic characteristics of group members (for example, gender, race, class standing) are important to the purposes of the study.

Group Composition

Should focus groups be heterogeneous (made up of persons representative of the whole sample) or homogeneous (made up of specific subgroups of the whole sample). Of course, this decision depends in part upon the purpose of the study, and whether responses by subgroups are important. But a very damaging bias may be infused into a study based on this decision, because heterogeneous focus groups can yield different results than homogeneous groups, given the same sample. For example, asking a focus group of men and women to discuss gender roles may yield quite different results than asking the same question of separate focus groups of men and women, because each may react quite differently in the presence or absence of the other gender. So some decision must be made about the potential bias created by the composition of the focus group. If there is reason to believe that bias may exist, then both heterogeneous and homogeneous focus groups should be conducted.

Ultimately, the investigator must decide, based on all of the above factors, whether the focus group or the individual interview is most appropriate. The best solution, of course, if time and resources permit, is to use both, taking advantage of the benefits of both.

Data Analysis

Once collected, the data must be codified, organized, and sequenced in ways that make analysis possible. This phase of an investigation is not an easy task and can require substantial time, energy, and cost. But there are some ways in which these factors can be mitigated.

To a great extent, data collection and analysis are conducted simultaneously. That is, while conducting interviews or reviewing documents, the investigator is learning more about what people think and developing new avenues for inquiry. For example, interviewers may want to write a memo to themselves which contains preliminary thoughts based on spending a few days in the field or conducting interviews (Bogdan and Biklen, 1992). During this process, suppositions will be developed and very tentative conclusions drawn. Still, at some point, the collection of data must stop and formal data analysis begin. It is at this point that researchers will need to find ways to streamline the task of analysis.

Data Reduction

Miles and Huberman (1988) and Lincoln and Guba (1985) provide excellent guidance for analyzing data. One basic approach is to try to reduce the information to individual data bits and record them. This information could come from interviews, field notes observations, or notes from document reviews. From these individual data bits, the themes, trends, and patterns will emerge upon which the investigator will base the final report.

Metaphors

Second, the investigator might think in terms of metaphors. Metaphors can help translate what is unfamiliar in a setting into elements that are more familiar to the investigator. While the fit may not be perfect, the use of the metaphor is an excellent tool that the investigator ought to consider, especially if the setting contains a number of characteristics unfamiliar to the investigator. For example, say investigators are studying the culture of a mythical organization, Company X. If in this study the investigators find that Company X operates with a great deal of attention paid to hierarchy and status and many regulations governing daily business, they might use the armed forces as a metaphor to describe Company X. While the purpose of Company X might be very different from the armed forces, using the armed forces as a metaphor generates vivid images which can help a person unfamiliar with Company X understand its culture.

Themes and Patterns

The investigator might want to share emerging themes and patterns with subjects. After conducting a few interviews some rough themes about the investigation might begin to emerge. It could be very useful to explore these themes with other respondents to see if they make sense. Respondents may confirm or disagree with these very tentative conclusions; the observations may stimulate further discussion and exchange. In one project, an assessment team concluded that respondents joined their organizations to become more familiar with certain aspects of their heritage. When this theme was shared with the respondents, they rejected the concept, indicating that they did not join for those purposes (Schuh, Triponey, Heim, and Nishimura, 1992).

Understanding the Data

On a more practical level, we have drawn from our experience several specific suggestions for analyzing interview data. The first issue is to get an accurate description of the data. Decide, for example, whether or not to transcribe tapes of interviews. On the one hand, transcriptions give the investigator the exact words of the participants, so there is no misunderstanding about what was said. On the other hand, transcribing hour-long interview tapes is a very time-consuming and costly process, often unreasonably delaying data analysis. It is particularly difficult when focus groups are used, because the transcriber is often unable to identify who is speaking.

A more practical alternative to transcription is for the investigator to listen to the tape several times, taking notes on key concepts, themes, and trends, and extracting direct quotes. This saves time, avoids the cost of transcription, and if there is any question about what was said, there is still an accurate record. Having several people listen to the tapes, either individually or in a group, is a good way of making sure that the analysis is thorough.

Another alternative is to code responses in ways that can be entered into a computer program. This may be especially appropriate if large amounts of data are being managed. For a detailed discussion of computer analyses in qualitative analysis, see Pfaffenberger (1988). Software programs are being developed not only for recording data, but for organizing, managing, and analyzing data as well.

Organizing the Data

Organizing data is more of a problem when the conversational interview format is used, because of the lack of consistency among the interviews. One must struggle to find a way to organize data that makes sense. Organizing data is somewhat less of a problem when the interview outline is used, because the outline can form the basis for organizing data. When the structured interview protocol is used, the questions may provide a way to organize data. However, there are times when the original interview format just doesn't seem to provide a good organizing format. In such a case, Patton (1990) recommends other alternatives, including describing data chronologically, presenting critical incidents or major events, describing various places, sites, settings, or locations, presenting case studies of groups or individuals, identifying key processes, or identifying key issues.

Analyzing the Data

Another hurdle that must be cleared is deciding "what it all means." It is quite possible for investigators to agree on the data collected, and how that data will be organized and analyzed, while disagreeing on the conclusions. In quantitative analysis, the data more easily determines the conclusions. In qualitative analysis, the connections between data and conclusions will be more elusive. As Patton (1990) points out, "The challenge is to . . . construct a framework for communicating the essence of what the data reveal" (p. 372). But according to Miles and Huberman (1988), "We have few agreed upon canons for qualitative data analysis, in the sense of shared ground rules for drawing conclusions" (p. 16). The solution is for the investigators to keep discussing, probing, and thinking until a consensus is reached on "what it all means." As pointed out above, this may mean going back to the respondents themselves, or bringing in persons not involved in the original study to offer their thoughts and ideas. Whatever is done, however, Patton (1990) argues that "analysts have an obligation to monitor and report their own analytical procedures and processes as fully and truthfully as possible" (p. 373).

To the inexperienced investigator, this process of describing, organizing, analyzing, and drawing conclusions may seem very intimidating at first glance. It has been our experience, however, that it is much less daunting than initially imagined. Most of the time, themes "jump out" and are confirmed over and over again. Areas of disagreement among respondents are easily identified. Conclusions are more easily drawn when a group of investigators engages in the process. All we can say is that in most instances, it is in fact easier done than said.

Examples of Qualitative Studies

As pointed out many times in this chapter, qualitative methods serve the investigator best when the study's aim is to determine why students behave the way they do in a natural setting and how they make meaning of their experiences. Quantitative methods can help the investigator learn about the "what" in students' lives, but qualitative methods open the door to the answers to such questions as "how" and "why." Also, qualitative methods allow students to determine the range of responses they can provide to certain questions, whereas the investigator provides the range of answers when quantitative methods are used. In Chapter Two, the reader was provided with a step-by-step example of a study which used both qualitative and quantitative methods in assessing the underuse of counseling services by African American students. Three examples follow which illustrate how qualitative methods can be used to provide answers to routine problems facing student affairs administrators and others on campus.

Qualitative methods are particularly useful when one wants students or others to assess their own learning experiences. In this first example, the problem lies in what appears to be a declining interest in serving terms in student government positions. The interview method is used to assess what students have learned from serving as officers in the student government association. Questions can be asked of student leaders, such as the following:

- What were your reasons for deciding to get involved in student government?
- How, if at all, did things work out for you?
- What, if anything, do you wish you could have done but could not in fact do?
- If you had it to do all over again, what, if anything, would you change?
- What, if any, were the most valuable learning experiences during your student government experience? How were they valuable?

- If you were in charge of this institution for a day, what would be the one thing you would not change?

Clearly, these open-ended questions cannot be answered in one or two words, forcing the respondents to elaborate and discuss their experiences and attitudes. These interview questions can be used in both individual interviews and focus groups, providing the advantages that both formats have to offer. Using current student leaders provides the most direct and valuable data to help solve the problem.

A second example stems from trying to determine the history of a campus issue. Suppose your college has a new president who has asked you to prepare a short report on the most significant issues for students over the past two years. How would you go about preparing the report? In this instance, document review is the most appropriate method. Going to the student newspaper "morgue" and reviewing the last two years of the paper may provide useful information. The stories and letters to the editor could reveal what was of concern to editorial writers, the people who contribute to the paper, and those students who write letters. From this analysis, a picture of campus issues could emerge. Should this be the end of your work? Probably not, since annual reports and other documents could be other potentially rich sources of information for your report.

A third example illustrates how another qualitative method can be used to meet a need on campus that emerged from observing student behavior. On this campus, for years students had taped flyers and posters on the sidewalks as a way of informing each other about events, programs, and the like. This taping of notices made for quite a mess, especially after high winds and rain. What the taping represented was a need for students to communicate with each other. To tell students they could no longer post notices on the sidewalks (in the name of campus tidiness) would not address the larger issue of their need to communicate. So, a number of kiosks were constructed on campus specifically for posting notices. Less litter resulted and communication among students was maintained.

These three stories—illustrating learning about student government experiences, summarizing issues through the use of documents, and determining need by observing student behavior—are good examples of how qualitative methods can be used in daily stu-

dent affairs practice. As one contemplates some of these assignments, which are routinely assigned to student affairs administrators, it is evident that qualitative methods have a very important role
in administrative decision making.

Ensuring Rigor

The principles and methods of qualitative assessment tend not to
conform to traditional standards of scientific rigor, such as reliability and validity (Crowson, 1987). This does not mean, however,
that qualitative research need not or cannot be rigorous; like all
researchers, those doing qualitative research must prove that
their study is "worth paying attention to" (Lincoln and Guba,
1985, p. 290).

Many qualitative investigators use the standard of trustworthiness, developed by Lincoln and Guba (1985), to establish the rigor
of their assessment. Criteria for trustworthy qualitative approaches
include credibility (data, interpretations, and conclusions are credi
ble to the participants in the research and others); transferability
(the study might be useful in another setting); dependability
(changes over time are accounted for); and confirmability (the
data and interpretations can be confirmed by someone other than
the researcher) (Lincoln and Guba, 1985).

Methods for satisfying these criteria are described in detail in
Lincoln and Guba (1985), Merriam (1988), and Whitt (1991), but
one example must suffice here. Credibility of data and interpretations can be established by triangulation (using multiple methods
of data collection and multiple data sources); peer debriefing
(using a peer to ensure that researchers are aware of their personal
perspectives, and to help develop next steps); and respondent
debriefing (reviewing and testing data, interpretations, and conclusions with assessment participants) (Whitt, 1991). Debriefing
with respondents is absolutely necessary because the "success or
failure [of a qualitative study] depends on the degree to which it
rings true to natives and colleagues in the field. . . . They should
recognize the details of the description as accurate" (Fetterman,
1989, p. 21). Respondent debriefings take place throughout the
assessment process, including during data collection and after each
phase of writing the research results (Kuh and others, 1991).

Other Qualitative Methods

Other approaches available to the qualitative investigator are worth mentioning, although they can be quite complex. The reader is referred to the original source material for a more complete discussion of these methods. Other approaches include the following:

1. Connoisseurship (the art of appreciation) and criticism (the art of disclosure) have their roots in the arts rather than the sciences. Eisner (1988) has written persuasively on this interesting topic, observing that the "language of criticism, indeed its success as criticism, is measured by the brightness of its illumination. The task of the critic is to help us to see" (p. 143). Eisner describes some of his practical work at Stanford in connoisseurship and criticism as creating new ways of looking at the phenomena that constitute educational life within classrooms. What does the critic do? "One describes, one interprets, and one evaluates or appraises what one sees" (p. 144).

2. According to Smith (1988), metaphors, which were referred to earlier in this chapter, are the devices for using one object to create a new perspective on another. Smith suggests that "as a qualitative, investigative tool, the metaphor proved to be a provocative and productive alternative strategy for conducting exploratory research" (p. 155). Among the potential sources for metaphors that Smith introduces are the law, journalism, economics, geography, and photography. For example, Smith discusses the concept of "least protest," a geographical concept that is used in decision making which posits that decisions are made which will generate the least amount of protest. It can be applied, in his view, to studies of, for example, school closures and employee transfers (pp. 164–165).

3. Phenomenography, the third approach, is defined by Marton (1988) as being "about the qualitatively different ways in which people experience or think about various phenomena" (p. 179). Phenomenography is a research specialization aimed at mapping the qualitatively different ways in which people experience, conceptualize, perceive, and understand various aspects of, and various phenomena in, the world around them. Marton points to a study of political power as one example of the use of phenomenography. In this study, people protested against the selection of

a particular site for the construction of a garage; their protest resulted in the halting of the project.

Conclusion

In this chapter, we have argued strongly that qualitative methods are appropriate for certain types of student affairs assessments. Qualitative and quantitative methods have been compared and contrasted. Specific techniques have been identified and the role and responsibility of the investigator have been described. We may have been a bit overzealous in this discussion, but we believe it is necessary, given the current skepticism within the higher education community about the validity and rigor of such studies. The solution in many cases is to use both qualitative and quantitative methodologies. But there are times when qualitative methods are appropriate, and quantitative methods are not, and student affairs professionals must know why, when, and how to do qualitative studies.

Chapter Four

Using Quantitative Methods

Patrick T. Terenzini and M. Lee Upcraft

More often than not, to most student affairs practitioners assessment in student affairs means conducting a quantitative study. While we would dispute the notion that quantitative assessments are the only valid means of conducting true assessments, conducting quantitative assessments are very important, and can be very powerful when done correctly.

In Chapter Two, we identified some of the key assessment issues in both qualitative and quantitative studies, and offered a step-by-step example (the underuse of counseling services by African American students) of how to conduct a particular type of quantitative study. In Chapter Three, we contrasted quantitative methods with qualitative methods. In this chapter, we will offer a more detailed discussion of quantitative methodologies, outlining an eleven-step process, consisting of (1) defining the problem, (2) defining the purpose of the study, (3) determining when to use a quantitative approach, (4) defining the population and sampling techniques, (5) selecting and constructing an instrument, (6) determining the types of statistical analyses, (7) developing and implementing a plan for data collection, (8) recording the data in usable form, (9) conducting the appropriate statistical analyses, (10) determining what the analyses mean for policy and practice, and (11) developing a strategy for how the results of the study will be used.

This chapter does *not* provide an exhaustive and definitive summary of all aspects of quantitative methodologies. We found Linda Suskie's *Questionnaire Survey Research: What Works* (1992), to be particularly helpful, and we drew heavily from this source in writing this chapter. We highly recommend this very "user friendly" resource to practitioners who have limited knowledge of quantitative methods. The reader is also referred to such texts as Kerlinger's *Foundations of Behavioral Research* (1986), Borg and Gall's *Educational Research* (1989), or Hinkle, Wiersma, and Jurs's *Applied Statistics for the Behavioral Sciences* (1994).

Definition and Use of Quantitative Methods

In Chapter Three, we discussed in detail when and how qualitative methods should be used. There are several instances in which student affairs assessments can use quantitative methods as well (many of which are discussed in much greater detail elsewhere in this book), including tracking students who use services, programs, and facilities, student needs assessments, student satisfaction studies, outcome studies, certain environmental assessments, and many others. Quantitative studies give us a very firm foundation for describing and analyzing what "is," and offer some insights into "why" it is the way it is.

Let's start with a basic definition. According to Rossman and El-Khawas (1987), quantitative methodology is the assignment of numbers to objects, events, or observations according to some rule. Patton (1990) adds that quantitative methods require the use of standard measures so that the varying perspectives and experiences of people can be fit into a limited number of predetermined response categories to which numbers are assigned. Thus it's possible to measure the reactions of a great many people by way of a limited set of questions, facilitating comparisons and statistical aggregation and analysis of the data. According to Shulman (1988), in quantitative research, samples are drawn from populations in ways that ensure that those chosen are *representative* of the population, according to some criteria. If the sample is, in fact, representative, then one can confidently *generalize* the findings from the sample to the whole population.

Steps in a Quantitative Study

We believe the best way to illustrate and expand these quantitative methods concepts is to walk the reader, step-by-step, through a basic quantitative study of an actual problem in student affairs. The reader should also refer to Chapter Ten, where a more sophisticated quantitative study, illustrating outcomes assessment, is discussed.

Step One: Define the Problem

As discussed earlier, all assessment flows from some problem. In this example, the problem was that the placement service of a large university had received a few complaints from corporate recruiters about the way they were treated when they came to the campus to interview students. Since students consider job placement an important and expected service, the placement service could not afford to have dissatisfied interviewers who might not come to the campus anymore. In fact, what made an assessment all the more urgent was the threat to discontinue campus visitations by a recruiter from a company that traditionally employed many graduates of this institution. More information about recruiter perceptions of the placement service was definitely needed, and needed quickly.

Step Two: Determine the Purposes of the Study

The placement service needed to know more placement recruiter perceptions about the placement services. More specifically, the purposes were:

1. To determine why recruiters chose this institution to interview students.
2. To determine how recruiters rated various placement services.
3. To determine if recruiter responses varied by gender, race or ethnicity, size of company, and number of previous visits to the placement service.

Step Three: Determine the Appropriate Assessment Approach

The selection of a quantitative approach was dictated by the purpose of the study, the size of the population, time limitations, and resource limitations. The problem was a vague sense that recruiters were dissatisfied, so the nature of that dissatisfaction needed to be verified. Looking at a smaller group in greater depth might have been misleading, because the placement service was not certain of the extent of recruiter dissatisfaction. It could have been that only a handful of dissatisfied employers were motivated to call and complain. It had been the previous experience of the placement service that satisfied customers were much less likely to call than dissatisfied ones. So some assessment across the whole population of recruiters was necessary, to determine if the problem extended beyond those who had complained.

The size of the population also entered into the decision to use quantitative methods. Approximately twenty-five hundred individual recruiters conducted interview schedules in the previous year. Time and resources prohibited the assessing of all of those interviewers, so it was possible to obtain only a sampling of them. Further, there were subgroups within the population (men and women, white and nonwhite, service and manufacturing businesses) which needed to be assessed. The amount of time available to design the study, gather the data, and analyze the results was also taken into account, as were the human and fiscal resources. For all these reasons, a quantitative approach, using a representative sample, was more feasible.

Step Four: Define the Population

As stated above, there was not enough time or resources to gather information from the entire population of twenty-five hundred interviewers, so taking a sample of that population was more appropriate. According to Borg and Gall (1989) there are four different sampling techniques.

1. *Simple random sampling:* a procedure in which all the individuals in a defined population have an *equal* and *independent* chance of being selected as a member of the sample. In this context, "independent" means that the selection of one individual does not affect in any way the likelihood of the selection of any other individual. Random samples can be drawn using a table of random numbers (usually available in a statistics text) or by computer software programs.

2. *Systematic sampling:* a procedure in which the total population is placed on a list, and, for example, every fourth person is selected until the sample size has been reached. Systematic

sampling can only be used if one is confident that every *n*th person does not share some characteristic with a subset of the entire population. It differs from random sampling in that each member of the population is not chosen independently. Once the first member has been selected, all the other members of the sample are automatically determined.

3. *Stratified sampling:* a procedure which selects the sample in a way that assures that certain subgroups in the population will be represented in the sample in proportion to their numbers in the population itself. Stratified samples are particularly appropriate in studies where comparisons between various subgroups are important. Proportional stratified sampling means the proportion of subjects randomly selected from each group is the same as the proportion of that group in the target population. The size of the sample is usually determined by the minimum number of cases needed in the smallest subgroup, which is typically about thirty-five cases.

4. *Cluster sampling:* a procedure which is used when the sampling unit is not an individual but rather a naturally occurring group of individuals. Cluster sampling is used when it is more feasible or convenient to select groups of individuals than it is to select individuals from a defined population. For example, in this study, we could have drawn a random sample of companies which send recruiters to interview, and then included all recruiters in each of these companies in our sample.

In this study, stratified random sampling was selected, because one of the purposes of the study was to compare various subgroups within the population. For example, recruiters were not spread out evenly over the companies which visit the campus. Smaller companies typically send one recruiter, whereas larger companies may send several. Also, most recruiters are white men. A simple random sample, therefore, might have resulted in an overrepresentation of larger companies, men, and whites, and an underrepresentation of smaller companies, women, and minorities.

Sample Size

There are several considerations regarding sample size which were reviewed in Chapter Two, one of which is *sample error.* According to Suskie (1992), sample error describes the possible difference in findings and results if one were able to obtain valid responses from the entire population. For example, in this study, if 35 percent of the respondents in a sample of eleven hundred cases said the level of service provided was outstanding, with a sample error of 3 percent, this means we can be quite sure (actually 95 percent sure), that between 32 percent and 38 percent of all respondents thought the service was outstanding. The more people in the sample, the lower the sample error will be, up to about ten thousand cases, when the sample error is less than 1 percent. The following table (from Suskie, 1992) lists the sample size needed for each amount of sample error.

Random Sample Size	Sample Error
196	7 percent
264	6 percent
384	5 percent
600	4 percent
1,067	3 percent
2,401	2 percent
9,604	1 percent

In general, the overall size of the sample does not affect sample error estimates. For further details on how sample error is calculated, see Suskie (1992).

So how many recruiters should be sampled? When considering minimum numbers for subgroup analysis, at least thirty recruiters in each of twelve subgroups (based on gender, size of company, race or ethnicity) were needed, requiring at least 360 usable responses. Since we wanted a sample error of no larger than 5 percent, we would need at least four hundred *usable* responses. The reader should be cautioned, however, that the 5 percent error margin applies to the entire, usable sample. The sample error for an individual unit of analysis (such as recruiters from small companies) will be larger.

Further, we must estimate the return rate. If our past experience has been that we may expect a 40 percent return rate, we may need to sample more than twice as many interviewers to get the four hundred usable responses needed.

The reader will remember the many earlier admonitions about the fact that assessment is a series of compromises. This study is a good example of what we mean. A sample size of one thousand was chosen, based upon an anticipated return rate of 40 percent, yielding a usable sample of approximately four hundred. This was large enough to do subgroup analysis, reduce the sample error for the total sample to 5 percent, remain within time and resource limitations, and establish "face validity" with the intended audiences.

Step Five: Determine the Instrument to Be Used

The first question to be asked in this step: Is there an instrument available which meets our needs? As pointed out in Chapter Two, we need an instrument that yields results that can be statistically analyzed, whose validity and reliability have been verified, that has norms against which our own results may be compared, and that is easily taken, scored, and analyzed. On the other hand, such an instrument may not be available, and if it is, it may not precisely meet our needs. In this study, no instrument was available, so one was developed. For an overview of the limitations of locally developed instruments, and guidelines on how to develop them, see Chapter Two of this book and Suskie (1992). For the purposes of this chapter, however, we will go into much greater detail on the issues important to instrument development, because choices made about the types of measurement scales used determine in part the appropriate types of analyses.

Types of Measurement Scales

In constructing a question for a quantitative instrument, some considerable thought must be given to how the array of possible answers is constructed. There are four types of measurement scales: nominal, ordinal, interval, and ratio.

A *nominal scale* simply categorizes objects; it "names" them. Thus, gender, race or ethnicity, religious preference, and type of institution (liberal arts, university, community college) are all nominal variables. An object is either in a category (and is "scored" accordingly because it possesses the trait or characteristic that defines the category), or it is not. No ordering along any dimension is implied. "Yes/no" responses also fall into this category. Obviously, if one responds "yes" to a question, then one cannot respond "no."

An *ordinal scale* rank-orders objects according to the amount they possess of the defining characteristic of the variable. For example, the order of finish in a horse race is an ordinal variable. Education-related ordinal variables include achievement (when measured by rank in class), educational attainment (reflected by the highest degree earned), and college choice preferences (measured as the rank order of colleges a student would prefer to attend). Ordinal variables reflect varying amounts or levels on the variable (rankings from high to low), but the measure has no absolute zero (we don't know if an object has none of the property; does the horse finishing last never enter the race?). Moreover, the intervals between the rankings in ordinal variables are not the same from one point to the next: measuring achievement by rank in class tells us the student who ranked first "achieved" more than the student ranking second, and both achieved more than the students ranking third or lower. But the measure does not tell us if the difference in achievement between the first and second student is the same as that between the second and third student, and so on down the line.

An *interval scale,* like an ordinal one, can be used to rank-order objects or people according to the amount of some trait they possess, but interval variables have the added advantage of equal-intervals score values. A Likert-type scale (where, say, 1 = Strongly Disagree, 2 = Disagree, 3 = No Opinion, 4 = Agree, and 5 = Strongly Agree) is presumed to be an interval measurement scale. The numerically equal distances on such scales are presumed to reflect equal differences in the property being measured. Thus, the difference between 1 and 2 is presumed to be the same as that between 4 and 5. Measurement specialists and statisticians disagree about the validity of this assumption (some argue that such scales are ordinal, at best), but for analytical purposes, such scales are commonly treated *as if* they were interval variables. Note, however, that no absolute zero is assumed. Thus, SAT or IQ scores have no "zero" on their scales, since we are unwilling to assert that someone has zero intelligence or academic aptitude.

Ratio scales are the highest form of measurement. Ratio scales have all the ordering characteristics of nominal, ordinal, and interval scales, plus the advantage of having an empirically meaningful zero. Family income, age, years of formal schooling completed, number of times a student meets with a faculty member—all are variables measured on a ratio scale.

These measurement scales are very important because the types of statistical analyses chosen is, in part, determined by the measurement scales used. (For more on this point, see the analysis section of this chapter.) When to use each of these scales also depends on the purposes of the study. In this study, the basic demographic information was collected using nominal scales. Information about why recruiters chose this institution to interview was collected using an ordinal scale (rank-ordering reasons). Information about ratings of the quality of services used was collected using interval scales (a Likert type scale), and information about the number of previous visits to the placement service was collected using a ratio scale.

The nominal scales included gender, race, and company size:

Gender: _____ female   _____ male
Race: _____ white   _____ Asian   _____ Hispanic
            _____ African American   _____ American Indian
            _____ Other
Number of Company Employees   _____ < 25   _____ 26–100
                                _____ 101–500   _____ 500+

The ordinal scales asked recruiters to rank the reasons for choosing the institution to interview, with 1 indicating the most important reason, 2 the next more important reason, and so on:

_____ quality of academic programs
_____ quality of students
_____ rate of success of graduates in our company
_____ quality of placement services
_____ reputation of the institution
_____ other (please specify) _____

The interval scales asked respondents to rate various services on a 1–5 scale, with 5 being the highest rating and 1 being the lowest rating:

_____ scheduling of interviews
_____ interview facilities
_____ parking
_____ advanced screening of applicants
_____ interviewee credentials packet
_____ recruiter checkout form
_____ advanced information on applicants
_____ ventilation system
_____ clerical staff cooperation
_____ printed instructions and materials
_____ handling of interviewee no-shows
_____ placement staff cooperation
_____ vacancy listings
_____ overall quality of placement service

The ratio scale asked respondents to state the number of times the interviewer had interviewed previously on this campus at this placement service.

_____ number of previous visits to this placement service

Step Six: Determine Types of Statistical Analyses

As pointed out many times, very rarely do student affairs professionals possess the expertise to determine the methods of statistical analyses. So the use of a statistical consultant is highly recommended. But this does not mean that practitioners should not be informed about statistical analysis. While practitioners may not need to know how a particular statistical analysis is calculated, they do need to know, at the very least, why a particular statistical analysis is appropriate (and why others are not), and what a particular statistical analysis will reveal about the data.

Analysis, according to Kerlinger (1986), "means the categorizing, ordering, manipulating, and summarizing of data to obtain answers to research questions. The purpose of analysis is to reduce data to intelligible and interpretable form so that relations of research problems can be studied and tested" (p. 125). This analysis is done through *statistics.* The two purposes of statistics, are to (1) manipulate and summarize numerical data *(descriptive statistics),* and (2) compare the the results with chance expectations *(inferential statistics)* (Kerlinger, 1986; Hinkle, Wiersma, and Jurs, 1994).

The first purpose of statistics is "to 'describe' the data we have collected. The mean, median, and standard deviation are the main descriptive statistics; they are used to indicate the average score and the variability of scores for the sample. The advantage of descriptive statistics is that they enable the researcher to use one or two numbers (such as the mean and standard deviation) to represent all of the individual scores of subjects in the sample" (Borg and Gall, 1989, p. 336).

According to Best and Kahn (1986), four types of statistical measures can be used to describe and analyze data in meaningful ways, including measures of central tendency, spread or distribution, relative position, and relationships.

1.   *Measures of central tendency.* The *mean* is the arithmetic average of the scores in a distribution. The *median* is the middle score in the rank-ordered distribution of scores. The *mode* is the most frequently occurring score in the distribution.

2.   *Measures of spread or dispersion.* The *range* is the difference between the highest and lowest scores, plus one. The *deviation from the mean* is a score expressed as its distance from the mean. The *variance* is the sum of the squared deviations from the mean, divided by the total number of scores in the sample (Best and Kahn, 1986). The *standard deviation* reflects the extent to which scores in a distribution, on the average, deviate from their mean. Each score is subtracted from the mean. The resulting deviation score is then squared. All squared deviations are then summed and divided by sample size to get the standard deviation (Borg and Gall, 1989).

"The mean and standard deviation, taken together, usually provide a good description of how members of a group scored on a particular measure. For example, if we know that a group of subjects has a mean score of 10 on a test, and a standard deviation of 2, we can infer that approximately 68 percent of the subjects earned scores between 8 and 12, and that approximately 95 percent of the subjects earned scores between 6 and 14" (Borg and Gall, 1989, p. 344).

3.   *Measures of relative position.* According to Best and Kahn (1986), *percentile rank* is the point in the distribution below which a given percentage of scores fall. For example, if the eightieth per-

centile rank is a score of 65, then 80 percent of scores fall below 65. *Standard scores* provide a method of expressing any score in a distribution in terms of its distance from the mean in standard deviation units.

4.   *Measures of relationships.* A *correlation* is the extent to which two variables are related. According to Hinkle, Wiersma, and Jurs (1994), a *correlation coefficient* is an index that describes the extent to which two sets of data are related; it is a measure of the relationship between two variables. "A correlation coefficient can take on values between -1.0 and +1.0, inclusive. The sign indicates the direction of the relationship. A plus indicates that the relationship is positive; a minus sign indicates that the relationship is negative. . . . The value of a perfect positive correlation coefficient is +1.0, and the value of a perfect negative correlation is –1.0. When there is no relationship between two variables, the correlation coefficient is 0" (pp. 104–105).

The reader should be cautioned, however, about the exact meaning of a correlation coefficient for two variables. "The correlation coefficient does not imply a cause-and-effect relationship between variables. . . . Similarly, a zero (or even a negative) correlation does not necessarily mean that no causation is possible" (Best and Kahn, 1986). The interpretation of the magnitude of a correlation is also very important. Unfortunately, too often lower correlations are touted as important when, in fact, they are not. This may be crucial for the lay reader to recognize, particularly if an important decision or policy is a stake.

One way to learn more about the meaning of a correlation coefficient is to calculate the *coefficient of determination* by squaring the coefficient correlation. This figure is interpretable as the proportion of the variability of scores in one variable that can be associated with another variable. For example, if the coefficient correlation between college grades and SAT scores is .50, then 25 percent (.50 squared) of the variability in SAT scores and college GPA can be predicted or explained with reference to aptitude or achievement. Put another way, with an r of .30, and an r^2 of .09, 91 percent of the variability of GPA is unrelated to academic aptitude.

As a rule of thumb, we can say that correlations of less than .30 indicate little if any relationship between the variables (Hinkle,

Wiersma, and Jurs, 1994). Here are some crude criteria for evaluating the magnitude of a correlation:

Correlation Coefficient	Coefficient Determination	Strength of Relationship
.00 to .20	.00 to .04	Negligible
.21 to .40	.05 to .16	Low
.41 to .60	.17 to .36	Moderate
.61 to .80	.37 to .64	Substantial
.81 to 1.0	.65 to 1.0	High to very high

Several ways are available to describe samples and responses to the items in an instrument. According to Suskie (1992), the method used to describe data depends on what one wants to know, and what kind of data (measurement scales) were used. The first and most primitive way of describing data is to depict data through frequency distributions, graphs, scattergrams, or a cross-tabulation table. According to Hinkle, Wiersma and Jurs (1994), a *frequency distribution* is an arrangement of values that shows the number of times a given score or group of scores occurs. A *graph* is a pictorial representation of a set of data. A *line graph* shows the relationship between two variables plotted on a horizontal and vertical axis. A *bar graph* illustrates the relationship between two variables when the scale of measurement of one of the variables is nominal. A *scattergram* is a graph that illustrates the relationship between two quantitative variables, plotted on a horizontal and vertical axis. According to Selltiz, Jahoda, Deutsch, and Cook (1962), a *cross-tabulation* is the "number of cases that occur jointly in two or more categories—for example, tabulation of the number of cases that are both high in education and low in income" (p. 407).

To summarize and simplify these concepts, Suskie (1990) developed the following table, which determines what method should be used, based on what one wants to do and what kind of measurement scales were used. (We have adapted the Suskie tables reported in this chapter to include ratio data.)

In the study of recruiter perceptions of placement services, the first level of analysis was descriptive. The first task was to describe the respondents. In this instance, the response rate was about as expected, so there were 410 usable responses. The reader will remember that information about the sample was collected through two measurement scales: nominal (gender, race, and number of company employees) and ratio (number of previous visits to this placement service). For the nominal scales, a frequency distribution and bar graphs were the appropriate means of describing the sample. Such a distribution would list the number and percent of males and females, whites and nonwhites, and the persons represented by the various sizes of businesses listed on the instrument.

For the ratio scale, a frequency distribution was also appropriate in describing the sample. This scale asked respondents to indicate the number of previous visits to the placement service. Such a distribution would list the number of recruiters who had interviewed previously and the number of times that person had interviewed.

The second task was to describe the responses of the sample. Again, referring to Table 4.1, frequency distributions were used to examine the responses of one group to one question (the responses of males to their ratings of parking facilities), for all kinds of data. Paired frequency distributions were used to compare the responses

Table 4.1. How to Describe Group Responses.

What do you want to do?	What kind of data do you have?	Use this method.
Examine the responses of one group to one question	Interval, ratio, or ordinal	Frequency distribution, bar graph/line graph
	Nominal	Frequency distribution, bar graph
Compare the responses of two groups to one question	Any kind	Paired frequency distributions or graphs
Compare the responses of one group to two questions	Interval or ratio	Scattergram
	Ordinal or nominal	Cross-tabulation table

Source: Suskie, 1992, p. 64. Reprinted by permission of the Association for Institutional Research.

of two groups to one question (the responses of males and females to their ratings of parking facilities). A scattergram was used for interval and ratio data when comparing the responses of one group to two questions (the responses of males to their ratings of parking facilities and vacancy listings); and a cross-tabulation table was used for the ordinal and nominal data when doing the same.

The second way of describing data is through the use of statistical analyses. Again, the method used to describe data depends on what one wants to know, and what kind of data (measurement scales) were used. Suskie (1992) offers the following way of using statistics to describe data:

The average response to a question for interval data (rating of parking facilities) or ratio data (number of previous visits to the placement service) is best described using a mean or median. The average response to a question for ordered data (ranking of reasons for choosing the institution to interview) is best described using the median, while the average response for nominal data (the rating of parking facilities) is best described by using the mode. The reader may consult Table 4.2 for other ways of statistically analyzing responses.

While these descriptions are informative, and give the investigator an overall notion of the sample and the responses, they offer little insight into the meaning of the data, and certainly do not provide a basis for solving the problem which motivated the study. At this point, inferential statistics become very important for the reader to understand.

Inferential Statistics

The second purpose of statistics is to compare the results with chance expectations (Kerlinger, 1986; Hinkle, Wiersma, and Jurs, 1994). Inferential statistics, as contrasted to descriptive statistics, are used to make inferences from the sample to the population, and to "allow us to *generalize* from the situation that was studied to the situations not studied" (Borg and Gall, 1989, p. 336). Of course, there is always the chance that the results obtained from the sample do not apply to the population. According to Borg and Gall (1989), the investigator must ask: Is this a chance finding? Is it possible that if we studied new samples we would get the same results? The answer lies in tests of significance.

Table 4.2. Using Statistics to Describe Responses.

What do you want to describe?	What kind of data do you have?	Use this statistic.
The average response to a question	Interval or ratio	Mean or median
	Ordinal	Median
	Nominal	Mode
The spread or variability of responses to a single question	Interval or ratio	Standard deviation
	Ordinal	Semi-interquartile range
	Nominal	Proportion falling outside mode
The degree of relationship between responses to two questions	Interval or ratio	Pearson's product-moment correlation coefficient
	Ordinal	Spearman's rank-order correlation coefficient
	Nominal	Cramer's index of contingency
The degree of relationship among responses to three or more questions	Interval or ratio	Multiple correlation
		Partial correlation
	Ordinal	Kendall's partial rank correlation

Source: Suskie, 1992, pp. 65–66. Reprinted by permission of the Association for Institutional Research.

When a study reports that "differences were significant" just what does this mean? In most cases, the reference is to *statistical* significance. Such references are generally of the following kind: "This difference was significant at the $p < .05$ level." Someone with limited statistical training might conclude that a result significant at the $p < .001$ level is much more "significant" than one at the $p < .05$ level. The level of statistical significance, however, is a reference only to the probability that the relation identified (say, the difference between the means of two groups on some measure of critical thinking or psychosocial development) is due to chance rather than to any "real" difference between the two groups. The "$p < .05$" means that one would expect to find a difference by chance only five times in one hundred; "$p < .001$" means one would expect to find such a difference by chance only once in a thousand times. Note that the interpretation of the level of statistical significance says nothing about *how strong* the relation between the two variables is. It reflects only the degree of confidence we can have that a difference or relation between two variables is real and not due to chance.

One other caveat: statistical significance is linked to sample size. With a large sample (say, fifteen hundred to two thousand or more), even very small differences (or correlation coefficients) will be "statistically significant" at .05. This problem can be overcome by raising the level of significance to at least .01.

Thus, saying a finding is "statistically significant" does not necessarily mean it is educationally, pedagogically, programmatically, or administratively meaningful or important. To judge whether an effect warrants attention, one must also know the *magnitude* of the difference, the *strength* of the relation. Most studies and reports stop with determining statistical significance, a necessary but insufficient condition for evaluating whether a finding is administratively or programmatically useful. To evaluate *substantive* significance, an estimate of the magnitude or strength of a relation will be far more informative. Administrators will make programmatic, policy, and budgetary decisions based at least in part on outcomes assessment information. They have a right to know—and those doing an assessment have an obligation to provide information on—whether the impact of college or some aspect of the college experience is large enough to warrant attention, resources, and action. Such estimates are sometimes called "effect sizes."

Types of Inferential Statistics

There are two basic types of inferential statistics: *bivariate analyses* and *multivariate analyses*. Bivariate analyses refer to statistical analyses designed to test whether a relation exists between two variables. Bivariate statistics include such familiar tests as the chi-square (χ^2) tests of association or goodness-of-fit, *t*-test, and the one-way analysis of variance.

A *chi-square test* evaluates whether two nominal variables (say, gender and major field), or one nominal and one ordinal variable (such as race or ethnicity and highest degree sought), are related. This test yields no information about the *strength* of the relation. The significance test simply reflects the likelihood that the relation is real rather than a chance occurrence.

The t-*test* is used to determine whether a relation exists between a *two*-group nominal or ordinal variable (such as gender, full-versus part-time enrollment status, or class year with only two years represented) and a second variable measured on an interval or ratio scale. The *t*-test evaluates the difference between the two groups' mean scores on the ratio or interval variable. For example, a *t*-test would be appropriate to answer the question of whether women had higher grade-point averages than men, or whether differences existed between full- and part-time students on a measure of critical thinking ability.

Analysis of variance (ANOVA) is the multigroup extension of the *t*-test. Like the *t*-test, it is used to determine whether a relation exists between one grouping variable (whether nominal or ordinal) and one interval or ratio variable. When the grouping variable has more than two categories (such as academic major, race or ethnicity, or year in school), however, analysis of variance, rather than a *t*-test, must be used. With three or more groups, the ANOVA test will indicate only that no fewer than one of all the possible pairs of group means are different at a statistically significant level. The overall F-ratio the test will not indicate is *which* of those possible pairs are significantly different. Some form of post-hoc testing would be needed. Discussion of post-hoc tests, however, is beyond the scope of this chapter.

Theoretically, there is no limit to the number of grouping categories one can have for the grouping variable (at a large university, there may be over a hundred academic majors). The difficulty of identifying and interpreting differences between specific groups increases, however, as the number of categories within the grouping variable increases.

One use of bivariate analyses is to determine whether the usable respondents in the sample are truly representative of the population. In this instance of the placement interviewer study, the question is whether the 400 interviewers who responded to the survey were representative of the population of all 2,000 interviewers who used the placement service. Here again, the measurement scales used determine which statistical test is most appropriate. Since there were two different measurement scales used to describe the sample, then two different statistical analyses are recommended. Referring to Table 4.3, the nominal demographic data (gender, race or ethnicity, and size of business), a chi-square test of goodness of fit is appropriate. For the ratio data, a t-test is recommended.

If we are fortunate, the tests will confirm a good fit between the sample and the population distributions, and we may proceed with some confidence (of about 95 percent) that this sample is a good representation of the population.

Table 4.3. Analyses Used to Test Differences Among Groups.

What kind of data do you have?	How many subgroups do you have?	Use this analysis.
Interval or ratio	Two	t-test for two independent means
	Three or more	One-way analysis of variance
Ordinal	Two	Mann-Whitney U-test
	Three or more	Kruskal-Wallis one-way analysis of variance
Nominal	Two	t-test for two proportions
	Two or more	Chi-square test of association

Source: Suskie, 1992, p. 69. Reprinted by permission of the Association for Institutional Research.

But what if we're not so lucky? Suppose these analyses reveal that the usable sample is not representative of the population. For example, it may turn out that the proportion of women in the sample is much larger than their proportion in the population. Here we have two choices. First, we could simply caution the reader that the fit is not a good one, describe how the sample differs from the population, list this lack of fit as a limitation of the study, and let the reader beware. This is probably not a good alternative, because this lack of fit casts considerable doubt on the credibility of the study. A second and much more viable alternative is to weight the responses of the usable sample in proportion to the population. That is, if there are fewer females in the sample than in the population, then the responses of females are given more relative weight in the analysis than males, thus overcoming the overrepresentation of males in the sample.

The second use of bivariate analysis is to determine if two or more subgroups are different from each other. Again, which bivariate analysis is used depends upon the scale of measurement and how many subgroups are involved. Suskie (1992) summarizes the appropriate uses of bivariate analyses in the following way:

In our placement interview study, gender differences were important to analyze. Since the reasons for choosing the institution to interview were gathered using an ordinal scale, thus it follows that when comparing the responses of males and females, the Mann-Whitney U-test is the appropriate statistic. The same is true for the race or ethnicity category. The ratings of services, however, were gathered using an interval scale, so that when making both gender comparisons, the t-test for two independent means is most appropriate. However, when making comparisons among the six race or ethnicity categories, one-way analysis of variance should be used.

However, in the instance of the size of business scales, there were four groups, so the appropriate statistic for the ordinal scales (rank-ordering of reasons for choosing the institution to interview), according to Table 4.3, is the Kruskal-Wallis one-way analysis of variance. For the interval data (rating of services), a one-way analysis of variance is appropriate.

A third use of bivariate analysis is to determine whether the responses from the sample to two or more questions are different from each other, or whether the sample has changed over a period of time. Again, Suskie (1992) argues that the type of bivariate analysis used depends upon the measurement scales used and the number of responses to be compared.

In our placement interview study, the only analysis appropriate to this use of bivariate analysis was the rating of services. In other words, is there a relationship (correlation) between types of respondents (for example, men and women) and their ratings of the fourteen services identified? According to Table 4.4, since these were interval data, the appropriate analysis is a one-way analysis of variance.

The reader should note, however, that bivariate analyses, while widely used and appropriate to this study, do have serious limitations. For example, if one is interested in more than just two variables, common sense logic would dictate conducting a series of bivariate tests (quite often a very large number of them), one for each pair of variables of interest. As discussed above, which bivariate test is chosen will depend on the nature of the measurement

Table 4.4. Analyses Used to Test Differences in Responses.

What kind of data do you have?	How many responses do you want to compare?	Use this analysis.
Interval or ratio	Two	t-test for matched pairs
	Three or more	One-way analysis of variance
Ordinal	Two	Sign test
		Wilcoxon matched-pairs signed-ranks test
	Three or more	Friedman two-way analysis of variance
Nominal	Two	McNemar test for significance of change
	Three or more	Cochran Q-test

Source: Suskie, 1992, p. 70. Reprinted by permission of the Association for Institutional Research.

scales of the variables being studied. The common sense logic is simple and straightforward enough: If you want to know whether two variables are related, test for that relation.

This logic, however, is flawed. When used in this way, bivariate tests of statistical significance are inappropriate for several reasons. First, as the number of such bivariate tests increases, so does the likelihood of obtaining a false "significant" finding. For example, one is likely to obtain five false significant results in every hundred tests (that's the meaning of "$p < .05$"). If one does one hundred t-tests, say, and finds ten statistically significant differences, half of those differences could be expected by chance alone. But *which* five are the "real" ones and which the false ones? Unfortunately, one can never know.

Second, and more important, bivariate tests (by definition) are limited to evaluating the relation between only two variables at a time. In many instances, the outcomes of a study are not independent of one another (that is, they are correlated). We know, for example, that a number of students' pre-college characteristics (including socioeconomic status, race or ethnicity, high school performance, admissions test scores), as well as a number of college experiences (frequency of contact with faculty, living on campus rather than off, peer interactions, and levels of academic and social integration), are *all* related to student persistence and other college outcomes. All of those variables cannot be equally influential, but which one(s) are the more powerful? If we take into account the pre-college characteristics that make some students "at risk" for college completion, which of the college experiences are the more powerful in helping students succeed? These two questions cannot be answered with bivariate statistical procedures. One can analyze data *as if* all the variables were unrelated to (or independent of) one another (which one must assume when using repeated bivariate tests), but such an assumption has little standing in the real world or the research evidence about college students. For example, assessing college impact and student change are just more complicated than that. Thus, repeated bivariate tests are not only unparsimonious, the results they produce are also virtually impossible to interpret with any degree of clarity or confidence. In order to evaluate the relative importance played by multiple variables, one must use multivariate statistical procedures, some of which are discussed below.

Multivariate Analyses

If, as argued above, bivariate statistics are fraught with problems that can lead to misleading, if not outright inaccurate, results, what sort of analytical procedures *should* one use? Multivariate analyses allow for studying the relationship of several responses to one response or outcome.

Multiple Regression

This is really a family of statistical procedures rather than a single statistical method, and includes stepwise regression, hierarchial regression, logit analysis, and probit analysis. Since the example used in this chapter did not use multivariate analyses, we will defer a more extensive explanation of these methods to Chapter Ten, where outcomes assessments are discussed.

Step Seven: Data Collection Plan

The data collection plan for this study consisted of mailing the instrument to the stratified sample of one thousand placement interviewers. The reader should refer to Chapter Two for a more detailed discussion of how to conduct a study using a mailed questionnaire.

Step Eight: Record the Data in Usable Form

As pointed out in Chapter Two, there are several ways of converting data from an instrument to computer data files. The easiest, of course, is to use a machine readable instrument form, which can then be scanned and compiled into a computer data file. This method may also be very cost effective, particularly with large samples. If the instrument is not machine readable, then the responses must be converted from the instrument to the computer file by a data analyst. In the placement interview study, the second procedure was followed.

Step Nine: Conduct the Appropriate Analyses

With the data in an appropriate computer data file, the next step is to choose a commercially available computer software package, such as the Statistical Analysis System (SAS) (available from SAS, Inc., Cary, North Carolina) or the Statistical Packages for the Social Sciences (SPSS) (available from SPSS, Inc., Chicago) to conduct the statistical analyses described above. Space does not allow us to report all of the results of the statistical analyses, but the following selected results will give a sense of what the analyses revealed:

1. Using a chi-square test of goodness of fit, the usable sample was representative of the population with respect to gender, race, and size of company, so no weighting of responses was necessary. Further, there were at least thirty-five usable responses in each of the subgroups chosen for analysis.
2. Using a frequency distribution, the highest ranked reason for choosing the institution was the quality of academic programs, followed by the rate of success of graduates in the program, the quality of students, the quality of placement services, the reputation of the institution, and others.
3. Using the Kruskal-Wallis one-way analysis of variance to analyze the rank ordering of reasons for choosing the institution to interview, no differences were found by gender, race or ethnicity, or size of company.
4. Using the Pearson product-moment correlation to analyze the ratio scale of number of previous visits to the institution, no differences were found.
5. Using the mean response to each of the services rated, the highest rated services were advanced information on applicants (4.52), scheduling of interviews (4.43), and overall quality of placement services (4.41). The lowest rated services were parking (1.52), ventilation system (1.98), and the handling of no-shows (2.74).
6. Using a one-way analysis of variance, no differences in ratings of services were found by race or ethnicity. However there were differences by gender and size of company:
   • Male interviewers rated clerical staff cooperation, placement staff cooperation, and handling of placement interviewee no-shows higher than women. Women rated advanced information on applicants higher than men.
   • Larger companies rated clerical staff cooperation, placement staff cooperation, and handling of no-shows higher

than smaller companies. Smaller companies rated vacancy listings higher than larger companies.

7. Using a one-way analysis of variance, no differences in ratings of services were found in the number of previous visits to the institution.

Step Ten: Evaluation, or the Meaning of Analyses for Policy/Practice

Several things were evident from these findings. First, overall, the reasons for choosing this institution to interview had to do with things over which the placement service had little or no control: quality of academic programs, rate of success of graduates, quality of students, and the reputation of the institution. The quality of placement services, however, finished fourth, leaving some room for improvement.

Second, while the overall ratings of various placement services were high (a new advanced scheduling system was put in place a year ago, and it received very high ratings), there were some points of dissatisfaction, including parking, ventilation, and handling of no-shows. Each of these services received very low ratings, and were obviously a source of interviewer dissatisfaction.

Third, race or ethnicity and number of previous visits to the institution did not appear to influence any of the responses. Gender and size of company, however, did have an influence. For example, men rated clerical and placement staff cooperation higher than women. Likewise, larger companies rated clerical and placement staff cooperation higher than smaller companies. It was clear that the personnel of this placement service, for whatever reasons, appeared to treat men better than women, and interviewers from larger companies better than those from smaller companies.

Step Eleven: Strategy for Use of Results

One part of the strategy was to learn more about certain findings. Another study, this one qualitative, aimed at gaining more insight into the apparent bias of placement and clerical staff toward interviewers from smaller companies and women, toward the goal of eventually revising in-service training programs and performance appraisals to deal with these issues. Problems of parking and ventilation were pursued by the placement services director with the appropriate administrators within the institution. It was also decided to replicate this study in two years to determine if interviewer perceptions had changed.

Conclusion

The purpose of this chapter was to familiarize the reader with the use of quantitative methodologies in the assessments of student affairs. We have presented a step-by-step outline for conducting a quantitative study, using a study which was designed to learn more about placement recruiter perceptions of placement services. In the process of describing this study, we tried to help the reader better understand some basic tools of quantitative research, including sampling, instrumentation, statistical analyses (both descriptive and inferential), data collection, data recording, and how to use findings to influence policy and practice.

Please remember that this is a cursory review of these methodologies, and the reader should consult the sources referred to throughout the chapter for a more sophisticated and complete discussion. We also strongly recommend that design and statistical consultants be used in the development of quantitative studies, for two reasons. First, the use of consultants can help ensure that the study is of the highest quality in terms of design and statistical analyses. But perhaps more important, good consultants can help the practitioner better understand the findings: what they mean, their strengths, and their limitations. This enables the practitioner not only to defend the study, but to proceed, with confidence, to applying its findings to policy and practice.

Part Two

Dimensions of Assessment in Student Affairs

Tracking Clients' Use of Services, Programs, and Facilities

As identified in Chapter Two, the first component of a comprehensive student affairs assessment program is keeping track of who use student services, programs, and facilities. More specifically, the question is how many clients use student affairs offerings, and how are they described by gender, race, ethnicity, age, class standing, residence, and any other important variables. Are there clients other than students who must be counted and described? In this chapter, we will review the reasons why keeping track of users is important, and offer several examples of how this can be done, with a special emphasis on computer information systems as an essential technique in keeping track of clientele.

Why Track Clientele?

Many reasons underscore why tracking clientele use and participation is important. The first and most obvious reason is that if our intended clientele do not use what we offer, then our intended purposes cannot be achieved. The primary assumption of student affairs is that interventions in the lives of students make a difference. Impact on the lives of students will not result unless students participate in the various offerings of a student affairs division.

Second, student affairs divisions want to keep track of who and how many use our services, programs, and facilities because this information can help determine what services, programs, and facilities we should offer. Sheer numbers can be one of many indicators of whether or not what we offer is needed, or needs to be revised. For example, client waiting lists in counseling centers may tell us that we need to devote more resources to counseling, or deliver counseling services in more efficient ways (such as increasing the use of group counseling, or instituting session limits). Likewise, consistent lack of use by critical numbers of clientele, after marketing and other considerations are taken into account, may mean a service or program should be revised or eliminated.

Third, we must track clientele because sheer numbers, while important, do not tell the full story. We also must be sure that users or participants are representative of our student population. Another important objective of the student affairs profession is that our offerings are inclusive, that is, they meet the needs of all of our clientele. In Chapter Two, we used the example of a counseling service whose total number of participants was acceptable, but within that total the number of African American users was very small compared to their representation in the student population. Without race or ethnicity tracking, there would have been no indication that these services were, in fact, not being used by African Americans.

Fourth, student affairs should track clientele because tracking can assist us in determining resource allocations and resource requirements, examining alternatives of providing a particular service, program, or facility, and determining if there is a need to expand what we offer.

Fifth, we should track clientele because other components of assessment are based on the assumption that we know who uses our services, programs, and facilities. For example, user satisfaction studies are based on knowing who the users are. Likewise, outcome studies typically are based on pre- and post-test comparisons of people who actually used services, programs, and facilities. In each instance, demographic information about users is important because it makes possible some more sophisticated analysis—by gender, race or ethnicity, age, class standing, and other important variables.

And finally, knowing who uses student services, programs, and facilities provides a foundation for establishing benchmarks for improvements in the quality of what we offer. We cannot show improvement if there is not some point in time when we know who used our services, programs, and facilities.

So for all these reasons, keeping track of who uses our services, programs, and facilities is very important. But how important? While such information is very valuable, collecting and analyzing it can also can be very time-consuming, costly, and, in some instances, may detract from the amount of time spent by staff in their primary role of providing the very services, programs, and facilities they wish to improve.

It is also much easier to collect information about clientele in those student affairs units with a discrete and identifiable clientele, such as counseling centers, health services, and residence halls. In student activities and facilities such as student unions, where clientele are not as easily identified, this kind of study becomes quite difficult. It is also difficult for some educational programs (such as AIDS education), where participants may not want to be identified.

What Information to Collect

The first and most obvious proposition is to determine what information should be gathered about students and other clientele who use student services, programs, and facilities. As mentioned previously, keeping track of sheer numbers is important, particularly when compared to the total number of potential users. The second step is to decide what other information is needed, and which is most important. We see three levels of information: basic, desirable, and optimal.

At the *basic level,* at the very least we should know the following things about users:

Gender

Race or ethnicity

Age

Class standing (semester; grad/undergrad)

Place of residence

Disability (if any)

Nationality

Enrollment status (full- or part-time)

College of enrollment

Number of credit hours enrolled

Retrieving this information about students who use our services, programs, and facilities enables us, at a basic level, to determine whether our offerings are accessible to all of our students, regardless of their status or other characteristics.

At the *desirable level,* taking into account the characteristics of our users will enable us to do more sophisticated analyses, particularly outcomes assessments. This information includes not only selected background characteristics but also experiences after enrollment in college:

Socioeconomic variables: family income and education

Prior academic record: high school achievement and SAT/ACT scores

Current grade point average

Major

Entry status (transfer or original enrollee)

At the *optimal level,* many types of information can be helpful but more difficult to retrieve. Among these types of information are the following:

Family values, support, pathology, and stability

Time between high school and college

College expectations

Religious preference

Motivation

Social and interpersonal skills

Maturity, self-esteem, confidence

Clearly defined educational goals

General mental health

Career aspirations, maturity

Involvement and participation in college life

Peer relations

Faculty relations

How to Retrieve and Store Information

The most obvious approach to this matter is to retrieve information directly from students at the time the service is provided, a program offered, or the facility used. This approach, however, is not always feasible, for many reasons. Providing information at the time of participation may require too much time and students may resist providing information at a time when they want to use a service or get involved in a program. In some instances (such as family income), students are notoriously uninformed, or in other instances (such as GPA), they are prone to exaggeration. But in those instances, or those institutions or units which do not have student databases, this may be the only way to collect important information.

The next most obvious approach is to take advantage of information already collected from students by other institutional units. For example, race, gender, ethnicity, age, prior academic achievement, and other variables may already be included in the admissions or registrar's databases. Information about family backgrounds, college expectations, and other such information may be included in students' academic databases. In those institutions that have developed integrated student information systems, information is more readily retrieved than in institutions where student information systems are decentralized.

It may be the case, however, that other institutional databases do not exist, or that they are not integrated, or that access is limited or impossible. Then the issue of developing student affairs or unit-specific databases becomes very important. Very few, if any, institutions have a general student affairs student database (although in many ways such a system would be desirable). More often than not, individual student affairs units keep information about students specific to those units, typically collected from their clientele. And some units keep no information at all.

While unit-based systems are better than no systems at all, they do present some problems, one of which being the fact that students are asked to supply the same information over and over again, from unit to unit, and sometimes within the same unit. But perhaps more important, cross-unit assessments become more difficult when several databases are involved because, typically, different information is collected, or collected in different forms, making comparability virtually impossible. And even if there is compatibility, merging data files is always challenging.

An Integrated System

The Pennsylvania State University has an Integrated Student Information System (ISIS), which is a single database containing pertinent data on all students who are taking or have taken courses in the past ten years. Component subsystems include Admissions, the Registrar, the Bursar, Housing and Food Services, Financial Aid, and the Graduate School. The primary functions of these databases are to provide an electronic warehouse for student information and to allow reporting capabilities based on that information.

ISIS is a secured system with access limited to authorized users only. Selected information can be downloaded to a desktop computer for review and analysis. It provides an on-line database for currently enrolled students, and also a longitudinal database containing information on students who are currently or formerly enrolled.

On-line report generators allow retrieval of ISIS data without using a computer programming language or the services of a programmer. These report generators include a Prospect and Applicant file, a Registration file, an Enrollment file, a Retention, Progression, and Mobility file, and an Instructional Activities Reporting file.

Using an integrated student information system has several advantages. First, and perhaps most important, comprehensive information on all students is readily available and does not need to be collected from students each time the need arises. Second, information can be retrieved from one source, eliminating the problem of having to retrieve information from several sources with the often frustrating process of merging files. Third, the report-generating capability is very user-friendly, and eliminates the necessity of writing programs to manage downloaded data. Fourth, because all relevant background information is available, and it is not necessary to collect this information from students, the information is much more reliable.

A Student Affairs Database

A second approach is to establish a stand-alone student longitudinal data file. In this approach, freshman cohorts are selected every few years and are followed over time. Variables are selected, and information is collected from existing institutional databases as well as from questionnaires administered to students. These questionnaires include locally developed instruments as well as commercially developed instruments.

Information can also be gathered by way of questionnaires from the Cooperative Institutional Research Program, the National Center for Higher Education Management Systems (NCHEMS), College Board Student Outcomes Information Services, the American College Testing Program Evaluation Survey Service, and others. From all these sources, a data file can be constructed, and information can be added as students continue through the course of their education and if they leave the institution. This database can then be used as a source from which to conduct various studies, and provide a benchmark for post-enrollment studies.

A Student Affairs Unit Database

One of the most interesting developments in the area of departmental databases has been in career planning and placement. Students prepare their resumes on computer disks provided by the office, using one of several formats that are compatible with the overall database. The resume is then downloaded onto a department data file which includes resumes from all the students registered with the office. Prospective employers can call the placement office and ask for resumes from students who have particular degrees, majors, certifications, or proficiencies. Examples of certifications include teaching licenses or licenses to practice nursing, physical therapy, or other health-related professions. Proficiencies in foreign languages or computer programming languages also can be included in the database.

Only a few problems are associated with the development of this kind of database. Foremost is the problem created by students who accept positions but do not inform the office which keeps their resume in the database. In addition, some of the students would prefer to develop their own resume format rather than use one of the formats provided for them on the disk from the office.

The advantages of this kind of system are obvious. Quick service is provided to potential employers, and positions can be called to the attention of students who might otherwise miss reading a posting on a bulletin board or in a periodic newsletter. This process can be used for students to arrange for interview appointments on campus, and it provides an accurate listing of all the positions available at any given point in time. In addition, a variety of statistics on placement activities in the office can be developed. Similar applications of this kind of database are available for internships and cooperative education experiences.

A Model for Gathering Information

One of the major problems in keeping track of who uses student services, programs, and facilities is deciding what information to collect. In the extreme, data collection can become so intrusive to staff that more time is spent in that activity than providing services and programs to students. In other words, the data collection procedures that are devised should be user-friendly, both to those collecting the information, as well as to those providing the information. Some definitional problems surrounding what constitutes "use" of student services, programs, and facilities need to be clarified.

Use of Services

At a minimum each student affairs unit should record student contacts for services and the nature of those contacts. Where the routine collection of such information is not feasible, or would be intrusive to staff and students, a time-limited sample is recommended. For example, keeping track of every telephone inquiry for the whole year would be intrusive and take far too much time. But sampling such contacts in three or four "typical" weeks during the year is an acceptable alternative.

But just what is a student "contact"? For the purposes of this discussion, there are two types of student contact: *informational contacts* and *assistance contacts*. An informational contact occurs when a student is provided with information relevant to his or her question, problem, or concern, and is typically handled in a very short period of time by clerical or professional staff. An assistance contact occurs when a student is provided with assistance with his or her question, problem, or concern, and is typically handled over a sustained period of time by a professional staff member.

As a general rule, for informational contacts handled in person or over the telephone, the staff member should record the number and nature of the contacts, and, if possible, a tally broken down by gender and race or ethnicity. For assistance contacts handled in person, where feasible, the student affairs employee may also take additional information such as enrollment status, age, and other basic information identified earlier in this chapter. A shortcut to collecting all this information from each contact is to ascertain each contact's student number, and retrieve this basic information from an existing database. If this approach is used, however, the student should understand just what providing his or her number means, and what information will be used.

Use of Educational Programs

At a minimum, each student affairs unit should record the number of programs conducted, the number of students attending, and, except where anonymity is important to the goal of the program, other selected information. There are two types of structured learning experiences: *educational programs* and *academic courses*. An educational program is defined as any effort to provide information, create awareness, or educate persons in a group setting. Academic courses are those in which the educational, informational, and awareness goals of student affairs are implemented through courses for credit, and are taught wholly or in part by student affairs staff.

For educational programs, information collected should include the number of programs, the number of persons attending, and the nature of the programs. When time permits, basic information described earlier in this chapter, such as gender and race or ethnicity, should also be collected. For each academic course, information collected should include the number of enrolled students, the number of credit hours generated, the title and content of the course, the number of contact hours, the number of hours spent in training and preparation, the number of staff involved, and basic information described earlier in this chapter.

Use of Facilities

Keeping track of the use of facilities is very difficult, especially in those facilities such as student unions, where unscheduled, informal gatherings happen at a moment's notice. At a minimum, each student affairs facility should record the scheduling of the facility and the nature of use, and establish a way of estimating the number of persons using the facility. Facilities may include scheduled or unscheduled events, meetings, and activities. For scheduled use of facilities, information collected should include the scheduling organizations or persons, the nature, frequency, and time of use, and, when feasible, "basic" information described earlier in this chapter. For unscheduled use of facilities, information collected should include the nature of use and time estimates of the number of users. It is especially important to use "time slices" in keeping track of facilities usage.

Investigators' Use of Computer Technology

Obviously, keeping track of who uses student services, programs, and facilities is much easier if assisted through the use of a computer. For example, asking clerical staff to record "hashmarks" on notepads to keep track of telephone calls is time-consuming, not to mention requiring additional time to record and summarize data collected in this way. Database software programs such as D-Base or Lotus can be adapted to record and summarize information collected from students. Scheduling software packages also are available, such as event management system (Dean Evans and Associates, 1994), which can be of tremendous help in collecting and reporting facilities usage.

The plain truth is that without computer-assisted information collection and databases, in whatever form is possible at your institution, keeping track of who uses student services, programs, and facilities is virtually impossible, causing assessment activities, in turn, to be virtually impossible. Data collection procedures, and databases, if properly constructed, will keep time spent collecting and storing data to a minimum, so that more time can be spent serving our clientele.

Some basic problems are associated with computer-assisted information collection and databases. First of all, putting the hardware and software in place can be expensive and time-consuming, and they must be designed very carefully. Second, someone with appropriate knowledge and skills has to be available to keep these systems up and running, and to train staff to use them. Finally, the staff assigned to collecting information must see such systems as a help, not a hindrance.

A Caveat: The Issue of Confidentiality

No matter what information is collected, or how it is analyzed, interpreted, reported, secured, or used, students and other clientele must be treated in ways that are ethical, and confidentiality must be ensured. Typically, two forms of gathering information about students are available. In the first instance, data are collected somewhat routinely for admissions, enrollment, and financial aid purposes, and students assume that the information will be used for internal purposes only. For example, an admissions office might want to construct routine reports on students by gender, or test the predictive validity of their admissions criteria. In these instances, where information is used for internal purposes clearly related to the office which collected the information, formal informed consent is usually not required. It would be desirable, however, even in these instances, to inform students how their information will be secured and used.

In the second instance, data collected by one office may become part of a general, integrated information system, or transferred to another office for assessment purposes. Again, if the information is used for internal purposes only (for example, to compare the retention rate of men and women), generally no formal informed consent is required. However, if the information is used in any public way (for example, to convince a legislative committee to appropriate funds to the institution, or to convey the results through a formal, public document), then formal, informed consent must be obtained, even for the most basic demographic information.

There are, however, some general guidelines regarding the collection and use of information about students. First, when any information is collected, students and others should fully understand why the information is being collected, even when the information is collected routinely as part of an individual unit procedure, but especially if such data are to be used for purposes other than those originally intended. A clear statement of purpose is essential.

Second, students and others must be assured that information about individuals will be kept confidential, and some detail must be provided about how that information will be secured. If such information is to be reported in the aggregate, this should also be explained.

Third, students and others must know how the information will be used. And finally, students and others must be informed about who is responsible for the information (name, title, office location, and telephone number are all essential), and where they can direct questions or inquiries.

Some of the aspects of informed consent may not seem to be necessary, but protection of human subjects is not only the right thing to do, it may also, in some instances, be required by law (see Chapter 14). Most institutions have policies regarding the use of human subjects in research, typically based on compliance with Title 45 of the Code of Federal Regulations, Part 46, and promulgated by the federal Office for Protection from Research Risks (OPRR) at the National Institutes of Health. Even when collecting basic information about students, these regulations, if applicable (and sometimes collection of data for administrative purposes does not fall under these regulations), should be used to guide the activity and protect those providing information.

Other Issues

Tracking clientele use of services, programs, and facilities requires the cooperation of many persons within the institution. Too often, systems are developed without regard to those who will actually have to do the work. It is important, therefore, to involve end users in the design of the tracking systems. For example, if clerical staff will be involved in data entry, then they need to be involved in the design just as much as the director and staff of a student affairs functional unit must be involved.

Also, any tracking system must be flexible enough to allow different student affairs functional units to collect different categories of information. Not every unit will need the same kinds of information, but there should be a common data core and flexible data elements that are unit-specific.

Further, a well-designed tracking system should allow the division of student affairs to examine the combined impact of multiple programs, services, and facilities. Any given program may not have as much impact as the collective impact of several.

Conclusion

Assessment begins with knowing who uses student services, programs, and facilities, because such knowledge can help us (1) determine what programs, services, and facilities to offer, (2) ensure that users represent our student population, and identify groups that may be underusing our services, programs, and facilities, (3) assist in allocation of resources, (4) provide baseline data for other types of assessments, and (5) establish benchmarks for quality improvement.

We must know why we are collecting such information, what information to collect, how to collect it, how to use it, and to collect it in ways that protect the confidentiality of clientele. Subsequent assessment efforts such as needs assessments, client satisfaction, and especially outcomes studies are almost wholly dependent on the institution's ability to describe its students and their use of services, programs, and facilities.

Chapter Six

Assessing Student Needs

Needs assessment may be a little bit like the weather—people talk about it all the time but don't do much about it. In the case of the weather that may be because not much can be done. But there are some techniques that, when properly employed, can produce a very effective assessment of student needs. This chapter is dedicated to discussing how to conduct an effective student needs assessment. How are student needs separated from student wants? Should a needs assessment be theory-based? What techniques seem to work well in conducting a needs assessment? What problems will one encounter in conducting a needs assessment? These questions and others are the focus of this chapter.

A number of issues related to needs assessment will be introduced as well. To provide a framework for needs assessment, definitions will be offered and thoughts about who is the target of the assessment will be discussed. Various methods for conducting needs assessment, some described in greater detail in other parts of this book, will be identified. And finally, various steps and perspectives in the needs assessment process will be compared and contrasted. When student affairs officers have read this chapter, they should have a reasonable idea about how to conduct a needs assessment on their campus.

Definitions of Needs Assessment

Several authors have provided good definitions of needs assessment. In viewing needs assessment through a human resource development lens, Rossett (1990) defines needs assessment as "the careful study of the context, job, skills, knowledge and job incumbents prior to implementing an intervention" (p. 191). Stuffle-beam, McCormick, Brinkerhoff, and Nelson (1985) define needs assessment as "the process of determining the things that are necessary or useful for the fulfillment of a defensible purpose" (p. 16). They add that needs assessment can fulfill two primary functions: determining what needs exist and how best they can be addressed, and providing criteria against which a program's merits can be evaluated.

One of the difficulties with needs assessment is that it can be difficult to separate student needs from student wants. For example, many college students, even those who attend residential colleges, seem to need automobiles (often, the more exotic the better!). Do students really need cars, or do they simply want them? Even if the need is legitimate, determining what it will take to meet the need without being extravagant or wasteful is not easy. Lenning and MacAleenan (1979) provide conceptual guidance to help in understanding this issue, reporting that "a need is considered to be a combination of discrepancy and level of necessity" (p. 188). They add that "the amount of need varies directly with both the level of necessity and the amount of discrepancy" (pp. 188–189). Let us return to the example of college students and automobiles. Does a college student really need to drive an expensive sports car? Probably not, but some form of reliable transportation will expedite a student's ability to get to an off-campus job in times of poor weather. A sports car is not the only form of automobile transportation that will help a person stay out of the rain on the way to work. A reliable used car very well may get the job done and it certainly beats riding a bicycle or walking in the rain. Both the used car and the sports car meet the need; the used car does so more economically and is a satisfactory solution, although perhaps not the most desirable from a student's perspective.

Kuh (1982) offers another approach to student needs by defining them as what the majority of a group decide. Of course, a variety of problems can be associated with this definition, especially on a campus with sizable groups of students which are underrepresented in the total student population, or marginalized in the decision-making processes of the institution. Commuter students, for example, often are overlooked in the program planning process for campus activities (see Jacoby, 1991). Student affairs staff can easily be seduced into thinking that programs are available which meet the needs of the student body as a whole if they listen to the majority. Techniques which will be described later in this chapter will help student affairs officers broaden their perspective in determining how to meet the needs of students who are not part of the majority culture.

Stufflebeam and his colleagues (1985) offer two other conceptual approaches to the concept of need. One approach they identify as *analytic*, meaning that if something is not provided, a problem may result. For example, if the graduate, academic preparation of potential student affairs staff did not include rudimentary familiarization with certain legal issues, problems might ensue. Practically speaking, this might result in an entry-level staff member's making available a student athlete's academic transcript to the local newspaper, which would be an egregious error and a clear violation of law. The other approach that Stufflebeam and his colleagues identify is referred to as *diagnostic*, meaning that the absence of something will result in harm. An example of a diagnostic need would be the failure to have fire extinguishers on every residence hall floor consistent with appropriate fire and safety codes. The absence of the appropriate fire-fighting equipment could result in tremendous problems in an emergency, as is clear to anyone who has been involved in residence hall administration.

Based on our analysis of these definitions, and our understanding of needs assessment, we have arrived at a definition which will guide our thinking throughout this chapter. Our definition is as follows: *Assessing student needs is the process of determining the presence or absence of the factors and conditions, resources, services, and learning opportunities that students need in order to meet their educational goals and objectives within the context of an institution's mission.*

Purposes of Needs Assessment

Various reasons exist for conducting needs assessments. Quite obviously, needs assessments are conducted because student affairs staff members have limited resources and they want to plan programs or create learning opportunities for students that will be useful and popular. Nothing is more deflating to the entry level program planner than to schedule a program in the campus center and have only a few people attend, or to plan a workshop on leadership development that, according to the evaluations completed by the participants, misses the mark! So, one purpose of conducting needs assessment involves making sure that programs meet the needs of the participants.

There is much more behind the conducting of needs assessments than we have suggested so far. Kuh (1982) identifies five reasons in his scheme for conducting needs assessments, as indicated in Table 6.1. As is the case with many aspects of student affairs, these purposes do not operate independently of one another (see Kuh, Schuh, and Whitt, 1991). Note that advantages and disadvantages exist for each of these purposes. Nevertheless, Kuh's scheme provides an excellent point of departure for staff who are thinking of conducting a needs assessment but are not quite sure how to develop a conceptual framework for the project.

It is probably useful to point out that needs assessments may very well be used in one way for purposes internal to a student affairs unit, and in another for external constituencies. Internally, a needs assessment will help student affairs staff make decisions about policies, programs, and services. The assessment can play a crucial role in helping staff determine what the unit's activities will be as they relate directly to students. Externally, needs assessments can be used to provide justification for initiating programs, for eliminating them, and for defending policies and activities to more senior level administrators, members of the governing board, the legislature, and the public. It should also be remembered that needs assessments can be very helpful in explaining to students why certain experiences are required of them, such as living in a residence hall, having to participate in a community service activity, or taking freshman English.

As one might imagine, there can be a dark side to conducting needs assessments. People do not always have the purest motives for these activities. Stufflebeam and others (1985) have identified several questionable, perhaps unstated, motives for conducting a needs assessment. One of these is to use the assessment on a post hoc basis to justify an administrative decision to cancel a program. At times, certain programs will have to be canceled, but the needs

Table 6.1. Purposes of Needs Assessments.

Kind	Purpose	Advantages	Disadvantages
Monitor stakeholder perceptions	Generate ideas and document perceptions about various issues	Exploratory in nature; relatively threat-free	Needs and wants may not be differentiated; not linked directly to action
Program policy justification	Collect information to support likely alternatives	Allows input into decision making	Needs and wants may not differentiated
Satisfaction index	Estimate relative acceptability of various alternatives	Allows input; helps identify potentially controversial issues	Tends to emphasize *wants* over *needs*; may generate support for questionable or controversial activities
Participating policy-making	Select the most acceptable policy or program from alternatives	Allows stakeholders to influence institutional response to needs	Potential to generate support for questionable or controversial practices
Measurable improvement	Determine whether needs have been met	Document effectiveness of unit; assesses client functioning	May not attend to present problems or needs; focus on concerns previously functioning

Source: Kuh, G. D. "Purposes and Principles of Needs Assessments in Student Affairs." *Journal of College Student Personnel,* 1982, 23(3), p. 205. Reprinted by permission.

assessment should be done in advance of the decision, not afterwards. Similarly, the discharge of an employee should not be justified by a needs assessment after the fact.

While it is nearly impossible to conduct value-free needs assessments (Kuh, 1982), conducting an assessment for the purpose of attacking an adversary's credibility is an anathema to the process. It can be difficult to separate organizational politics from a needs assessment, but in general the focus of the assessment should not be on strengthening a political position. However, as pointed out in Chapter Two, sometimes we must justify services and programs to important political constituents and needs assessments may be important to that justification. Similarly, trying to enhance one's visibility or credibility undeservedly should not be a purpose of needs assessment. The assessment may point to good work being conducted by certain persons in the organization, but that should be a by-product of the activity, not its central purpose. The National Association of Student Personnel Administrator's *Standards of Professional Practice* (1992–1993) speaks directly to the ethical considerations of conducting an assessment and is well worth reviewing in advance of conducting an assessment.

Theory-Based Needs Assessments

One of the first decisions one needs to make in adopting a methodology to conduct a needs assessment is to determine whether or not the assessment will be based on theory. Theories about human needs have been available for many years, and Maslow's hierarchy of needs (cited by De Coster and Mable, 1980) has been integrated into student affairs literature for decades (Riker and De Coster, 1971; De Coster and Mable, 1974). Examples abound of theory-based programming, including those reported by Andreas (1993) and Rodgers (1990).

How theory might or might not be used can be illustrated by considering how to assess prospective students' needs for orientation to a given college. An atheoretical way to approach this problem would be for the investigators to survey students after their first year, asking them what they recall they needed to know about the college as they entered the institution. It would also be useful as part of this process to ask them what was not but should have been included in the orientation process. These data could be aggregated, and a needs assessment instrument could be prepared for incoming students. Based on all of this information, drawn from both students after the first year and students ready to enroll, needs could be identified and orientation planned. This assessment was atheoretical, that is, not based on student development theory.

Another way to examine this problem would be to use theory to guide the development of questions for incoming students. Chickering's psychosocial theory of student development (1993), for example, would indicate that students, especially in the early postsecondary years, most likely would be addressing vectors one through three (developing competence, managing emotions, and moving through autonomy toward interdependence). Using this approach, needs assessment questionnaires and interview protocols would be based on the theory, with individual items speaking directly to the various aspects of Chickering's first three vectors. On the basis of what is learned from surveys and interviews, orientation programs and experiences could be planned.

Evans (1985) conducted a study of needs assessment methodology to determine if using a questionnaire based on theory was more relevant to students than one empirically based. Her results favored the theory-based instrument. Evans concludes, "These results suggest that items on the theory-based survey were generally more relevant to students than those on the empirically based survey" (p. 112). She also observes that a "well designed questionnaire with a solid theoretical base can provide a comprehensive and accurate overview of student concerns" (p. 114). The theory selected by the person conducting the assessment will depend on a variety of issues, including the target of the assessment and the skills of the researcher. Nonetheless, grounding the assessment in theory seems to enhance the quality of the project.

Needs Assessment Techniques

As has been discussed earlier in this book, a variety of techniques are available to the person planning to conduct a needs assessment. Evans (1985) indicates that "the purposes for the assessment, the size of the project, and the time and money available to carry out the assessment must be considered" (p. 114). Probably the most difficult decision to make is to identify the techniques to employ, since such a wide variety of them is available. As a result of their study of this matter, Barrow, Cox, Sepich, and Spivak (1989) recommend that multiple techniques be used. They conclude that the "results of this study support the contention that multiple sources of information should be used in assessing students' need" (p. 80). Several of these techniques will be identified in this chapter, along with some of their advantages and disadvantages.

Questionnaires

Rossett (1990) presents an excellent discussion of tips for improving needs assessment questionnaires and avoiding problems associated with them. What follows is based largely on her discussion of this issue.

The use of questionnaires in conducting a needs assessment has several advantages. Among them are relatively low cost, ease in scoring the results, guarantee of respondent anonymity, and strong public relations value.

The cost of conducting a survey can be quite modest. The primary expenses of developing this approach include printing and postage (although campus mail can eliminate postage costs for students with on-campus mailboxes), and staff time. The students completing the instrument can be guaranteed anonymity simply by not writing their names on their answer sheets. A separate postal card should be sought from respondents to facilitate follow-up with non-respondents. By using score sheets that can be analyzed mechanically, the time needed for securing results is minimal, and a final report can be produced quickly. The production of a final report on a timely basis inspires confidence on the part of the participants, reinforcing the impression that the needs assessment is a serious attempt at determining how to plan interventions which meet participants' needs.

The needs assessment process can be improved by implementing the following guidelines, although this list is by no means complete; Chapter Two provides more ideas about how to improve the quality of survey instruments.

The number of items should be kept relatively short. Remember that students have many activities competing for their time, and completing a survey will probably not be high on their list of priorities for the day. By keeping the number of items short, one improves the chances for a high rate of participation.

Follow up at least once. By using the postal card arrangement described above, a follow-up can be completed without great effort. Undoubtedly, a few respondents will forget to send in the postal card, which may mean that they will have to be contacted more than once, but conducting a second mailing to nonrespondents will improve the participation rate markedly.

Pilot test the instrument on a group of students. The size of the pilot group need not be large. After the students have completed the instrument, ask them questions such as: Were the items easy to understand? How long did it take you to complete it? Do you think this kind of activity will be attractive to your colleagues? Is there anything we can do to improve the chances that students will complete the survey?

Finally, the needs investigator might want to publicize the survey before it is conducted, with the hope that this will stir up a bit of interest in the project among the people whose needs will be assessed. This can be done through the student newspaper, residence hall newspaper, campus radio station, bulletin boards and so on.

Of course, problems are associated with using questionnaires. Rossett has identified several of these, including the fact that surveys are not interactive; that is, the person conducting the survey cannot ask follow-up questions beyond what is on the questionnaire. In addition, poorly worded questions will result in responses that are nonsensical. Unless the items are constructed with great precision, it can be quite difficult to determine what the responses mean. And, of course, typographical errors, lots of white space, and sloppy layout can distract the respondent from focusing on the items. While written questionnaires can be of great utility, they tend to yield results that are less rich than a second commonly used technique, interviews.

Also, as discussed in Chapter Two; telephone surveys can be used to assess student needs, overcoming many of the problems inherent in mailed questionnaires, such as cost, response rate, and student convenience.

Interviews

Interviews tend to produce richer data than questionnaires (Evans, 1985), but are usually a more time-consuming and expensive method of collecting information. Students can be interviewed individually, or in small groups often referred to as focus groups (Carnaghi, 1992). Whitt (1991, 1993) provides a strong overview of the use of interviews as a data-gathering technique. The reader is referred to Chapter Three for more information about conducting focus groups and interviewing individuals.

Other Needs Assessment Techniques

Two other techniques, document review and observations, can be used in certain circumstances. These techniques are not used as commonly as questionnaires and interviews, but they certainly have a place in the process, depending on the nature of the needs assessment. For example, observing student behavior was instrumental in determining the need for child care at Wichita State University. The Associate Dean of Students, after hearing that students were leaving their children in their parked cars while they went to class, systematically walked through parking lots at various times to determine how widespread this practice was. She found that it was all too common and this information provided the impetus for conducting a more systematic needs assessment, which resulted in the university's developing a comprehensive child care program.

Documents also can provide useful information about student needs. Just reading the letters to the editor in the student newspaper will provide a hint about what is in the minds of students. Obviously, further investigation beyond reading letters to the editor would be necessary before committing substantial funds to new programs or services, but if students write many letters to the editor expressing concern about some aspect of campus life, this area may need to be reconceptualized and perhaps changed.

Brown and Podolske (1993b) recommend several other forms of needs assessment that are less formal but still quite useful to the student affairs staff member charged with trying to determine the needs of students. They recommend polling students by asking them to rank program possibilities at residence hall floor meetings, interviewing particularly insightful students informally over lunch or dinner in the cafeteria, and asking for a show of hands of students in a meeting. While none of these techniques will provide a complete picture of the needs of students by itself, like the letters to the editor they can provide points of departure for further investigation. Sometimes, simply asking students how they feel about life on campus and the quality of their education will yield very interesting information. However, one should never make major decisions on the basis of an informal chat with one student; still, as is indicated above, valuable information gathered in a casual manner can help the investigator to frame additional, more systematic inquiry.

Needs Assessment Process

After thinking through some of the issues presented above, including theory-based needs assessment and various methods that might be employed, once these matters have been decided, the next step for the investigator is to follow a process. A variety of processes appear in the literature about how to conduct needs assessments. What follows is based upon ideas from Rossett (1990) and Stufflebeam and others (1985); the questions frequently asked about how to conduct assessment studies discussed in Chapter Two; and thoughts based upon our hands-on experience in conducting needs assessment studies. To illustrate the needs assessment process, we have a scenario based on a real-life situation.

The Scenario: Old Ivy College

What's the Problem?

As stated in Chapter Two, problems drive assessments; thus, problems drive needs assessments. The overall problem is that many times, our services and programs lack a coherent basis for students needs, often severely limiting their effectiveness. So all needs assessments are driven by a lack of information about students. Generally speaking, needs assessments are conducted in response to three problems: (1) there is absolutely no institutionally based information on student needs in general; (2) general information is available, but specific information on one or more student sub-populations, such as women or African Americans, is lacking; or (3) specific information on particular issues important to student learning, such as alcohol and drugs or career development, is lacking.

So the first question to be asked is which of these problems must be addressed in designing a needs assessment. A general needs assessment may be constructed in a way that addresses all three problems, and there are commercially available instruments which can do this (see the Appendix). In some instances, these instruments can offer not only information on general student needs, but specific information on specific issues. Further, data can be analyzed by student subpopulations. But it has been our experience that while general needs assessments are helpful in understanding students in general, it is often difficult to use this information to change or improve services and programs.

Thus, needs assessments which are focused more narrowly and developed institutionally may have more direct applications to student services and programs. It makes sense to design studies which are more specific, and the Old Ivy College example illustrates such a study.

Old Ivy College (OIC) is a private institution which is in its second century of service. The college is dedicated to providing a high-quality liberal arts education, and until the late 1960s it admitted only men. Today, the college enrolls nearly as many women as men.

Historically, OIC has had very strong intramural programs. Men formed teams through their living units and Greek letter organizations, vigorously competing for championship trophies in fifteen sports. After women were admitted to OIC, similar team sport opportunities were made available to them, but the women's intramural teams and leagues were not as successful as the men's.

In response to this imbalance, recent women presidents of the student body have campaigned on the promise to rethink OIC's approach to student recreation, which was built historically on a male intramural sports model. Each woman president held that women were as interested in recreation as men, but that the nature of their interest was different, that is, they were more interested in aerobics classes, fitness machines, wellness instruction, and weight training than in competitive intramural sports. Not only did OIC offer nothing in these areas of recreation, it resisted changing the strong tradition of campus intramurals.

After the three years of debate, the college decided it was time to find out more about recreational programs for women, as well as how widespread apparent dissatisfaction was among the student body, faculty, and others. The president appointed a blue ribbon committee consisting of faculty, students, recreation administrators, and two local graduates with the specific charge to "determine the extent to which a need exists on campus for expanding the nature and variety of recreation programs to better meet the needs of our increasingly diverse student body."

What's the Purpose?

As discussed in Chapter Three, the purpose for an assessment study should flow directly from the problem. In this instance, the purpose of the investigation (translated from the president's charge to the committee) was to assess the recreational needs of students, and offer recommendations.

Who Should Be Studied?

Because OIC was relatively small (1,570 students), and virtually every student lived on campus or in facilities adjacent to it, the committee decided to include the entire student body in the study—in other words the entire population was used, rather than some smaller sample.

What Is the Best Assessment Method?

The committee decided upon a combination of quantitative and qualitative methods. First, the committee would survey the entire study body to form a basic understanding of their perceptions. Information was collected about students' backgrounds and characteristics so that analyses by gender, class standing, and other variables could be conducted.

The committee used three qualitative assessment methods to generate a greater depth of information about the situation. These methods were developed after the quantitative analysis was completed, so the committee had some guidance as to what issues they should explore in greater depth. First, the committee decided to conduct focus groups consisting of those who participated in recreational programs and those who did not. The needs of nonusers are a very crucial element in any needs assessment and should not be overlooked. Second, they held open forums on campus to discuss this issue with anyone who was interested. Finally, several committee members spent some time in OIC's recreational facility and talked with student users informally.

Who Should Collect the Data?

For the quantitative part of the study, the committee decided to use the good services of the Institutional Research Office to mail the questionnaire to students, retrieve information, and analyze results.

For the qualitative part of the study, the committee decided to conduct the focus groups, open forums, and observations with committee members, for two reasons. First, they felt very strongly that they needed direct contact with students to better assess their needs. Second, the composition of the committee was sufficiently representative (students, faculty, recreational administrators, and local graduates) to provide a variety of perspectives and perceptions.

What Instrument Should Be Used?

For the quantitative assessment, a locally constructed questionnaire was developed by the committee, in close consultation with experts on survey construction from the Institutional Research Office. This questionnaire explored the reasons why students participated or did not participate in current recreational programs, and what programs they wished would be offered but were not currently available.

For the qualitative assessment, interview protocols were developed for the focus groups, consisting of two basic questions: (1) What do you think of our current recreational program? and (2) How might the current recreational program be improved?

No particular protocol was established for the open forums, except that any and all students were invited to share their perceptions of the recreational program, and the committee would be there to listen. For students using the current recreation facility, committee members had two tasks. First, they simply observed how students used the facility, roaming the building from time to time and noting which facilities were used and by whom. Second, in informal conversations with users they asked two basic questions: (1) Why do you use this facility? and (2) How might our current recreational program be improved?

At Old Ivy, the assessment began. As stated above, questionnaires were mailed to every student and the response rate was gratifying. Since over 50 percent of students completed the instrument, the committee decided not to conduct a follow-up. From the responses to the questionnaires, participants and nonparticipants in the recreation program were identified, and focus groups were formed, each conducted by a two-person team from the committee. Students were eager to participate, and freely shared their opinions about what they liked and did not like about the recreation program. However, the campus forums were a bit of a disappointment. Not too many students participated and the information generated tended to repeat what was learned from the survey and the focus groups. The conversations in the recreation facility provided more depth to what was learned from the users.

How Should the Data Be Recorded?

Data from the questionnaire was recorded from machine readable instruments to a computer-based data file. Data from the focus groups and open forums were audiotape recorded, and observations were recorded through observers' notes. Themes were identified. (For a more extensive discussion of recording data, see Chapters Two, Three, and Four).

How Should Data Be Analyzed?

Data from the questionnaire were analyzed using multivariate analyses, which provided not only descriptive results, but helped explain responses according to various subgroups. Data from the focus groups, open forums, and observations were summarized and analyzed, yielding selected themes from participants.

At Old Ivy, the analysis of the data indicated that the student body presidents had been mostly right. Many women, indeed, were looking for different recreational activities than those currently available. Surprising to many committee members, however, was the large number of male students who were interested in different recreational opportunities as well, including camping, hiking, rock climbing, boating, and other outdoor recreational activities. In addition, more women would have participated in intramural competition if different sports were available.

How Should the Data Be Reported?

After extensive discussion and deliberation, the committee reported its finding and recommendations to the president, along the lines suggested in Chapter Thirteen. They submitted three reports. The first was the full report, which included what was done, why it was done that way, and all the findings and conclusions. The second was a short report (five pages) based on the full report; it provided more detail than the executive summary without burdening readers with a full report. The third report was an executive summary intended for general student, faculty, and public perusal.

The final report contained recommendations for changes in recreational programs, including a change in philosophy starting with the development of a new mission statement. The committee also recommended that the recreation programs' advisory board be more representative of all students, and that a person be hired to coordinate a wellness program that could be offered not only in the recreational facility but also in residence halls and Greek letter houses. And of course, the committee recommended additional funds be allocated to improve and expand already existing recreational facilities.

How Should the Study Be Used?

Unfortunately, the actual change may not be that easy to implement. If an assessment study indicates that a variety of student needs are not being met, then work will have to be done to change what is in place, or create new structures, services, programs, and learning opportunities. This is not easy in the environment in which colleges and universities currently operate. Money is short; staff members are overloaded with assignments; other priorities may be more important; and, as we stated earlier in this book, just because an assessment project concludes that certain students' needs have not been met, we cannot expect people to step forward immediately to fund new initiatives. Student affairs staff have been known to plan programs because of their own interests or skills rather than to meet student needs (Hurst and Jacobson, 1985).

At OIC, the president received the report, gave it wide circulation in the campus community, discussed it with his cabinet, and instructed the student affairs staff to develop an implementation plan, including funding. Ultimately he approved the diversification of the recreation program, the reconfiguration of the advisory board, and the hiring of a wellness coordinator. He did not approve the expansion of physical facilities, however, because of a lack of funds, but he did include this project in the institution's development program.

Commentary on the Process and the Example

The process described in this section has excellent potential for assessing student needs on virtually any campus. One should not assume, as has been suggested earlier in this chapter, that change will come easily. Nor should one assume that answers to the complex problems that face college campuses will come easily. As a case study, this example was fairly simple with clear-cut logical solutions. Real life dilemmas, however, are not always resolved so elegantly. Further, in this case, multiple methods of needs assessment were used, but please note that approaches that work well in one circumstance may not be transferable to others. Local exigencies nearly always influence the needs assessment process. Finally, one should not conclude that because some of the techniques used in this example worked better than others, that therefore they are inherently superior. The purpose of indicating that some techniques worked better than others was to illustrate that everything will not be as successful as one might plan, and that a variety of techniques promotes confidence among members of the assessing team that they will be able to generate enough useful information upon which to write a meaningful report.

Potential Needs Assessment Problems

A variety of issues and problems related to needs assessment merit at least cursory discussion as one contemplates conducting a student needs assessment. Some of these issues have been touched upon briefly in the previous discussion. In this section these issues are aggregated so that they can be addressed before a needs assessment project is undertaken.

Organizational Politics

The reader will recall that in Chapter One, one of the reasons for doing assessment in student affairs is "political." Brown and Podolske (1993b) and Stufflebeam, McCormick, Brinkerhoff, and Nelson (1985) discuss the role of politics in conducting a needs assessment. From the perspective of Brown and Podolske, the role of politics in the decision-making process should not be under-estimated. They observe, "It is important to recognize the political nature of decision making about needs, whether it involves differ-ent opinions among student groups, among staff, or between stu-dents and staff" (1993, p. 408). If the president decides that the university is going to provide student housing living arrangements so that women and men do not live on the same floor, conducting a needs assessment to determine if students have needs that run counter to the president's wishes will not be productive. The pres-ident has decided this issue already; no matter what a study shows, men and women are not going to live on the same floor.

In addition, if the president or other senior administrators interpret needs assessment results by taking certain actions that run counter to the interpretations of those conducting the assess-ment, that is their prerogative. The investigators do not have to like the senior administrators' interpretation, but they do need to realize that senior administrators may have to deal with a different set of problems and issues, and within their framework for deter-mining how to solve problems they may choose to act differently than those who have conducted the assessment.

Stufflebeam, McCormick, Brinkerhoff, and Nelson (1985) view the political problems related to needs assessment in a different way, but still provide useful advice: "One must keep in mind the capability a needs assessment has to affect people and resources, especially money, in order to be aware of the potential to arouse political forces" (p. 11). The fact is, when a needs assessment is undertaken, the potential exists that the results of the assessment may point to certain student needs that are not being met as well as they should be. Needs that are addressed poorly can be interpreted as caused by specific people who are not performing their jobs up to the standard that has been set for them. Will that discovery result in tasks being reassigned? Will resources be diverted? Will people be replaced? All of these questions have dramatic implications for the needs assessment process. It is one thing to think about conducting a needs assessment in a hypothetical situation, but it is something altogether different when one considers that certain people's careers may hang in the balance of the results of the assessment.

Perhaps one of the ways to avoid the potentially emotionally charged nature of an assessment would be to agree before conducting the assessment that the results will be used to make certain judgments about the direction of a program and the way it has been implemented. All concerned should agree in advance that if certain problems surface, staff will be retrained and supported so that they can do their jobs more effectively rather than being demoted, reassigned, or removed.

Crisis Orientation

Closely related to the political problems associated with needs assessment is what happens when this kind of study is conducted as a result of a crisis, such as when an institution's retention of students is so poor that enrollment is affected. In this scenario, a needs assessment might be conducted to determine if the needs of those students who do not persist are being met. Another crisis situation would occur when residence hall occupancy declines precipitously. Or after a student is assaulted, in which case assessment of campus safety would be required. Needs assessment under the cloud of a crisis creates a very difficult situation for all concerned.

Routine Needs Assessment

A needs assessment may be triggered by a campus problem, but from a conceptual perspective, needs assessment ought to be a continuous process rather than a single method utilized to resolve a crisis. Student needs ought to be assessed on a routine basis within the calendar of events for a student affairs division. If they are, a variety of useful byproducts are likely to occur. Kuh (1982) speaks to this point: "Experience has shown that needs assessments that follow a predetermined but flexible plan often have a variety of side effects that prove to be beneficial both from an educational and personal development perspective" (p. 208). These byproducts are less likely to occur if the needs assessment is conducted in an atmosphere of crisis.

Lack of Coordination

Needs assessments, according to Thomas (1984), frequently are not coordinated with other organizational activities, or with other needs assessments that are conducted continuously within the life of the institution. An illustration of this potential problem is as follows. The student health service conducts cholesterol screenings of the entering class and determines that students need more exercise and a lower fat diet. Simultaneously, student government reviews the fee structure and recommends to the governing board that their contribution to the recreation and wellness programs be reduced. Independently, the food service director conducts focus groups and learns students want more fast food in the union building without regard to their diet. The director decides to develop a hamburger, French fries, and malt shop in place of a salad and yogurt bar. The result is that cholesterol counts do not improve. This example, quite obviously contrived, points out how units can work in opposite directions, all trying to be helpful to students. Closer coordination might have averted the undesirable outcome.

How much are the results of needs assessments shared? We suspect not very much (see Chapter Thirteen). Rather than a variety of uncoordinated, perhaps overlapping, needs assessments conducted by various departments each year, such studies ought to be coordinated so that time, money, and effort can be saved. Determining which office will handle the coordination of these activities is a major decision, as is how the information can be shared. On a complex campus perhaps no single office can coordinate all assessment activities. But, as a start, a perspective needs to be developed so that as various departments learn about student needs, their knowledge is shared with other departments. Reports, no matter how informal, ought be sent to each department head in student affairs and routed to appropriate staff. It might be possible to hold a yearly miniconference at which each department that has collected needs assessment information shares this information, giving a brief presentation followed by reactions from their colleagues. Another step would be to identify skilled assessment consultants who might be willing to work with various departments as they contemplate conducting needs assessments.

Utilizing Only One Data-Gathering Technique

Thomas (1984) observes that needs assessments frequently rely on only one data-gathering technique, a tendency which has been addressed earlier in this chapter. The use of multiple data-gathering techniques will result in much richer information for the people conducting the assessment. Admittedly, the more complicated the data-gathering plan, the more expensive the project will become, in terms of both time and money. The alternative, however, which is to utilize only one technique and run the risk of developing an incomplete project, is hardly desirable.

Multiple data-gathering techniques should be employed whenever possible. Brown and Podolske (1993a) argue persuasively that using questionnaires alone may be the wrong approach in conducting a needs assessment. They conclude that questionnaires "become massive undertakings taxing the staff's time and energy to construct, mail, process, and tabulate the results" (p. 407). They also question the validity of homemade instruments. They believe that alternative means of assessing student needs may be more useful to the student affairs staff members as they analyze assessment data. Their point is well taken. If alternative means of identifying student needs can be developed, they should be used. Clearly, more than one method of identifying student needs will add substantial richness to a needs assessment project.

Target Populations for Assessment

Barrow and his colleagues (1989) identify a very interesting issue in their analysis of a needs assessment project they conducted. They concluded that survey data may be "more valuable when used to identify subpopulations with special needs than when used to provide a needs profile for the general student population. A need idiosyncratically expressed by one subgroup may be a more reliable indicator of a genuine area of interest than a need endorsed highly by the overall sample" (p. 81).

This is a point well taken, and was illustrated in the Old Ivy College scenario. It may be more useful to target needs assessments at definable groups of students within the overall student body rather than all students on campus; it may be more effective to look at the needs of the freshman class, master's students in specific departments, and so on. For example, if one really wishes to determine the special needs of people who are physically challenged, ask people from that group, not everybody. Similarly, female students can best speak to their needs, as can students from other historically underrepresented populations. As needs assessment projects are contemplated, it may be more useful to work with identifiable subgroups of students rather than the larger group from which they are drawn.

Conclusion

Conducting a credible needs assessment is not an easy task. Too often needs assessments are conducted the wrong way for the wrong reasons. This chapter has identified some of the salient issues related to needs assessment, including (1) determining substantive purposes for doing a needs assessment, (2) identifying various assessment techniques, (3) following a process that will generate useful information, and (4) avoiding a variety of problems that can contaminate the process. Armed with the information contained in this chapter, a student affairs officer should always be ready to conduct a needs assessment.

Chapter Seven

Assessing Student Satisfaction

How does a student affairs administrator determine if students are satisfied with their experiences on campus? Traditionally, satisfaction has been measured by distributing questionnaires to students and analyzing the results of their responses to these instruments. Or, in recent years, focus groups have been used in an effort to learn what students report about their experiences. These approaches are valid and commonly used with good results. Other approaches, however, are available that can be used to determine, at least in part, how satisfied students are with their experiences on campus. This chapter will present and describe a variety of techniques.

Several major themes will be addressed. First, a few words will be offered about developing criteria to measure satisfaction. Second, a variety of approaches will be discussed which make use of what have been identified as "static measures" of satisfaction. These approaches use techniques other than the quantitative or qualitative measures. Third, more active approaches to measuring satisfaction will be introduced, including quantitative and qualitative techniques. Finally, some concluding thoughts and guiding principles will be provided.

Definition and Purpose of Satisfaction Assessment

A useful way of looking at student satisfaction is to frame one's conceptualization of this matter by what makes for a high-quality experience on campus. Bogue and Saunders (1992), define quality as "conformance to mission specification and goal achievement—

within publicly accepted standards of accountability and integrity" (p. 20). If one assumes that high-quality experiences make for satisfied students, then a high level of student satisfaction should result when students have high-quality experiences on campus. The purpose of assessing student satisfaction, then, if one accepts this framework, is to determine whether students have high-quality educational experiences that foster their learning and growth. Bogue and Saunders (1992) present the case that all campuses have the potential to provide high-quality experiences for students.

As a caveat to the reader it is important to point out that student satisfaction, or a lack of it, may not necessarily be equated with good educational practice. Just because students find a faculty member to be engaging and friendly does not mean that they are learning much in that person's courses. Similarly, because some students like living in a residence hall, where they can do anything they want at virtually any time without adherence to institutional guidelines, may not be consistent with a good group-living experience. As a result, the student affairs administrator has to be careful not to assume that just because students are satisfied, it necessarily follows that good educational experiences have occurred. This chapter is dedicated to identifying methods that can be used to determine student satisfaction with their experiences.

Measuring Satisfaction

First and foremost, the student affairs administrator who is charged with assessing the level of student satisfaction has to determine what criteria will be used to measure it. A good place to start with this process is to revisit the institution's mission and statement of purpose. Lyons (1993) describes the importance of an institution's mission as the "most important factor that determines the shape and substance of student affairs" (p. 14).

While some may discount the value of a mission statement, a variety of studies have found it to be extremely helpful in that it describes what an institution of higher education hopes to accomplish with its educational program (see Kuh, Schuh, Whitt, and Associates, 1991). Mission statements vary widely from institution to institution, depending on their hopes and aspirations, who they attempt to serve, and how they plan to go about achieving their goals.

After reviewing the institution's mission statement, the investigator must review the mission statement or statement of purpose for the individual units that are being included in the satisfaction assessment. Again, these can vary dramatically from institution to institution. For example, the role and scope of the housing program at a residential institution that serves traditional-aged undergraduates will be quite different from that of a metropolitan institution which houses primarily international students. The individual units, then, should conduct a thorough review of their mission statements so that a realistic appraisal of student satisfaction can be assessed.

From this point, a framework can be constructed that will measure student satisfaction. Simply learning that students are satisfied with their experience does not, however, provide a complete picture. Rather, determining that students are satisfied with their experiences, and that those experiences are consistent with institution's goals, will provide a much better understanding of student experiences on campus.

Total Quality Management

While this commentary is not designed to be a primer on Total Quality Management (TQM), it is important to note that in many ways TQM can be used to measure student satisfaction and develop mechanisms so that students' experiences can be improved. TQM is concerned with improving the performance of an entire institution (Krueger, 1993), with a special focus on enhancing systems. According to Krueger (1993), "85 to 90 percent of all problems are the fault of the system, not the individual" (p. 274). Hence, if systems are improved, student satisfaction will increase. Hogan (1992) adds that one of the benefits of TQM is that faculty and staff come to acknowledge the concept of customer satisfaction.

Implementing a TQM system can involve a number of techniques. Interestingly enough, many of these can involve using data that are already at hand within an institution, such as the number of course sections with fifteen or fewer students, the overall faculty-student ratio, the average ACT or SAT scores of entering freshmen, and the number of internships and practical or other practice-oriented courses (Krueger, 1993). These kinds of measures point to the quality of a student's experience which, in turn, will likely lead to satisfaction with the college. For more details on TQM and high-quality educational experiences, the reader is referred to Deming (1986) and Chickering and Gamson (1987).

Static Measures of Satisfaction

A variety of measures exist which are available on virtually any campus and which provide evidence of student satisfaction with a particular event, service, or activity. We have characterized these measures as "static" because they are available to the student affairs administrator who is interested in measuring satisfaction without undertaking a complex research study. A brief discussion of these measures follows in this section of this chapter, with observations about why the investigator needs to be cautious about drawing definitive conclusions from these measures. Also included is a word or two about where to find the information.

Persistence

One of the ways of measuring student satisfaction with their overall experience at a college or university is to determine the extent to which they persist from year to year and finally to graduation. These statistics are required by federal law and are readily available.

It is important to note, however, in looking at persistence statistics that whether or not students persist to graduation may not reflect satisfaction entirely with an institution. For example, students may enroll at an institution with the intent to transfer after a year or two. They may plan to enroll in pre-professional courses at one college and then transfer to another to complete their education. In this circumstance, failure to persist does not reflect dissatisfaction with the institution in which they were first enrolled.

Other students may not plan to finish a college degree at all, either at their institution of first enrollment or anywhere else. For example, a recent study of entering first-year students at Wichita State University (Schuh, 1993b), indicates that 2.6 percent of the respondents indicated that even though they were enrolling in degree-bound programs, they did not intend to complete a college degree at Wichita State or anywhere else.

As is mentioned above, persistence records are kept on all campuses because of the federal law. The information should be available from the registrar's office, the institutional research office, or a similar department.

Participation Rates

A second way of measuring student satisfaction is to consider the extent to which they participate in various activities and programs. Chapter Five includes a more extensive discussion of how to keep track of who uses which services, programs, and facilities. One can make the presumption—which may not always be correct—that students participate in those activities which give them satisfaction. And students avoid experiences that they do not find satisfying.

Participation, however, may not always reflect student satisfaction. Students may participate in certain activities because they perceive that this may elevate their status on campus, enhance their prospects for employment, or assist their admission to a prestigious graduate school. One example of this kind of thinking may be the motivation students have for attending some events on campus because their organization, such as a fraternity, will receive "credit" toward winning a competition among all the Greek letter organizations on campus.

Most organizations keep track of the number of students who attend their events, or at least have a reasonable estimate of that number. For example, the student activities office should know how many students attend dances, movies, or concerts, especially if the purchase of a ticket was necessary for admission.

Spending Patterns

Many students will argue that they do not have enough money. Based on their financial aid commitments (see Schuh, 1993a), it is clear that many students do not have tremendous amounts of disposable income. Nonetheless, students have many opportunities to spend their money on campus, ranging from taking care of their basic needs by living in student housing, to buying their textbooks and other educational supplies at the college bookstore, or attending to some of their entertainment needs through the student union, athletic department, and other entertainment venues. It may be valid to conclude that if students do not spend their money on campus, but rather for other, off-campus opportunities, then what is offered on campus may not be satisfying to them.

Now, it may not be entirely correct to conclude definitively that, because students do not spend their disposable income on campus, they are not satisfied by what is available. Certain items may not be available on campus because of the college's mission (such as birth control devices being unavailable on a "religious" campus). Restrictions on student life may be part of campus policies (such as twenty-four-hour visitation in the residence halls), or certain products may not be available on the campus (such as cigarettes) because it is policy at the institution not to sell them. In these and other cases idiosyncratic to specific institutions, students have to make their purchases of certain items elsewhere.

Since fees are collected for the on-campus services and products described in this section, records comparing collections from one year to the next should be readily available. Comparing gross sales from one year to the next will provide a start in making judgments based on students' spending patterns. Should spending patterns vary dramatically from year to year, such fluctuations may reflect changes in student satisfaction. Or, they may not. In any case, such changes do point to avenues of inquiry that can be explored in measuring student satisfaction.

Membership Recruitment and Retention

Some student organizations seem to encounter relatively few problems recruiting and retaining members. Others struggle mightily to build their membership rolls. Why is that? One reason, quite obviously, might be that organizations that meet the expectations of members attract and retain them, while those that do not have membership problems. It might be worth the effort to study what elements contribute to member satisfaction and why some organizations seem to do well year after year.

On the other hand, as has been pointed out for the other measures identified above, there may be reasons why students join organizations that do not meet their needs. Peer pressure, which can be extremely powerful (see Astin, 1993), may contribute to students' decisions to join certain organizations, as well as perceptions that membership will accelerate career opportunities. Nonetheless, one clear way to measure students' satisfaction with an organization is to measure the extent to which its membership grows.

Often, organizations are required to submit member names and addresses on an annual basis to the department on campus charged with registering student organizations. The student activities office, residence life office, dean of students office, or other

location of organizational records will have this information. Therefore, this information is readily available for the investigator.

Programs

Within organizations, a way of looking at member satisfaction is to
look at the overall series or variety of programs that are offered.
Those organizations which have a growing number and variety of
programs exhibit vitality, while those whose programs are shrink-
ing in number and quality very well may be experiencing trouble.

Again, leaping to conclusions based on an increasing number
and variety of programs may be incorrect. Just looking at the numbers will not reveal an organization's qualitative aspects. For example, perhaps members were required to go to an event or join an
organization (which often can be the case for fraternity and sorority pledges). More investigation may be necessary before definitive
conclusions about the attendees' satisfaction can be reached. Nonetheless, an increasing number of programs may very well point to
a viable organization on the wane.

Some organizations may keep track of such information because of their purpose, traditions, or longevity, while others may
not. All student organizations should be encouraged to do so. For
records of more major campus events, the investigator should
check the institution or campus newspaper archives.

Student Newspapers

The student newspaper has been described as a potentially aggra-
vating element on the college campus, depending on how accurately the paper reflects student opinion and campus life (Schuh,
1986). Virtually any student affairs administrator (Asher, 1986),
president (Magrath and Magrath, 1986), or even newspaper adviser (Siddons, 1986) would agree that the student newspaper can
be a source of tremendous pride as well as frustration. Remem-
bering that student newspaper staffs can have their own agendas
and may not always accurately reflect student attitudes about campus life, the newspaper can provide two sources of information
about how well satisfied students are with life on campus.

First, the articles that the paper staff prints will provide information about their view of campus life. These stories can border on
the sensational since neither good instruction nor a well-managed

and fiscally prudent college generally are news. But an investigator can often count on the student newspaper to identify points of tension where the level of student satisfaction may not be acceptable. News stories combined with editorials prepared by the paper's editors will provide at the very least the issues the student body considers worth debating, and it may well hint at the majority opinion of students about an issue. Student newspaper staff certainly should not be entirely discounted as a bunch of rabble rousers whose ultimate goal is to embarrass the college. The fact is that members of the senior staff of student papers are among the very few students on campus who have a reasonably global view of life on campus, especially if the campus newspaper covers all campus news well.

Second, it is a good idea to read the letters to the editor that are printed in the student newspaper. These letters, which usually included mention of the student authors' names, can reflect a general level of satisfaction or dissatisfaction with some aspect of the college. Sometimes a letter may reflect a misunderstanding about how a policy has been developed or a procedure implemented. At other times, however, the student may really have a point. Depending on the circumstance, it might make sense for a student affairs administrator to place a telephone call to the student to get more information on what precipitated the letter. If the student misunderstands the situation, additional information might be supplied, but the student affairs officer also might find the perspective of the student very helpful as a means of gaining a better understanding about why this student, and perhaps others, are unhappy with some aspect of the college. In this instance, the educational process certainly can work both ways.

Institutional Databases

Chapter Five provides detailed instruction about how to use institutional databases for tracking clientele. Such resources can provide a variety of interesting data which, again, in and of themselves will not provide a complete picture of the satisfaction students feel with certain aspects of their experience, but such data can raise questions that will point the person engaged in assessment in the direction of further assessment activity. Two examples of institutional databases will illustrate how this material can be used to help provide a sense of the level of student satisfaction with the college.

Institutions keep records of student registration activity, including drops and adds of courses, as well as which instructors' courses fill to capacity and have waiting lists. Lots of reasons contribute to why students take certain courses, including whether the course is required, if it is perceived as being not particularly rigorous, if the course is of high quality, and if the instructor is relatively friendly and approachable. If courses fill to capacity during preregistration, that may be a signal that students are well satisfied with them. On the other hand, if substantial proportions of students drop courses offered by specific instructors, that may indicate lack of satisfaction. Registration data will not provide definitive information about the level of satisfaction that students experience with instructors and courses, but it can provide clues about where to conduct further inquiry if student satisfaction with courses is of interest.

Another institutional database located in the college's library can be used to provide information from which further inquiries may be conducted. Libraries tend to keep track of such data as how many people use the library in general, how many use specialized services, and which materials are checked out for student use. Use patterns can be very helpful in trying to understand what books and other materials students read. Are these materials likely to be used to help students meet classroom requirements, or are they used for personal reading? How would faculty evaluate the materials that students read for pleasure? If students appear to do little or no reading for pleasure, what does that mean? These questions will not necessarily be answered by the library database, but they will provide a point from which one can do further investigation. In addition, if the library database indicates that students generally do not use the library, this information may suggest additional inquiry. If one assumes that the college's library is at the intellectual heart of the institution, then reviewing the use patterns of the library would provide an interesting beginning to assessing student satisfaction with the college as a whole.

Food Services

Many colleges indicate that promoting the health and wellness of students is an important part of the educational experience they wish to provide for students (Leafgren, 1993). Central to this objective is providing healthy, well-balanced meals for students. Food services keep records of participation rates for students with meal plans; these records can provide helpful information for those trying to assess the extent to which students are satisfied with meal programs and maintaining a healthy diet.

Students often have choices with regard to the kind of meal plan they can select (see Fairbrook, 1993). These choices range from the number of meals they can contract for in the residence halls, to the use of debit cards and other means of providing food services in the student union and other places on campus. These programs use automated systems to keep track of the items food outlets sell to students. A review of the records of the food services programs will begin to provide a picture of the kinds of items students purchase and whether or not the food they purchase on campus will contribute to a healthy diet. Do students tend to eat the same kinds of food throughout the entire year? Does the participation rate for either the meal plan or cash operation decline or increase over the course of the year? If so, how much and why? Information about on-campus eating habits can provide a good start in assessing student satisfaction with the campus food service.

From these static measures we move on to discussing active measures of student satisfaction.

Active Measures of Student Satisfaction

An excellent way of complementing static measures of student satisfaction is to engage in active means of assessing student satisfaction. Before we discuss these methods, however, it will helpful to review a more specific model of satisfaction assessment, drawn from the marketing field and developed by Zeithaml, Parasuraman, and Berry (1990). This model helps answer the question an investigator will need to ask before beginning an assessment, "What specific aspects of student satisfaction should be assessed?"

Using extensive focus groups, these researchers identified ten dimensions of service quality (which were subsequently reduced to five) as they developed an instrument for measuring client's perceptions of service quality (SERVQUAL). They stress that these dimensions are not mutually exclusive in the minds of clients and actually overlap significantly. They include the following:

1. *Tangibles:* Appearance of physical facilities, equipment, personnel, and communication materials.
2. *Reliability:* Ability to perform the promised service dependably and accurately.
3. *Responsiveness:* Willingness to help customers and provide prompt service.
4. *Assurance:* Includes four subdimensions:
   Competence: possession of the required skills and knowledge to perform the service
   Courtesy: politeness, respect, consideration, and friendliness of contact personnel
   Credibility: trustworthiness, believability, honesty of the service provider
   Security: freedom from danger, risk, or doubt.
5. *Empathy:* Includes three subdimensions:
   Access: approachability and ease of contact
   Communication: keeping customers informed in language they can understand and listening to them
   Understanding the customer: making the effort to know customers and their needs [Zeithaml, Parasuraman, and Berry, 1990, pp. 21–22, 24].

We believe this model provides an excellent beginning point for discussing active measures of assessment, as well as a model for developing instruments and protocols to measure student satisfaction of services, programs, and facilities. Within this framework, however, it is doubtful that one method of assessing student satisfaction will paint a complete picture of just how happy students are. Rather, using a variety of methods will result in a more accurate understanding of how satisfied students are with their college experience. Several methods are described in this section which the student affairs administrator may want to employ.

Secret Shoppers

Commercial enterprises often use the technique of a "secret shopper," or a person who reports on his or her experiences as a customer. Secret shoppers are briefed before they begin their activities with the enterprise so that they understand its mission, what is expected of employees, and how to report their experiences. The type of information they report can include such items as how long they had to wait before being helped, whether materials such as forms were readily available in the area where the transaction was completed, how cordially they were greeted, how long it took to complete their transactions, if the transactions were accurate, if they were thanked for using the enterprise, and if their overall impression of the activity was satisfying. In addition, the secret shopper is asked to report on the appearance of the area, who assisted them, the friendliness of the employees, and the knowledge of the staff.

In a higher education setting, secret shoppers are asked to complete forms shortly after they have completed an experience on campus, such as a transaction at the bursar's office or library. The forms are sent to an office where information from all the secret shoppers on campus is compiled. Composite information is provided to the heads of the departments where the secret shoppers conducted their business, and they, in turn, are supposed to provide feedback for the employees who actually served the shoppers. On a periodic basis, this information can be aggregated for the employees, who should then receive instruction about how to improve their service to students and other clients.

Use of secret shoppers will not necessarily transform the quality of student experiences overnight, but it is an effective way of measuring just how satisfied students are. While in a commercial enterprise this kind of assessment activity is geared toward purchasing goods or services, there is no reason why it cannot be applied to circumstances where students use services or participate in activities on campus, such as using the recreation center, the student union, or the campus telephone operator. If properly structured, use of secret shoppers should not result in employees' fear for their jobs; rather, it should provide useful information to improve students' experiences.

The quality of the information provided in this kind of assessment activity will rest to a great extent on how well the secret shoppers are trained. The secret shoppers, who are students, need to understand that at times good educational practices or institutional policies will not allow them to do just anything they want (such as take a course before they have satisfied the prerequisite for it), and that they will not see change overnight; they will have to wait to be served better by employees of the college. Assuming that the students' training is conducted properly, and that the secret shoppers are accurate in their reports, this kind of assessment of student satisfaction can provide extremely useful information.

Quantitative Measures of Satisfaction

Chapter Four includes details on the use of quantitative methods in assessment projects. In this chapter, we point to a variety of quantitative studies, in and out of higher education, which report the level of satisfaction people experience with selected aspects of their lives. Among these are reports from Silverman and others (1983) on members' satisfaction with their churches, Kennedy (1989) on students' satisfaction with their families, and Meredith (1985) on students' satisfaction with their campus experiences. One common thread running through all of these reports is that quantitative methods are used to measure the degree of satisfaction people feel with regard to their experiences. As these studies show, measuring student satisfaction by way of quantitative methods is a well-accepted practice.

In his recent book, Astin (1993) reports an analysis of student satisfaction with their college experiences. In this particular study he indicates that students were asked to rate over twenty different aspects of their college campus using a five-point scale. They could choose from responses such as very satisfied, satisfied, neutral, dissatisfied, can't rate, and no experience. The responses "can't rate, no experience" were eliminated from further analysis and a factor analysis was conducted to combine the items into five general categories. The results were then reported as measures of the satisfaction students had with their campus experiences, both inside and outside the classroom. Pace (1979, 1987) has asked similar questions in surveys he has conducted and analyzed.

In his study, Astin (1993) also asked the penetrating question about whether or not a student would enroll in his or her college given the opportunity to make the choice again. This question provides extremely useful information about the level of satisfaction students express about the aggregate of their experiences, since, presumably, satisfied students would enroll again, while those who were unhappy would not.

Erwin (1991) indicates that a variety of quantitative approaches are available to a person wishing to conduct an assessment. The first choice the researcher needs to make is whether to use a standardized instrument or to develop one specifically designed for the project. Erwin is quick to remind us that "for assessment information to be useful in decision making, an assessment method must have both good reliability and evidence of validity" (p. 59). Erwin provides excellent guidance about how to construct instruments that meet the criteria of good reliability and evidence of validity; his suggestions are well worth reviewing for anyone planning to develop their own instruments.

For those who wish to develop an instrument which meets the specific needs of their campus, a variety of formats exist. Among these are surveys and questionnaires, rating scales and checklists. Again, Erwin (1991) provides excellent advice about how to develop these instruments which is worth reviewing before embarking on a project based on campus-based instruments.

Another option the student affairs officer has in assessing satisfaction on campus is to use an instrument that is standardized, that is, one which has been used on many campuses and has well-developed norms based on numerous applications. One of the most useful instruments to be developed in recent years is the College Student Experiences Questionnaire (CSEQ), developed by C. Robert Pace (1979). Included in this instrument are questions that examine the college environment, students' estimates of gains or progress they have made while enrolled at the college, and their opinions about the college, including the extent to which they like the college and would enroll again, if they could go back and do so. The CSEQ is extremely well constructed and useful as an instrument that can measure student satisfaction as well as elicit a great deal of other information about students' experiences on campus. This instrument provides an excellent option for those who do not wish to develop their own.

Another standardized instrument that has been used in a series of college student satisfaction studies (Robertson, 1980; Wesley and Abston, 1983; Dillard, 1989) is the College Student Satisfaction

Questionnaire (CSSQ) (Betz, Menne, Starr, and Klingensmith, 1971). This instrument measures six dimensions of student satisfaction, including policies and procedures, working conditions, compensation, quality of education, and social life. It also asks students to respond to a series of items (ranging from 92 to 139, depending on which form is used) using a five-point Likert-type scale. The reliability and validity data of the CSSQ are quite positive. This instrument provides a viable alternative for the person who wishes to use a standardized instrument as a substitute for the CSEQ.

A third nationally standardized and recognized instrument is the Student Satisfaction Inventory, published by Noel Levitz, Inc. (1994). It measures how important various areas are to students, as well as assessing their satisfaction with academic advising, campus climate, campus life, campus support services, concern for the individual, instructional effectiveness, recruitment and financial aid, registration effectiveness, safety and security, service excellence, and student centeredness. Results can be reported through comparison to national norms, and by student target groups. There is a four-year college and university version, and a version for community, junior, and technical colleges.

Nationally developed instruments can also be used to measure satisfaction with specific student services and programs. The Appendix contains a listing of selected instruments that might be useful in this kind of project.

Qualitative Methods of Measuring Satisfaction

Of course, another approach to measuring satisfaction is to use qualitative methodology, as was discussed in Chapter Three. If the owners of a restaurant wanted to find out how two people enjoyed their meals, they could ask their customers as they paid their bills. This kind of assessment is referred to as summative (Brown, 1979), meaning that something is evaluated after the event has ended. Formative evaluation, the opposite of summative evaluation, refers to evaluating something in process, or as it is taking place. If the owners of the restaurant used formative evaluation, they would ask diners at their restaurant if they are enjoying their meals while they are in the process of eating. Similarly, students can be asked about their experiences either while they are in the middle of them or after they have ended. The studies reported by Pace (1979) are excellent examples of how investigators can work with graduates to learn what effect their experiences had both during their time at college and after their graduation. Qualitative methodology, while somewhat more complex than simply asking people what they think of their dinner, has an excellent place in assessing satisfaction, whether students are in the middle of their college experience or after they have graduated.

Qualitative methods, the reader will recall, include such techniques as interviewing students, reviewing documents, and observing the behavior of students. Several qualitative techniques that the student affairs officer might want to employ include structured interviews and the use of diaries or journals. Erwin (1993) points out that interviews can be conducted with individual students or in groups, where "group members can play off each other's responses" (p. 94). The reader is referred to Chapter Three for more information about qualitative methods.

Guiding Principles about Satisfaction Assessment

Assessing students' satisfaction with their educational experiences is not easy but can be very rewarding. A variety of tools and techniques are available to the student affairs officer who wishes to conduct a satisfaction assessment. In the final portion of this chapter a few concluding thoughts and guiding principles about satisfaction assessment will be offered.

Role of Mission

The investigator should remember that trying to determine students' level of satisfaction will hinge on factors other than simply trying to determine if they are happy. Satisfaction needs to be framed by the institution's mission and the mission and goals of the various programs, services, and learning opportunities that are part of the assessment. The framework, at times, may not necessarily engender immediate pleasure on the part of students, since certain educational policies or practices may be more demanding than some students want. As a result, it is important in designing the assessment and analyzing the results to make sure that what is assessed is consistent with the college's goals and objectives for students' experiences.

Static Measures

A variety of measures which were defined as static in this chapter are available to the student affairs administrator. Many of these can be part of the administrator's routine, such as reading the student newspaper or studying routine institutional reports, while others could be used in conducting a satisfaction assessment. None of these measures will provide a complete picture of student satisfaction with all of their educational experiences, or even some of them, but many will open avenues for further investigation and study.

Active Measures

Active measures also were discussed in this chapter. These are specific techniques that can be used when conducting an assessment that requires that the investigator take specific initiatives. Active measures include both quantitative and qualitative methods. The quantitative methods require the student affairs administrator to choose between selecting a standardized instrument or developing a questionnaire on campus. Qualitative methods, described briefly earlier, include interviewing students, reviewing documents, and observing student behavior.

Blending Methods

In the final analysis, a thorough assessment of student satisfaction will be accomplished most successfully when a blend of methods and techniques is used. Since really no specific method or technique will result in a complete understanding of student satisfaction, using a combination of active and static measures will generate the best results possible. A realistic attitude will temper one's hopes for the results of a satisfaction assessment. Such variables as the amount of time that can be devoted to the project, the financial support available for the project, the expertise of the researchers, and, perhaps most important, what is being measured—all of these things will limit the assessment project. In the end, however, a blend of techniques and methods will result in a satisfaction assessment that will yield extremely useful information about students' experience, and will point to what can be done by the institutions to provide richer educational experiences for students.

Conclusion

This chapter has been designed to provide the student affairs administrator with ideas about how to measure student satisfaction. Student satisfaction is best measured within a framework of providing high-quality experiences for students shaped by an institution's mission. Student satisfaction can be measured by static techniques, active techniques, or both. Qualitative and quantitative techniques can be used in conducting satisfaction assessments.

Chapter Eight

Assessing Campus Environments

If a member of a governing board were to ask a senior student affairs officer to describe the environment on campus for students, a relatively simple inquiry at first blush, an appropriate response might be: Which student? Students take different classes, live in different places, have different sets of friends, come from different families, and so on. Consequently, every student has a unique environment since each individual attending the college has a different set of factors influencing his or her experiences.

Perhaps because of the circumstances described above, assessing the environment on campus is not easy. Astin (1993) observes the following about environmental assessment: "Environmental assessment presents by far the most difficult and complex challenge in the field of assessment. It is also the most neglected topic" (p. 81). This chapter is designed to discuss several aspects of environmental assessment. First, a bit of theoretical background will be presented about the interaction of people and their environment. Then, several models will be introduced which describe different approaches to environmental assessment; common elements from these approaches will be distilled. Finally, examples will be presented which illustrate how an environmental assessment project can be conducted in order to address specific situations on campus.

The reader should realize that a number of excellent discussions on the topic of environmental assessment and ecological management have been written in the past few years. The topic is complex and reviewing other discussions is imperative for the person who desires a thorough understanding of it. The approach taken in this chapter is to try to provide specific information which should facilitate conducting an environmental assessment on campus. As mentioned, a wealth of material exists on this topic which provides wonderful supporting information. Much of this material (such as Huebner, 1989; Huebner and Lawson, 1990; and Strange, 1991) should be read in its entirety to gain a more complete picture of the issues associated with environmental assessment.

Definition and Purpose of Environmental Assessment

Environmental assessment determines and evaluates how the various elements and conditions of the college campus milieu affect student learning and growth. These elements and conditions vary from campus to campus. For example, a college located in a large metropolitan area dedicated to technical education will have a fundamentally different physical and psychological environment than one located in a rural setting which focuses on the liberal arts. It would not be hyperbolic to claim that every campus has a unique environment.

What is the purpose of environmental assessment? It helps those responsible for the campus environment to provide the best possible circumstances where students can learn and grow. One of the challenges that face those who manage the campus ecology (see Banning, 1989) is that the campus environment has many dimensions, including the physical facilities and physical environmental characteristics; the curriculum and the cocurriculum; the human elements, including faculty, staff, and students; and the social and psychological climate and university philosophy (Huebner and Lawson, 1990). Every person is affected differently by the campus environment; you might even say that every person's environment is unique, a fact that creates tremendous challenges in conducting an assessment.

Lewin's Formula of Person-Environment Interaction

Decades ago, Kurt Lewin (1936) took the position that psychology should be concerned not only with time, but also with space. He believed that the mathematical discipline "topology" would help make psychology a "real" science (p. vii). Accordingly, Lewin conducted research that was committed to describing human behavior in scientific terms.

One of Lewin's interests was explaining human behavior in terms of a formula based on laws. He observed that without laws, the behavior of individuals could be interpreted merely as random events. However, Lewin believed that a large number of individual cases would have to be studied before it would be possible to offer meaningful generalizations about human behavior.

Lewin pointed out that at the time of his research, psychology was evolving from a science concerned with describing events to one that was interested in predicting outcomes. Lewin thought that the development of psychology as a science would be advanced if laws were developed that could be used to predict human behavior. Even with laws, however, predicting human behavior would not be an easy task: "The application of the laws presupposes the comprehension of individual cases. One can apply a law only if one knows the nature of the concrete case with which one is dealing. Considered from this point of view the laws are nothing more than principles according to which the actual event may be derived from the dynamic factors of the concrete situation" (Lewin, 1936, p. 11).

One way of describing human behavior was by way of the formula $B = f(S)$, meaning that behavior (B) is a function of the whole situation of a person $f(S)$. This formula, in Lewin's view, was incomplete. He thought it was important to determine "the relationship between an object and its surroundings. It is not thought then that the environment of the individual serves merely to facilitate or inhibit tendencies which are established once and for all in the nature of the person" (Lewin, 1936, p. 12).

Lewin observed that every psychological event depends upon the state of the person and the state of the environment, although the relative importance of one to the other depends on the specific situation. As a result, Lewin developed a formula, $B = f(PE)$ (roughly meaning that behavior is a function of the interaction of the person and the environment). This formula took into account the relationship between the person and the environment. He concluded that "every scientific psychology must take into account whole situations, i.e., the state of both person and environment" (Lewin, 1936, p. 12). Lewin's line of thinking, then, provided a foundation for contemporary environmental theory.

Those who have attempted to build on Lewin's pioneering work have not been totally successful in developing and manipulating environments. Huebner and Lawson (1990) offer a critique of Lewin's paradigm and identify six issues that contribute to a lack of progress in manipulating college environments successfully. Included in their list are the following:

1. Inability to identify the most powerful environmental and personal variables to study or manipulate in a given setting.
2. Unsatisfactory definition of the concept of interaction that does justice to human complexity or environmental richness.
3. Lack of agreement on outcomes, how to measure them or relate them to the interests of the various constituencies of higher education.
4. Many variables cannot be controlled since they are outside of the range of influence of student affairs officers.
5. Resources and time are spent by student affairs officers on other matters more closely related to routine, daily work.
6. The number of environmental variables that affect students is nearly infinite, and the complexity of the interactions of these variables is difficult to understand and even more difficult to manipulate [p. 143].

Nevertheless, Huebner and Lawson (1990) are quite complimentary about Lewin's work. They observe the following about his formula: "It is consistent with the most realistic, accurate, and appropriately complex understanding we have about how human beings function. Any other approach, although perhaps more easily understood or applied, will be less satisfying and less powerful" (p. 144).

Thus, Lewin's explanation of the interaction of people with their environment provides an excellent theoretical point of departure that can be used to guide environmental assessment activities. Other approaches also may be employed as alternatives to Lewin's. Strange (1991) provides a comprehensive discussion of several models that explain the nature of human environments and their effect on students. These models include the following:

1. Physical models which address the natural and synthetic physical features of human environments.
2. Human aggregate models which stress that environments are transmitted through people and reflect the collective characteristics of the people who live in them.

3. Structural organizational models which emphasize the importance of the goals and purposes of environments leading to organizational structures that enhance or inhibit certain environmental characteristics or outcomes.
4. Perceptual models which posit that a critical element in understanding how individuals experience an environment is a result of how they subjectively interpret that environment [p. 161].

A review of Strange's analysis of these models would be very helpful to a person seeking an alternative to Lewin's paradigm.

The decision to select a theory to guide an environmental assessment probably is more important than the actual selection of the theory itself. The person contemplating an environmental assessment project will be well served to have the assessment theory-based, since theory will provide a way of framing and understanding the activity.

In contemporary literature, Lewin's formula has been represented as $B = f(P \times E)$, and it represents an elegant approach to understanding the interaction between an individual and the environment. The challenge, of course, in assessing a student's environment lies in trying to isolate those variables which have the greatest influence on a student at any given time. If the student's environment is understood more completely, then interventions can be developed to reduce the negative impact of poor experiences on students and to accentuate the positive ones. Many of the environmental assessment techniques that will be discussed in this chapter are dedicated toward that end.

Environmental Assessment Models

In this section, several models will be introduced that can be used to guide an environmental assessment. The reader should realize that models summarized here are rather complex; they should be reviewed in their entirety for a complete understanding of them.

WICHE's Ecosystem Model

In the early 1970s, the Western Interstate Commission for Higher Education (WICHE) produced a model for designing campus environments called the "ecosystem model" (1973). WICHE observed the following about campus environments: "From an ecological systems approach, the question of whether the campus environment is supportive of learning becomes very important. The environment becomes an important element in obtaining educational objectives" (p. 5). The design philosophy of this model was based on several assumptions, two of which quite obviously come from Lewin's pioneering work. They include the assumption that the campus environment consists of all the stimuli that impinge on the students' sensory modalities, and that a transactional relationship exists between college students and their campus environment. Put more simply, students shape their environment and are shaped by it.

According to the WICHE model, every campus has a design, whether it is intentional or unintentional. The campus, in this view, should be dedicated to designing an environment that complements the wide variety of individual characteristics found among students. Whether or not it manages to do this stems from the institution's philosophy, planning, and dedication.

The ecosystem design process that WICHE developed consists of seven steps. The steps can apply to an entire campus, or a part of the campus that is well defined, such as a residence hall, Greek letter organization, academic program, or major. It is important to note that the steps of the design process are interdependent and interactive. Each affects all the others and no one step stands by itself. A person using this model, however, can start at any place in the design process and work through all seven steps.

In *step one,* the designers of the campus environment join members of the collegiate community in selecting the educational values of the campus. These values may already be chosen and identified as part of an institution's mission.

Step two involves the translation of values into specific goals. The goals of an institution may or may not be consistent with the goals students have for their education. For example, students may be strongly committed to translating their learning experiences into training for specific employment opportunities, while the college may see students' learning as preparation for broader life experiences. If a lack of congruity of goals exists, the college can change its goals, define them differently, or do a better job of articulating what it hopes students will gain from their experiences.

Step three consists of developing environments for each of the goals identified in step two. If, for example, one of these goals is to make sure that every entering student has a small group learning experience with a senior faculty member, then the campus might develop a series of tutorials for every first-year student. Similarly, other goals are operationalized in the environment in this step of the model.

The environment is then fit to students, which is *step four.* An appropriate analogy for the process at this point is buying a pair of jeans. If a customer wants to buy a pair of jeans, but after trying on a pair finds the size is too big, the solution is not for the buyer to gain twenty pounds. Instead, trying on a smaller pair to find a better fit makes good sense. There is nothing wrong with the first pair of jeans, nor is there anything wrong with the buyer. A better fit will serve everyone better. So, too, is the case with the college environment. A good fit between student and environment serves everyone well.

In *step five,* students' perceptions of the environment are measured. This can be done by using instruments developed specifically for this process, or by using standardized instruments which are described elsewhere in this book.

As important as it is to measure students' perceptions of the environment, student behavior within the environment should be monitored, which is *step six.* Are students dropping out? If so, why? Do students spend time on campus or leave as soon as classes are over? What facilities do they use? What facilities are avoided? These questions and others are useful in deciding how student behavior will be monitored.

Finally, in *step seven* feedback on the design is provided. With this information in hand, changes can be made. The information can be factored into the process at step two or three, and the process can begin all over.

The ecosystem process can be applied to three levels of students. *Level I* refers to large numbers of students, such as all sophomores, or all residence hall students. *Level II* is designed for well-defined groups of students, such as those with a specific major or those who are members of a fraternity or sorority. *Level III* is targeted at individual students and uses very specific tools.

The WICHE approach suggests that this process has the potential to be implemented by any staff member regardless of responsibility on campus, depending on their range of responsibilities and interests. Obviously, more senior staff would have a broader point of view and as a result, might want to look at the entire campus, while a person with more limited responsibilities might want to take a more narrowly defined approach.

Ecomapping

Huebner and Corrazini (cited by Paul, 1980, and by Huebner, 1989) developed a ten-step process model to assess person-environment interaction. In this model, the student possesses certain needs and wants, the environment provides the resources to meet those needs, and person-environment interaction is reflected by the extent to which the student's needs are met. This model consists of ten steps which are reported by Paul (1980) and Huebner (1989). The approach is more complex than the ecosystem process model developed by Aulepp and Delworth, and perhaps more cumbersome (Paul, 1980).

Ecomapping involves the use of multiple sources of data, including questionnaires, interviews, and observations. *Step one* consists of securing permission and establishing an on-site planning team. Charting the actual environment is *step two*. *Step three* involves identifying the needs and goals of the various subgroups within the environment. In the case of a college or university, a vast array of subgroups exist. Consequently, identifying student needs has the potential to be a complicated task. This activity leads to *step four,* identifying matches and mismatches in the environment. In some cases, resources will be available in the environment to meet the needs of the subgroups, while in other cases, those resources will not exist. From this point, apparent matches and mismatches are compared with the actual environment. Environmental referents are collected from students about how to remedy problems and enhance positive aspects of the environment.

In *step six,* the investigator examines how students have coped with mismatches with the environment. Do students avoid the problem altogether (by dropping out, for example), or do they develop mechanisms that compensate for what is lacking in the environment? *Step seven* results in returning data to the design team, which leads to *step eight,* determining where changes can be made. Very possibly, some changes are going to be much more feasible than others, and some aspects of the environment may not be change-able at all. *Step nine* results in the implementation of design changes, and the final step, *step ten,* involves reassessing the environment to determine if the mismatches have decreased.

Paul (1980) considers application of this model to be difficult and time-consuming. While the approach has the potential to gen-erate extremely rich information with powerful implications for the campus, Paul (1980) concludes that "there has been little actual use of the model and those conceptual pieces which have been used are incorporated into the less cumbersome ecosystem model" (p. 71).

Multiple Perspective Model

Paul and Huebner (reported by Paul, 1980) developed an approach to visualizing the interaction process between a person and the envi-ronment. According to Paul (1980), this model "attempts to view both the person and environment in terms of process" (p. 74).

Paul (1980) also proposes an eight-step sequence using the indi-vidual as the problem-solver. The individual gathers information about alternatives in the environment and then acts to "produce outcomes that are satisfying, need-reducing and/or self-sustaining" (p. 71). According to Paul, all individuals may not go through the eight steps in the same sequence.

The steps that the student will follow are as follows:

1. Take in information.
2. Interpret the information.
3. If a problem or need is identified, this may be expressed to others.
4. Alternative solutions may be identified by the student.
5. Alternative solutions are sought out in the environment.
6. Alternate solutions are evaluated.
7. One of the solutions may be applied.
8. The outcome of the solutions is assessed by the student.

While the student is going through the process described in the preceding paragraph, the environment also is undergoing a process by which analysis and redesign is occurring. The steps Paul (1980) identifies for the environment are similar to those for the individual person:

1. The environment furnishes a passive arrangement of resources to meet students' needs.
2. Input is received from members of the community.
3. Input from the community is actively sought (perhaps through a "comment board" in the lobby of a university facility).
4. Agents may provide additional information about the environment to members of the community. This step parallels the active seeking of information external to the person identified in step five above.
5. Students are trained in developing new skills.
6. Perceptions and attitudes about the environment are changed.
7. Modification of the environment may occur.
8. Assessment of outcomes of the changes is undertaken to determine if improvements in the environment occurred.

A more detailed explanation is provided by Paul (1980), and the steps identified above are a brief synopsis of a fairly complicated, albeit attractive and intriguing, process.

In commenting on this model, Paul (1980) observes that for any single environmental problem, two steps can be taken simultaneously to improve the situation. One step is to train people how to be more effective in their environment, and the other is to provide better services to meet people's needs. This is a different approach than that proposed in the models identified above, since the models tend to focus more on changing the environment rather than changing the people within the environment. This two-step approach is highly attractive from a conceptual point of view, and it has intriguing potential for student affairs administrators.

Behavior Engineering Model

One other model that is reported in the literature from time to time (see Paul, 1980) is the behavior engineering model, also known as the human competence model. The model was developed by Gilbert (1978) and it is another variation on the theme of person-environment interaction.

Gilbert (1978) suggests that "all instrumental human behavior . . . has two aspects of equal importance: a person with a repertory of behavior (*P*) and a supporting environment (*E*). The person's repertory and the supporting environment together form a transaction that we call behavior" (p. 81). To improve human performance, several aspects of the environmental supports and the person's repertory of behavior must be understood.

The environmental supports and the person's repertory of behavior that Gilbert identifies consists of six components of behavior. All six occur in a single event, and provide a framework for looking at that event. The resulting model helps provide a mechanism for engineering human performance.

The environmental supports and the repertory of behavior each consist of three components, but the definitions of each are slightly different. The environmental supports consist of information (data), instrumentation (instruments), and motivation (incentives). The repertory of behavior also consists of information (knowledge), instrumentation (response capacity), and motivation (motives).

Using Gilbert's model, student behavior in an academic course might be defined this way. A series of environmental supports must be in place for students to succeed. For example, to do well, the students must be placed in a course where they can do well (environmental support/information), the equipment the course requires must be in good repair (environmental support/instrumentation), and they must realize that if they do well in the course, they will be able to take other courses (environmental support/motivation). In addition, the student's repertory of behavior must be appropriate for the course, including having completed the appropriate academic prerequisites for the course (repertory/information); knowing how to use the equipment required for the course (repertory/instrumentation); and wanting to do well in the course (repertory/motivation). For students who have problems doing well in the course, various interventions can be developed to address the various aspects of the circumstance so that the student can improve. For example, if the equipment does not work all of the time, it can be repaired. For students who do not know how to use the equipment, their skill level can be improved.

This model was designed originally to improve performance in settings other than higher education, such as business and industry. Nevertheless, it provides an interesting approach to dealing with improving student performance and satisfaction in an academic environment, and it builds on the person-environment interaction theme first developed by Lewin. Paul (1980) summarizes this model this way. From Gilbert's perspective (1978), this approach suggests that the interventionist can alter the person's repertory, the environment, or both in order to improve inadequate performance. The choice becomes a pragmatic one of selecting the most effective approach. Paul (1980) adds, "The model's value on the campus remains to be tested, but there is no reason to believe it cannot be applied with equal success to improving performance on specific accomplishments there as well" (p. 76).

Elements Common to Environmental Assessment

Models

The models identified in the previous section share a number of elements. This section will identify some of these elements so that as the reader thinks about conducting an assessment project, these elements can be used to help conceptualize the task, whether one were to choose to implement one of the models or to develop a model idiosyncratic to the specific campus situation.

Influence of Lewin

Each of the models identified above has its roots in Lewin's ideas. The models put their own twist on how to address person-environment interaction, but they are all used as a means to the same end: to determine how people interact with their environment, and how specific interventions can be developed to improve the fit between people and their environment. Implementing Lewin's concepts, however, has proved to be challenging. As Huebner and Lawson (1990) put it, "There is little doubt that researchers in the student development area, as well as those in psychology and other disciplines, have made a substantial investment in defining salient dimensions of the Lewinian paradigm. Interventions using these concepts, however, lag far behind" (pp. 142–143).

Student-Environment Interaction

At the heart of each of these models is the interaction of students with their environment. Students affect and are affected by their environment. What is more difficult to determine, however, is the extent to which each influences the other, since every student has a unique environment. Those who developed these models struggled with the question of how to tailor each person's environment so that it facilitates student growth and development to the maximum. At best, environments are studied in gross terms and much progress needs to be made to provide more specific interventions for each individual student.

Studying the Environment

Much of the focus of these models has been on studying the student environment, but they place less emphasis on dealing with the political realities of changing students' environments. At the latter stages of each model, the student affairs staff member is instructed to make changes in the student environment based on the results of collecting and analyzing data, and then to determine how well the changes worked. Change can be very difficult. The political aspects of bringing about change are very complicated. Organizations, almost invariably, do not change without vigorous debate. The reader should not assume that once armed with a persuasive model and substantial data, change will come easily. Even when the arguments are compelling, change can be difficult.

Focus on Redesign

Even though change may be difficult, each of the models is concerned with change as an integral part of the process. These models are action-oriented. Simply conducting a study which yields rich, potentially useful data is not enough. Staff are challenged to bring about change so that students will function at a higher level of effectiveness in their environment.

Ongoing Process

Please note that these models propose that, once change is brought about and studied, the process begins again. Those who developed the models believe that the process of environmental assessment and design is integrated into the normal cycle of institutional business, and that assessment should be performed routinely and regularly. That may not be easy, since each process requires time and effort. Nevertheless, none of the models is designed to be a single-purpose activity.

Change Is Participant-Oriented

One other common element is that students are seen as partners rather than passive recipients in the change process. These models do not propose activities that are performed either for or to students. While the level of involvement of students varies somewhat from one model to the next, all of the models place an emphasis on forming partnerships with students. The environment is evaluated through a student lens and ideas are sought from them in terms of how the environment can be changed and improved.

Applying the Ecosystem Model

Environments

Aulepp and Delworth took the conceptual work of WICHE and developed a five-stage operational approach to implementing the ecosystem model. They reported their work in 1976 after the model had been field-tested on several campuses. Their approach to the ecosystem model has been applied in a number of circumstances, including a medical school (Huebner and others, 1979), an office of services for persons with disabilities (Schuh and Veltman, 1991), a dean of students office (Hurst and Ragle, 1979), and an entire campus (Treadway, 1979). While a number of issues related to the implementation of the model remain unresolved, the ecosystem model as refined by Aulepp and Delworth has tremendous utility in assessing students' environments and has been used with great success. It is particularly effective in assessing environments that affect a well-defined group of students, such as those who live in a residence hall. Reports that assess the quality of student life in residence halls using this model have appeared in the literature for more than a decade (see Schuh and Allan, 1978; Schuh, 1978). More recently, the model has been used to assess the services and programs of an office dedicated to meeting the needs of students with disabilities, and to assess the services of a campus child care center.

Describing how to use the ecosystem model to assess the environment of two disparate groups of students is the purpose of this section of this chapter. One group includes those who lived in a residence hall system, while the other consists of those who used the services and programs of an office, called the Resource Center for Independence (RCI), for students with various disabilities (see Schuh and Veltman, 1991). As was mentioned above, a number of issues related to the application of the ecosystem model remain unresolved (see Schuh, 1990), but the foundation for using this model has been established firmly enough that it can be applied in a variety of circumstances. And, lessons have been learned from the repeated use of the model in assessing these environments, so that it can be used to assess a wide variety of distinctive student environments on campus, such as those for students who are members of Greek letter organizations, specific student majors, or participants in clubs or other activities. This brief discussion will provide a few tips on applying the model using two distinct situations as examples.

Stage One: Organizing a Planning Team

In stage one, a group of people, including staff, students, and perhaps an interested faculty member or two, are organized into a planning team. These people guide the process and do most of the work involved in assessing the student environment. Team members should have an interest in the project, a commitment to seeing it to conclusion, and a willingness to implement change as a result of the process. Ground rules for the operation of the team are established at the start of the process, and care can be taken to limit the number of meetings of the team (Schuh, 1979). Many of the people involved, perhaps all, will have a substantial portfolio of responsibilities and they will be taking on this activity in addition to their normal work load.

The members of the team should be committed to following through on the project, and if the information generated by the project dictates, they should be willing to make changes in their areas of responsibility. Presumably, in the case of assessing a resi-

dential environment, staff from residence hall operations, programs, and food service would form the core of the planning team
and would be joined by several student leaders, staff from the student affairs division, and a faculty member with special interest in
the residence hall environment on campus.

In the case of the office that provides services for students with
disabilities, a smaller team was organized, including office staff, staff
from the student affairs division, and students served by the office.

Stage Two: Determining What to Assess

After a planning team has been assembled, the work of determining
what to assess can begin. Based on the questions posed in Chapter
Two, in this stage the group should be (1) identifying the problem
or problems to be addressed by the assessment, (2) defining the pur-
pose(s) of the assessment, and (3) identifying the population to be
studied.

Since mission statements determine the shape and substance
of student affairs programs (Lyons, 1993), the mission statement
for the service or program to be assessed provides an excellent
point of departure. Reviewing this statement helps the assessment
team to understand the conceptual approach of the program. The
mission statement for the residence life department held that it
aimed at providing the best possible environment for residential
students, providing support for students so that they could achieve
their academic objectives, and developing learning opportunities
for students which would complement what they learned in the
classroom. The mission statement for RCI held that it would offer
services and programs to eligible students so that they could achieve
their educational objectives at the university.

The general purpose of the residence life study was to assess
the programs, services, and personnel of the residence halls at the
university. From this general purpose, it became necessary for more
specific items to be assessed. At this stage, a process is introduced
for brainstorming ideas and generating categories of issues to be
assessed. From this point, lists of potential topics for assessment
need to be generated and some thinking must be devoted to the
extent to which the assessment will generate data which are useful
to the program as a whole, in addition to providing information

useful to specific aspects of the program. For example, if the residence hall system has a number of special interest halls, such as units where foreign languages are spoken, it might be useful to provide an opportunity for the students and staff from those units to ask a few questions about their special programs. Put in the language of the model, the levels of assessment need to be clarified and the team members may determine that they wish to assess the macro-environment of the students living in the residence halls, in addition to a variety of selected micro-environments, such as floors or wings that exist within the residence hall system.

Two general objectives for the RCI study emerged: (1) to evaluate the services offered by RCI from the perspective of its clients, and (2) to determine how clients would prioritize their needs. Then, an inventory of services and programs was compiled to determine the scope of the activities and services of the unit. These services and activities provided the basis upon which specific items for the instrument were constructed.

One of the challenges the planning team will face in this phase of the project is to determine how many items to include in the instrument. So many things could be asked of students that it is easy for a planning team to be seduced into developing a list of items so lengthy that what may very well result is an instrument so complex that students will not complete it. The team will have to determine a ceiling on the number of topics for inquiry and stick to it. The reader should note that the layout and design of the questionnaire, as well as the formatting of individual items and the potential responses, also will influence the length of the questionnaire. Obviously, the goal in questionnaire construction is to develop an instrument that is visually appealing and clear.

A third step involves the planning group's identification of the population to be studied. The population in the residence hall study was made up of all the students living in the residence halls on campus. The population in the RCI study was made up of all students and faculty with disabilities at the university.

Stage Three: The Assessment Technique

The next important stage for the planning group is to determine the assessment methodology. Based on the questions posed in Chapter Two, this stage includes deciding (1) what is the best assessment method(s), (2) who to study (sampling decisions), and (3) what instrument should be used.

In previous chapters, we have discussed the advantages and disadvantages of qualitative and quantitative methodologies, and argued that (1) this decision as to what type of study will be used should be based on the purpose of the study, and (2) in some instances, both methodologies can be used in the same study. In the residence hall study, a quantitative approach was considered best because of the size of the population (over 12,000). In the case of the RCI study, also, a quantitative approach was considered best since most students lived off campus and worked more than twenty-five hours per week, making arranging interviews or even reaching participants by telephone very difficult.

Sampling is always an issue. For a large, residential system, a random sample of 10 percent of residents was chosen. An inverse relationship exists between the number of students in the population and the percentage of students drawn; hence, a higher percentage should be drawn when the size of the population is fairly small. By drawing a random sample, the planning group was confident that the respondents represented a diverse resident population, and the results could be generalized to the population. In the RCI study, since the population was quite small ($N = 248$), the planning group decided to study the entire population. (For a more complete discussion of sampling and sample size, see Chapter Two.)

After the team has identified a number of topics for inquiry, it has to determine which assessment technique to use. One possibility is to use a previously published instrument such as the University Residence Environment Scale (URES), for the residence hall study, or for the RCI study, the Disabled Student Survey, the purpose of which is to measure disabled students' sense of inclusion in the campus environment. More general environmental assessment instruments (such as the Environmental Assessment Inventory), and instruments designed to assess more specific campus climates such as the Campus Diversity Survey, the Campus Opinion Survey, and others identified in the Appendix, also are available. (See the Appendix for a more complete description of these instruments.) Excellent reasons support the decision to use standardized instruments, including detailed studies on the reliability and validity of the instrument; and there are some drawbacks as well, such as cost. Equally powerful incentives, as well as some problems, are associated with using an instrument developed specifically for the project. This matter is worthy of careful consideration by the planning team because, quite frankly, if a poor instrument is used, the value of the project will be diminished greatly. The advantages of previously constructed instruments are discussed in detail in Chapter Two.

There are advantages to using locally constructed instruments, particularly when studying environments. Aulepp and Delworth (1976) recommend a two-part questionnaire. The first part includes items that examine specific aspects of the students' environment that can be changed. The second part consists of environmental referents (ERs), which are written responses provided by the respondents to the items included in the first part of the questionnaire. The ER format is very attractive, though it is not often mentioned in discussions about collecting information through the use of surveys or questionnaires. After completing the first part of the questionnaire, the respondents are asked to go back through the instrument and select a limited number of items (perhaps no more than five), comment on them, and offer suggestions for change. This process results in a partnership between the students and the planning team and is an important feature of this process. Rather than using an instrument designed specifically for this process as the first part of the questionnaire, a standardized instrument could be substituted.

The two-part questionnaire recommended by Aulepp and Delworth, and developed specifically for the assessment project, has been used many times with success (see Schuh, 1990) and has the added advantage of examining issues idiosyncratic to the campus. If this type of instrument is used, the items need to be specific and uncomplicated and should represent areas that can be changed by the planning team. In the residence hall study, after selected demographic information was solicited, students were asked to respond to the following:

1. I am able to study in my room when I wish to.
2. I know the rules of my residence center.
3. I look forward to meal time in my residence center.
4. The custodian in my unit keeps the area clean.

The RCI study included these items:

1. RCI staff were helpful when you applied for a handicapped parking decal.
2. There is an adequate number of parking spaces for those driving vehicles with handicapped decals.
3. RCI provided an interpreter who was helpful to you in class.
4. RCI staff have demonstrated concern for you at the university.

It is useless for the planning team to raise questions about certain aspects of the environment that cannot be changed, such as a governing board policy which the president of the board has been emphatic about not changing, or activities which must be conducted because of legal requirements. In addition, there is little point in raising questions about issues that fall outside the portfolio of the planning team members, unless the person who is responsible for the area is consulted and his or her cooperation in raising the issue is sought. The politics of change can be very delicate and team members should be sure not to embarrass colleagues as a result of this process.

Demographic questions should be chosen with care. Demographic information about students should not be sought unless this information will be used in the data analysis. In other words, why ask for a student's major, for example, unless that information will be used in analyzing the data?

Assuming that a questionnaire is developed specifically for the campus, having a section seeking environmental referents (ERs) is highly desirable. This gives students a chance to identify items about which they feel very strongly, in either a positive or negative sense, and to make recommendations for change. The involvement of students in the change process makes this approach to environmental assessment highly valuable in terms of the information it generates, and very credible among students.

Stage Four: Assessment and Data Analysis

In this stage, the planning teams needs to decide (1) who should collect the data, (2) how data should be collected, (3) how data should be recorded, and (4) how data should be analyzed. In answer to the first question, in both studies, the planning teams decided to collect the data by mailing questionnaires to the sample; postpaid reply envelopes were enclosed to facilitate a reasonable rate of return (for a more extensive discussion of how to ensure a reasonable return rate, see Chapter Two).

Recording and analyzing data from the first part of the two-part questionnaire proceeded along lines suggested in Chapter Two. The questionnaires were machine-scored and stored on a computer disk for analysis. A description of the results, including frequency distributions and measures of central tendency, was generated. Analysis of variance was used to determine if responses differed by gender, class standing, race or ethnicity, or other variables. Setwise multiple regression (see Chapter Ten) enabled the team to determine how much each of these variables contributed to the results.

Analyzing the second part of the questionnaire (the ERs) takes more time. Each response needs to be read and studied. Patterns and trends should be identified. Ideas can be developed as students provide recommended changes for certain problems. One of the ways to determine which items need the most attention is to rank the forced choice items from the least favorable responses (by mean score) to the most favorable responses. (This can be written on a chalkboard.) Next to this list, the items should be ranked from those receiving the most ERs to those receiving the least. Those items with lower mean scores and the most ERs should be addressed first. Those with higher means (assuming the higher the mean, the more favorable the response) and fewer ERs can be analyzed later.

Stage Five: Redesign and Evaluation

Stage five is the evaluation phase of environmental assessment, defined in Chapter Two as the reporting and use of a study's results. In both of the sample situations described above (following the guidelines suggested in Chapter Thirteen), each planning team wrote a report that included an executive summary prepared for general consumption, and a summary report for interested members of the collegiate community. Although a full report was written, it was not distributed widely (it was available, however, for anyone who was interested). Each team also decided upon a general distribution of the results to student leaders, key faculty, and administrators.

Since the ecosystem model as conceived by Aulepp and Delworth is action-oriented, there is an expectation that some aspects of the environment will be redesigned based on the information generated by the assessment process. Some changes, most likely, can be effected quite easily while others take time. For example, providing more and better information to students suggest a need for a departmental newsletter or a residence hall radio station. Such initiatives would not be terribly complicated. But to develop a faculty involvement program because residence hall students are concerned about a lack of contact with faculty—this would take care and considerable planning. Similarly, organizing a tutoring program for RCI users, for example, could not be accomplished overnight.

As was mentioned above, the ecosystem model has been applied a number of times in the residence hall setting. After this process becomes institutionalized, people associated with the college will expect annual reports on the quality of the residence hall environment. That can be a blessing and a curse. The positive side is that interest and concern about the quality of student life across a broad spectrum of an institution means that people care about student experiences and will not treat them with benign neglect. The problem, however, is that in some years it may not be possible to conduct the assessment, and if a report is not produced hard questions will be asked as to why. If one has to choose between the rewards of doing this activity routinely, as compared with the potential problems, the advantages of systematically assessing the campus environment outweigh the potential problems, and the ecosystem approach has stood the test of time.

The same situation has evolved in the assessment of the RCI. This activity has been undertaken twice in a three-year period and students and others who use the services of the RCI are very interested in the results; in fact, they expect the assessment to be conducted on a biennial basis.

At the time of this writing, the ecosystem model has been used in assessing a third distinctive situation, a university child care center. This assessment focused on the quality of care provided for the children from the perspective of their parents, and it paid special attention to evaluating the quality of the teaching staff. The results were heartening (Baldridge, 1993), and the most important finding of the study was that parents sincerely appreciated the quality of care provided by the center's teachers.

The process developed by Aulepp and Delworth made the conceptual work of WICHE practical. Their work operationalized the theory to the point where it could be implemented on virtually any campus. Their guidance on this topic has facilitated the implementation of the ecosystem model and has resulted in viable technology for environmental assessment and redesign.

Conclusion

This chapter began with an observation about the difficulty of assessing students' environments. In spite of all the models and techniques, the reader should be cautioned to remember that, while the technology of environmental assessment has been advanced dramatically in the past two decades, the fact remains that current approaches do not provide precise information about specific environments. Instead, generalizations about the various student environments are generated. These generalizations can be helpful in developing impressions about the environment of the campus as it affects students. But, since each student has a unique environment, there is no way to know how the environment has facilitated or inhibited an individual's growth and development without having a discussion with that student. In the end, environmental assessment is a useful tool for accessors who wish to gain an understanding of what is occurring on campus. Other steps need to be taken to more fully understand how individual students function in their environment, the simplest of all, and perhaps most effective, being to talk to individual students and listen to what they have to say. This approach is time-consuming, and perhaps not terribly realistic on large campuses, but one can learn the most about the lives of students by talking with them.

Chapter Nine

Assessing Student Cultures

Elizabeth J. Whitt

Commenting on efforts to improve college student learning out-comes, John Van Maanen (1987) made the following statement: "We probably know far more about our students before they enter and after they leave than while they are with us. . . . If we are to manage education better, it is with the process of education we must begin. . . . Process entails experience and experience is best captured by narrative" (p. 12).

Therefore, increasing interest in, and commitment to, assess-ment of college student learning and development demands exam-ination of students' experiences "while they are with us," including—perhaps especially—their experiences with peers. This chapter de-scribes a process for studying student cultures and students within cultures with qualitative research methods, producing a narrative of students' experiences.

The chapter begins with an overview of the use of cultural per-spectives in student assessment, and continues with a discussion of the importance of assessing student cultures. Guidelines and tech-niques for studying student cultures follow, and the chapter con-cludes with an outline of a student culture assessment.

Cultural Perspectives in Student Assessment

Cultural perspectives offer effective frameworks for understanding all aspects of colleges and universities, including student learning and behavior. In addition to the more visible elements of institu-tional life, such as policies, procedures, structures, and processes, cultural perspectives reveal the impact of taken-for-granted elements, including history, symbols, myths, and language, all of which influence student experiences (Kuh and Hall, 1993). For the purposes of this chapter, culture is defined as the collective, mutually shaping patterns of institutional history, mission, physical settings, norms, traditions, values, practices, beliefs, and assumptions, all of which guide the behavior of individuals and groups in an institution of higher education, and which provide frames of reference for interpreting the meanings of events and actions on and off campus (Kuh and Hall, 1993, p. 2).

This definition acknowledges the role cultural elements play in shaping the meanings, perceptions, and behaviors of persons within the culture, as well as those persons' utility for understanding the meanings, perceptions, and behaviors. Also, this definition illustrates the complicated nature of studying culture, in that all cultural elements—history, traditions, values, the external environment—influence one another in visible and invisible ways, creating a complex, unique, and evolving picture—a "tapestry" (Kuh and Whitt, 1988)—of the whole. Pulling this "tapestry" apart to identify separate threads—such as characteristics, sources, and patterns of student cultures—is not only difficult, but can actually obscure one's view of the entire picture.

This is not to say, however, that cultures in institutions of higher education are impossible to discover and understand. Several frameworks are available to assist in studying the "threads" and the "tapestry." One such framework was developed by Kuh and Whitt (1988) and provides four levels of analysis of institutional cultures: (1) the cultures of the external environment, including time in history, geographic location, economic conditions, social and religious mores, sources of students, and ethnic backgrounds; (2) the culture(s) of the institution, including mission, history, responses to crisis, traditions, interactions among people, structures, academic programs, and practices; (3) subcultures within the institution, such as faculty, students, and staff; and (4) individual roles and actors, such as the college or university president, student leader, senior professor.

Schein (1992) offered another framework for analyzing cultures. Schein described institutional cultures as encompassing three levels, which are arranged hierarchically from most obvious to most tacit: artifacts, espoused values, and basic assumptions. Artifacts are what we are most likely to notice about cultures—"the visible products of the group" (Schein, 1992, p. 17), including history, traditions, stories, heroines and heroes, norms, organizational processes, physical settings, and ways people interact with one another. Although artifacts are easily observed, they are not easily interpreted; outsiders cannot assume they know the meanings insiders give to artifacts (Schein, 1992). At Randolph-Macon Woman's College, for example, the stairway sweeping upward to the left and right from the foyer in the main entryway appears, to an outsider, simply a beautiful welcome to the college. To students, however, the stairway is a means to reinforce an important college tradition—"sister" classes: first-year students and juniors use one side of the stairway, sophomores and seniors, the other (Whitt, 1992b).

Espoused values are shared beliefs about what is most important, such as teaching, student development, research, service, or liberal arts. Values can be unspoken as well as spoken, and acted upon or merely espoused (Schein, 1992). A student government might, for example, espouse the value of representative government. On the other hand, it is possible that only members of certain student groups feel comfortable running for office.

Basic assumptions constitute an "all-pervasive system of meaning" (Morgan, 1986, p. 133) that influences what people in the culture think about, how they behave, and what they value. Assumptions are implicit; "in fact, if a basic assumption is strongly held in a group, members will find behavior based on any other premise inconceivable" (Schein, 1992, p. 27). Examples of basic assumptions include assumptions about the purposes an education serves, who should receive an education, who can learn, and what it means to be human (Kuh, Schuh, Whitt, and Associates, 1991).

These frameworks provide lenses with which to discover both the threads and the tapestry of institutional cultures. How these lenses might be used is discussed in the section on methods for assessing student cultures.

Student Cultures

Student interactions with peers and others in the college environment, as well as with institutional processes and structures, can lead to the formation of student cultures (Hughes, Becker, and Geer,

1962). Student cultures are "a collective response" (Bolton and Kammeyer, 1972, p. 379) to the problems students face as college students and as young adults in today's society: making and maintaining friends, achieving academic and social success, having an impact on their world, and connecting the values and expectations of students to those of the institution (Love and others, 1993), or sustaining values and expectations inconsistent with those of the larger community (Bolton and Kammeyer, 1972; Gottlieb and Hodgkins, 1968).

The characteristics of student cultures—persistent interaction; socialization processes for shared norms, values, and expectations; mechanisms for social control; sustained existence across time and generations of students—enhance students' potential for exerting peer influence beyond that of ordinary peer groups. According to Coleman (1966), "A student culture is, at its strongest, nearly a society in itself. . . . members are turned inward, looking to one another for social rewards; their associations are almost completely with one another; and they have many of the accoutrements of a society" (p. 245).

The nature and strength of student cultures vary across and within campuses, as different student problems evoke different collective responses. Thus, there are at least three levels of student culture (Coleman, 1966; Horowitz, 1987; Kuh, 1990; Love and others, 1993). First, the national level of student culture comprises attitudes, beliefs, and experiences common to traditional-aged undergraduate students across the country. Evidence of a national student culture can be found in Helen Horowitz's (1987) description of "college life," or recent writings about "Generation X" (see Howe and Strauss, 1992).

The second level of student culture is the institutional, encompassing predominant values and expectations of an entire student body. One example is the "Greeners" of Evergreen State College, described by Lyons (1991) as "a politically active and socially conscious student body that is more liberal than conservative, more casual than formal, and clearly not interested in the more usual careers (e.g., business, engineering, medicine)" (p. 188).

Third, the subcultural level of student culture reveals distinct groups within a single institution. Social sororities and fraternities; political or social activist organizations; residents of a dorm floor;

major- or career-related groups; students who share common racial or ethnic backgrounds, or age, or life experiences; or groups formed around a common interest, such as a marching band—all are examples of student subcultures.

The focus of this chapter is institutional and subcultural levels, although none of the three I have defined above is completely separable from the others.

Student cultures are powerful agents of socialization, communicating to their members "who, when, and where should do what and how and why" (Wallace, 1966, p. 12). Because peer cultures determine which peers with whom students spend time and from whom they seek approval, these cultures influence the values, attitudes, and beliefs students explore, accept, and reject, as well as the ways in which students direct their attention and energy (Coleman, 1966). In short, these cultures teach their members "how we do things here": how to spend time and energy, how to have fun, with whom to associate, what work is worth doing, and how to get rewards and avoid punishment—indeed, which rewards and punishments matter (Kuh and Hall, 1993).

Perhaps most important, student cultures influence the extent to which students are integrated into the academic life of the college, affecting majors, time spent on studying and dealing with academic issues, courses and teachers taken and avoided, and the importance placed on intellectual activities and academic success (Katchadourian and Boli, 1985; Kuh, 1993a; Weidman, 1989; Whitt and Nuss, 1994). "Student cultures offer their members thick and thin guidelines for how to get an education and thus define for students just what an education means" (Van Maanen, 1988, p. 5). And students learn from other students "what an education means" despite the orientation and socialization efforts of the college. No matter what institutional agents say or do, within four to six weeks following the start of an academic term, new students are exposed to the prevailing student culture, which tells them what classes and instructors are to be taken seriously, and when and how much to study (Kuh, 1993a, p. 36).

Thus, student cultures shape what students learn, both in class and out of class, as well as the nature and directions of intellectual and social development. As a consequence, student cultures affect the achievement not only of individual student goals, but the achievement of institutional educational purposes as well (Weidman, 1988).

Persons interested in studying student cultures ought to be familiar with the ways in which such cultures form, what student subcultures have been identified, and how student cultures influence the institutions in which they live. These topics are beyond the scope of this chapter, but detailed descriptions of the formation and characteristics of college student cultures can be found elsewhere (see Bolton and Kammeyer, 1972; Clark and Trow, 1966; Horowitz, 1987; Katchadourian and Boli, 1985; Kuh, 1990; Kuh and Whitt, 1988; Leemon, 1972; Magolda, 1994; Moffatt, 1988; Newcomb, 1962; Newcomb, 1966; Rhoads, 1992; Wallace, 1966).

Warrant for Studying Student Cultures

Astin (1993) asserts that "the student's peer group is the single most potent source of influence on growth and development during the undergraduate years" (p. 398). If students are the most important people in other students' lives, and if student cultures shape student learning, then the nature and impact of student cultures have important implications for college outcomes and, therefore, institutional effectiveness (Katchadourian and Boli, 1985). Yet current student culture assessment—especially at the institutional and subcultural levels—is scarce. The few recent examples include Moffatt's study of residence hall students at Rutgers (1988), Magolda's study of students in a residential college (1994), and Rhoads's examination of a social fraternity (1992).

Demands for assessment of student outcomes for the purpose of accreditation or accountability have, for example, encouraged colleges and universities to measure what their students learn, but the influence of student cultures on student learning remains a "black box" (Kuh, 1994, p. 2), in that little is known about how that influence is exerted and in what specific ways learning is shaped by other students. Understanding "the native" (Van Maanen, 1987, p. 4)—that is, the student—has often been neglected in efforts to identify and improve educational outcomes. We do not know, for example, whether involvement in particular student cultures fosters particular outcomes (Kuh, 1994). Thus, to be useful, institutional assessment of student learning outcomes must consider elements of the college environment, including other students (Erwin, 1991; Weidman, 1989). "The educational process in college can only be meaningfully understood in the larger context of the students' broader life experiences. . . . Treating students as disembodied intellects makes no sense" (Katchadourian and Boli, 1985, pp. 248–249).

For student affairs practitioners, student culture assessment offers a means to foster student learning and development in ways that support the educational purposes of the institution, and to assess the impact of campus environments on student learning. In-depth understanding of campus student cultures is necessary to influence those cultures, as well as to create campus environments that promote student learning (Love and others, 1993). If, for example, you want to change the emphasis placed on alcohol in the social life of your institution's student culture, you must first discover how alcohol is used—and not used—by whom and under what circumstances, what traditions and norms pertain to alcohol use on your campus, the values espoused and enacted by the institution and students with regard to alcohol, as well as the meanings alcohol has for all types of students.

How to Study Student Cultures

The following sections present guidelines and methods for studying student cultures. Although qualitative methods are emphasized, the use of quantitative methods and both qualitative and quantitative methods is discussed. Because detailed descriptions of techniques for designing, implementing, and writing studies of student cultures exceed the space limitations of this chapter, useful resources for such techniques are identified.

Guidelines for Assessing Student Cultures

All aspects of a study of student cultures—how it is conducted, by whom, over what time period, what data are collected and how—are determined by the purpose and focus of the assessment. Some assessment questions, for example, lend themselves to quantitative answers, whereas other research foci are suited to qualitative methods.

The applicability of the following guidelines also may be influenced by your assessment focus or purpose, but the guidelines provide some issues to think about if you are considering an assessment of student cultures on your campus.

1.   *Study student cultures from students' perspectives.* This means, first, that although the perspectives of others in the context are important, the students' meanings, experiences, and language should be the primary sources of data about student culture. This also means that students should be involved in the collection of data about student cultures and that those data should be analyzed and interpreted using the lenses of students as well as others. Finally, if you want to understand student cultures, talk to students (Kuh, 1993a); this implies the use of qualitative research methods, a topic to which I shall return.

2.   *Obtain as many and as diverse perspectives on student culture as possible.* Do not assume that there is a single truth to be learned about student cultures or subcultures on your campus; there are, rather, many truths (Erlandson, Harris, Skipper, and Allen, 1993; Whitt, 1993). A student's experiences of intellectual life on campus, for example, may be influenced by his or her motivation for attending college, age, gender, place of residence while a student, involvement in student groups or organizations, country or region of origin, or membership in a racial or ethnic minority. Be particularly careful to obtain the perspectives of students who have been marginalized, by age, for example, or gender, race, place of residence, interests, or employment (Kuh, 1994).

3.   *Be prepared to hear what students say about their experiences.* Studies of cultures, including student cultures, can involve examining the underside of rocks long left undisturbed. If you (or "significant others" in your institution) are unwilling to see and hear things that surprise or disappoint or challenge, do not undertake a study of student cultures (Van Maanen, 1987).

Also, precedents for trust, listening, and openness should be established before attempting to study student cultures. Students are likely to be suspicious of questions about their experiences if they are not accustomed to such questions, or have learned that answers to such questions can have negative consequences.

4.   *Respect the uniqueness and integrity of the student cultures and of the students themselves.* Although perceived need for change might

motivate the study of student cultures, remember that they must be understood before they can be changed effectively (Love and others, 1993). And, in order to understand a culture, one must approach it—and its members—with the assumption that there is much to be learned, and much one does not know or understand. The privilege of having members of the culture share their perceptions and experiences entails a responsibility to treat them, as well as their experiences and perceptions, with respect and an open mind (Whitt, 1993).

5. *Be aware of your own biases, assumptions, and values before attempting to study student cultures.* It is very difficult to approach the study of student cultures with openness and respect if your assumptions about how students should and should not behave, think, or feel are allowed to influence what you see and hear. This does not mean that the assessment is value-free, that no judgments can be made about the appropriateness of certain elements of student cultures, or that student culture assessment should not be undertaken with culture change as a motive (Kuh, 1994). What it does mean is that, for the purposes of discovery and understanding, you should be willing to suspend expectations, judgments, and "shoulds" so that you can truly listen to the students' descriptions of their experiences (Whitt, 1993).

6. *Study student cultures in context.* Just as any study of the culture of an institution must include consideration of the cultures of the external environment, so a study of student culture must take into account the institutional and other cultures in which the student culture is embedded (Kuh, 1994; Van Maanen, 1987). The framework of analysis of levels of culture (Kuh and Whitt, 1988) described in the introduction to this chapter can be helpful here. One cannot understand the culture of a particular social fraternity, for example, without learning about the Greek system in which it operates; the national organization of which it is a part; the backgrounds of its members; the history of Greeks at the institution; dominant institutional and student cultural values, such as freedom of association, intellectualism, or egalitarianism; and institutional assumptions about what a college education ought to include.

7. *Use multiple methods to study student cultures.* The assessment questions to be answered should determine what methods will be used (Whitt, 1991). Some questions lend themselves to the use of qualitative methods, others call for quantitative methods, and some

require a combination of both. Regardless of the questions to be answered, however, studying cultures requires triangulation: multiple data collection techniques, such as observations, interviews, and document analysis; multiple data sources, such as students, graduates, and faculty; and multiple collection instruments, including people (Schein, 1992; Russell and Stage, 1992; Van Maanen, 1987). Specific recommendations about research methods are offered later in this chapter.

8. *Use insiders and outsiders to study student cultures.* This guideline refers, first, to the use of students (both inside and outside the dominant culture) as data sources in order to obtain the necessary diversity of perspectives. If, for example, you are interested in studying the student leadership culture on your campus, you might want to talk with students who are not leaders to find out what, if any, obstacles exist to involvement in leadership experiences. For the purposes of this study, the focus of the research determines who is an insider and who is an outsider, and what perspectives are most useful.

This guideline also implies that persons both within and outside the institution should be involved in the study of student cultures (Kuh and others, 1991). Insiders need the assistance of outsiders to "transcend their own immersion" (Chaffee and Tierney, 1988, p. 4), to see what is so familiar to insiders that it might be overlooked. Long-standing room assignment practices might, for example, create barriers to student interaction and thereby limit the number and diversity of peers with whom a student can form relationships.

Outsiders also can ask questions that might be off-limits to insiders. In a study of student cultures at an institution that had recently been transformed from a women's college to a coeducational institution, outside researchers were able to draw attention to the ways in which the women's traditions of the college were being eliminated, and to urge an examination of the impact that turning away from the former women's culture was having on the current status of women at the college (Schuh and Whitt, 1990).

But outsiders also need the assistance of insiders (Whitt, 1993). Ongoing feedback from insiders is necessary to ensure that the information, impressions, and interpretations that emerge during data collection and analysis accurately reflect insiders' experiences and perceptions.

9.   *Be prepared to commit institutional resources to study student cultures.* The discovery of an institution's cultures demands lengthy engagement with that culture, and can be time-consuming and expensive (Whitt and Kuh, 1991). In determining just how expensive and time-consuming, consider the following: the institutional resources available for the study, including the number of investigators involved and their need for compensation, training, and time for research; the scope of the study (for example, the dominant student culture of an entire institution, a subculture, a residence hall); and the resources required by the research methods chosen, including purchase and analysis of survey instruments, fees for outside investigators, and costs of equipment involved in qualitative methods (such as tapes, transcriptions, and tape recorders).

The need for resources implies the need for an institutional commitment to the purposes, foci, and processes of the assessment (Kuh, 1994). The scope, significance, and motivations for the assessment determine whose imprimatur is required to proceed with the study. A large-scale longitudinal study of the student cultures of an entire college or university might require widespread institutional commitment and the blessings of all senior-level administrators, whereas an examination of a single student group might not. Such decisions will be influenced, however, by the norms, politics, expectations, structures—that is, the cultures—of the institution (Whitt, 1993).

10.   *Acknowledge the fact that student cultures might not be ready or willing to be studied.* Do not undertake such a study without the informed consent of the persons involved, and if they are unwilling, do not proceed (Lincoln and Guba, 1985). Also, do not interview anyone without being clear about your purposes and the ways in which the information obtained from them will be used (Lincoln and Guba, 1985; Schein, 1992). In addition, be very clear about the ways the outcomes of the study can and cannot be used (1) in an accreditation self-study? (2) as a basis for policy decisions? (3) in information distributed to prospective students and parents? Studying student cultures requires scrupulous attention to the ethics of research, a topic that will be described in detail later in the chapter.

11.   *Tolerate ambiguity.* Studies of student cultures are scarce, in part, because they can be messy (Kuh, 1994). Trying to identify and follow threads—artifacts, values, assumptions—and to discover

the picture the tapestry portrays is complicated by multiple and contradictory perspectives; hidden, unarticulated, or unknown meanings; pressures of time and money; and the evolving and flexible nature of qualitative research. Because you are not aware of all that you do not know before embarking on the research, you cannot necessarily specify in advance all of whom or what you will or will not study, nor can you be certain of the time the study will take (Lincoln and Guba, 1985; Whitt, 1991). The elements of the research that can be specified are discussed in the section on research methods.

12.   *Be patient.* Do not be eager to come quickly to closure—to find "the answer." Take the time to allow the culture to reveal itself to you in all its complexity (Whitt, 1993).

Patience also is required when exploring areas of disagreement as well as agreement. A temptation in studying cultures is to disregard inconsistencies and contradictions and look for those things about which there is consensus (Kuh, 1994; Martin, 1992). It is much simpler—even comforting—for example, to focus on what the members of a Greek system have in common while dismissing differences among sororities and fraternities, or among or within chapters.

Martin (1992) offers three perspectives to keep in mind when studying cultures: (a) an integration perspective, which looks for what is shared and common and disregards ambiguity, (b) a differentiation perspective, which finds consensus within subcultures only and describes inconsistencies between subcultures and in the larger culture, and (c) a fragmentation perspective, which focuses on "ambiguity as the essence of organizational culture. . . . Clear consistencies and inconsistencies are rare" (Martin, 1992, p. 12). Using all three perspectives for studying student cultures provides a more detailed picture of those cultures and, therefore, deeper understanding, than using only one perspective (Martin, 1992).

13.   *"Just do it."* After reading the previous guidelines about patience, ambiguity, and the complexities of student culture assessment you might have decided to read no further. It is the case that not everyone enjoys the flexibility and messiness of such studies, but it is also a very effective way to assess and understand student cultures, and it can be a very rewarding experience. The best way to learn how to assess student cultures is by doing—and how to "do it" is the topic to which I shall turn next.

Assessment Methods and Procedures

This section provides suggestions for ways to approach assessing student cultures. After a brief overview of the possible uses of both quantitative and qualitative research methods, a step-by-step qualitative assessment of student cultures is described.

Quantitative Assessments

Although the primary focus of this chapter is using qualitative methods to study student cultures, some assessment questions or purposes are suited to quantitative methods. If, for example, you want to know about the experiences of a very large number of students, or to compare many student subgroups over time, a survey instrument might be more efficient than interviews. Quantitative studies of student culture are likely to use local or standardized questionnaires (for example, the College Student Experiences Questionnaire, College Characteristics Index), checklists, or surveys to gather student self-reports of perceptions, behavior, and attitudes (Kuh, 1990). Detailed descriptions of the use of quantitative methods, and a combination of qualitative and quantitative methods to assess student cultures, can be found in Chapters Three and Four of this book, as well as in Attinasi and Nora (1992), Baird (1988), Kuh (1990), and McMillan (1989).

Qualitative Assessments

As mentioned earlier, studies of culture are more likely to use qualitative assessment methods—that is, the data are words and all data are collected and analyzed by the researchers themselves (Lincoln and Guba, 1985; Whitt, 1991)—because qualitative methods are most effective for studying the complicated constructs and processes of student cultures, such as values, assumptions, mission, and socialization (Morgan, 1986; Kuh and Whitt, 1988; Whitt, 1993). Qualitative data also "allow for thick data to be collected that demonstrate their interrelationship with their context" (Erlandson, Harris, Skipper, and Allen, 1993, p. 16), and are essential for understanding student cultures.

Defining the Problem

As asserted many times in this book, all assessment starts with a problem, and so the first step in assessing student cultures is to define the problem. As discussed earlier in this chapter, student culture is such a complex and pervasive influence that almost any problem has a student culture dimension. However, some problems, such as racial tensions, campus violence, interpersonal relationships, and others, are especially appropriate to study from a campus cultures perspective.

Developing the Purpose

The second step in conducting a student cultures assessment is to decide on the purpose of the investigation, and the questions to be answered by the assessment—that is, what do you want to know and why? All of the other decisions about the assessment—what techniques to use, whom to involve, and so on—flow from the decisions about focus and purpose (McMillan, 1989). A study of the cultures of and for student leadership on your campus in order to plan leadership training will, for example, differ in many ways from a study of the impact of student cultures on student learning outcomes for the purpose of an accreditation self-study. The latter would probably require a much broader perspective and much broader campus participation than the former.

Let us assume, for the purpose of the following description of assessment methods, that we have decided to discover and assess the influence of campus student cultures on student learning and development experiences at a midsized private college, Ivy Hall. Assume, also, the impetus for the study is twofold: (1) the new senior student affairs officer needs information to plan student affairs division priorities, and (2) senior administrators and faculty perceive that the values and behaviors of the predominant student cultures at Ivy Hall undermine the educational purposes of the college and the learning potential of students.

Given that the focus of this assessment is fairly broad, assessment questions might include any or all of the following: What student cultures are present and how do they form? How do students become involved in student cultures? What are the artifacts, values, and assumptions of the student cultures? What do students believe are the college's values, assumptions, and expectations? Who "fits in" and who doesn't and how do they know? (Love and others, 1993). What socialization processes are used to bring new members into the cultures? What behaviors do the student cultures reward and punish and how? In what activities and behaviors are students involved? How does membership in particular student cultures influence involvement? How does membership in particular student cultures shape learning outcomes? (Kuh, 1990; Kuh, 1994). What are the artifacts, values, and basic assumptions of relevant aspects of the external environment and institutional cultures? (Kuh and Whitt, 1988).

Van Maanen (1987) advocated asking "the hard questions" in studies of student culture, including to what extent do they support or inhibit achievement of the institution's educational purposes, in what ways are they supportive or disruptive of campus community, do they embrace values and artifacts that support student learning and development, and how do students spend their time? Many other research questions are possible, of course, but these are offered to prompt thinking about alternatives.

Developing an Assessment Plan

Once the problem, purposes, and questions have been identified, an assessment plan should be developed which parallels the outline suggested in Chapter Two. That plan should include determining the best assessment methods, deciding who should be studied, deciding what instruments and protocols should be used, designing a data collection and recording procedure, choosing who should collect the data, and outlining how data will be analyzed.

Other issues to be considered in planning our assessment of student cultures at Ivy Hall include these:

1. *Timing:* What times of the school year should data be collected? Formal orientation might, for example, provide a good opportunity to hear the college's official expectations of new students, but interviews of first-year students six weeks after the beginning of the year might provide useful information about informal socialization by peers.

2. *Permission:* What permission is needed to conduct the study and from whom must that permission be obtained? Some campuses have formal processes for approving all research projects, and the scope, visibility, and sensitivity of the student culture assessment will determine what additional permission is needed.
3. *Investigators:* What use will be made of inside and outside researchers, who will they be, and what training will be needed for insiders?

Selecting the Assessment Team

In most of the other assessment approaches described in previous chapters, one or two individual investigators assume the responsibility for planning, conducting, analyzing, and reporting assessment results. However, in conducting student culture assessments, the use of multiple investigators offers the potential for discovering and understanding more of the many and complex elements of cultures (Whitt and Kuh, 1991). The composition of the external team is, however, critical to the success of the assessment; "the human instrument is a wonderful data-processing organism" (Erlandson and others, 1993, p. 107), but the qualities of the individual "human instrument" determine her or his effectiveness and the combined skills and relationships of multiple human instruments influence the effectiveness of the study (Whitt and Kuh, 1991).

A number of personal qualities and skills are useful—if not required—for any qualitative investigators regardless of the focus of the study. Many of these qualities were alluded to in the guidelines for assessment: open-mindedness and curiosity, the ability to place oneself into the experiences and position of another, ability and willingness to take criticism and questions, a high energy level, flexibility, tolerance for ambiguity and little structure, and varied experiences and perspectives relevant to the study (Whitt, 1991). Also essential to the effective human instrument are strong communication skills (listening, writing, speaking) and familiarity—if not expertise—with qualitative research methods (Whitt, 1991).

Assessments of student cultures have human instruments as their foci. The purposes of the study influence the specific competencies and perspectives needed by the investigators. Issues to consider when selecting researchers for a student culture assessment are (1) credibility with students, faculty, and others; (2) the potential for roles and statuses to help or hinder obtaining accurate data; (3) the need for diversity of personal characteristics (backgrounds, experiences, age, class level) and perspectives, including marginalized or discordant views; and (4) relevant expertise (qualitative methods, experience with student cultures, and so forth).

The composition of the assessment team is also critical to the effectiveness of the assessment (Whitt and Kuh, 1991). A decision must be made early on about what use will be made of investigators from outside the institution; recall the guideline that recommended the use of both insiders and outsiders. Other issues to be considered include complementary skills and perspectives, effective working relationships, and communication skills. For a detailed discussion of team assessment using qualitative methods, scc Whitt and Kuh (1991).

Once the team members have been identified, a coordinator of the team should be designated for the purposes of communicating with the institution. Team members also should discuss expectations for working together and for the assessment, special skills and interests that would influence division of labor (such as writing a case report, developing interview questions, or obtaining institutional documents), and concerns and questions that should be answered (for example, with training) before the study begins. The potential for misunderstandings and unexplored assumptions should be acknowledged and addressed. Expectations for meeting deadlines, dealing with conflict and differences of opinion, following through on commitments, and working effectively as a team, all ought to be clear from the beginning. However, some issues might need to be revisited as problems arise (Whitt and Kuh, 1991).

A contact person should be appointed by the college to work with the team and make the necessary arrangements for travel, research facilities, interview scheduling, and so on.

Identifying Data Sources

Data sources for a qualitative assessment of student cultures include people, documents, events and activities, and settings (Whitt, 1993). People are likely to be your primary source of information about student cultures. Recall the importance of studying student cultures in context; you will want to interview faculty, administrators, graduates, and others. Students, however, should be your primary sources of data about student cultures.

Useful sources of written information—documents—about student cultures include student newspapers, student handbooks, yearbooks, campus advertising of student events, T-shirts, orientation information, and minutes of student organization meetings. Documents helpful in understanding the contexts of student cultures include admissions publications, development publications, planning documents, policies and procedures manuals, job descriptions, budgets—each of which describes ways in which the institution represents its mission, values, and assumptions about students and student life to others. Some of these documents will be obtained and analyzed prior to talking with community members to obtain an outsider's view of the culture as well as to help develop interview questions (Whitt and Kuh, 1991). You will become aware of other important documents as the study proceeds.

Other sources of data about student cultures range from daily activities, such as between-class breaks, organization meetings, residence hall floor gatherings, and class sessions, to special events, such as Homecoming or Greek Week, to spontaneous events, such as protests or parties. Once the focus of the assessment is established, obtain schedules and calendars to plan for the events that must be attended; other important events and activities will become evident as the assessment proceeds.

Opportunities to learn about student cultures occur in any settings in which students interact with one another. Settings that might provide data for the assessment include residence hall floors, lounges, and lobbies; other student housing areas, including Greek houses, apartments, or cooperatives; offices and reception areas; classrooms and the hallways and stairwells of classroom buildings; student unions, post offices, and other gathering places; cafeterias; sidewalks; and recreational facilities (Whitt and Kuh, 1991).

Selecting the Sample

As discussed in Chapter Three, the qualitative investigator's goal in identifying data sources is to obtain the broadest range of information and perspectives possible (Lincoln and Guba, 1985). Because, however, studying all of the students and all of the events, processes, and contexts of student cultures is probably not possible, some sampling techniques must be used (Whitt, 1991). Sampling in qualitative methods is purposive, not random (Lincoln and Guba, 1985); this means that decisions about what to observe or whom to interview are based on the research purposes, foci, and potential of the data source to provide useful information about the phenomenon being studied (Erlandson and others, 1993). The process of sampling in qualitative methods is as emergent as the research; ongoing purposive sampling expands "the scope of the study, refines questions or constructs under investigation, [and] generates new lines of inquiry" (Goetz and Le Compte, 1984, p. 69). For an elaboration of qualitative sampling methods, see Chapter Three.

Criteria for selecting data sources—for the purposive sampling process—include (1) who and what would provide "the most meaningful information" (Morgan, 1988, p. 45) given the research purposes, (2) knowledge about the cultures being studied, (3) roles held in the cultures, (4) communication skills, (5) willingness to participate (Johnson, 1990), and (6) accessibility to the researchers (Whitt, 1991). For our assessment of student cultures at Ivy Hall, then, we must first identify what people, events, settings, and documents are the best sources of data in light of our research foci. Keep in mind, however, the need to obtain as many and as diverse perspectives as possible.

Collecting and Analyzing Data

In more traditional quantitative assessment approaches, data are collected and then analyzed, but in qualitative assessments, data collection and analysis are concurrent. However, particularly in the instance of student cultures assessment, data collection and analysis may be concurrent: data obtained from people, events, and documents inform the further collection of data (Erlandson and others, 1993). Particularly useful techniques for collecting data during an assessment of student cultures include interviews, document analysis, and observation.

Interviews should be conducted in a variety of formats, including individual interviews and focus groups, to gather as many perspectives from as many people as possible. Focus groups (Brodigan,

1992; McMillan, 1989; Morgan, 1988) are discussion groups that meet only once for a specific purpose, such as talking about the values expressed in the dominant student culture. Focus groups "provide higher quality and greater richness of information because of shared opinions, ideas, and discussions of a small group who have similar experiences, [and] an in-depth understanding" (McMillan, 1989, p. 8).

Individual interviews and focus groups are especially important in student cultures assessment as ways of gathering as many perspectives and to give "voice" to as many people as possible. Focus groups can, for example, demonstrate the language students use and the ways in which they interact with one another; they also allow participants to share opinions and experiences as they discuss the issues raised by the investigator (Brodigan, 1992; Morgan, 1988); in short, focus groups are "peer conversations" (Morgan, 1988, p. 77), rather than group interviews. Although specific techniques for planning and implementing focus groups and analyzing focus group data are beyond the scope of this chapter, good sources of these techniques, in addition to Chapter Three of this book, include Brodigan (1992), McMillan (1989), and Morgan (1988).

Some students and other community members, such as graduating seniors, student leaders, students of color, the college president, or student organization advisers, might be particularly rich sources of cultural information, and so individual interviews would be appropriate to obtain their unique perspectives (Whitt and Kuh, 1991). Helpful sources of information for planning and conducting interviews for the purposes of student culture research include Carnaghi (1992), Fetterman (1989), Lincoln and Guba (1985), Manning (1992), Patton (1990), and Spradley (1979).

Another source of suggestions about foci for interview questions is the Involving College Audit Protocol, included in *Involving Colleges: Successful Approaches to Fostering Student Learning and Development Outside the Classroom* (Kuh and others, 1991). The Protocol is based on conclusions about successful approaches to student learning and involvement developed in the College Experiences Study. Although Protocol is a misnomer in the sense that the document does not provide a set of interview questions, it does identify—and provide suggestions for examining—many aspects of student experiences that a student culture assessment might need to address, such as the institutional mission; the nature of campus environments (both physical and psychological); campus cultures; the roles of faculty, administrators, and other students in students' lives and learning; and institutional practices and policies that influence student experiences.

Documents, including student handbooks, student publications, and institutional histories, are reviewed before and during the site visit in order to obtain information and gain impressions about student cultures and their context, and to generate interview questions (Whitt and Kuh, 1991). For additional information about analyzing documents for the purposes of assessing student cultures, see Guba and Lincoln (1981) and Whitt (1992a).

Observations of events, activities, and programs can be a useful source of information about student cultures as well as a source of additional interview questions (Fetterman, 1989; Ely and others, 1991; Merriam, 1988; Whitt, 1991). Some activities or times of the year, such as commencement, homecoming, and the beginning of the fall semester, may hold more promise for cultural exploration than others. At such times, the history and values of the institution are vividly portrayed in ceremonies, traditions, and speeches.

Analysis of qualitative data after all data are collected—"final" data analysis (Ely and others, 1991)—can be a complex process, especially with a team of researchers. Very large amounts of data must be organized and themes and patterns identified. For more detailed descriptions of analysis of qualitative data, in addition to Chapter Three of this book see Lincoln and Guba (1985), Ely and others (1991), and Whitt and Kuh (1991).

Reporting the Results

Writing the results of a student cultures assessment is, perhaps, the most difficult aspect of the study, as the assessment is only as effective as the investigators' ability to convey their findings, their interpretations—the "tapestry"—to others (Van Maanen, 1988). As pointed out in Chapter Three of this book, there is no standard format for writing qualitative assessment and there is likely to be a very large amount of data and interpretations to be included (Merriam,

1988; Patton, 1990). A number of decisions must be made with regard to the writing of an assessment of student culture, including the following:

1. Who will do the writing? Will it be a group effort or will one individual take primary responsibility?
2. Who forms the audience for the report and who will receive it? The intended audience influences the style and organization of the report, as well as the content. If, for example, the report is intended for policy makers, a set of recommendations for changes might be appropriate.
3. How will the data and interpretations be presented? Is an executive summary appropriate? To what extent will respondents' words be used? Should certain respondents' perspectives be emphasized? How will the author(s) distinguish between data and interpretations? How much narrative is needed?
4. Who will review the report for accuracy before it is presented to persons at the study site?

No matter what format or organization is selected, a report of qualitative assessment should constitute a story that will engage the attention and expand the understanding of the reader (Van Maanen, 1988). An effective report will put the reader in the setting studied and present the participants' views from their perspectives (Lincoln and Guba, 1985). Useful descriptions of the processes of writing qualitative research can be found in Erlandson and others (1993), Van Maanen (1988), and Wolcott (1990). For a more detailed discussion of reporting results, see Chapter Thirteen of this book.

A Sample Student Culture Assessment

Here, in outline form, is a sample assessment of the student cultures of Ivy Hall, using qualitative methods. The assessment is divided into phases and assumes that persons inside and outside the institution will be involved in conducting the assessment. This assessment also assumes an assessment plan that allows for two phases of data collection and analysis—referred to here as "site visits." Any actual assessment must, however, be planned and conducted to suit the specific purposes of the assessment, the cultures of the institution, and the needs of the investigators (Kuh and others, 1991). For details about each element of this outline, pleases see the previous section on research methods.

Phase One: Getting Ready

Tasks to Be Accomplished

1. Determine foci for the assessment; clarify purposes of the study; clarify expectations of the institution for the outcomes of the assessment. That is, what will be included in the assessment and what will not? How will the assessment data be used, and who will have access to the findings? Will the final product of the assessment be a written report, a presentation, or both? Does the institution want the assessment team to make recommendations based on the findings, or is a description enough?
2. Assessment team works with campus contact person to make all arrangements: space for investigators, travel arrangements for outside investigators, interview places, permission to observe, appointments with respondents, etc.
3. Develop an assessment team.
4. Develop tentative plan for assessment process; plan and prepare for first phase of data collection and analysis. Include data sources and sampling decisions; plan for interviews and observations; plans for ensuring trustworthy and ethical research.
5. Contact persons who will be interviewed: explain the purpose of the interview and the sort of information you will seek.
6. Develop consent forms for use with all respondents; respond to requirements of ethical research and "human subjects" policies. Forms might include descriptions of assessment purposes and procedures, means to ensure confidentiality, ways in which the data and results will be used, and rights and responsibilities of respondents and researchers.

Team Development

1. Decide who will coordinate the work of the assessment team, including site visits, crisis management, deadline implementation, and so on.

2. Identify team members.
3. Divide tasks among team members, according to roles, skills, interests.
4. Discuss and clarify expectations of and for team members, including deadlines and time schedules, responsibilities for data collection and analysis, and ethical research; discuss and clarify assumptions about students and student cultures, cultures of the institution, culture research, and qualitative methods; discuss and clarify perspectives and roles that might influence what is seen and heard.
5. Provide training and development (in such things as data collection techniques, assumptions and principles of qualitative methods, and cultural perspectives) for team members as needed.

Advance Data Collection

1. Obtain and analyze institutional documents relevant to the study.
2. Develop interview questions based on document analysis; develop interview protocols for each set of respondents (for example, students, faculty, staff, graduates). The focus of the assessment and information obtained from documents will provide information for initial interviews; new questions will emerge as the assessment progresses.

Phase Two: Data Collection and Analysis, First Site Visit

Tasks to Be Accomplished

1. Collect data.
2. Analyze data.
3. Identify additional data sources, interview questions, assessment processes.
4. Begin to identify tentative findings and interpretations to be checked in next phase of data collection and analysis.
5. Begin planning for next site visit and next phase of data collection and analysis.

Data Collection

1. Interviews with individuals and focus groups as identified in purposive sampling.
2. Observations (for example, of special events, daily activities of students, student gathering places).

Data Analysis

1. Concurrent with data collection.
2. Conducted by individual investigator and as an assessment team. Team members should plan to meet at the end of each day to discuss experiences, generate additional interview questions, identify additional persons for observation of interview or events, and begin to identify themes and patterns emerging in the data. These meetings should be recorded for future use.
3. Identify needs for additional data collection: interviews, next interview questions or areas to explore, observations, documents.
4. Meet with insiders to check data collected and emerging impressions and interpretations.

Phase Three: After the First Site Visit

Tasks to Be Accomplished

1. Identify tasks and deadlines for team members: writing tentative case report, arranging next visit, planning for next data collection and analysis, planning for respondent debriefing.
2. Additional data analysis: expanding on team analysis conducted on site.
3. Write the interim case report and circulate it among the team members; revise as needed.
4. Submit the interim case report for respondent debriefing during second site visit; ask persons at the site to read the report for errors, impressions, reactions.
5. Plan for second site visit.

Additional Data Analysis

1. Organize data by pulling together all products of data collection and analysis from individuals and team meetings.

2. Identify themes, patterns.
3. Identify what else you need to know (agenda for second visit).

Writing the Interim Case Report

1. Decide what to say and how: Who is the audience? What are areas of agreement and disagreement? Will recommendations be made at this stage? How much information should be provided about assessment methods? Should an executive summary be prepared? How should the report be organized? How will the data and interpretations be presented?
2. Decide who will write the report (the entire team? one individual? distribute the pieces among team members?).
3. Consider language issues: thick description, cultural terminology, use of respondents' words.

Planning for Second Site Visit

1. Make visit arrangements.
2. Identify data sources and means to collect additional data.

Phase Four: Data Collection and Analysis, Second Site Visit

Tasks to Be Accomplished

1. Collect additional data via interviews, observations, documents. Fill in the gaps, expand understanding.
2. Conduct debriefings with respondents regarding the interim case report. Have extra copies available for those who have not received it.
3. Conduct additional data analysis, including feedback from debriefings. Again, data analysis will be conducted by individuals and the team.
4. Prepare to write "final" case report, including making team assignments.

Respondent Debriefings

1. Based on interim case report and ongoing data analysis.
2. Intended to obtain feedback on accuracy of facts, validity of interpretations. Questions might include these: Is this your

experience? What did we miss? Who did we miss? What isn't accurate? What did we get right? What should be added to accurately portray student cultures on this campus? With whom should we speak to develop a more thorough picture of student experiences?

3. Format for debriefings includes both focus groups and individuals (depending on role) and both persons who were respondents during the first site visit and new respondents.

4. Issues to be considered: what to do if there are disagreements; how to handle defensiveness; what to do if the report was not distributed as requested; how to handle challenges to accuracy of facts. If there are disagreements among persons in the college about the researchers' interpretations, try to understand the differences and why disagreement exists, since absence of shared views of student cultures can be an important finding. Work with respondents to negotiate a final product with which both respondents and researchers can agree.

Phase Five: The "Final" Report

Tasks to Be Accomplished

1. Write final case report and send or deliver to site.
2. Identify additional needs of institution, additional tasks for the team (if any).
3. Thank campus contact person(s) and respondents for their cooperation.

Writing the "Final" Case Report

1. Decide what to say and how to say it. Issues to consider: What information must be included? What additions and other changes from first report?
2. The report is never really "final."

Communicating the Report to the Site

1. Decide on most appropriate format: Should there be in-person discussions? With whom should they be conducted? What role will students play?

2. Decide what, if any, role researchers will play in helping the college make use of the report.
3. Decide the extent to which researchers are willing and able to accommodate additions and changes in the report—when is "final" final enough?

Conclusion

The importance of peers in the lives of college students, and the influence of student cultures on student learning and development, should not be ignored in efforts to assess the impact of a particular college on its students. The messiness and challenges of cultural assessment and qualitative methods should not discourage anyone from undertaking a study of students' experiences in their own words and from their own perspectives. Not only can such assessment provide useful data, it can have an impact on the education and development of students as well as the institution: "Those who are concerned with renewal and reform must realize that the real enemies of undergraduate education are apathy and ignorance. . . . One of the best ways of combating them is to provide reliable information in palatable form. Such efforts keep undergraduate education on the institutional agenda. The more we know about our students, the more likely we are to care; and from such caring comes the will to do the best we can" (Katchadourian and Boli, 1985, p. 252).

Chapter Ten

Assessing Program and Service Outcomes

Patrick T. Terenzini and M. Lee Upcraft

Perhaps the most intimidating question posed to a student affairs practitioner goes something like this: "Sure, the students like your programs and services, but what evidence do you have that what you are doing is making a difference?" Unfortunately, this question seldom is asked by someone who is sympathetic to the mission and goals of student affairs. In some cases, the question may be asked as a genuine effort to improve quality. But in many cases the "evidence" question is posed by someone who (1) doubts the value of student affairs, and (2) is convinced that the money allocated to student affairs could be spent better elsewhere (mostly likely in the questioner's own department!). However, the "evidence" question can also be posed by regional accrediting agencies, who are now incorporating outcome assessments into their accreditation criteria.

Regardless of who poses this question, it typically sends the student affairs practitioner running back to his or her organization in a panic, because in most student affairs organizations, little or no systematic "evidence" of the impact of student services, programs, and facilities is available. This situation typically leads to a hurried rush into "outcome assessments" not only as the answer to the evidence question, but as the "cure" for everything else that ails student affairs. The fact is that while assessing the purported outcomes of our efforts with students is probably the most important assessment we do, it is seldom done, rarely done well, and when it is done, the results are seldom used effectively.

The purpose of this chapter is to offer an overview and definition of outcome assessment, present and discuss the most commonly used and highly credible model of outcome assessment, and offer a step-by-step process of conducting outcome studies, including a discussion of multivariate analysis, the most appropriate statistical tool for analyzing outcome studies.

Outcome Assessment: An Overview

In Chapter One, we identified assessing outcomes as the fifth and perhaps most important component of a comprehensive student affairs assessment program. Of those persons who use our services, programs, and facilities, is there any effect on their learning, development, academic success, or other intended outcomes, particularly when compared with nonusers? Can institutional interventions (for example, programs, services, and policies) be isolated from other variables which may influence outcomes, such as background and entering characteristics, and other collegiate and noncollegiate experiences? Outcome assessments attempt to answer the most important question of all in student affairs: Is what we are doing having any effect, is that effect the intended one, and how do we know?

While assessing outcomes is important, it is also extremely difficult, for reasons which will be elaborated later in this chapter. But outcome assessment must be done, and done well, because without it, other forms of assessment become trivial. For example, in and of itself, keeping track of who uses student services, programs, and facilities is a meaningless exercise if no impact on students can be demonstrated. The same can be said for student satisfaction with services, programs, and facilities. So the impact question is the cornerstone of a comprehensive student affairs assessment program, the foundation upon which all other forms of assessment rest.

Astin's Model of Assessing Outcomes

There are many viable sources for learning more about outcome assessment (Ewell, 1985; Erwin, 1991; Banta, 1993; and many others); perhaps the most widely recognized and frequently used framework for assessing outcomes is Alexander Astin's input-environment-outcome (I-E-O) model (1991). This model provides investigators with a parsimonious but conceptually rich set of guidelines for the design of outcome assessments. The primary purpose of Astin's I-E-O model is to identify and estimate institutional effects on how students grow or change during the college years. In particular, this model is a useful tool for identifying and estimating effects of those college experiences over which institutions have some programmatic or policy control, such as student experiences, which can be shaped to educational advantage through an institution's programmatic or policy actions. Applied to student affairs, this typically means examining student experiences outside the classroom, and students' participation and involvement in student services, programs, or facilities.

Inputs

The first dimension of Astin's I-E-O model is inputs. Students come to college differing (often substantially) on a wide variety of personal, background, and educational characteristics. Astin (1993) identified some 146 possible input variables, including high school grades and admissions test scores, student expectations, high school courses taken in eight different subject matter fields, preliminary choice of a career, preliminary choice of a major field of study, the importance given to reasons for attending college, degree aspirations, religious preference, parental occupation, parental income, parental education, and a variety of demographic measures including race or ethnicity, age, gender, marital status, and citizenship.

Each of these precollege characteristics (Astin's inputs) can influence educational outcomes. As Astin (1991) states, "Outputs must always be evaluated in terms of inputs" (p. 17). Institutions ought not to take credit (although they often do) for producing high-performing or highly developed students when they admit primarily high-performing or highly developed students. What is at issue is the "institutional contribution" to student development above and beyond the student's level of development at the time of admission.

To estimate institutional effects on students, ways must be found to take into account ("control") initial differences. Such controls, in a sense, put all students on the same starting line as they begin their college careers. Unless such controls are part of an assessment study, one will be unable to distinguish between those senior-year differences among students that are attributable to the institution's educational programs, and those differences that were present when the students first arrived on campus.

Environment

Astin (1991) argues that attention must be paid to those things which might influence what and how much students learn or change, or the environment component of the model. As noted earlier, a fundamental purpose of assessment is to help identify not only those influences which shape student learning and change, but also those influences over which colleges and universities have some policy or programmatic control and which can be shaped to maximum educational advantage. Knowing how much students learn or change (such as measuring the difference between a student's knowledge, ability, or "condition" at the start and end of college) is insufficient. Such information gives no insight into why change may have occurred. Answering the "why" question, which is essential if programmatic or policy changes are to enhance educational effectiveness, requires gathering information on the kinds of experiences students have while in college.

Astin (1993) identified seven classifications of environment variables, constituting some 192 different environmental measures, including institutional characteristics (such as type, control, size); student's peer group characteristics (such as socioeconomic status, academic preparation, values, attitudes); faculty characteristics (such as favored methods of teaching, morale, values); curriculum (such as true core, type of requirements); financial aid (such as Pell grants, Stafford loans); major field choice; place of residence (such as college dormitory, private room); and student involvement (such as hours spent studying, number of classes taken in different fields, participation in honors programs).

The environment part of Astin's model assumes collecting data on students over some period of time, thus becoming "longitudinal" in nature. The fundamental educational mission of colleges and universities is to help students learn and develop in various ways. Learning and development imply change, and change occurs only with the passage of time, whether brief or long. Thus, studying student change requires doing longitudinal research. Assessment of student learning and change, as Astin's model demonstrates, can be accomplished only with the collection of information on students at no fewer than two points in time. These data collections typically occur at the beginning of students' first year in college and at the end of the first or the senior year, or at the beginning and end of some program or activity whose effectiveness is under examination. Useful information may be gathered at intermediate stages, of course, but the point is that students' "condition" (for example, how much they know, their developmental status) must be tracked or monitored over time.

Owing to the longitudinal character of assessment, like student change, an effective assessment takes time. Certain cross-sectional designs are available that yield relatively immediate estimates of student change (for example, comparing a sample of first-year students with a sample of seniors to infer change due to the college experience), but all cross-sectional designs are methodologically inferior to following the same students as they move through their college careers or some particular experience. Longitudinal research requires patience on the part of administrators and investigators alike. Student change cannot be rushed, no matter how urgent an administrative decision may be.

A second implication of the longitudinal nature of assessment is the need for analytical procedures capable of dealing with the complexity of estimating change over time. The process is more complicated than comparing scores on some measure at "time one" with those taken at "time two." These procedures are described in some detail below.

Similarly, collecting information on student change at only two points in time (for example, before and after freshman year or freshman and senior years) is also likely to be insufficient if we are serious about enhancing educational programs and activities. Pre- and post-college information certainly is important, but it reveals nothing about when those changes occur. We actually know very little about whether change is linear and occurs in relatively equal increments, or whether it is episodic and discontinuous over the college years. It seems reasonable to suggest that the pacing of change varies across outcome areas. For policy and program development purposes, it is not enough to know simply whether change occurs, we must know when it occurs and why it occurs. These requirements suggest the need for several data collections throughout the college career of an entering cohort of students.

Outcomes

The third component of Astin's model is outcomes. What are the desired effects of college? The easiest and most measurable collegiate outcomes are grades and retention. The more difficult and less easily measured outcomes identified by Pascarella and Terenzini (1991) include development of verbal, quantitative, and subject matter competence; cognitive skills and intellectual growth; psychosocial outcomes such as identity, self-concept, self esteem, and relating to others and the external world; attitudes and values; moral development; career choice and development; the economic benefits of college; and quality of life after college. Likewise, Astin (1993) identified seven classifications of student outcomes, including political orientation, personality and self concept, attitudes, values, and beliefs, patterns of behavior, academic and cognitive development, career development, and satisfaction with the collegiate environment, constituting 82 different individual variables.

Historically, student affairs typically has focused on out-of-class "nonacademic" outcomes such as psychosocial outcomes, attitudes and values, moral development, and career choice and development. In the 1970s and 1980s, however, studies were done which showed the relationship between student out-of-class experiences and "academic" outcomes such as grades and retention. Examples included student's place of residence (Astin, 1973; Chickering, 1974), participation in orientation (Upcraft, 1984), participation in extracurricular activities (Upcraft, 1985), and many other student experiences.

Thus, as Astin (1991) points out, an adequate assessment design requires gathering three distinct kinds of information on students: what they are like when they come to college, the nature of their experiences while in college, and what they are like when they leave college. As Pascarella and Terenzini (1991) make clear, students change in a wide variety of ways during the college years, and those changes are shaped by a complex combination of students' precollege characteristics and college experiences. Unraveling that complexity can be a daunting task, but it is by no means impossible.

"Incomplete" Outcome Models

The reader might now assume that the I-E-O model makes a lot of sense and should be used as the outcome assessment model. However, there are many variations of the I-E-O model that are too often erroneously identified as outcome assessment, when, in fact, they are so inherently flawed that they are at best worthless, and at worst, dangerous. Astin (1991) identifies four such frequently used models: outcome-only assessment, environment-outcome assessment, input-outcome assessment, and environment-only assessment.

According to Astin (1991), outcome-only assessment is probably the fastest growing approach of all. This approach involves using some kind of end-of-program assessment designed to determine whether selected outcomes are being achieved. A good example would be retention. An institution looks at the percentage of students who survive the first year, and then either pats itself on the back for a high retention rate, or anguishes over what is felt to be an excessively high dropout rate.

This gross retention outcome measure, however, is difficult, if not dangerous, to interpret for many reasons. First of all, one has no idea to what one may attribute the result. It could well be that a high retention rate is a result of a very selective admissions process, in which only the most academically qualified and highly motivated students are accepted, and for whom the prognosis for success is very high. Further, it is impossible to discern how much of the retention rate, if any, is attributable to environmental influences. With outcome assessment only, we literally have no idea what the results mean or how they were achieved.

Astin (1991) is also critical of a second "incomplete" assessment model, the environment-outcome assessment, for many of the same reasons. Again, using retention as an outcome measure, an institution may conduct studies which point to selected environment variables which it believes contribute to retention, such as living in residence halls, faculty contact, class attendance, hours spent studying, involvement in extracurricular activities, and other factors. On the one hand, there is substantial evidence that these experiences affect retention. On the other hand, without taking into account input variables such as prior academic achievement, socioeconomic status, race or ethnicity, gender, and other pre-college variables known to affect retention, there can be no valid conclusions drawn regarding the relationship between environment variables and retention.

A third "incomplete" outcome assessment model identified by Astin (1991) is input-outcome assessment. In this instance, an institution may measure some trait, ability, or level of development when students arrive on the campus, measure those characteristics at the end of some specified time period, and conclude (without any evidence) that the institution had something to do with those traits as outcomes. The problem with this approach is that change is equated with environmental impact. Just because change occurred during college does not mean that one can attribute that change to some particular set of collegiate experiences. It tells us how students change over time, but nothing about why they change.

The fourth of Astin's "incomplete" outcome assessment models (1991) is environment-only assessment, in which we focus on some environment variables themselves and assess their various components. Astin believes the best-known example of this model is the regional accreditation process in higher education, which traditionally involves an examination of the institution's libraries, physical plant, faculty-student ratios, teaching loads, required and elective courses, and the academic qualifications of the faculty. A corresponding example in student affairs might be accreditation of counseling services by the International Association of Counseling Services, Inc., or health services by the Accreditation Association for Ambulatory Health Care, Inc. The problem with this method is that no matter how detailed the descriptive information, no data concerning the actual impact or effectiveness of the environment are provided, so we can only infer such impact.

The bottom line is that the I-E-O model cannot be used piecemeal, in spite of the fact that this is frequently done. At best, there are too many limitations when only part or parts of the model are followed. At the worst, worthless and misleading results are obtained, which form a very poor basis for solving problems, making decisions, and developing policy.

Steps in the Outcome Assessment Process

The steps in the outcome assessment process (which closely parallel the assessment questions discussed in Chapter Two) are best exemplified by using a rather simple example of an outcome study.

In practice, the "state of the art" outcome study would be much more complex, taking into account many more input, environment, and output measures. The example selected here is a quantitative study of first-year attrition, using a study published by Terenzini and Pascarella (1978) as a guide.

The reader should note two caveats to the material that follows. First, while we have chosen a quantitative study as an example of outcome studies, it is possible to conduct outcome assessments using qualitative methodologies. That is, through interviewing or focus groups, it is possible to examine student perceptions of their collegiate experiences, taking into account their background characteristics and relating those backgrounds and experiences to some measurable or perceived outcome.

Second, there are good reasons for using personal development outcomes as well, and the reader is referred to the Student Development Outcome Assessment Model, developed by Winston and Miller (1994), as an excellent example of developmental outcome assessment.

Step One: Define the Problem

As discussed previously, all assessment flows from some problem. In this example, a medium-sized (approximately ten thousand students) private research university became concerned about why some freshmen were voluntarily leaving the institution, while others survived the first year. The voluntary attrition rate was of concern because of the educational and fiscal implications for the institution. Up until this time, the institution had very little data on what the attrition rate was, and even less information on how to explain it. It was hoped that the results of this study would provide some guidelines for institutional policy or program action.

Step Two: Determine the Purposes of the Study

Once the problem was identified, the next question to be asked and answered was, "What is the purpose of the study?" Based upon the problem, two purposes were identified:

• To determine the relative influences on attrition of students' precollege characteristics.

- To identify those features of the freshman experience which were most closely associated with attrition and which were amenable to institutional program or policy action.

Step Three: Determine the Appropriate Assessment Approach

Since this study attempted to measure change over time, it was decided that Astin's input-environment-outcome model was appropriate, for the reasons identified above.

Step Four: Determine the Outcomes

Although outcome is the third dimension of Astin's I-E-O model, it should be the first to be determined because the selection of the input and environment dimensions is determined by possible or demonstrated relationships between the outcomes and these other variables. The next question to be asked was "what are the outcomes that are most important to the problems identified and the purposes of the study?" Obviously, voluntary attrition was the outcome the institution was interested in explaining. Voluntary attrition was operationally defined as those first-year students who voluntarily withdrew from the institution by the end of the second semester, or had failed to re-enroll for the third semester.

Step Five: Identify the Input or Control Variables

Identifying the input variables is easy, but retrieving them is another matter. As discussed above, Astin (1993) identified some 146 input variables. Of course, it is unlikely that an individual institution would have access to all these variables, so some tough choices have to be made, primarily on the basis of what is most important, and more practically, what is available. This brings us to an issue which will inevitably complicate and limit outcome assessment. While it would be ideal to include all of Astin's input variables (1993), it is almost always impossible. It is very unlikely that any given institution would be able to access all 146 input variables (the exceptions might be those that participate in Astin's annual Cooperative Institutional Research Project). Also, it may not be necessary to include all of them, given the outcomes studied. For example, if a literature review indicates that a particular input variable is unlikely to influence a particular outcome, then that variable could be eliminated. To cite a somewhat absurd example, if there is no known relationship between retention and birth order (an input measure), then there is no need to take this variable into account in studying retention.

In this study, a combination of availability and appropriateness led to the selection of the following pre-college characteristics:

- Sex
- Racial or ethnic origin (nonminority or minority)
- Academic aptitude (combined Scholastic Aptitude Test scores)
- High school achievement (rank in high school class and class size)
- Personality (four Activities Index Area Scores)
- Mother's education (six ordinal categories)
- Father's education (six ordinal categories)
- Expectations of the academic program (on four dimensions of the Adjective Rating Scale)
- Expectations of the nonacademic life (on four dimensions of the ARS)
- Expected number of informal contacts with faculty (per month, of ten minutes or more outside the classroom)
- Expected number of extracurricular activities (of two hours per week or more, on the average)

The omission of other possible input variables was identified, and noted among the limitations of the study.

Step Six: Identify the Environment Variables

Now begins the fun and frustration of dealing with the complexity of student experiences. It would be impossible, of course, to account for every possible relevant collegiate experience of every student. We can only look to previous research through a literature review and reasonable estimates of which collegiate experiences are most influential, given the outcomes studied. Again, it might be ideal to use all 192 of Astin's environment measures (1993), but in reality few, if any, institutions could include most of them. So, important decisions must be made about which measures to include and which to exclude, based on the purpose of the study and the ability to collect such data.

Thus, in this study, importance and accessibility of data were critical variables in determining environment variables. These variables were selected on the basis of Tinto's model of student attrition (1975), in which he argues that first-year students who become integrated into the academic and social systems of the institution are more likely to persist than those who do not. For the purposes of this study, the following academic and social environmental measures were used:

Academic Integration Set

- Perceptions of the academic program
- Affective appeal
- Practical value
- Dullness
- Challenge
- Cumulative grade-point average (on a scale of 1 to 4, where 4 = A)
- Intellectual development progress (one-scale score)

Social Integration Set

- Perceptions of nonacademic life (on four ARS dimensions)
- Affective appeal
- Practical value
- Dullness
- Challenge
- Actual number of informal contacts with faculty (total, of ten minutes or more, outside the classroom)
- Actual number of extracurricular activities engaged in (two hours or more per week, on average)
- Personal development progress (one-scale score)

Step Seven: Select the Measurement Instruments

The Adjective Rating Scale (ARS) (Kelly, Pascarella, Terenzini, and Chapman, 1978) was used to measure students' expectations (and perceptions) of their academic program and their nonacademic life.

The ARS consists of twenty-four adjectives (for example, enjoyable, demanding, useless) against which respondents rate certain statements on a four-point scale (from 1 = extremely to 4 = not at all). Students were asked to rate the statements "I (expect/have found) my academic program at this institution to be . . ." and "I (expect/have found) my nonacademic life at this institution to be . . ."

Data from Stern's Activities Index (AI) (1970), a measure of personality needs, were also collected. This study used four AI Area scores (achievement orientation, dependence needs, emotional expression, and educability). Data on other variables listed earlier were collected on either the pre- or post-registration questionnaires or taken directly from students' admissions or academic records. Where a respondent had a missing data element, the mean value of the appropriate group (voluntary "leaver" or "stayer") was assigned.

Step Eight: Determine the Population to Be Studied and the Sample to Be Drawn

The population included all 2,400 first-year students at the institution at the time of the study. From this population, a random sample of 1,008 persons was drawn by computer for inclusion in the study. A random sampling procedure was chosen because, for the purposes of this study, it was essential that all the individuals in the population have an equal and independent chance of being selected. The sample size was chosen because, based upon an estimated return rate, it was large enough to conduct the analyses described below. (For a more extensive discussion of sampling procedures, see Chapter Four.)

Step Nine: Determine the Modes of Statistical Analysis

Very rarely do student affairs professionals possess the expertise to determine the modes of statistical analyses. In Chapter Four, we identified many different types of statistical tools and explained how they can be used. The reader will recall that we discussed the limitations and even dangers of using multiple bivariate analyses to assess change over time. On the other hand, multivariate analyses allow for a study of the relationship of several responses to a single response or outcome. In this study, it should be obvious that a multivariate analysis is most appropriate, because the authors were examining the relations between several independent variables (in this instance, multiple background characteristics and environmental experiences) and one dependent variable (attrition). The results will show to what extent, if any, attrition is influenced by various environment variables, taking into account the influence of background characteristics. But we do have some choices to make within a range of multivariate procedures.

As pointed out in Chapter Four, multiple regression is really a family of statistical procedures rather than a single statistical method, and includes stepwise regression, hierarchical setwise regression, logit analysis, and probit analysis. Thus, we will consider only two of these regression approaches, because of the frequency with which they are used and because they are easier to understand and interpret. The reader will note that discriminant function analysis was also a possible method of analysis (because there are nominal dependent variables: "leavers" and "persisters"), but space limitations do not allow for a discussion of this method, or why Terenzini and Pascarella (1978) decided setwise regression was more appropriate for this study.

Stepwise Regression

This method is best suited to answering the question "Which of a set of independent variables are the best predictors of (or the most strongly related to) the dependent or outcome variable?" Note that this question implies an equal interest in all independent variables, both control (background) and main independent (environment) variables. The analysis, in essence, produces a reduced list of variables that (as a set) are most strongly related to the outcome. In this approach, the identification of the most important independent variables for inclusion proceeds in a stepwise fashion, one variable being selected at a time. The computer program controls whether an independent variable will be included in the model (that is, on the list) and, if so, at what "step" it will be selected. In essence, the computer asks which one of all the independent variables under examination is most strongly related to the dependent variable (that is, which one explains the most variance in the outcome variable). That independent variable is then added to the model (or list). The computer then tests all remaining (so far unselected) independent variables to identify the one that can explain the most of what variance remains unexplained after the inclusion of the first variable. That second variable is then added to the model. Then, the process is repeated: all variables unselected thus far are tested to identify the one that explains the most of the variance left unexplained by those variables already selected for inclusion. The process continues until the addition of another variable would not further reduce the remaining unexplained variance. At this point, the optimal set of independent variables for explaining the most variance in the dependent measure has been identified, and one would turn to examine the beta weights of each of those variables to evaluate the relative individual importance of each variable selected for inclusion in the model. (It is possible that a variable may enter the model at some point and subsequently be dropped as other variables are included. For present purposes, this phenomenon need not concern us.)

Basically, stepwise regression is a data reduction technique. All of the independent variables identified by the researcher for examination are evaluated and only those showing the strongest relations to the outcome variable are selected. The others, presumably, can be safely ignored.

This approach does have its limitations, however. Not every independent variable has its day in court. It is well to remember that "independent" variables (a designation given them because of their role in the research design) are not uncorrelated. If two variables are correlated with one another and with the outcome measure, the variable with the higher correlation with the outcome measure will be selected and the other will not (no matter how slight the difference between them, and computer programs calculate these correlations to seven decimal places). Only if the ignored variable has some power to explain variance in the outcome measure above and beyond that explained by the other independent variable will it be included in the model. Thus, the possibility exists that a variable of theoretical or practical interest to the investigator may be overlooked.

Moreover, while this method may produce a parsimonious result, it is also decidedly atheoretical. It is the computer, not some conceptual plan developed by the researcher, that decides which variables are included in the model. The computer will not permit identification of the relative importance of specific sets of variables. For example, one would not use this method to estimate how much of the differences among new students at the end of their first year are attributable to their college experiences rather than to the characteristics they brought with them to college.

Hierarchical Setwise Regression

This type of regression analysis has considerable potential to illuminate the relations between and among input and environment variables and how they may shape changes in the outcomes of interest. The hierarchical or setwise method is similar to stepwise regression to the extent that the order in which independent variables are included in the model is controlled. But there the similarity ends. Hierarchical models differ from stepwise models in two important ways. First, the order in which variables enter the analysis is determined by the researcher, not by the computer, and second, groups or sets of variables can be entered in a predetermined order or hierarchy.

How the person doing the assessment orders the entry of variables may be guided by a particular theory. For example, Tinto's model of student persistence (1987), Pascarella's model of learning and cognitive development (1980), and Astin's more generalized I-E-O model all specify a temporal order among the independent variables as they shape the outcome measure of interest. All three models begin with a given set of students' pre-college characteristics believed to interact, subsequently, with various features of the institutional environment which, in turn, are thought to influence the degree and nature of change on some outcome measure. Within each set, the individual variables are normally entered simultaneously in a single step, since typically there is no conceptual or logical basis for believing one collegiate experience variable within a set should be entered before another. The computer can, however, be programmed to enter them in a stepwise fashion within each set of variables if there is a reason to do so.

For example the pre-college characteristics "happened" or were present before the student came to college. These are all potential sources of variance in first-year retention that are beyond the institution's ability to control and, thus, must be taken into account (controlled) before looking to see how much influence the students' college experiences (those things over which an institution does have some control) have on first-year retention. This setwise procedure makes it possible to "partition" the total variance into three pieces: (1) that due to students' pre-college (input) characteristics, (2) that due to their college experiences (the environment), and (3) the remaining variance that is unexplained by either of the input or environment variable sets.

It is important to note that this analysis yields a variance estimate (an estimate of the importance of that set in influencing the outcome variable) that is unique, a proportion of the total variance explained over and above that attributable to input characteristics alone. Put another way, hierarchical regression analysis has estimated the effect of those college experiences on first-year retention after statistically equating the students at the time of their enrollment with respect to gender, academic ability, and the other input variables studied. Other potentially confounding pre-college characteristics, of course, could have been included in the model and, thereby, been controlled.

In fact, this hierarchical method is a conservative approach to estimating college effects. Any variance estimate attributable to collegiate experiences probably underestimates their effect, because any variance the inputs and environments share jointly is, in this method, attributed entirely to the pre-college variables, since they entered the model first. This underestimation is not particularly problematic. One simply needs to keep in mind that the estimates of the unique variance attributable to the college experience variable set is probably a "lower-bound" estimate.

It is worth noting that this method of analysis, particularly with pre-college estimates of academic ability included as a control (background) variable, provides a conservative, but "clean" and easily interpretable, estimation of effects of college experiences. Though one might conclude that the estimated amount of variance attributable to the environment variables may be small (perhaps 10 percent) and therefore not very important substantively, one is on solid ground in asserting that the estimate is statistically sound and the estimates of college's effects unconfounded by any of the input variables included in the analysis. Further, for reasons explained by Astin (1991), even small regression coefficients (one percent) may be of practical importance.

Returning to our study, hierarchial setwise was chosen as the most appropriate multivariate analyses because it was important to clearly identify the relative influence of input (background) variables and environment (collegiate experiences) variables on the retention of first-year students.

Step Ten: Develop and Implement a Plan for Data Collection

The best-constructed study will fall on its face if it does not have a well-designed data collection procedure, that is, one that collects accurate data about subjects from as many sources as possible. The procedure must be "user friendly" to encourage students to participate, and information that can be retrieved about students from other institutional sources should be utilized. For more details about how to achieve maximum collection of data from a variety of sources, see Chapter Two. This study involved accumulating data about first-year students during the summer before their first semester, and again approximately two-thirds of the way through their second semester. Some 1,009 sample members were sent a detailed questionnaire designed to assess pre-college characteristics and perceptions, including their expectations on a variety of aspects of the college experience, as well as selected background information. Usable responses were received from 766 who subsequently enrolled. These respondents were sent a second questionnaire during their second semester, seeking information about their first-year college experience. After a mail and telephone follow-up, usable responses were received from 536 freshmen (70.0 percent; 53.2 percent of the original sample). Statistical tests indicated that the 536 respondents were representative of the institution's freshman population with respect to sex, college of enrollment, and academic aptitude, so weighting of the sample was not necessary. A subsequent review of each student's records indicated that ninety students had voluntarily withdrawn from the institution at the end of their freshman year, and these students were identified as "voluntary leavers."

A design problem which always confounds attrition studies became readily apparent. Remember that attrition was defined as those students who were enrolled during their second semester, but failed to re-enroll for their third semester. Those who dropped out included other cohorts: those who dropped out during their first semester, those who completed their first semester but failed to re-enroll for their second semester, those who dropped out during their second semester before the second data collection procedure.

While persisters and dropouts could be compared on all of the input (background) variables, it was not possible to collect data on the environment variables for those students who dropped out before the second data collection. So the conclusions of this study are based on those first-year students who were still enrolled at the time of the second data collection procedure.

Step Eleven: Record the Data in Usable Form

There are several ways of converting data to computer data files, and the reader should decide how that should be done on the basis of locally available computer-based data file capabilities. However, data files for most institutionally based studies can be compiled on floppy disks for use in desktop computers. Likewise, most desktop computers have the capability of using commercially based statistical packages, such as Statistical Analysis Systems (SAS) or Statistical Package for the Social Sciences (SPSS) cited in Chapter Four. A locally based computer consultant can best advise how to record data in a usable form, given local resources.

Step Twelve: Conduct the Appropriate Analyses

As stated earlier, in this study, a hierarchical setwise multivariate analysis was used to analyze the data, using the .05 level of significance. While it is not the purpose of this chapter to present a detailed description of the analyses, a brief summary is appropriate.

Mean scale scores for each respondent on each component were computed. Attrition status (stayer/voluntary leaver) was used, as the dependent variable is a series of multiple regressions. The independent variables were the variables listed above comprising three variable sets: (1) pre-matriculation characteristics (twenty-one measures), (2) academic integration variables (six measures), and (3) social integration variables (seven measures). In the main analysis, three setwise multiple regressions were performed: (1) pre-college characteristics were entered first as a set, then followed in order by the social integration set and the academic integration set; (2) pre-college variables were entered first as a set, but the order of entry of the social and academic integration sets was reversed; (3) pre-college characteristics were entered first as a set, followed by the social and academic integration variables as a combined set, all prior to entering the interaction vectors as a set.

Overall, the amount of variation in attrition status, explainable with reference to the four variable sets, was 25.6 percent. This means that the variables included in this study "explained" approximately 26 percent of the variation in the attendance behaviors (staying or leaving) of the 534 students in the study. Put another way, there were other unknown variables, not included in this study, which "explain" the other 74 percent.

More specifically, the results indicated that pre-college characteristics explained less than 4 percent of the variance in attrition status, a statistically nonsignificant amount. However, social integration variables explained 3 percent of the variance in attrition status after controlling for precollege characteristics and academic integration. (This represents the "unique" contribution of the set.) These results suggest that after taking into account pre-college differences and subsequent integration in the academic domain, such considerations as students' perceptions of their nonacademic lives, the frequency of their informal contact with faculty members, the number of extracurricular activities in which they engage, and the amount of progress they feel they have made in their personal development, all are modestly, but statistically, significant at the .05 level, related to the decision to remain or withdraw from this particular institution at the end of the freshman year.

The results also indicated that the degree of integration in the academic systems of the institution, after all pre-college characteristics and social integration variables have been controlled, is also statistically related to attrition decisions. The academic integration variables (perceptions of the academic program, cumulative grade-point average, and perceived progress in intellectual development)—as a set—explained nearly 6 percent of the variation in attrition status, nearly twice as much as the social integration set, and statistically significant at the .001 level.

At this point, the concept of *interaction effects* must be introduced. According to Hinkle, Wiersma, and Jurs (1994), when investigating two independent variables (in this study, pre-college characteristics and academic and social integration measures), we can also test whether the levels of one independent variable affect the dependent variable in the same way across the levels of the second independent variables. If the effect is not the same, we can say there is an interaction effect between the two independent variables.

In this study, the interaction vectors, taken as a set, made a statistically significant contribution at the .05 level to the prediction of attrition status, even after pre-college traits and academic and social integration measures had been controlled. As a set, the interaction terms explained an additional 10.6 percent of the variance—nearly twice as much as the academic integration set and more than three times as much as the social integration measures. This finding led to an investigation of individual interactions.

When the focus was on the unique contributions of each variable, the amount of informal contact with faculty members outside the classroom for ten minutes or more made the largest contribution to the prediction of attrition, followed by the amount of affective appeal and the amount of dullness that students found in their academic program. No other single variable made a significant contribution to the prediction of attrition.

Other analyses indicated that the amount of self-perceived progress in intellectual development is virtually unrelated to attrition among minority students, but much more important among nonminority students. With respect to the interaction of race or ethnic origin, and the amount of affective appeal found in the academic program, however, the stronger the impact of the academic program on students' affective or emotional lives, the lower the probability they will drop out, especially for minority students. The amount of challenge males find in their academic programs is unrelated to subsequent attrition decisions, but females who find their academic programs less challenging than do other females are more likely to leave the institution. (For a more in-depth reporting of these results, see Terenzini and Pascarella, 1978.)

Step Thirteen: Evaluate the Analyses for Policy and Practice Implications

This study revealed several implications for policy or practice; only a few of them will be reported here. First, the analyses strongly indicated that even at an institution with a more selective admissions policy, what happens to a student after matriculation may be more important in subsequent voluntary attrition among freshmen than are the attributes the student brings to college. Therefore, predicting attrition *solely* on the basis of students pre-college characteristics is suspect. The findings suggest that efforts to reduce current attrition levels are more likely to succeed if they are focused on what happens to students after their arrival on campus, rather than on what they are like at the time of admission.

Second, the results of this study also suggest that what happens in students' academic lives may be more influential than their social experiences in subsequent attrition decisions. In addition, two of the three best individual predictors of attrition status were associated with students' perceptions of their academic programs. The implications for the classroom might include faculty giving greater attention and commitment to students' positive affective reactions to their classroom experiences.

Third, it is also clear from these findings that the frequency of students' interactions with faculty outside the classroom made the largest unique contribution to the prediction of attrition status. Thus it may be fruitful for administrators seeking to retain students to explore ways to bring students and faculty members into more frequent informal contact, perhaps through orientation or residence hall programming.

Step Fourteen: Develop a Strategy for Using the Results

As pointed out in Chapter Thirteen, strategies for how to use assessment results often are dictated by several factors, including the original purpose for the study and other institutional factors. In this instance, the results of the study were reported to the administration, and many of the findings were discussed and subsequently implemented.

Conclusion

Outcome assessment is the most valid way of demonstrating the effectiveness of student services, programs, and facilities, especially in defending and promoting student affairs, but also in meeting accreditation criteria. It is also the most difficult, complex, and misunderstood of all the assessment methodologies discussed in this book. It has the potential, however, when done correctly, of being a very powerful tool in solving problems, developing and reconsidering policies, and making decisions in student affairs.

As Astin (1991) states, "The input-environment-outcome (I-E-O) model is predicated on the assumption that the principal means by which assessment can be used to improve educational practice is by enlightening the educator about the comparative effectiveness of different educational policies and practices. The I-E-O model is specifically designed to produce information on how outcomes are affected by different educational policies and practices. Use of this model should allow those responsible for assessment activities to enhance their understanding of how student or faculty development is affected by various educational policies and practices" (p. 37).

Chapter Eleven

Benchmarking: Comparing Performance Across Organizations

There is a time-honored tradition in student affairs of consulting with other institutions when confronted with a particular issue or problem. We do this primarily because we want to benefit from the wisdom and success of others so that we don't have to "reinvent the wheel." If others have solved a problem similar to ours successfully, we want to benefit from their experience and, if we are lucky, save ourselves the time and agony implementing untried approaches.

In recent years, the practice of comparing organizations to one another has become more sophisticated and systematic through the concept of "benchmarking." Benchmarking has its origins in "total quality" approaches to organizations, in which "best practices" of comparable organizations are studied to improve products, services, or processes, in order to become "best in class" among competitors. Therefore, as argued in Chapter Two, a comprehensive assessment program must include ways in which comparisons can be made with other organizations.

The purposes of this chapter are to define benchmarking and identify the different types; discuss the various uses of benchmarking; outline the steps in the benchmarking process; offer some examples of benchmarking in student affairs; and discuss the keys to successful benchmarking.

Definition and Types of Benchmarking

According to Spendolini (1992), benchmarking is a "continuous, systematic process for evaluating the products, services, and work processes of organizations that are recognized as representing best practices for the purposes of organizational improvement" (p. 9). He identifies three major types of benchmarking. The first is *internal benchmarking*, which is to compare practices of administrative units within your own organization or institution (Spendolini (1992). This can occur within units in student affairs, or among units outside student affairs but within your institution.

For example, a problem frequently encountered by health services is an unacceptable "wait time" for appointments. It may well be that your counseling service has a much shorter wait time. Studying the process by which appointments are made in a counseling service may be a useful way of improving wait time for appointments in the health service. Or, if both the health service and the counseling service have a problem with wait time, it might be useful to look at the appointment process in another unit of the institution which has demonstrated a shorter wait time, such as an academic advising center. In other words, it may be possible to learn about "best practices" from within your own institution.

The second form of benchmarking is *competitive benchmarking*, which is to compare the products, services, and work processes of your organization's direct competitors (Spendolini, 1992). The idea behind competitive benchmarking is the same as that behind internal benchmarking, except that comparisons are made to functions or processes outside the institution rather than within it. The key here is to choose institutions, functions, and processes which are comparable to your own. For example, to help solve the wait time problem in counseling and health services, you might want to contact an institution of similar type, size, and mission which has counseling and health services that have demonstrated shorter wait times.

The third form of benchmarking is *functional* or *generic benchmarking*, which is to compare the products, services, and work processes of organizations that may not be your direct competitor, but which have similar products, services, or work processes (Spendolini, 1992). This means making comparisons with comparable functions *outside* of higher education. Using the same wait time example, perhaps a private hospital with a demonstrated shorter wait time would be an appropriate benchmark.

Uses of Benchmarking

The primary use of benchmarking, of course, is the improvement of products, services, and processes. But knowing "best practices" of comparable organizations can be helpful not only for improvement, but for many other things as well. Spendolini (1992) identifies several other uses of benchmarking. First, benchmarking can be useful in strategic planning, both in the short and long term. Bellow, Morrisey, and Acomb (1987) define strategic planning as the systematic process which provides a framework for strategic thinking, goals, and action in an organization, leading to the achievement of consistent and planned results.

Using other comparable organizations as models can help your organization in its strategic planning. For example, if a student affairs operation is reconsidering its mission and goals, it might be useful to know more about the mission and goals of successful student affairs operations in comparable institutions. Again, the key is selecting the right institutions and identifying measurable criteria for determining "successful" student affairs operations.

A second use of benchmarking is forecasting, or predicting trends in relevant areas. Here the advantage of learning more about other successful institutions is to try to predict not only what is needed today, but what might be needed tomorrow. If a student affairs operation wants to make sure it is preparing for the future, it might compare itself with student affairs operations that have the reputation for keeping up with and staying ahead of trends important to higher education. For example, if enrollment at a particular institution is expected to move away from traditional-aged students toward older students, it would be essential for a student affairs operation to anticipate changes in the delivery of services and programs. What better way to react to this trend than to benchmark student affairs operations at institutions which have made a successful transition from younger to older students.

A third use of benchmarking is in generating new ideas, or, as Spendolini (1992) puts it, thinking "out of the box." Benchmarking allows an organization to reach beyond its own thinking and the limits of its own resources, thereby expanding creativity and innovation. For example, if there was evidence that new students were not reading or digesting the information sent to them in advance of their enrollment, it might be useful to review new and creative ways of communicating important information by looking at the orientation programs at other institutions which appear to be more successful in these efforts.

A fourth use of benchmarking is to provide data for analyzing and determining affordability. Certainly one organization's experience of funding a service, program, or facility can be useful to another organization's attempt to project costs, improve cost effectiveness, or manage budget reductions. This may be an especially important use of benchmarking at institutions where budget reductions have forced student affairs administrators to make difficult decisions about which programs to downsize or eliminate, and more important, which staff to lay off.

Whether implementing strategic planning, forecasting, generating new ideas, or analyzing and determining affordability, there is no question that benchmarking is a necessary part of a comprehensive assessment program.

Steps in the Benchmarking Process

So how does one go about benchmarking? The following steps are suggested, based on several models of benchmarking (Spendolini, 1992; Capezio and Morehouse, 1992; Camp, 1989).

Step One: Define the Problem

Benchmarking almost always flows from some problem. In a student affairs division which is assessment-driven, problems may have been identified from student use studies, student satisfaction studies, student needs studies, outcome studies, or other types of assessment. Problems also may be identified by less formal means, typically from staff, students, faculty, administrators, or governing boards, or by the institution's various publics, including alumni, parents and families, the local community, state legislatures, or federal legislation or mandates.

Step Two: Determine If Benchmarking Is Appropriate

The second step in the benchmarking process is to determine if benchmarking is an appropriate approach for dealing with the problem identified in step one. Here a basic question must be asked: Can information from other organizations help my organization and solve my problem? It is not a foregone conclusion that analysis of other organizations will be helpful. It may be that no other comparable organization is any further along in solving your problem than you are. To determine if benchmarking is appropriate, you will need to do some preliminary investigation; you must find out if others have been more successful in dealing with a problem like yours than you have. It may also be that your problem is not best addressed through benchmarking, but rather through other forms of assessment.

Step Three: Determine What to Benchmark

Depending on the problem identified in step one, you must make many choices about what exactly you should benchmark. As stated earlier, products, services, or processes may be benchmarked. For example, you made need to improve a product, such as a student affairs publication or an educational program, based on customer feedback. Or student use assessments may have revealed low student usage of an important service. Or a basic process may need to be improved, such as the "wait time" problem discussed above. It is important to know just what is being benchmarked, and why.

Step Four: Determine Who Should Be Involved

Benchmarking will not work unless the people directly affected by the benchmarking process are involved from the very beginning. Benchmarking most often fails when it is dictated and controlled from the top down. While this principle of involvement is an important element of all assessment, it is especially important in benchmarking, for two reasons. First, the benchmarking process (through every step suggested here) should involve the staff who deal directly with the problem, or to use total quality terms, those "closest to the customer." Using one of the examples cited previously, benchmarking "wait time" in a health service involves more than a phone call from one student affairs vice president to another seeking advice on how to improve wait time. It requires continuous communication and exchange of ideas, information, and workable solutions by clerical staff, nurses, and other support staff, all of whom actually monitor and implement the wait time process; these people know more about the problem than anyone else.

Second, if the staff who are closest to the problem have been involved in the benchmarking process, there will be greater ownership of the results, and a greater likelihood that the solutions will be implemented. Further, morale is likely to be improved when the leadership empowers staff in ways that demonstrate respect for their expertise, autonomy, and judgment.

Which staff to involve depends upon what is being benchmarked and why. In general, benchmarking is best accomplished by a team of people, each of whom has a vested interest in the outcome. If the problem is one that crosses two or more individual student affairs units, the team leader should probably be a student affairs mid-level manager with no vested interest in the outcome other than improving service to students. For example, "wait time" could be a problem for health services, counseling services, academic advising services, or any other student affairs offices providing direct service to students. In this instance, the team leader should be an assistant vice-president or other central management staff. Team members should include staff from each of the units affected (who are closest to the problem), and when appropriate, there should be students. While directors of units may be members, it is not necessary for them to be involved.

When the problem being addressed is unique to a particular unit (such as reducing the time it takes to process and adjudicate a discipline case), the team leader should come from the discipline office, and team members should include those people who are closest to the problem. Again, the unit director need not be directly involved. In either instance, team members should be involved in all subsequent steps identified below.

Step Five: Determine Which Comparable Organizations Will Be Benchmarked

Deciding which organizations to benchmark is a very important decision. Be sure to remember that while institutions of higher education are the most likely candidates for benchmarking, institutions outside higher education with similar products, services, or processes can also be used in this process. However, making comparisons to organizations whose products, services, or processes are not similar will not only be useless, but may well be misleading. Thus, the criteria you use to determine which organizations will be benchmarked are very important. In general, one should select organizations which have the following characteristics:

- *Products, services, or processes which are similar to your own.*
  The most obvious choices are those student affairs organizations in institutions with similar missions and resources, and of similar size and type. But non–student affairs organizations inside or outside higher education may also be viable choices, so long as there is some logical connection between your own products, services, or processes and theirs.
- *Reputations for quality products, services, or products.* Spendolini (1992) suggests that companies which represent best practices may be identified through special awards and citations, media attention, professional associations, independent reports, word of mouth, and consultants.
- *Valid information to offer.* Does the organization have information to begin with? Sometimes reputations for quality are built on hearsay rather than evidence. If information exists, is it correct and verifiable?
- *Reliable information to offer.* Are the sources of information trustworthy? Is there consistency over time? Is there consistency from one source to another in the same organization?
- *Leadership which values benchmarking.* Institutions which do not value benchmarking are unlikely to cooperate seriously with you, because it would take them a lot of time and resources to provide valid and reliable information. Often the best benchmarking organizations are ones with which you have a past history, particularly if that past history includes your cooperation with them.
- *Easy accessibility.* Time and resources may limit the organizations with which you can feasibly benchmark. For example you may only have the resources to benchmark those institutions within reasonable travel distance from your institution.

Once the criteria have been considered, you must choose between internal benchmarking, or doing a comparative study between your institution and another administrative unit within your organization; competitive benchmarking, or comparing your institution with a student affairs operation from another institution; or functional or generic benchmarking, or comparing your institution to a non–student affairs organization which has products, services, or processes similar to your own. Here again, a little preliminary investigation may help. Also, it is not necessarily a good idea to benchmark only with other student affairs organizations. For example, if the problem is the quality of publications, a publishing company may be more helpful than organizations within higher education.

One other caveat: while two institutions may be quite comparable with regard to larger institutional or academic characteristics, it does not necessarily follow that the student affairs divisions, or units within student affairs, are comparable. Therefore, it is important not only to identify comparable institutions, but determine if the student affairs units within those institutions have comparable missions, goals, staffing, funding, and other important characteristics.

Step Six: Determine What Information Will Be Gathered

This can be a difficult problem because different organizations keep different information in different forms. Nevertheless, the benchmarking team must determine what information is needed to improve the product, service, or process. Further, it is probably a good idea to develop a format or protocol which provides a framework within which information can be gathered.

Step Seven: Determine How the Information Will Be Collected

Spendolini (1992) identifies five methods of information collection:

- Telephone interviews are easy to plan and conduct, enable contact with large numbers of resources, can be conducted at almost any time, and are relatively inexpensive. But they can also be time-consuming and difficult to arrange, and people are often less likely to spend a lot of time on the telephone.

- Personal meetings and site visits can establish personal and professional relations, provide more quality time, and are more likely to produce a good deal of information. But they are expensive and time-consuming; scheduling difficulties can arise, and the information collected at times is not easily analyzed.
- Surveys allow the collection of information for a large population, are fairly easy to construct, are relatively inexpensive, and allow for the easy transfer of information for analysis. But the return rate is often low, with no opportunity for follow-up questions. Also, surveys typically offer little chance for detailed responses, and they are impersonal.
- Publications and the media provide easy, inexpensive collection as well as access to a wide variety of sources. Large quantities of information can be collected from many organizations. Like other methods listed here, however, the process is time-consuming, the validity of the sources can be hard to establish, and determining which information is most important may be difficult.
- Archival information is easy and inexpensive to collect, but data often are missing, poorly organized, and have limited applicability.

Spendolini (1992) points out that each of these methods requires planning. For example, telephone interviews, while easy to conduct, should be scheduled in advance with the people in the organization who can provide you with the information you need. Simply deciding who to call can be difficult. "Cold calling" almost never works, except as a preliminary inquiry. Further, an interview schedule should be sent in advance for the person to review, so that he or she may review and check sources of information before the telephone interview.

The planning required for a site visit is even more complicated. Schedules must be developed, and appointments confirmed; you must decide who to interview, and address any other logistical problems. In addition, surveys must be carefully developed. User-friendly surveys increase the response rate and are more easily analyzed.

Critical to all of these methods is the necessity of insuring that the people and organizations being benchmarked have a clear idea about why you are gathering information, how you will gather it, and, most important, how the information will ultimately be used. This is especially important if confidential information is shared. There should be clear understandings about all of these issues before the data-gathering process begins.

Step Eight: Analyze the Data

Once the data are collected, a method of organization must be developed to help solve the problem that triggered the benchmarking process in the first place. In many respects, analyzing information culled in a comparable institutions assessment can be conducted using techniques described in previous chapters of this book on quantitative and qualitative assessment. With the exception of surveys, most of the data collection techniques outlined above are qualitative in nature, and thus best analyzed through the means discussed in Chapters Three and Nine.

Spendolini (1992) offers some other pointers for comparable institutions assessment. He believes that information collected should be screened to uncover misinformation. This is most easily performed by comparing data from different sources and methodologies. For example, a written report may contain information which is at variance with interview data. Also, common trends or patterns may emerge from different sources. In addition, missing information also may be instructive, prompting the question, "What didn't they tell us, and why?"

In the end, however, the data analysis should yield information that addresses the problem identified initially, and in a form that is usable. It should include specific recommendations and solutions which address specific problems. Again, data analysis should involve the whole benchmarking team.

Step Nine: Take Action

It may seem obvious that the benchmarking process should result in concrete action, but this is not necessarily the case. The easiest actions to take, of course, are those which save resources, or require little or no additional resources. When substantial resources are required to solve the problem, action may be more difficult to take. To solve the problem, the leadership must acquire additional resources, or other programs, services, and processes must be down-sized or eliminated. These are not easy decisions, and are probably best addressed in advance of the benchmarking process; that is, the leadership should clearly state at the outset that only those solutions which are within available resources should be considered.

Step Ten: Assess the Action Taken

Once action is taken, there should be assessment mechanisms in place to determine if the action taken actually solved the problem—whether it improved the service, product, or process. For example, as a result of changes made in the health service "wait time" study, was "wait time" actually reduced, and if so, were students and staff satisfied that the steps taken did not create other problems?

Keys to Successful Benchmarking

First, benchmarking should be done correctly or not at all. When steps in the process described above are skipped or ignored, the credibility of the whole process will suffer, and the results will be less useful.

Second, benchmarking should involve those who are directly affected. The general rule is to involve those people closest to the problem or the client served, and give them the authority to make changes based on the benchmarking process. In student affairs, it is especially important to involve students at all stages in the proc-ess. To be sure, their contributions will vary depending on the prob-lem being addressed, but they should not be excluded.

Third, benchmarking should have the support and commit-ment of the leadership of the organization. The leadership can demonstrate its support by clearly stating the purposes and limita-tions of benchmarking, providing resources for the benchmarking process, and taking appropriate action once the process has been completed.

Fourth, benchmarking is most useful when the organizations selected are comparable, willing to participate and cooperate, and can offer reliable and valid information. One of the keys to find-ing such organizations is to select those for which reciprocation is possible. The whole process can be enhanced through a quid pro quo arrangement, in which your organization becomes a benchmark for the other organization in exchange for their cooperation in your benchmarking assessment. As time passes, networks of benchmarking organizations make possible ongoing benchmarking relationships.

Conclusion

In this chapter, we have tried to make the case for benchmarking as a viable part of a comprehensive student affairs assessment program. When conducted correctly, a benchmarking study can (1) justify the existence of student affairs, (2) improve quality, (3) demonstrate affordability, (4) develop strategic plans, (5) formulate policy, and (6) aid in making decisions. Benchmarking is a time-honored way of proving one's worth in higher education, and should a part of any student affairs assessment program.

Chapter Twelve

Measuring Effectiveness Against Professional Standards

Theodore K. Miller

As noted in other chapters, in order to be effective, student affairs assessment must be based on a thorough understanding of its institutional context, so that this context influences the assessment processes and procedures and is in turn influenced by them. In effect, student affairs assessment does not (and cannot) function outside of its institutional context. Valuable assessment always operates as an integral part of the larger whole, which in this instance is the institution of higher education and the larger society in which it functions.

Consequently, when student affairs assessment is contemplated, it must be conceptualized and operationalized within the system of which it is a part. To do otherwise is to act as if the field of student affairs is an autonomous, self-contained, and self-directed social agency that is neither responsible to those outside its ranks nor accountable to its highly diverse group of constituents.

This means that a comprehensive student affairs assessment model must measure any student affairs operation against professional standards that have been promulgated by professional associations, regional accrediting agencies, and others. The purpose of this chapter is to identify sources of these professional standards, and to present several criterion-based assessment models, focusing on those promulgated by the Council for the Advancement of Standards for Higher Education (CAS). Other models, including regional accrediting agencies, peer review, reputational rankings and ratings, and certification and licensure review, are also discussed. Finally, two approaches to the application of assessment strategies, program review and strategic planning, will be outlined and discussed.

Models of Professional Standards

CAS Standards and Guidelines

The Council for the Advancement of Standards in Higher Education was chartered in 1979 as a consortium of professional associations dedicated to developing, publishing, and promulgating standards of professional practice and preparation for student services and student development programs in higher education. The enormous impact of CAS on the field of student affairs has been noted in the professional literature (Bryan, Winston, and Miller, 1991; Mable and Miller, 1983, 1991; Miller, 1984). CAS takes the position that each institution, and each functional area within, is responsible for achieving its goals and purposes through self-regulation.

CAS has developed and promulgated some nineteen functional area standards and guidelines (S&Gs) for student programs and services, and is currently developing additional sets of functional area standards. The standards were created with the intent of providing higher education professionals with criterion measures against which they could assess and make judgments about the character and quality of their programs, services, and facilities. This self-regulation approach assumes that both institutions and individual departments wish to assess the extent to which they are accomplishing their stated purposes using a set of nationally derived norms as criterion measures against which to make judgments. In effect, CAS S&Gs were promulgated for the sole purpose of providing criteria that individual institutions and programs could use to implement self-evaluations.

CAS functional area standards and guidelines have been published for academic advising, admissions programs and services, alcohol and other drug programs, career planning and placement, college unions, commuter student programs and services, counseling services, disabled student services, fraternity and sorority advising, housing and residential life programs, judicial programs and services, learning assistance programs, minority student programs and services, recreational sports, religious programs, research and evaluation, student activities, student orientation programs, and women student programs and services. In addition several others are in the process of being developed for financial aid programs and services, international student office programs and services, registrar programs and services, student leadership programs, and others.

In the name of user utility, an operational version of each functional area standard adopted by CAS has been created and organized into a *CAS Self-Assessment Guide* (SAG), which practitioners can use when assessing a given student support program or service. Each SAG has thirteen components, each of which is designed to focus upon an essential aspect of a comprehensive student program or service area, including mission, program, leadership and management, organization and administration, human resources, funding, facilities, legal responsibilities, equal opportunity, access, affirmative action, campus and community relations, multicultural programs and services, ethics, and evaluation.

The SAG is composed of three major sections, the first of which introduces the guide, details the roles of documentation and assessment in the self-study process, and outlines follow-up action steps that can be implemented to assure maximum benefit. The second section has been organized into a workbook format, which includes each of the thirteen components and offers opportunity to focus attention on specific details of the standards by providing lists of criterion measures that can be rated on a Likert-type scale. Space also is provided within each component for identifying and summarizing the documentation used to evaluate to what degree the program is in compliance with the standard. In addition, space is available to describe discrepancies noted between the assessment criteria and functional area practice; space is also available to delineate corrective actions needed and/or recommendations for ways to improve a program. The third and final section of the SAG is a reprint of the functional area S&Gs that integrate the CAS general standards, common to all functional areas, with the standards and guidelines specific to the functional area under consideration, which are unique to that particular program or service.

Standards are distinguished from guidelines by the use of auxiliary verbs and print. Standards invariably include the auxiliary verbs *must* or *shall,* while guidelines use *should* or *may.* Likewise, standards are printed in bold type, while guidelines are not. Because the CAS S&Gs are viewed as minimal standards of practice, functional area programs under review may, at their discretion, identify selected guidelines to be used as standards. In other words, institutions and programs can hold themselves to higher standards than those promulgated by CAS if they so wish. In this way, CAS S&Gs set a lower limit for all institutions and their departments to follow, but allow for individual institutions to increase the standard level they wish to pursue.

A CAS Self-Regulation Example

Those wishing to use the CAS S&Gs to evaluate departments will benefit from reviewing *Putting the CAS Standards to Work* (Yerian and Miller, 1988). This training manual was prepared especially to instruct practitioners on using the *CAS Self-Assessment Guides* (Miller, Thomas, Looney, and Yerian, 1988) effectively for program development and related self-study purposes. The manual includes thirty-one transparency masters, which can be used to prepare overhead transparencies for group training purposes. Although the functional area example presented in the manual focuses on the Academic Advising standards and guidelines, it is relatively simple to create complementary transparencies for use with the other eighteen functional area standards, such as housing and residential life, student activities, and student orientation programs.

The following example of implementing a self-assessment process in a housing department should help the reader understand the various steps commonly involved in a CAS-based self-study. No matter what functional area is being assessed, a similar evaluation process can be used assuming one has access to a *CAS Self-Assessment Guide* for the functional area under review.

Eight separate steps are recommended for implementing a CAS self-study. They include (1) decide on a self-study approach, (2) identify guidelines to include, (3) clarify criterion measures to be used, (4) identify and summarize evaluative data, (5) describe discrepancies between criteria and practice, (6) delineate required corrective actions, (7) recommend program enhancement actions, and (8) prepare an action plan.

There are at least two basic approaches that the housing staff members can use to implement a self-study. Staff members can either (1) seek to develop a collective consensus through group discussion and review or (2) combine the individual judgments of the various internal reviewers to determine the group's general perspective. Whichever approach is used, it is important to remember that simply rating criterion statements does not a self-study make. Rather, it is essential that the criterion measures be carefully studied and judged so as to stimulate critical thinking about housing activities and the implications routine staff behavior has for achieving the department's stated mission. In most instances, the former approach is superior to the latter because it demands that group consensus be achieved. This approach also requires that a staff dialogue be established to examine, debate, and ultimately come to a consensus about how the housing and residence life program will proceed. The latter approach, on the other hand, reflects a kind of majority rule perspective that can be divisive if there are significant differences of opinion among the staff members about the extent to which the department is meeting the standards.

Once the self-study approach has been determined, it is necessary to decide whether to include any of the *guidelines* from the CAS Housing and Residential Life standards as evaluation criteria in addition to the standards. That is, the department may wish to use criteria that go beyond the minimal standards established by CAS. For example, a guideline appears in the CAS Housing and Residential Life standards which states that the department's goals *may* include opportunities for students to *develop and exercise leadership skills*. If it were decided by the housing office to include leadership development as an expected learning or developmental outcome for students living in the halls, then a criterion measure statement to that effect would be added to the other standards for evaluation purposes. If the guideline is not included as a standard, the housing department could be in compliance with the CAS standards and yet have no student leadership program whatsoever. Consequently, it is important to consider the level of expectation the department has established for itself. For a comprehensive, well-developed, and professionally staffed housing department, minimum standards may be viewed as less than challenging and in need of enhancement. For a housing program on the other end of the organizational continuum, the minimal CAS standards may constitute a major challenge that could take several years of concerted effort to bring into compliance. Whatever the situation, inclusion of guidelines as criterion measures in the self-assessment process is completely up to the department's determination.

The next step involves systematically rating the department on the CAS criterion measures to determine how staff members judge the functional quality of the various housing programs. The SAG provides assessment criteria for each of the thirteen components. Using a five-point rating scale, where 1 represents noncompliance and 5 represents full compliance, practitioners can obtain both individual and collective estimates of the degree to which a given criterion has been met. Although interrater reliability may be initially low among staff members judging the department's functioning, intrastaff dialogue about how to interpret criterion statements will usually result in increased levels of reliability among raters as to how well the various criteria are being met.

For example, one of the mission criterion statements calls for *a well-developed, written set of housing and residential life goals that are consistent with the stated mission of the institution.* If ten staff members rate this criterion with a range of responses from 1 to 5, then interrater reliability is a concern. On the other hand, if all raters judge the criterion at a 1 or 2 level, there is evidence that the raters are in relative agreement that the department is not in compliance. Even when general agreement exists, there is value in discussing why raters judged the criteria as they did. Although SAG criterion measures were designed to be highly specific and unambiguous, it is still possible that individual raters may interpret them differently. If at all possible, structured discussions to increase interrater reliability should be initiated as part of a training process early on. One way to do this is to establish what a given rating means. For instance, a rating of 1 would reflect the lack of any written goals, while a rating of 2 might indicate that written goals exist, but are not accessible to staff members. A 3 rating (midpoint on the scale) reflects a somewhat neutral judgment and might imply that the written goals exist, but that there is ambivalence about how well they reflect the institution's mission. A rating of 4 might indicate that a set of written goals exists that is consistent with the institutional mission, but that these goals were prescribed by the housing director without staff input. A 5 rating, on the other hand, would imply that all elements of the assessment criterion statement are fully met.

The fourth step in the process is to identify and summarize the evaluative evidence that supports the preliminary rater judgments, which are necessary, but not sufficient, to a final determination. Consequently, this calls for a review of tangible evidence that supports rater judgments. It is one thing to agree on a given criterion measure, but something altogether different to provide documentation in support of that judgment. A crucial point here is that rating the assessment criteria in the S&Gs alone is not the goal of the self-study process. Rather, the process also requires documentation, which typically includes both quantitative and qualitative data.

Quantitative data concerning the existence of a written mission statement would include the written statement itself along with specific department goals. It might also include the results of staff surveys as to the appropriateness and effectiveness of the statement as a guide for department practice. The qualitative data, on the other hand, might include written or transcribed notes about the process used to develop the goals, and subjective review responses of staff members to the mission statement. It is possible that another criterion statement example would provide increased understanding of both quantitative and qualitative documentation efforts. A SAG Human Resources component criterion measure states that *there must be a sufficient number of professional staff members to carry out all aspects of housing and residential life.* Quantitative data concerning this criterion might include information about the length of time a student has to wait after requesting assistance, or the results of a student survey rating the quality of service provided or the level of security available. Qualitative data, on the other hand, might include student satisfaction checks done by random follow-up phone calls, or student interviews conducted by resident assistants. In many instances, the self-study rating process will identify the housing department's need to collect additional data to measure against various criteria. For example, a program component criterion measure stating that *the housing and residential program is responsive to the developmental and demographic profiles of the students served* can be objectively judged only if the staff members have access to data describing the profiles of students in residence. Consequently, the self-study assessment process may well stimulate considerable additional data collection for purposes of providing documentation to support the rating process.

Logic suggests that only when a problem is clearly defined can one find a viable solution. Therefore, it is important to identify and describe any discrepancies that may exist between the assessment criteria and actual housing practice. Only by outlining discrepancies fully can housing leaders be sure they are addressing all aspects of the problem, rather than simply shifting the problem to a new form. Consequently, each SAG component includes space to identify the discrepancies between standards and practice that require attention. Although most often viewed from the perspective of failure to meet a criterion measure, these discrepancies can likewise reflect positive accomplishments. That is, a housing department may well have programs, personnel, or organizational patterns that exceed the expectations of a given criterion measure. In such an instance, commendation is in order and the department should be recognized accordingly.

Once discrepancies between practice and minimal expectation have been identified, it is necessary to delineate corrective actions required to bring the department into compliance with the standard. This action calls for department staff members to determine, in some detail, the desired state of affairs or end-result being sought. To accomplish this it is often necessary to subdivide the larger change task into manageable parts. For the earlier mission statement criterion example, the approach here might be to draft a statement of goals that a subcommittee believes have been implicitly agreed upon, circulate the statement to the total staff for comment, and prepare and promulgate a final statement. This three-step process would very likely bring the department into full compliance with the criterion statement.

Even excellent housing departments have areas that can be further refined to provide residents with improved services or enhanced learning outcomes. To accomplish this, it is first necessary to recommend special actions for program enhancement. For example, a well-developed set of written goals may need more attractive packaging in order to be widely read and used. As with the resolution of discrepancies, one must identify first what is desired and then establish a set of steps that can be taken in sequence to improve quality.

Finally, after all data and related documentation are in place, all judgments made, all discrepancies noted, and all enhancements determined, it is essential for the housing department to establish an overall self-study follow-up action plan that identifies and prioritizes future directions, comparing past performance with desired outcomes.

A four-step process can be used to accomplish this task. First, review the self-study assessment for areas in which the housing department excel. Second, determine what actions are required to bring the department into compliance with the standards. This can be accomplished by identifying each criterion for which a discrepancy has been observed, listing each specific action required to achieve compliance, and establishing priorities for action on the basis of the discrepancy's overall importance. Third, identify areas in which department enhancement is desired, list each specific action recommended to strengthen and enhance the department beyond minimal standards, and prioritize the actions to be taken. Finally, finalize a department action plan to implement required changes and program enhancement action. It is wise to establish a schedule or time-line for completion of specific actions, and to identify who is responsible for completing the action tasks desired. To do otherwise may result in a situation where much energy goes into the self-study assessment process with little organizational change accomplished—to be sure, a needless waste of time and resources.

Accreditation

Accreditation has become a major force in higher education during the past half century. Readers unfamiliar with institution and program accreditation processes and procedures will benefit greatly from reviewing a special edition on accreditation of the *Journal of Higher Education,* edited by Thrash (1979), and the book *Understanding Accreditation* by Young, Chambers, Kells, and Associates (1983). The latter defines accreditation as "a process by which an institution of postsecondary education evaluates its educational activities, in whole or in part, and seeks an independent judgment to confirm that it substantially achieves its objectives and is generally equal in quality to comparable institutions or specialized units" (p. 21). The accreditation process is typically accomplished through an institutionwide or program-specific self-study which tests programs and activities against the criteria established by the accrediting agency to which the institution or program voluntarily adheres.

Young (1983) and his colleagues also made special note of what accreditation is *not*. For instance, it is not governmental, not mandatory, not a rating system, not a policing mechanism, and not an individual student or course approval system. Nevertheless, institutions and programs which seek accreditation from external agencies are highly dependent upon those bodies for formal recognition as worthwhile and high-quality institutions and programs. Although no accrediting agency holds that it functions as an "accreditation godfather" to its constituent institutions or programs, many institutions and agencies alike tend to act as if this were the case. Likewise, accrediting agencies strongly resist the notion that institutions and programs initiate their periodic accreditation self-studies because the agency requires this activity for continuing accreditation, but many constituent groups act as if this were true, because they are dependent on the agency for accreditation recognition. Consequently, it is not uncommon for institutions and programs alike to view the accrediting agency and its established criteria as obstacles that must be overcome if the institutions are to be recognized as legitimate or of high quality.

To a very significant extent, institutions and programs with this attitude tend to carry out the accreditation self-study process as if it were an academic exercise rather than an act of self-worth enhancement and program development. Although others may mandate assessment as a requirement for continued existence, its true value has great potential for transcending such a minimalist, even survivalist, viewpoint.

Both regional and specialized accrediting bodies typically establish and publish written standards that are generally agreed on by member institutions, which hold voluntary membership in accrediting agencies. These accreditation standards, which represent the criteria that member institutions and their programs use to judge quality, take various forms depending upon the accrediting body involved. Complexity in the selection of appropriate standards is compounded by the fact that there are six regional accrediting agencies, including those for the middle states, New England, the north central United States, the northwest, the southern, and the western; as well as four specialized institutional accrediting bodies including Bible colleges, independent colleges and schools, trade and technical schools, and home study institutions; and over forty agencies that accredit academic preparation programs. Most of the ten regional and specialized institutional accrediting bodies have established and published standards against which to judge the quality of student affairs programs and services within the institutions seeking accreditation under their auspices.

Although few in number, there are other accrediting agencies that accredit particular functional areas in student affairs, including the International Association of Counseling Services, Inc., which accredits counseling centers; the Accreditation Association for Ambulatory Heath Care, Inc., which accredits college health services; and the American Psychological Association, which accredits professional psychology internship programs.

Although the standards vary considerably for student affairs and student services practice promulgated by institutional level accrediting bodies, from highly prescribed to relatively ambiguous criteria, each agency's standards can be used to assess student affairs divisions. Fortunately, any given institution will likely be a member of only one of these bodies, depending upon the type and/or location of the institution. In light of this, it is essential that the chief student affairs officer include a copy of the most recent version of the regional or institutional accreditation criteria in the office library so that all staff members can access it. Although most regional accrediting agencies require a formal accreditation self-study assessment and review only once a decade, it is prudent always to keep the criteria in mind and use them conscientiously as part of the institution's continuing process of program development. For instance, many student affairs leaders have found it prudent to use the standards in outline form to frame the annual report format.

Although the agencies that accredit academic preparation programs typically do not promulgate specific standards for student affairs practice, they usually include standards concerning student matriculates' support, such as admission and retention, financial assistance, academic advising, and student records criteria (Crosson, 1988). In only rare instances, however, would an institution's student affairs or student services programs use these academic preparation criteria.

Typically, the standards established for accreditation purposes are considerably more general than the CAS or other functional area standards. For example, the Southern Association of Colleges and Schools (SACS) devotes approximately three pages of its standards (1992) to student development services, compared to the CAS standards and guidelines, which devote approximately eight pages to each functional area for which standards have been promulgated. Most other regional accrediting agencies provide even fewer student affairs related standards than SACS does. Consequently, the use of regional accrediting body standards for program assessment purposes is fraught with considerable ambiguity and lack of specific guidelines. Even the SACS criteria, which are comparatively comprehensive for regional accrediting agency standards, identify only ten student affairs areas by function and even then in relatively terse terms. Because of the limitations inherent in these accrediting body criteria, some colleges and universities have used more comprehensive standards as criteria for self-study and other program assessment purposes (Bryan, Winston, and Miller, 1991).

Although only institutions in the southern United States will use the Southern Association of Colleges and Schools Commission on Colleges *Criteria for Accreditation* (1992) for self-study purposes, exposure to the SACS accreditation approach has utility for all colleges and universities. Section 5.5, Student Development Services, contains some twenty-three *must* criterion measure statements, which represent the essential criteria for all accreditation self-study purposes. Although additional criteria may be incorporated into the self-study process by an institution under review, SACS requires that these twenty-three criteria be met if a division of student affairs is to be found in compliance with the standards. Nine criterion measures to judge the scope, accountability, and resources of the division and its departments are in place, while fourteen other criteria are used to judge the quality and effectiveness of programs and services, including academic advising; counseling and career development; health services; student government, activities, and publications; student behavior, records, and financial aid; and residence halls.

SACS criterion measures include statements such as "The institution *must* clearly designate an administrative unit responsible for planning and implementing student development services," "Human, physical, financial, and equipment resources for student development services *must* be allocated on the basis of predetermined needs and *must* be adequate to support the goals of the institution," and "The institution *must* publish a statement of student rights and responsibilities and make this available to the campus community" (Southern Association of Colleges and Schools, 1992, pp. 49–51). These examples represent the essence of the SACS criteria promulgated to assess student affairs units throughout the southern states. Although limited in scope, such criteria promote a level of quality assurance for all who associate themselves with SACS-accredited institutions. Though voluntary in nature, the regional accrediting agencies provide an important service of quality assurance to the country at large.

Peer Review

It is quite common for institutions and programs desirous of accreditation to focus on self-study reviews. Although a limited number of accrediting agencies require formal peer review visitations only when the self-study fails to provide adequate information for making an informed accreditation judgment—for example, the Council on Rehabilitation Education (CORE)—the vast majority have built formal peer review into the evaluation process. This approach puts the onus of responsibility for determining program quality on a visiting team of well qualified colleagues, usually from comparable institutions, who spend a period of time—typically two to four days—reviewing and validating the institution's or program's self-study report. Consequently, the visiting team's peer review report is prepared using the accrediting agency's criteria for judging institution or program compliance. The peer review is then used by accrediting agency leaders to make final decisions about whether accreditation will be granted. Although expensive and time-consuming, peer review is considered one of the most effective ways of assuring that the institution or program is in compliance with the accrediting agency's standards.

Likewise, peer review is often used separately from the accreditation process, usually as part of an academic or student affairs program development or internal review process. Employing well-qualified professionals with high levels of expertise to provide peer review judgments is an increasingly common practice, especially in instances where institutional leaders wish to ascertain from objective others how well the institution's programs and services are functioning. As noted later in this chapter, peer review can aid the self-regulation approach also, in that it can be helpful to have external evaluators visit and review a student affairs department or division for purposes of validating a program's self-study findings.

Reputational Rankings and Ratings

Closely related to accreditation and peer review processes is the reputational ratings approach to measuring institutional quality. This approach, which relies heavily upon subjective judgment, is somewhat flawed. Although Astin and Solmon (1981) identified two major dimensions, (1) scholarly and professional accomplishment and (2) commitment to undergraduate teaching, they concluded that reputational ratings of undergraduate programs may be unnecessary because comparable, and perhaps more objective, data can be obtained through other means. Reputational ratings, which often include reference to institutional image, conditions, or resources (such as national rankings, library holdings, endowments, number of nationally recognized faculty or Nobel Laureates, rigorous admission criteria, and numbers of students served), have increasingly lost credence over the years, largely because there are few if any ways to correlate the relationship between reputation and results. In effect, higher education institutions and programs have sought to transcend subjective judgment as a primary means for ascertaining quality. Although an institution's image may well influence the perceptions of its constituents, reputation does not and cannot assure the quality of education at a particular institution.

Certification and Licensure

Often, especially when professional education programs are involved, governmental or professional association credentialing processes can be used for assessment purposes, albeit indirectly. From this perspective, professional certification and public licensure criteria can be brought into play. Use of these evaluation processes and procedures, however, is peripheral to direct assessment, for their primary job is to ensure that individuals, not programs, are qualified to provide the public with services that would not only be viewed as unprofessional, but also would be illegal without official sanction. For example, the certification of teachers and the licensing of professional counselors and psychologists, as well as many other professional service providers, has become commonplace throughout the country in order to protect the general public from unqualified or unscrupulous individuals who may take advantage of them. Whether it likes it or not, higher education is inextricably involved with licensure, even when controversy rages over whether public regulation of practice is in the best interests of academe.

Bogue and Saunders (1992), for instance, note several criticisms common to licensure that deserve attention. These criticisms suggest that licensure (1) is self-serving, (2) has not been proved to exclude incompetents, (3) excludes many competent and deserving individuals, (4) mitigates the voluntary nature of accreditation, and (5) exhibits disturbing and counterproductive contradictions to the actions of policy makers. In other words, although licensure's very existence influences academe, academic programs and faculty have limited autonomy for establishing and amending the content and process of their professional academic offerings if society expects practitioners to meet specific license criteria upon completing academic programs.

To a lesser extent, the same is true of other forms of professional certification, even when the regulatory agency consists of an association of professionals who seek to assure the public that practitioners are qualified (through education and experience) to function as professional service providers. Clearly, as with accreditation affirmation, the certifying and licensing agencies demand that the institutions which provide instruction to seekers of licenses offer programs of study compatible with licensure criteria. In other words, if a professional license to practice is the desired result of the educational process, then academic programs and curricula must provide the quality of instruction demanded by the regulatory agencies; if they do not, their graduates will not be well served. Consequently, licensure and certification standards become a driving force that promulgates the criteria by which academic programs can, and do, judge their quality and success. From this perspective, if its graduates cannot pass the licensure exam or meet certification criteria, then the academic program has failed to achieve its mission.

Applications of Professional Standards Models

The models described above can be applied in several ways to systematic efforts to assess student affairs, including program reviews, strategic planning, and outcomes assessments. Since outcomes assessment is covered in Chapter Ten, this discussion will focus on the first two applications.

Internal Program Review

An assessment approach that has great value is the internal program review, which focuses on how effectively a program is accomplishing its stated goals. Program review and its closely related counterpart, program development, lends itself well to self-regulation as an approach to assessment, although it may also have utility for accreditation purposes. Program reviews often utilize peer review as a method of evaluation, but external evaluation is not essential. However, criteria must be agreed upon for judging the capacity of the program to accomplish its stated purpose, efficiency, or effectiveness. Whether initiated by an individual program, by a single institution, or a system of institutions, or by a state government, program reviews (sometimes referred to as program audits) are most often used to evaluate financial, educational, political, or ethical areas of concern. Further, program reviews tend to be designed to answer certain questions: Are program goals relevant and being met? Are program resources adequate and well applied? And how can the program be improved? (Bogue and Saunders, 1992).

While program reviews can be quite comprehensive or can focus on a particular area of concern, multiple measures are strongly encouraged. Further, the more clearly defined the purpose of the review, the more likely the results will have value. Prior to initiating the program review, a decision must be made regarding what criterion measures will be used. In instances where relevant professional standards, such as those promulgated by CAS, are in place, the review process can be initiated with relative ease. Where written standards are not available, considerable time may be required to decide which criteria to use and how to use them. In either instance, however, a consensus must be reached regarding program reviews, among those who will carry out the review as well as those who will use the results. There is little utility in implementing a program review if those involved are not clear about why the process is being initiated, what it is intended to accomplish, and how the results will be used.

Strategic Planning

An institution's strategic plan invariably will be value-driven and founded on values shared by members of the academic community (Bryson, 1988). Consequently, the process begins with a values audit in which the institution seeks to identify and clarify those values held most dear by the academic community. As with all quality enhancement approaches to institutional and program development, strategic planning begins with the institution's mission statement as a foundation and moves to identify specific ways its designated purposes can be implemented. This process calls for reexamination of institutional purpose, identity, and philosophy, and raises questions such as: Does the existing statement of purpose reflect our current and most cherished values? What are the primary reasons for this institution's existence? In what do we believe? Into which endeavors do we wish to place our available resources? What do we wish to emphasize in both the short and long term? From these deliberations should come a series of institutional themes, which can be used to guide the subsequent planning process.

An institutional theme may be defined as a reflection of the college or university's mission and purpose. It provides a framework for the development of strategic direction and well-considered goals for the institution. A theme articulates the values of the institution, identifies areas of special emphasis, and suggests areas in which increased levels of excellence may be sought.

After conceptualizing several institutional themes, a strategic plan can be established. Such a plan typically begins by setting goals and objectives designed to give specific direction to the institution's activities. For example, what do we, as an institution of higher learning, want to accomplish? How do we wish our mission, purposes, and themes to become manifest? What types of educated people, scholarly products, and public services do we wish to encourage? In effect, what does this institution wish to accomplish in the immediate and long-range future within the context of changing social and institutional conditions? One of the most valuable products of a strategic planning initiative may well be that information which can be used to set policy and make operational decisions. In most instances, strategic planning can be accomplished at various levels of an organization. For example, a division of student affairs and its departmental subunits might establish strategic plans individually and collectively in support of the institution's strategic planning initiatives.

Other important strategic plan categories include such things as assessing current status, formulating action plans, establishing formative criteria, and determining outcome measures. Unless we know where we are in relation to established goals and objectives, it is virtually impossible to progress effectively toward the desired goals. One excellent method for this type of goal assessment is the Force Field Analysis method developed by Lewin (1936) in which institutional driving forces and restraining forces that impact goal achievement can be identified in order to judge a goal's current status within the institutional environment. Miller, Carpenter, Saunders, and Thompson (1980) describe in some detail the use of this method as part of an action planning model which has utility for those student affairs practitioners who wish to encourage and promote systematic change. Readers desiring an in-depth examination of strategic planning will benefit from reviewing Bryson's book, *Strategic Planning for Public and Nonprofit Organizations* (1988).

Applying Professional Standards

Though growing at a relatively modest pace, the professional literature in the area of professional standards and assessment criteria is slowly increasing. One of the most definitive publications to date in this area is Bryan, Winston, and Miller's *Using Professional Standards in Student Affairs* (1991). This 110-page monograph presents a historical perspective of professional standards and their use in the accreditation process; the application of standards in program evaluation and professional preparation; strategies and tools for using standards in outcome assessments; and five examples of the practical uses of CAS standards. In addition, the book includes four appendixes that provide contacts and addresses of accrediting agencies, standards councils, and institutions which have used CAS standards. Readers, especially those interested in applying CAS standards, are encouraged to examine this monograph.

Several institutions of higher learning, as well as state systems, have used professional standards for assessment purposes to good avail. In a midwestern state, for instance, the CAS standards and guidelines were used in conjunction with institutional personnel data during a state review of the salary structure for higher education student affairs personnel. Early indications suggested that the state's central personnel office viewed college student affairs staff members as little more than classified staff members who had minimal professional responsibilities for accomplishing the state institutions' educational missions. After considerable dialogue, documentation, and the sharing of CAS standards with officials to validate minimum professional qualifications and competencies required, the pay-grade levels for student affairs staff members (which leaders hoped could be maintained at their current levels) were increased from two to six pay grades, based on what the CAS standards called for and what was really occurring in the field. The student affairs professional most intimately involved in this review process indicated that the CAS standards provided the foundation and the support for people trying to understand the profession. Further, he noted that in all likelihood the student affairs practitioners would not have been able to bring about the pay-scale increases without the CAS standards.

Similarly, a western state college system used the CAS standards as a vehicle for framing job descriptions and outcome objectives for the various student affairs functional areas and departments throughout the system. In another case, an eastern state university used CAS, ACHA, and IACS standards to create an action plan for fourteen student affairs departments. The resulting action plan manual identified, for each department, areas of excellence that are currently in place, a list of desired actions stated in outcome objective form, the schedule for accomplishment, and the individual or individuals responsible for implementing the action. Examples of the more than 250 department outcome objectives: (1) hire a graduate assistant or intern to work with the existing divisional committee, (2) adopt written goals within the division and review department goals in relation to the division goals, (3) increase training for peer evaluators of student employees, (4) offer at least six study skills assessment and remediation sessions, (5) have the Greek Housing Task Force examine space in which chapters can store essential equipment and hold ritual or special ceremonies, and (6) promote the African American Scholars Program to faculty. Although not all of the desired objectives for developmental outcome assessment purposes are stated, the resulting document reflects a major effort to enhance the developmental quality of student life and the capacity of the institution to assess that quality.

Many professionals throughout the country have indicated that even when a full-blown systematic assessment process is not in place, the availability of professional standards such as those promulgated by CAS have great utility for staff and program development, position description, and departmental mission development purposes. Although professional standards reflect the criterion measures used to evaluate departments and institutions, they have educational functions as well, as indicated above, through staff development and explaining student affairs to wider audiences.

Conclusion

Applying professional standards when assessing student affairs is an essential part of an overall comprehensive assessment program. When conducted properly, this form of assessment must be conceptualized and operationalized within the systems framework of which it is a part; and the criteria that are used to judge effectiveness must reflect the mission and purposes of the institution as well as that of the student support services under examination.

Several viable assessment models are available to guide those providing support services to students in institutions of higher education. These include the CAS Self-Regulation Assessment Model, accreditation, peer review, reputational rankings, and certification. Each has potential for assessing service programs and student services, and all present measurable criteria against which to judge program quality and student outcomes achievement.

An important implication of using professional standards to assess student affairs concerns the forces that drive the assessment processes being initiated. Institutional values, as reflected in purpose and mission statements, drive functional area programs and services. It is essential that all who are assessing higher education institutions take this into account when they plan and implement programs designed to influence the education and development of college students. Further, whatever the reason for initiation or the department targeted, the assessment process is not an autonomous, freestanding activity. Accordingly, practitioners must keep in mind that both they and the programs and services for which they are responsible function within the context of a larger higher education system and that any action taken at one level has consequences for other levels within the system, influencing results throughout. Assessment has great potential for student affairs practitioners, but it carries with it great obligations as well. To be truly effective, investigators must consider very carefully the established criteria used to judge effectiveness and quality.

Part Three

Assessment Challenges for Practitioners

Chapter Thirteen

Reporting and Using Assessment Results

Nothing is more frustrating than to conduct an assessment study of high quality and then learn, usually over some period of time, that the decision makers failed to act on the study's findings. There are many reasons why some assessment studies end up on a shelf gathering dust, or filed under "I" for "Interesting." The most cynical view, of course, is that assessment studies are political acts that occur in a context where power, ideology, and interest are more powerful determinants of decision making than feedback about the effectiveness of a policy or program (Cook and Shadish, 1986). A more realistic view, based on our experience, is that political realities, public pressures, bureaucratic survival instincts, failure of leadership, and perhaps most important, scarcity of resources all can prevent assessment studies from being used to drive decisions, make policy, and improve effectiveness. Nevertheless, there are some things an investigator can and should do to increase the likelihood that a study will be used and become part of the evaluation process.

It is not just the investigator who ends up frustrated when a study is not used. If it is well known that a study is being conducted, and several audiences expect the results will have an impact on their lives, the failure to use the results increases these people's distrust of decision makers and cynicism about their motives. So the stakes are very high, both for decision makers, impacted audiences, and the investigator.

The basic question, then, is how should investigators develop, conduct, and report assessment studies in ways that draw them into the evaluation process and create an impact? The purpose of this chapter is to suggest some basic rules which, if followed, increase the likelihood that assessments will be applied to decision making, policy development, and problem solving. A plan for interpreting and using assessments will also be presented.

Rules for Making Good Use of Assessment Results

Rule One: Do Not Do a Study That No One Really Wants

It has been our experience that some assessments have no impact because they are studies that decision makers were never prepared to deal with in the first place. The reality is that in some instances, no one really wants to know or use the findings of a study. For example, commissioning a study may be a good way of enhancing decision making, or it may be the perfect way to buy time and delay a decision. Who can argue with the administrator who says, "We need some time to study this problem before we make a decision."

So the first thing an investigator must try to ascertain is whether or not the institution's decision makers are serious about using the results of a particular study. To be sure, this is not an always easy task, but attempts should be made nevertheless. It is better to prevent a study from being conducted than to face the awkward situation of ignoring or burying a study which may embarrass or, worse yet, put the institution at risk politically, legally, or publicly.

For example, a few years ago a study was proposed (and actually conducted) to determine if gender or race biases were reflected in the salaries of student affairs employees at an institution where the track record of hiring and maintaining women and minorities was not particularly good. Unfortunately, there was little, if any, discussion of what might be done if bias was found. The study did, in fact, find that women and minorities were paid less than other employees, even after factors such as education, prior relevant experience, length of time in the position, merit raises, and other factors were taken into account. Only after the study was completed did it become obvious that no money was available to address these inequities, the institution feared that if the findings fell into the "wrong" hands, both public relations and legal challenges might result, and, therefore, the institution had no intention of doing anything with the findings except to bury them as deep as possible. As a result, insofar as possible the investigator must determine, in advance of the study, if the institution is serious about using the study's results.

The best way to determine if decision makers *really* want the study is to pose the question, "If we find (fill in with some particularly sensitive or controversial results), what if anything will you do?" If the decision maker says he or she can deal with the findings, then at least there is some indication that the study will be used. If the answer is more equivocal, then the question of whether or not the study should be done should be reopened.

Rule Two: Determine How Confidential the Study Will Be

Two questions on confidentiality need to be asked in advance of a study: Who will know if the study is being conducted, and who will have access to the results? With regard to the first question, there may be some instances where decision makers will want to commission a study without anyone knowing it is being done, for whatever reasons. The investigator needs to know how "public" the study is, and what rules of confidentiality apply. Such secrecy is most easily maintained when the data gathering is restricted to institutional records. For example, an institution can conduct a retention study in relative secrecy, using institutional records alone instead of contacting students directly.

With regard to the second question, who will have access to the results, the choices range from total confidentiality to total public disclosure. The salary study mentioned above was completed in complete confidentiality; the investigators used information drawn from confidential institutional files as their source, and submitted their results to the chief student affairs officer only.

At the next level of confidentiality, it is possible to conduct studies which are accessible only to the unit(s) affected. For example, in the study of placement interviewers mentioned in Chapter Four, access to the report was restricted to the placement service employees, for their use in improving interviewer satisfaction. At yet another level of confidentiality, student needs studies might be made available to all student affairs units, as well as to other appropriate units within the institution.

At the most open level of disclosure, the entire campus community would share the results. For example, environmental studies and cultural audits are typically designed to engage the campus community in a dialogue about a particular problem or issue, and this dialogue should be open.

The problem comes, of course, when the findings of a study might upset an intended audience, or some other audience, and the temptation arises to change the conditions of the extent of public disclosure agreed upon at the outset. For example, if a study of the racial climate on campus finds that there is much bigotry and discrimination, does this information help or hurt efforts to build equitable and just campus environments? Administrators may believe such information would simply inflame racial tensions, while those who are victims of bigotry may believe such information would bring a level of awareness necessary for change.

One of the best ways to determine how confidential a study will be is to pose the question to the decision maker: "If we find (fill in with results that may upset some audiences), who should know the results?" If for whatever reasons, the decision maker opts for limiting the results to certain audiences, the investigator can design and report the study accordingly.

Rule Three: Determine Who Should Be Involved in the Study

Too often, the decision to conduct a study results from some negotiation between the decision maker and the investigator. The decision maker says, I need such and such information, and the investigator determines if the information is retrievable, how many resources will be needed, and how soon the study can be completed. However, because the effects of a study are seldom restricted to the decision maker and the investigator, if a study is to have an impact, those affected by the results must be involved from the very beginning.

According to Jacobi, Astin, and Ayala (1987), those persons affected by the research can and should be involved in all phases of the research, including the development of objectives, design, interpretation of results, and recommendations for action. Such involvement increases the likelihood that they will take the results seriously. For example, in Chapter Two, a study of the reasons why

African American students underused the counseling center was described. The reader will note that African American students and counseling center staff were very involved in the design and implementation of the study. As a result, the findings had much greater credibility with those affected, as well as with those who were most able to do something about the problem.

This is not to say that whether or not a study is conducted, or how it is conducted, is voted upon by those who will be affected by changes the study recommends. We do, however, argue for the involvement of and consultation with at least a representative sample of those to be affected by the results. One of the best indicators of involvement is to pose the question, "Who will be affected by these results, and how can they become involved in the study?" Such involvement not only goes a long way toward insuring that results will be used, but it also helps investigators build trust and confidence of those to be affected by the findings.

Rule Four: Conduct a Good Study

This rule may be too obvious to even mention, but the quality of a study may determine if it will be used by decision makers or have credibility with intended audiences. Here, the experience and expertise of the investigator assumes center stage, because the quality of a study is in his or her hands; the investigator must make sure that all those characteristics of a good study identified in earlier chapters are present.

The best way to determine the quality of a study is to pose the question, "If I were to be an unfriendly critic of this study, what would I attack?" Then, point by point, the investigator must deal with the criticisms, either by acknowledging limitations or by strengthening the study based on anticipated criticisms. Also, knowing where a study will be attacked will also help frame the way it is reported.

Rule Five: Write a Good Report

Even if everything we have recommended is taken into account, a study's findings may be ignored because the report is unreadable. The most common mistake investigators make is to send a complete and comprehensive report (most often modeled after a typical doctoral dissertation) to all intended audiences. While a comprehensive and complete report should certainly be written, sending the whole thing to everyone is a colossal mistake. It will be intimidating, it won't be read, and, as a result, it will likely have no impact. If, however, an intended audience *requests* the whole report, there is certainly no problem in meeting that request.

The basic question then, according to Erwin (1991), is, "How can educators adopt reporting strategies which allow assessment information to contribute in positive ways to the decision-making process?" Following from this question, the investigator must ask whether, given all the other realities mentioned above, a study should be reported in ways that result in better decisions and policies. In short, just how does one go about writing a report that will be read and used?

Suskie (1992) offers a series of suggestions about how to report the findings of a study. The first step is to determine the audience, or audiences; who will read and use the findings? Often, there is more than one audience. Depending on the study, potential audiences may include students, student affairs professional staff, the chief student affairs officer, the central administration, the board of control, alumni, the students' families, the local community, state legislatures, and the general public. If, as discussed above, audiences were identified before the study, then the task is relatively simple. On the other hand, if there is a change in the intended audience, this should be taken into account before writing the report. The following questions must be asked:

Will readers already be familiar with the study, or will you have to start from scratch?

Do readers have the time to review an extensive report or will they want only a short summary?

Will readers want only your findings, or will they want to know how you arrived at them?

Are readers knowledgeable about research methods, or will you need to explain them?

Are readers likely to be friendly or unfriendly toward the results? Can you anticipate criticisms?

Are readers likely to be questioned about the study by others?

The answers to these questions may determine not only how the report will be written, but whether several different versions are necessary. Our experience has taught us that it's best to write a total and comprehensive report, and then to issue subreports to various audiences, depending upon the answers to the questions.

The second step in reporting findings, according to Suskie (1992), is to determine the appropriate format, given the intended audience. Listed below are several options, from the simplest to the most comprehensive:

- A few *tables* summarizing the findings may be all that is needed, if the audience is already familiar with the study. However, even then, some readers may have difficulty understanding charts and tables. If this option is used, a couple of explanatory paragraphs should be included.

- A one- or two-page *executive summary* may be all that is needed for an audience that is only interested in the results. An executive summary gives a quick overview of the purpose, methods, findings, and recommendations of the study.

- A *short report* (three to five pages) based on the full report provides more detail than the executive summary without burdening readers with the full report.

- Creating *supplemental reports* is an excellent way to get the details of the study only to those people who would really be interested. For example, in a comprehensive study of student satisfaction with student services, a supplemental report focusing on student satisfaction with residence halls could be sent to the residence hall staff, which may be more appropriate than asking them to wade through an entire report.

- A *complete report* should always be written; it should contain a description of what was done, an explanation of why it was done that way, and discussion of all the findings and conclusions. (See the next section for the format we suggest for a complete report.) Even if it is sent to no one (and there are good reasons for doing that, as discussed above), it should nevertheless be written as a resource should anyone either require more information or wish to study the topic further.

- *Multiple reports* may be tailored to different audiences. For example, a college president with little time to read an entire report may only need an executive summary. Decision makers may want a complete report, while the institution's public relations office may want only a short summary upon which to base a press release.

The third step in the process of writing a report is to include in it the following components, based on Suskie (1992) and our own experience:

- *A meaningful title.* Very often, the title alone may convince potential readers to read or discard a report. Going back to the study of the underuse of counseling services discussed in Chapter Two, there are several options. The title might be very generic: "African Americans' Perceptions of Counseling Services." It might be tied more closely to the purpose of the study: "Why African Americans Underuse Counseling Services." Or it might be tied to the results of the study: "Ways to Improve African American Use of Counseling Services."

The pure researchers, of course, would choose the generic title, but as we have said many times in this book, assessment is not research. Based on our experience, the more eye-catching and specific the title, the more likely the study will be read, so either the second or third title above would be our choice.

- *An executive summary.* Based on our experience, the executive summary is probably the most important form of the report, because it will be the most widely read. It is also the most difficult to write. The executive summary should be accurate, reflecting precisely what is said in the study itself, not paraphrased or generalized. It should also be short; one page is preferable, two pages is tolerable, and more than two pages is unacceptable. The executive summary is difficult to write because on the one hand, it must be accurate and short, but on the other hand, it must not oversimplify or overreach for meaning. Because the executive summary is so important, we have included an example at the end of this chapter.

- *A statement of purpose.* The reader needs to know what problem was addressed in the study, why the study was conducted, and what it was designed to discover. In some instances, with an uninformed readership, some background or literature review may be appropriate. Throughout this book, we have stressed over and over the importance of defining the problem and identifying the purpose of a study before it is conducted, so that if the study was done properly, writing this part of the report should be relatively easy.

- *Design.* The reader needs to know not only what the design was, but why it was chosen. In several earlier chapters, we have discussed the appropriateness of qualitative versus quantitative research (or the use of both), and the report should explain why particular methodologies were chosen for the study. Instruments, interview protocols, sampling, data collection, analysis, and other appropriate design information should be included. But perhaps most important of all, the limitations of the design should be spelled out. This includes not only limitations inherent in the methods chosen, but subsequent limitations as the study progressed, such as a low response rate, the unrepresentativeness of the usable sample, confusion over interview or survey questions, and other issues.

- *Results.* Since readers' knowledge and sophistication will vary, reporting the results can become complicated. Our rule of thumb is to report the results as if all readers were well informed and sophisticated. For quantitative studies, reporting the results of statistical analyses and their meaning will be very important, but it is our preference to put the details of such analyses (graphs, tables, charts, and the like) in appendixes to the report. For qualitative studies, reporting themes that developed from the interview protocol questions, backed by selective quotes from respondents, is the best way to report results.

For readers who are not so well informed and who may be overwhelmed by detailed reporting of results, in the next section we present a more simplified, less complicated summary of findings.

- *A summary of results.* Next to the executive summary, this part of the report will be the most widely read, so it should be carefully crafted, based precisely on the detailed reporting of results.

- *Recommendations.* There are two schools of thought on recommendations. One is that the investigator should only report the results of the study, leaving the implications for practice to the practitioner. The other is that the investigator has a responsibility not only to report results, but to ponder what the results mean given the problem which precipitated the study.

We definitely support the latter option. That is not to say that the practitioner may ultimately decide against all or part of the investigator's recommendations; that can and will happen. But the practitioner, when considering the implications of the findings, should be guided by the investigator, who knows more about the findings than the decision maker. Put another way, what the findings mean for practice should be the result of a discussion among the investigator, the decision maker, and others affected by the results. That discussion is best facilitated when the report itself offers a starting point for that discussion, through the investigator's recommendations. Assuming that recommendations should be included, then it is the investigator's obligation to tie any recommendation directly to one or more of the findings. This is not only a very clear way of communicating recommendations, it is also the ethical obligation of the investigator.

It is also permissible for the investigator to *speculate* on the possible reasons for findings, so long as speculations are clearly labeled as the investigator's opinions, not the findings of the study itself. Suggestions for additional studies are also appropriate.

The fourth consideration in writing a report, according to Suskie (1992), is to keep it interesting and readable. For most of us, our experience writing graduate theses is a curse when it comes to writing assessment reports. Assessment reports should be "reader friendly" and much more casual in tone than a research report or a doctoral thesis. Use plenty of headings, keep sentences and paragraphs short, avoid research jargon, spell out abbreviations, minimize citations, and try to write as clearly as possible (Suskie, 1992). The best reports we have seen are those that "tell a story" in an engaging way, capturing the interest of the reader.

A final question to consider when writing reports—perhaps the most important based on our experience—is what to do with results which are very sensitive and controversial, and which might offend, embarrass, or anger intended audiences. Probably the most difficult situation for an investigator comes when he or she realizes that the results of a study will not please the decision makers who commissioned it. Worse yet is the situation in which the results show that the decision makers appear to be part of the problem. On the one hand, results that no one wants to hear must be included; in no way should results be toned down or omitted because certain audiences will be offended or threatened. On the other hand, the way in which sensitive or controversial results are reported may well determine the extent to which a study is used. There are no easy answers to this dilemma. As we discussed above, letting decision makers know about possible controversial results in advance of doing the study is one way of preparing for this dilemma.

Suskie (1992) suggests several strategies for reporting potentially controversial results. First, use praise as well as criticism. Include a positive aspect or context for every problem identified. For example, instead of saying "African American students want more people of color on the counseling service staff," one might say, "While the recent addition of an African American staff member is a step in the right direction, African American students believe there should be more people of color in the counseling center." The message is conveyed, but in a less strident tone, without diluting the results.

Second, phrase potentially controversial results gently. For example, instead of saying "African American students believe the counseling service is insensitive to their needs," one might say, "African American students believe the counseling service fails to provide the services they need." Again, the message is conveyed in a less threatening way, without diluting the results.

Third, avoid pinning the blame on anyone. For example, instead of saying, "The counseling center has made a very serious mistake in not hiring more African American staff members," one might say, "The counseling center needs to make a more concerted effort to hire more African American staff members." The first sentence clearly blames the counseling center, while the second sentence acknowledges the previous effort in the past while suggesting a stronger effort in the future.

Finally, if you know the report will upset some intended audiences, let them know in advance when the report will be released. It is possible that those discussions will lead to a better way of reporting potentially controversial results, or even influencing how the results will be interpreted. This strategy also gives intended audiences some time to think about their reactions, and to reduce the feeling that they were "blindsided" by the investigator.

Rule Six: Develop and Implement a Dissemination Plan

A mistake frequently made by investigators is to consider their job finished when the report is submitted to the person or office that commissioned the report. To be sure, the first obligation of the investigator is to report the findings to those who commissioned the report. But there should also be a dissemination plan agreed upon by the investigator and sponsor. Who should know about the findings? In what form should the findings be disseminated? What opportunities should the recipients have to react to the report? Perhaps even more important, when should the results be sent?

In disseminating assessment reports, timing can be everything. According to Jacobi, Astin, and Ayala (1987), reports should be released as decisions are being made, so that the findings and recommendations can become a part of the decision-making process. Again, the person who commissioned the study is in the best position to decide on the timing of a report's release.

Also, in this world of high-tech communications we live in, a written report, although important, should not be the only way in which studies are communicated. Press releases, press conferences, and even computer-accessible reports posted on an interactive computer bulletin board are all effective ways of making assessment results readily available to the people who should read them.

Rule Seven: Develop a Plan for Using the Report

Another mistake frequently made by investigators is to assume they have no responsibility in seeing to it that the study is used and not forgotten. To be sure, the final responsibility for using the study rests with those who commissioned it. On the other hand, to put it bluntly, the investigator should make it very difficult for the decision maker to ignore the report. The best way to do this is to negotiate an implementation plan with the decision maker which specifies when and how the findings of the report will be integrated into the decision-making process (see below).

Evaluation: How to Interpret and Use Assessments

The reader will remember that in Chapter One, we distinguished between assessment (any effort to gather, analyze, and interpret evidence which describes the effectiveness of institutions, departments, divisions, or agencies) and evaluation (any effort to use assessment evidence to improve the effectiveness of institutions, departments, divisions, or agencies). Even if a report is written following the rules identified above, it may never go beyond the "assessment" phase to the equally important "evaluation" phase.

A good example of an assessment study that had an enormous impact on improving institutional effectiveness is drawn from one of the authors' institutions. While not a specific student affairs example, it does point out the basic elements of an effective evaluation process.

A very important comprehensive and lengthy report on the status of women, commissioned at the president's request and conducted by representative groups of faculty, staff, and students, was submitted to the president. The first thing he did was to disseminate this report to his chief administrative and academic officers and to the faculty senate, asking for their feedback within two months. Within a month of receiving their comments, he made decisions on the recommendations, accepting most but rejecting others. He then parceled out each of the recommendations to the appropriate chief administrative or academic officer, asking that they report on their implementation within six months.

For every six months for the next three years, all chief administrative and academic officers received a memo from the president, asking them to update him on the progress toward implementing the study's recommendations or to state the reasons why a recommendation was not yet implemented. This delivered a very clear message to the entire university community, not to mention his chief administrative and academic officers. The report continued to be a force in policy development and decision making for many years thereafter, but only because the president held his administrative officers accountable for the implementation of the report.

What made this report effective, compared to other reports that weren't?

1. *There was a commitment of the leadership of the institution to address the recommendations of the study.* The president's actions upon receiving the report made this very evident. He didn't sit on it until the dust settled, bury it in his bureaucracy, or refer it back for further study. He began dealing with the report within a month after he received it.

2. *The recommendations were referred for consideration by the larger university community before any action was taken.* The president knew he would be making a big mistake if he simply decided upon the recommendations without further consultation with the rest of the

university community that would be affected by the recommendations. Therefore, he asked for feedback from his faculty and his administration before making final decisions, but again, within a specified time period.

3. *The leadership had the courage to openly accept some recommendations, and reject others.* Taking into account all the feedback he received, the president accepted most of the recommendations, while rejecting others. He also publicly stated the reasons for his decisions. There was a lot of controversy over both the recommendations he accepted (for example, providing services for gay, lesbian, and bisexual students) and those he rejected (such as fringe benefits for domestic partners of employees), but in spite of the controversy, the president kept communication open with those who disagreed with him.

4. *There was a plan for implementing the recommendations, and holding administrative and academic officers accountable.* The plan for periodically checking on the progress of key personnel as they implemented the president's decisions was the key to the success of this report. This plan established administrative accountability directly to the president every six months, something which chief academic and administrative officers could not ignore.

5. *The evaluation process was conducted in a timely fashion.* Throughout the process, deadlines were established, from the amount of time the president took to ask for feedback, to dates for receiving the feedback; from the timely decisions regarding the recommendations, to the subsequent timetables for reports on the implementation of recommendations. In this way, the assessment study became part of the evaluation process, and consequently, it has been a significant factor in policy and practice.

Conclusion

It is our belief, based on our experience, that if the rules presented in this chapter are followed, and the leadership has a plan for the timely consideration and implementation of assessment studies, they will not gather dust on a shelf, but rather be used to help make decisions, develop policies, solve problems, and in general improve effectiveness. That means (1) not doing a study no one wants, (2) determining how confidential the study will be, (3) determining who should be involved in the study, (4) conducting a good study, (5) writing a good report, (6) developing and implementing a dissemination plan, and (7) developing a plan for using the report.

What this all boils down to is the willingness and courage of the leadership to act upon assessment reports so that they are used in the evaluation process; we offered an example of how that can be done effectively, focusing on timely action, involvement of affected persons, and, perhaps most important, administrative accountability. It is also our belief that the investigator has a very important role in making sure that assessment reports are used, and thus become part of the evaluation process. Put another way, seldom do assessment reports speak for themselves; the investigator must speak for them, advocate their constructive use, and guide decision makers in the fine art of evaluation.

Chapter Fourteen

Maintaining High Standards of Ethics and Integrity

A publication on assessment in student affairs would be incomplete without a discussion of some of the more salient ethical issues related to assessment. A variety of ethical statements, principles, institutional regulations, and federal laws influence research and assessment activities on campus, and the student affairs persons conducting an assessment project should have an excellent working knowledge of them. Failure to have such an understanding could result, at the very least, in embarrassment to the staff member, and, at the very worst, potential harm to that person's subjects, the institution, or both. Indeed, as Marshall and Rossman (1989) have concluded, "The researcher cannot anticipate everything, but she must reveal an awareness and appreciation of commitment to ethical principles for research" (p. 71). We hope that those who read this material will gain a new appreciation for ethical principles in assessment.

This chapter will address selected ethical issues related to assessment in student affairs. It will not cover all of the ethical issues related to assessment. Rather we will present a commonly accepted framework for ethical issues in student affairs and then identify specific aspects of assessment that demand rigorous adherence to ethical principles. Suggestions for further reading and study will be offered. In this chapter, the terms *investigator, evaluator,* and *researcher* will be used interchangeably because the sources cited do so. While there are differences spelled out in Chapter One, our opinion is that similar ethical guidelines apply to all individuals engaged in assessment, research, and evaluation.

A Definition

Winston and Saunders (1991) offer an excellent definition of ethics which can be used a framework for further discussion of this issue. They indicate " 'Ethics' from a philosophical point of view is concerned with determining what acts or behaviors are 'right,' or 'ought to be done/not done' as well as determining the epistemological justifications for ethical statements or assertions" (p. 311). They identify two dimensions of ethics. "From the philosophical perspective, the first sense of ethics is normative in that the concerns are in specifying rules or principles which can guide individual decisions about conduct. The second sense of ethics has to do with asking questions about what does it mean to say 'one ought to' or 'that is good' " (p. 311). Building on this definition of ethics are Kitchener's five ethical principles which guide student affairs administration. Kitchener (1985) developed a series of ethical principles for student affairs administration. Her five principles form the basis for the following discussion.

Respecting Autonomy

Autonomy, according to Kitchener, has several aspects. First, it includes the right to live one's life as a free agent. Second it includes freedom of thought and choice. The principle of autonomy can be found in the ethical codes of several student affairs professional associations. According to Kitchener (1985), "These rules include the right of self-determination, the right to privacy or confidentiality, and informed consent" (p. 21).

Winston and Saunders (1991) describe this principle as "respecting one's right to make choices about life issues and freedom of thought and expression" (p. 325). But Canon (1993) reminds us that individuals have the right to decide how they live their lives "as long as their actions do not interfere with the welfare of others" (p. 330). As is the case with so many aspects of our lives, the freedoms addressed by this principle are not unlimited. For example, prior restraint of the student press at a public institution can be exercised only under the most unusual circumstances, but the press is barred by law from knowingly libeling other students, members of the faculty, administrators, or others.

Applications of this principle to the process of assessment can take many forms. If students do not want to participate in an assessment, the institution should not, under any circumstances, engage in retribution. For example, students who do not want to answer an assessment questionnaire about the financial aid office should not have their aid reduced because of failure to complete the instrument. Similarly, students who assess the performance of staff should have their anonymity protected completely if they were guaranteed such by the investigators.

Doing No Harm

Kitchener (1985) writes that many ethicists have suggested that "doing no harm to others is a basic [sic] ethical principle. All other things being equal, it is an even stronger ethical obligation than benefiting or helping others" (p. 21). Canon (1993) adds that the "obligation to avoid inflicting either physical or psychological harm to others and to avoid actions that put others at risk is a primary ethical principle" (p. 330). Winston and Saunders (1991) warn, "Because the risks of psychological harm are often subtle and difficult to predict accurately, decisions based on this principle must be made carefully" (p. 325).

In the work of assessment, this principle is particularly useful for guiding activities related to data collection. To protect students and others who are subjects in research projects (which would include assessment activities where data are gathered directly from respondents by way of questionnaires, interviews, and the like), institutions of higher education have adopted a process whereby review of a researcher's plan is conducted before data are collected. Under this process, all research plans involving human subjects are approved in advance. Consider one university's approach to regulations that were adopted to govern research on human subjects (Wichita State University, 1988): "The Faculty Senate [has] adopted general policies and procedures for the clearance of all research involving human subjects. The policies and procedures are consonant with those of the federal government and include research done by faculty and/or students. The policies and procedures are aimed at safeguarding the rights and welfare of the subject, the investigator, and the University" (p. 58). Student affairs staff who are planning to conduct an assessment would be well advised to review their institution's policy on research on human subjects and consult with members of the campus Institutional Research Board (IRB) if they have any questions about the nature of their work.

As a matter of standard practice, it might be best for the investigator to automatically seek approval from the IRB before collecting information from subjects. In most instances this approval can be expedited without much difficulty (see U.S. Department of Health and Human Services, 1991). With IRB approval, the investigator obtains official approval for the project and ensures that the subjects are not at risk.

Benefiting Others

The third principle Kitchener (1985) presents relates to the assistance provided by student affairs staff to others. She writes, "Benefiting others is an acknowledged goal of student services professionals" (p. 22). She adds, "acting ethically means not only preventing harm and respecting autonomy but actively promoting the health and well-being of others" (p. 22).

Canon (1993) adds to this discussion by pointing out that members of the helping professions "assume that the welfare of the consumer comes first when other considerations are equal" (p. 330). Winston and Saunders (1991) agree when they say that the student affairs profession has a mandate "to assist students in their personal development" (p. 325; see also Dobbert, 1982, pp. 78–79).

Assessments can certainly be conducted to determine the quality of services being provided to students or the growth that results from specific learning experiences. Obviously, activities and learning experiences which are designed to improve the quality of life on campus can have the direct implication of benefiting students and should be assessed on a periodic basis.

Being Just

Kitchener (1985) discusses two aspects of justice: fair treatment of individuals, and fairness in the distribution of resources. In her view both aspects of justice assume three standards: impartiality, equality, and reciprocity (p. 24). Canon (1993) characterizes this principle by indicating that "to be just in dealing with others means to offer equal treatment to all, to afford each individual his or her due, to be fair" (p. 330). Winston and Saunders (1991) add, "Justice is not simply a matter of equal treatment, equal access, or due process. It is a complex concept that must take into account individual differences and the effects of action taken" (pp. 325–326).

The standards Kitchener outlines, which are a part of the principle of justice, have a direct relationship to the assessment process. The assessment process is governed by impartiality; that is, data are collected using a rigorous process where accuracy is held to be sacred, regardless of what the information reveals. Moreover, the results can very well point to ways of conducting our work more efficiently and serving all campus constituencies better.

Being Faithful

The final principle Kitchener (1985) introduces is being faithful. She indicates that people in the helping professions "acquire a special obligation to be [faithful] by virtue of the roles ascribed to them: that is, to help, to be deemed trustworthy" (p. 25). Winston and Saunders (1991) observe that "this principle embodies the concepts of loyalty, keeping promises, trustfulness, and basic respect" (p. 326). Canon (1993) adds, "One should keep promises, tell the truth, be loyal, and maintain respect and civility in human discourse" (p. 330).

Assessment rests to a great extent on the premise that the process is conducted with scrupulous attention to finding the truth. The very purpose of the assessment is to determine what is true. To violate this "special obligation" is to destroy the project, and perhaps in the process, the credibility of the person conducting the assessment.

These five principles are an excellent guide to virtually all aspects of student affairs administration, not just assessment projects. From them we move on to a more narrow discussion of ethics in research, evaluation, and assessment projects.

Ethical Issues in Inquiry

Smith (1990) offers what he characterizes as an initial view of ethics in inquiry. He writes, "In recent years discussion of research implications and practices regarding the rights of human subjects have become more central and debated within the several disciplines and professions. The two most important principles for the protection of human subjects are informed consent and anonymity" (p. 260). Informed consent and anonymity relate directly to the principles offered by Kitchener. She indicates that those engaged in student affairs administration should do no harm, respect autonomy, be just, and be trustworthy. By paying careful attention to protecting anonymity and providing informed consent, those conducting an assessment will stay true to these ethical principles. (We will return to them later in this chapter when working with respondents is explored, but first, several other aspects of ethics in inquiry will be introduced.)

Major Elements

Erwin (1991) identified three elements that are central to successful higher education assessment projects: "accuracy, quality and confidentiality" (p. 149).

Accuracy can take on several dimensions. In the data collection and analysis phases of a project, the work must be conducted with careful attention to detail. Scoring and coding errors must be avoided. To make sure that computational errors do not contaminate a project, results must be reviewed and checked for accuracy. Accuracy also requires that the final report of the assessment project fairly represents what was learned. Results must be neither overstated nor underplayed. The reader of the report should have as accurate a picture of the results of the project as the researchers can produce. If those conducting the project have difficulty determining how to report results, they should seek help from an independent person who possesses the necessary expertise to assist them.

Quality in assessing requires that the project is conducted with the very highest level of assessing skills. The methodology used by the investigators must be rigorously applied and biases must be eliminated so that the project is not contaminated.

Finally, the *confidentiality* of the respondents must be guaranteed and protected. Again, when one refers to the ethical principles introduced by Kitchener and reiterated by Erwin in a different form, avoiding harm to the subjects is of paramount importance. Whether students complete questionnaires, participate in focus groups, or contribute information in some other way, they must be protected. Failure to do so is a serious ethical breach and may even make the researchers legally liable.

These three ethical elements provide an excellent framework with which to guide assessment projects. Those conducting a project would do well to review their assessment plans in the context of these elements before beginning the implementation phase.

Ethical Considerations in Field-Based Research

The National Commission for the Protection of Human Subjects of Biomedical and Behavioral Research identified three basic ethical principles for research (1979): "Three basic principles, among those generally accepted in our cultural tradition, are particularly relevant to the ethics of research involving human subjects: the principles of respect for the person, beneficence, and justice" (p. 4). Investigators cannot go wrong while adhering to these principles.

Dobbert (1982) has identified several other general ethical criteria that apply to field-based studies. While not all assessment projects are field-based in the narrowest definition of the term, Dobbert's thinking on this matter is of sufficient quality and importance that those conducting assessment in student affairs would be well advised to consider them. Four of Dobbert's considerations are introduced in this section of this chapter.

Confidentiality

As has been discussed earlier in this chapter, protecting the rights of the respondents is of critical importance to the investigator. Dobbert indicates that confidentiality has three aspects: (1) guaranteeing anonymity to the respondents, their families, others providing information, and the sites of the research activities; (2) keeping all information confidential; and (3) publishing nothing that could injure the respondents or the groups of which they are members. This can be a very delicate matter if the information provided by a person or small group of persons can be identified easily. Before revealing this information, the investigator should discuss the matter with the respondents. If they do not want it revealed—even if they have signed an informed consent response—it should be kept confidential.

Circumstances may arise when information must be shared because of potential harm to a student subject or others. An example might be substance abuse revealed by a subject. In a case such as this, confidentiality may be broken. When confronted with such a situation, the investigator is well advised to speak with a member of an IRB, the director of a counseling service, or a person equally well versed about the boundaries of confidentiality.

Honesty

In the view of Dobbert (1982), honesty requires the investigator to explain to potential respondents the purpose of the research; how the project will be done; what the benefits the researcher will receive for completing the project; who will have access to the final reports; and the potential risks to the respondents. Beyond these points the researcher has an obligation to keep subjects informed if any other changes occur during the course of the project, such as a substantial shift of purpose, or exposure of the final reports to an audience radically different from that proposed.

Responsibility

Dobbert (1982) claims that it is not possible for research to be done which "does not in some way interfere with or disrupt the lives of the people observed" (p. 79). Among the responsibilities that Dobbert advocates for the researcher to assume are trying to avoid and minimize all negative consequences of the research, freely admitting any mistakes in the conduct of the project, and being sure to write up a final report. Dobbert concludes that non-publication is a violation of ethics. As she puts it, "Every field-worker will probably goof on some project" (p. 80). This kind of mistake, and the others identified above, should be acknowledged and corrected as expeditiously as possible.

Fair Return

The investigator most likely will gain something by conducting the assessment project. The investigator might gain greater insight into how students perceive the services of a department, learn about ways to conduct departmental affairs more expeditiously, develop results that can be published or presented at a regional or national convention. Dobbert asserts that the researcher should identify for the respondents what benefits are likely to accrue from the project and attempt to arrange a reasonable return for them. What might be the basis of fair return for students? Once the study is concluded, the investigator might (1) send them an abstracted version of the final report, (2) provide information to them that could assist in their various activities on campus, (3) give them a token that could be exchanged for a free movie, ice cream, or another token of the investigator's appreciation. At times, determining fair return for students may not be particularly easy, but one way to find out is to ask some students in advance of the project what they think would be fair.

Working with Subjects

As was identified above in the reference to Smith (1990), working with subjects really forms the heart of ethical issues associated with assessment projects. In this section, five aspects of working with subjects will be discussed. To a certain extent, there is some overlap among these guidelines, all of which address the process of working with those who provide data. Protecting the rights of subjects cannot be overemphasized in the research and assessment process. Hence, some detail will be included in this discussion.

Protecting Subjects from Harm

When framing her discussion on ethical responsibilities of those engaged in student affairs work, Kitchener pointed out that protecting students from harm was absolutely crucial. Similarly, protecting subjects or respondents from harm in any assessment is essential. Guba and Lincoln (1989) argue that while the more overt and dramatic forms of subject abuse have been dealt within the law, such as "infecting inmates of mental hospitals with syphilis in order to study the progression of that disease over a lifetime" (p. 121), more needs to be done to protect subjects against other forms of harm, such as the loss of dignity, the loss of individual agency or autonomy, and the loss of self-esteem that occurs upon discovering that one has been duped.

Patton (1990) identifies a number of potential risks that people participating in a research project may take unknowingly. Among them are psychological stress; legal liabilities; ostracism by peers, program staff, or others for having talked; and political repercussions (p. 356). The person conducting the assessment ought to consider all of these risks when designing the study, and be prepared to respond to these types of problems should they arise in the course of the project.

While the examples given so far are more dramatic than what is likely to occur during campus-based assessments, the researcher needs to anticipate the worst possible consequences of conducting a study that goes awry. Accordingly, subjects need to be zealously protected from harm, and when the potential for harm raises its ugly head, immediate intervention must occur regardless of how inconvenient it might be for the project or the investigator. Under no circumstances should the subjects be put at risk to protect the assessment project.

Obtaining Informed Consent

A second safeguard when working with subjects is to obtain their fully informed consent. Rodriguez (1992) asserts, "Failure to inform students of their right to consent and to voluntary participation is a deceptive research practice" (p. 60). Guba and Lincoln (1989) also speak to the matter of complete and fully informed consent: "Informed consent cannot be given when participants are misinformed or not informed regarding the purposes of the evaluator or researcher. To deprive individuals of this right essentially robs them not only of their autonomy and control but also of their essential rights to be honored and respected as autonomous human beings" (p. 123).

So, based on these assertions, and the basic commitment student affairs staff make to respect the autonomy of students and others, before conducting an assessment it is essential that the investigator obtain fully informed consent from all participants. However, does one have to obtain informed consent from students in order to observe their behavior in public areas of the campus? Russell (1992) addresses this issue and provides some guidance. She suggests that the investigator consider the degree to which the behavior is public (for example, walking along a campus mall is more public than using a private carrel in a library), and the extent to which aides in observation are used, such as using powerful binoculars to watch subjects rather than the naked eye. In the end she recommends that the degree of risk to the subjects will be an important consideration for the researcher, and the use of review boards and "other scientific community expert panels" (p. 42) can be instructive. Huebner (1984) provides additional thinking about this topic: "In situations where informed consent is not obtainable without destroying the validity of the assessment, such as in naturalistic observation, the ethical issues are more subtle and complex. In such instances it becomes more crucial to insure the confidentiality of the data collected. . . . It is all too easy to fail to consider the ethical implications of data collection in situations where informed consent is not possible" (p. 4).

Another informed consent issue arises with the use of institutional records and databases for assessment purposes. For example, a "nonintrusive" retention study (conducted entirely from institutional records, with no data collection from subjects) does, in fact, use information from individual student records. Is informed consent from every student necessary in such a situation? The answer is a qualified "no." So long as (1) strict confidentiality of individual records is maintained, (2) no information on an individual student is reported, and (3) the results are analyzed and reported *in the aggregate,* the consensus among most investigators is that informed consent is not required to access and use institutional records. However, if the study is both nonintrusive and intrusive (additional data are collected directly from subjects), then the investigator must include the use of institutional records on the informed consent form.

The model presented in Exhibit 14.1 contains commonly accepted elements of an informed consent form. Accompanying the form, as Exhibit 14.2, is a checklist that provides a series of questions the investigator can raise in preparing an informed consent form.

Treating the Subjects with Respect

There is perhaps another way of stating what is presented in the two previous sections: treat subjects with respect and seek their cooperation in the research (Bogdan and Biklen, 1992). Bogdan

Exhibit 14.1. Model Consent Form.

(Put on university letterhead.)

You are invited to participate in a study of *(state what is being studied)*. We hope to learn *(state what the study is designed to discover or establish)*. You were selected as a possible participant in this study *(state why and how subject was selected).*

If you desire to participate, you will *(describe the procedures to be followed, including their purposes, how long they will take, and their frequency)*.

(Describe any risks, discomforts, and inconveniences that may reasonably be expected and any benefits to subjects or society that may reasonably be expected.)

Any information obtained in this study in which you can be identified will remain confidential and will be disclosed only with your permission. *(If you will be releasing information to anyone for any reason, you must state the persons or agencies to whom the information will be given, the nature of the information to be given, and the purpose of the disclosure.)*

(Describe any compensation or costs related to participation in the study.)*

Participation in this study is entirely voluntary. Your decision to participate or not to participate will not affect your future relations with *(institution or agency)*. If you decide to participate, you may withdraw from the study at any time without affecting your status as a *(patient, student, etc.)*.

If you have any questions about this research, please ask me. If you have additional questions during the study, I will be glad to answer them. You can contact me at: *(name, address, and phone).***

You will be given a copy of this consent form to keep.

You are making a decision whether or not to participate. Your signature indicates that you have read the information provided above and have voluntarily decided to participate.

_____   _____

Signature of Subject   Date

_____   _____

Signature of Parent or Legal Guardian   Date
(omit for subjects consenting for themselves)

_____   _____

Signature of Investigator   Date

(continued on the next page)

Exhibit 14.1. continued

*If participation of human subjects poses more than minimal risk, and/or involves physical activity, you must include the following paragraph:

> I have been informed and I understand that the college does not provide medical treatment or other forms of reimbursement to persons injured as a result of or in connection with participation in research activities conducted by the college or its faculty. If I believe that I have been injured as a result of participating in the research covered by this consent form, I should contact the Office of Research Administration at the college.

**If you are collecting data by means of a mail-out questionnaire, you may substitute the following format from paragraph seven through the end of the document:

> You are under no obligation to participate in this study. Your completion and return of this questionnaire will be taken as evidence of your willingness to participate and your consent to have the information used for the purposes of the study.

> You may keep this cover letter and explanation about the nature of your participation in this study and the handling of the information you supply.

Sincerely,

_____

Name of Investigator

NOTE: This letter must be signed by the principal investigator.

Exhibit 14.2. Consent Form Checklist.

Items	Yes	No	Comments
1. Is the general purpose of the study stated; what the researcher expects to learn?	____	____	_____
2. Is the subject's right to choose indicated?	____	____	_____
3. Is there a statement indicating how a subject was selected as a possible participant? Are the population and number of subjects identified?	____	____	_____

4. Are the procedures to be
followed in the study clearly
described (time, frequency,
nature of information asked,
observations, etc.)?   ____ ____ _____

5. Is there a statement of possible
risks, discomforts or inconveniences that the participants may
reasonably expect?   ____ ____ _____

6. Are any substantial or likely
benefits to subjects identified?   ____ ____ _____

7. Is any standard treatment with-
held or alternative procedures
disclosed?   ____ ____ _____

8. Is subject confidentiality
explained? (Use of tapes, photos,
data, etc.)   ____ ____ _____

9. Are subjects' compensation and
costs of participating in the study
explained?   ____ ____ _____

10. Is where the subject can contact
the investigator to have
questions answered indicated?   ____ ____ _____

11. Is the subjects' right to a written
copy of the consent form stated?   ____ ____ _____

12. Is there a statement that
expresses that the individual's
signature indicates a willingness
to participate?   ____ ____ _____

13. Are appropriate signature and
date spaces included?   ____ ____ _____

---

and Biklen indicate that researchers "should never lie to subjects
[or] record conversations on hidden mechanical devices" (p. 54).

In the case of on-campus assessments, students need to be
treated within the framework outlined by Kitchener (1985) and
reported above. Student autonomy must be respected. No harm
should come to them. They should be asked if they would be willing to participate in a project as opposed to being forced to participate as a course requirement. In short, the students or others

invited to participate in the project should be treated the same way the investigator would like to be treated if he or she were a subject in a research project.

Guarding Against Deception

Guba and Lincoln (1989) argue persuasively against deception of subjects by researchers. They say that according to some lines of thinking, deception is appropriate if the project is conducted for a " 'higher' order of truth" (p. 122). But Guba and Lincoln disagree; they believe that evaluators must be clear, direct, and undeceptive as they seek "to know how stakeholders make sense of their contexts" (p. 122). They add, "Deception is worse than useless to a nonconventional evaluator; it is destructive of the effort's ultimate intent" (p. 122).

One example of conducting deception in a research project would be the following. Suppose a housing director had concluded that matching certain personal, ascribed characteristics (such as the size of their home town) would lead to more compatible roommates. The housing director decides to test the theory by assigning some students from the home towns of the same size together as the control group, and students from towns of different sizes as the experimental group. Ultimately, using a series of measures including a questionnaire, interviews, and data from requests for change-of-roommate forms, a project is undertaken, and the students are not informed that they are a part of a study. While the project might yield useful results that would help in determining roommate compatibility, no one has agreed to participate in the study. No matter how laudable, this project would violate the ethics of conducting assessment and evaluation projects, in addition to potentially violating the institution's policy on research on human subjects and possibly federal regulations as well. Subjects should never be deceived about their voluntary participation in a study; they should be completely and fully informed. At a minimum, such a study must meet institutional IRB guidelines and be approved by the appropriate institutional body. Deceptive research practices have no place in student affairs assessments. Projects need to be conducted with the utmost commitment to integrity and to protecting the respondents from any danger.

Protecting Confidentiality

Finally, the investigator is responsible for protecting the confidentiality of the subjects. Patton (1990) asks the question, "What are reasonable promises of confidentiality that can be fully honored [for potential evaluators]?" (p. 356). Bogdan and Biklen (1992) state that the "subjects' identities should be protected so that the information you collect does not embarrass or in other ways harm them" (p. 54). Rodriguez (1992) argues that all data analysis should be conducted at the group or aggregate level in the case of conducting survey research. He also states that security steps should be implemented to protect the confidentiality of data left in offices or other places where carelessness could result in a breach of respondents' confidentiality.

Ethical dilemmas related to protecting anonymity will inevitably arise in the course of one's work. Bogdan and Biklen (1982) describe a series of problems one may encounter in field work, such as encountering physical abuse or the misuse of funds. They conclude by saying, "For many qualitative researchers, ethical questions do not reside narrowly in the realm of how to behave in the field. Rather, ethics are understood in terms of lifelong obligations to the people who have touched their lives in the course of living the life of a qualitative researcher" (p. 55).

To ward against accidental exposure of subjects' identities, assessments should be conducted so that individuals are not singled out and identified in report form. Nor should field notes or tape recordings be dealt with casually (such as leaving them around an office where they can be reviewed by anyone who wanders through). In addition, personally identifiable information should not be collected unless it is germane to the study. As Smith (1990) notes, striving to protect the anonymity of the respondents is a cornerstone of ethical behavior in conducting research.

Other Ethical Dilemmas

Other ethical dilemmas arise in the course of conducting assessments that are not as closely related to the respondents for the project, but are nevertheless an important part of the process. This section will discuss several of these problems.

Data Access and Ownership

Patton (1990) identifies this issue as worthy of consideration for the investigator. Who will have access to the data and who owns the data? Is it the investigator who owns the data or the institution? Can the head of the department being assessed have access to the raw data? These matters are best determined in advance of conducting the assessment, since failure to do so can result in very difficult discussions on a post hoc basis.

One way of looking at this problem would be to determine whether or not the investigator is an insider or an outsider. If an insider, meaning the investigator is assessing something on his or her own campus, the data probably belong to the institution. If an outsider, ownership of the data should be negotiated, because it could belong to the investigator, the campus, or both.

The head of the department being assessed may very well help in collecting data. In this case, it would be difficult for the head not to have access to the data, at least temporarily. One potential problem is if department heads collect data about themselves. It would be better if these data were collected by others, particularly if an element of the assessment has to do with department head effectiveness. To deal with this issue, a memorandum of understanding should be drafted so that all involved understand the extent to which access is temporary or permanent.

Negotiating an Agreement

It may very well be best to handle many of the details of an assessment project either in the form of a contract, a memorandum of agreement, or a letter of agreement. This is particularly true when conducting an assessment at another institution. On one's own campus, a memorandum of agreement would suffice. What issues might be considered? Among the issues identified by Bogdan and Biklen (1992): Can the results be published? Who owns the data? To whom will the data be revealed? These questions and others identified by Dobbert (1982) will need to be resolved before beginning the assessment project.

Dobbert (1982) suggests the following issues as negotiating points:

- Determine why the project is being conducted.
- Identify potential uses for the data the investigator will gather.
- Retain ownership to the data the investigator collects.
- Guarantee that one's professional autonomy in designing the project and data gathering not be compromised.
- Retain rights to publish the findings without client approval.
- Raise and discuss any potential conflicts of interest.

A sample memorandum of agreement is presented in Exhibit 14.3. Virtually every point listed in the sample is negotiable between the person commissioning the assessment and the person conducting the assessment.

Role Conflicts

Conducting an assessment in one's own institution can result in a role conflict for the investigator. As pointed out in Chapter Two, the question of who should conduct assessments is important. This conflict arises usually when those people most qualified to conduct assessment are also those who have a vested interest in the outcome. Or worse, the investigator is under some pressure from superiors to produce "appropriate results." Rodriguez (1992) indicates that the "role conflicts of institutional researchers are magnified when other persons in the institutional hierarchy place specific role expectations on the behavior of the researcher. The more members of the hierarchy that perceive themselves as stakeholders in the research, the greater the likelihood of [a] clash due to competing and specialized interests" (p. 64).

How does one avoid this dilemma? First, before beginning the assessment, the investigator must acquire a careful understanding of his or her role and the reasons for conducting the project. Administrators need to understand that investigators cannot ethically conduct studies in which the outcome is a foregone conclusion. Second, as pointed out in the previous chapter, a study that nobody wants should not be conducted. This means the investigator has an obligation to inform administrators of the many possible outcomes, and determine if they can live with them. If not, then the study is best not done. Third, as pointed out in Chapter Thirteen, there are ways of reporting assessment studies which maintain the

Exhibit 14.3. Model Memorandum of Agreement.

(Date:)

The following document will serve as a memorandum of agreement about the assessment project tentatively titled "*(FILL IN TITLE OF PROJECT)*," hereinafter referred to as "the Project."

1. This agreement is between *(fill in name of person commissioning the Project)* and *(fill in name of person who will do the Project)*.

2. The purposes of the Project are the following:

   a. _____

   b. _____

   c. _____

   d. _____

3. A preliminary report will be submitted by *(fill in name of person who will do the Project)* by *(fill in the date)*.

4. A final report will be submitted by *(fill in name of person who will do the Project)* by *(fill in the date)*.

5. When the Project has been completed, ownership of the data will revert to *(fill in the name of the person who will own the data. It can be the person commissioning the Project, carrying out the Project, or a third party or entity. This point is negotiable)*.

6. *(Fill in name of person who will do the Project)* will *(or will not)* be able to publish the results of the Project without the permission of *(fill in the name of the person commissioning the Project)*. *(This point is negotiable.)*

7. Permission to undertake the Project from the site's institutional review board will be secured by *(fill in the name of person)*. In addition, each person who is invited to participate as a subject will have to complete an informed consent form.

8. Upon completing the Project and submitting a final report, compensation in the amount of *(fill in the amount)* will be remitted to *(fill in the name)*.

AGREED:

_____	_____	_____	_____
Person who commissioned the Project	Date	Person who will do the Project	Date

_____

integrity of both the study and the investigator, often in the choice of language and tone of the report.

While freedom of inquiry is a cornerstone of academic freedom and ought to be one of the benchmark values of any institution (see Joughin, 1969), there is a substantial difference between a scholar's freedom to conduct research and pursue "the truth" and an institutional investigator's freedom to conduct assessments. As pointed out in Chapter One, there is a difference between research and assessment. While an institutional investigator has a responsibility to conduct assessments which are ethical, have integrity, and are of high quality, it is the institution, not the investigator, that determines what shall be studied and how the results will be used. However, the investigator does have a responsibility to assist the institution in ensuring that all assessments meet the ethical standards articulated in this chapter and the works cited herein.

Promises and Reciprocity

While it may sound obvious, Patton (1990) reminds researchers to keep their promises. By this he means that if a copy of the report is promised to interviewees, then a report ought to be supplied. "If you make promises, keep them" (p. 356). Canon (1989) also believes that promises must be kept to colleagues with whom the investigator collaborates. If one agrees to work with colleagues on a project, that commitment must be honored.

Telling the Truth

There are times when the data from a study reveal negative information. The investigator may be tempted to smooth over the results, or couch them in such a way that conceals the full impact of the information. Bogdan and Biklen (1992) provide this advice: "The most important trademark of a researcher should be his or her devotion to reporting what the data reveal. Fabricating data or distorting data is the ultimate sin of a scientist" (p. 54).

How does one deal with this dilemma? As pointed out in Chapter Thirteen, the investigator can prevent post facto administrative pressure to smooth over awkward or politically sensitive results, by making sure administrators are aware of possible outcomes in advance of the assessment. After the study, there are ways of reporting controversial results which may better communicate their meaning. Further, if a study reveals significant problems, the person who commissioned the report and other interested parties may be warned in advance. Using this strategy will ensure that no surprises will arise when the final report is submitted.

Evaluator Effects

Patton (1990) has identified three concerns worthy of our attention about the effect of the evaluator on a project. His thinking forms the basis of this discussion.

The first of these concerns is the extent to which the evaluator will influence the project. Patton concludes that "evaluator effects are often considerably overrated, particularly by the evaluators" (p. 474). His advice is that evaluators neither overestimate or underestimate their effects but rather "take seriously their responsibility to describe and study what those effects are" (p. 474).

Evaluators can affect a project by getting involved in the activities of the subjects and the site. For example, if one were evaluating the effects of a classroom, correcting mistakes of the students or the instructor would be an obvious intrusion that could affect a class session. This kind of behavior should be avoided.

Patton's second concern has to do with how an evaluator might be changed as a result of the assessing experience. In this case, he points to someone who evaluates the effects of a religious revival and, in the process, is converted to the religious orientation of the revival. Once converted, it is possible for the evaluator to become so personally involved with the process that he or she will lose sensitivity and objectivity. One way investigators can maintain an objective view is to work in teams. That way, one member can point out any changes that may occur in the behavior or orientation of another team member.

The third point that Patton makes has to do with the biases or predispositions an evaluator may bring to data analysis and interpretation. It is virtually impossible for evaluators to conduct value-free work. Most student affairs professionals, for example, believe that out-of-class experiences contribute positively to a student's education. If such people are asked to assess the student activities program at an institution, they should recognize their bias with regard to the value of student activities. Biases can be reduced considerably by using several techniques. As mentioned above, working in teams helps, especially if the membership of the team hold a variety of perspectives toward the topic that is being assessed. With a free and open exchange of opinions between team members who have varying perspectives about what has been found, the resulting report will be as objective and accurate as possible. In addition, member checking (see Chapter Three on qualitative methodology) will help determine if the data that have been collected are consistent with what the subjects have to offer. A comprehensive audit trail reviewed by a person external to the assessment team will help ensure that blatant biases have been kept out of the assessment process. This matter of predispositions and biases needs to be kept in mind by each investigator throughout the project. If the investigators allow their own biases to influence the project, the results will be flawed, possibly derailing the assessment completely.

A particularly challenging dilemma for the investigator who combines quantitative and qualitative methods is that quantitative methods generally strive for a completely bias-free approach to the project, while qualitative methods will recognize that investigator bias may be a necessary part of the project. Nevertheless, regardless of which approach is used, or if both are combined in a project, the investigator should strive to be objective (Borg, Gall, and Gall, 1993) and "neutral with regard to the phenomenon under study" (Patton, 1990, p. 55). The techniques suggested above will help reduce investigator bias so that assessment projects are not contaminated.

Accuracy of Secondary Data

It is highly likely in some assessment projects that the team will rely on data collected by other people or through other sources. In these situations the team will have to make sure that these data meet the level of rigor and integrity they have established for the rest of the study. Grose, Lauroesch, and Schiltz (1992) conclude that "the institutional researcher cannot avoid the responsibility to appraise the quality of all data used by the office, regardless of the source, and to inform users of any potential errors therein" (p. 27).

Dealing with flawed data can be a particularly delicate situation, especially if one is working with institutional colleagues. Nonetheless, to use flawed data in an assessment project would create greater difficulties. Consequently, problems such as this will have to be addressed in a firm, yet delicate, manner so as to protect the integrity of the process.

Ethical Fallacies

Ethical mistakes in the process of conducting assessment studies can happen if the investigator makes assumptions which turn out to be false. The following short discussion includes several fallacies identified by House (1993), such as doing whatever the client wants, which is also known as *clientism*. This kind of thinking occurs when, for example, an investigator who wants to study psychologically unstable people encounters a person who appears to be dangerous to others. This dangerous person has a plan to randomly shoot bystanders at a bus station, a plan the investigator knows about but does not notify law enforcement authorities. While this example is dramatic, it underscores the notion that circumstances can arise when the needs or wishes of the client or the goals of a project must be treated as subordinate to the larger good of society.

House (1993) also points to the fallacy of *contractualism*, which can be defined as meeting all the obligations of the evaluation or assessment contract, but doing no more. Contractualism would occur if one assessed an office and in the process became aware of the theft of equipment. While the contract might not require the investigator to play the role of financial auditor, the investigator's obligation to the greater good would require that since potential malfeasance has been uncovered, a more systematic, comprehensive audit could be conducted to sustain or refute the investigator's impression.

House (1993) identifies a third ethical fallacy which he calls *relativism*, meaning that the opinions of all persons involved as subjects in a study, particularly a study employing qualitative methods, have equal weight. In fact, some people have more information than others, and thus may have a better view of the circumstances that make for a certain situation. For example, an assessment of the student government on a campus should include the perceptions, quite obviously, of students. Students who are members of the campus senate, most likely, will know more about governmental operations than newly enrolled transfer students. The context of any subject's experience needs to be noted by the investigators. In some studies, a subject's bias may become apparent as data is collected. In any case, however, as House (1993) defines the relativism fallacy, "There is a sense in which everyone deserves to be listened to and to express his or her interests, but this does not mean that those expressions are to be judged morally equal. The racist does not rate equally with the victim of racism" (p. 170).

Conversely, House (1993) raises concerns about *pluralism* or *elitism* as a potential fallacy. He warns against the tendency to hold as more valid the opinions of those in powerful positions as compared to the opinions of those in positions of less influence. In the end, he urges those conducting an evaluation to include the interests of the widest range possible of different levels of authority and influence.

Codes of Ethics

Guidance for investigators is provided by the two professional associations concerned with the broad array of activities that comprise student affairs work. Both the National Association of Student Personnel Administrators (1993–1994) and the American College Personnel Association (1989) have published codes of ethics which ought to be readily available in all student affairs units. Each of these statements addresses issues related to confidentiality, research, and protecting human subjects. A citation for each appears in the reference list. In addition, other organizations which focus on more specialized aspects of student affairs work publish codes of ethics which will provide additional information to investigators.

Conclusion

This chapter has been designed to point out a variety of ethical problems and dilemmas that a person planning to undertake an assessment project might encounter. Also presented are strategies for addressing these issues satisfactorily. We think we have identified the most likely issues that the investigator would encounter, and we want to reinforce the fact that when the investigator is in doubt about how to deal with a problem, that help can be found in the various sources we have identified throughout the chapter. The investigator is never alone when making difficult ethical choices. In the final analysis, Whitt (1991) gives excellent advice about ethics and these kinds of activities when she writes, "The researcher should strive to maintain a high level of competence and rigor throughout the study—despite the pressures of time, people and finite energy levels—in order to protect the interests of the respondents. This means scrupulous attention to the purposes of the research, to data management . . . and to systematic data collection, analysis and interpretation" (p. 415).

Chapter Fifteen

Making Assessment Work: Guiding Principles and Recommendations

In summarizing the content of this book, we will first revisit the comprehensive model upon which this book is based, and review the basic questions about the assessment process. As a way of further summarizing this book, we developed a series of principles including purpose, timing, personnel, ongoing assessment, methods, funding, final reports, ethics, and the use of results. Without a doubt these principles will have to be modified according to the nature of a specific assessment, but in some form or other they will come up in every assessment. We list these principles here as a ready reference for the person who needs to look at a summary of what we have discussed more fully in preceding chapters. We conclude this final chapter by echoing the theme of the first: Assessment is a key to the survival of student affairs, as well as a tool for policy development, decision making, ensuring quality, accountability, and accessibility, strategic planning, and responding to political pressures.

A Comprehensive Model of Assessment for Student Affairs

This book was organized around a model of assessment which we believe can provide a comprehensive assessment program for student affairs. It consists of seven components:

- Tracking use of programs, services, and facilities
- Assessing student needs
- Assessing student satisfaction
- Assessing environments and student cultures
- Assessing outcomes
- Assessing through comparable organizations
- Using professional standards to assess

Basic Questions Guiding Assessment

For any assessment study conducted within this framework, we developed twelve questions to guide its design and interpretation:

1. What's the problem?
2. What's the purpose?
3. Who will be studied?
4. What's the best assessment method?
5. How do we decide who to study?
6. How should the data be collected?
7. What instrument or instruments should we use?
8. Who should collect the data?
9. How should we record the data?
10. How do we analyze the data?
11. How do we report the results?
12. How do we use the results?

Basic Principles That Guide Assessments

Purpose

Perhaps the most important of all assessment principles is contained in the question, "Why are we doing this study?" Each assessment must be conducted to meet a specific purpose identified in the overall goal or goals for the project. Out of the goals for the assessment will come more specific objectives. The goals and objectives for the project will need to be understood by those conducting the assessment, those being assessed, and those who will receive the assessment's report. It may take quite a bit of time to identify the goals and objectives of the assessment, but that is not necessarily a cumbersome dimension of the project. The fact is that misunderstood goals and objectives of an assessment project by those associated with it very well can doom a project from the start.

We have been involved in assessment projects where the goals and objectives have been misunderstood, obfuscated, or worse. In one situation, one of the authors was invited to join a periodic assessment of a student affairs department at another campus. Over the telephone the assessment was described to this person as routine, with no particular problems requiring the investigator's attention. As it turned out, the purpose of the assessment was to lend credibility to a plan to restructure the department and reassign many of the department's personnel. Obviously, this lack of understanding of the assessment's goals caused many problems for virtually everyone who was associated with it.

Timing

Some assessments can be done at virtually any time, while others must be conducted within specific time frames. The appropriate time to conduct an assessment will depend on a variety of factors, among them the purpose of the assessment, the nature of the activity being assessed, the academic calendar, and the availability of resources.

Traditional orientation programs for new, incoming students, for example, which are conducted over a period of a day or two in the summer, lend themselves well to an assessment that is done after the program has been completed. It is pretty difficult to ask students in the middle of orientation whether or not their concerns about the college have been addressed because, quite probably, they will have many unanswered questions.

On the other hand, if one were interested in assessing the quality of the environment in the campus residence halls, a study conducted in the middle of the fall term would be entirely appropriate. Based on the assessment's results, changes could be made to reshape the environment and improve those areas identified by students as weaknesses.

Personnel

In the best of circumstances, assessments are conducted by a combination of insiders and outsiders. What this means is that insiders will understand the department best and will have a feel for its subtleties that may not be apparent to those who are outsiders. Outsiders, on the other hand, have the ability to view a department with a fresh perspective, and may ask questions about issues that are not obvious to those who are deeply immersed in the department's activities on a daily basis.

Insiders generally are defined as people who have responsibility for the operation of the department or work very closely with it on a routine basis. For example, if one were evaluating a student activities office, members of that department clearly would be insiders as might the Greek organization adviser or the dean of students. Outsiders could be anyone from the campus, such as faculty, facility planners, or staff from the bursar's office. Outsiders also might include people external to the institution, such as individuals holding counterpart positions at other colleges.

Because of cost, it is unlikely that a large number of outsiders external to the institution will routinely participate in assessment. There are ways to deal with this issue, such as working out arrangements to "trade" assessments with other institutions in the same geographic area. In this scenario, one institution would use outsiders as investigators on a project and then make counterpart staff available for an assessment project at the other campus. For example, student health staff from one campus could work as outsider investigators for another campus. In turn, members of the counseling center staff from the second campus return the favor at the first campus later in the year.

Ongoing Assessment

At times, assessments are conducted on a "one-shot basis," as in the case of materials for decennial reviews by regional accrediting associations, for example. The assessment activity is completed and then everyone relaxes until it is time for the next accreditation visit. The purpose of the accreditation assessment may be fulfilled by a one-shot study (in other words, the institution receives full accreditation), but the opportunity for improvement in learning opportunities, programs, or services that should result from a careful review of these activities may be missed. For this reason, we recommend that assessments be conducted on a periodic basis.

How often is often enough? This question does not have an easy answer, but we believe that a series of assessments should be conducted not less than every two years. If one studies matriculation and attrition at many institutions, and the student body has a turnover of more than half every two years, to conduct assessments less frequently than every two years will result in the perceptions of a substantially different set of students whenever the assessments are conducted. For the reasons enumerated earlier in this book, following a group of students over four or five years to measure outcomes makes excellent sense. But one should not conclude that assessments should be conducted only once or twice a decade. Our view is that they need to be conducted on a routine basis and find their way into the annual calendar of a department.

Methods

Proponents of qualitative or quantitative methods abound. There are those who are particularly strident, meaning that they see little value in the methods used by those in the other camp. For example, some quantitative methodologists will argue that qualitative methods are nothing more than sloppy "science" yielding marginally useful information. On the other hand, one can find qualitative methodologists who have little time for quantitative methods.

The truth, in our opinion, lies between the two extremes. We believe that each method has strengths and weaknesses, and that each is appropriately rigorous. However, this is not an "either-or" choice, because often the most powerful study uses a combination of both approaches. The investigator needs to understand the purpose of the assessment, and choose methods which will generate the kind of information and provide the best answers to the questions raised by the assessment. Recall that we suggested that the goals and objectives of the assessment need to be well understood by all associated with the project. Assuming that such is the case, then methods should be chosen which will generate the best information for the project.

Investigators should put aside whatever research biases they bring to the project and realize that lots of useful information can be developed by using a combination of methods. The most successful investigators are those who are armed with a substantial arsenal of assessment strategies and techniques, and who understand that blending them in ways that best meet the needs of a specific project is essential.

Funding

Providing the necessary resources, both human and monetary, is an issue that must be addressed at the start of a project. Staff should not be deterred from a project by its cost, but nor should one be deluded into thinking that assessment can be done for free. Time is a precious commodity on a college campus, and for staff to be engaged in an assessment project means that they will be diverting time to that project from other activities. The time spent on the assessment can be limited by certain ground rules, such as by having only a few meetings, limiting the length of the meetings, and using electronic mail and other technological devices.

Not every project requires outside consultants or extra student workers, but it is a common practice to spend some money on supplies, computer time, and other operating or support activities to get the project completed. In the final analysis, it is useful to recognize that costs are associated with an assessment, and that the person or persons commissioning the project must agree to provide at least a minimum level of support before the project is begun. We advise those contemplating beginning a project to secure this support at the outset or decline to undertake the project.

Final Reports

Who receives the final assessment report? How widely should it be distributed? Would it make sense to release it to the student newspaper or the faculty senate? Should multiple reports be issued for specific audiences? These are difficult questions. Our general view is that it is the job of the investigators to deliver the report to the person or persons who commissioned it. At that point, this person or these persons can answer questions about distribution.

This is not to say that pressure will not be placed on the chair of the assessment team or members of the group to make a decision about distribution. Nevertheless, their most appropriate response would be to refer such questions to the person who commissioned the study.

What about assessments that uncover major problems in staff performance? A private conference with the person who commissioned the report would be in order here. This information may not be included in the final report, or may be included in less harsh terms if the information is particularly damaging. It is important for the investigator to realize that assessment is a serious activity with people's careers in the balance. If potential malfeasance is discovered, that information ought to be reported immediately so that the commissioner of the report can begin an investigation without delay.

We suspect that there is a direct, inverse relationship between the length of a report and the willingness of people to read it. So, for particularly busy people, such as a president, an executive summary is in order. That may also be true for those who have tremendous amounts of material to read, such as vice presidents, trustees, legislators, and so on. If their interest is kindled by a summary, they can always read the full report at a later date. (For a more thorough discussion of final reports, see Chapter Thirteen.)

Ethics

We will not discuss ethics at length, since ethical considerations have been identified throughout this volume. We will only reiterate our belief that it is absolutely essential that those involved in assessment projects pay scrupulous attention to the ethical considerations that frame the project. We believe that if ethical corners are cut in assessment projects, the results of those projects are not worth the paper on which they are printed. When faced with an ethical dilemma, we recommend that the investigator seek consultation from a well-experienced person external to the project, a colleague at an other institution, or a person recommended through a professional organization.

Using Results

As we pointed out in Chapter Thirteen, nothing is more frustrating than to conduct an assessment study and then learn that decision makers have failed to act on the findings, for whatever reasons (for example, poorly conducted and reported studies, lack of courage to implement results, fear of political repercussions if results are known, or lack of relevance of the study's results). While some would argue that the investigator's responsibility ends with the submission of the final report, we believe that although the investigator has a responsibility to conduct a good study and write a good report, he or she also should help decision makers draw the connection between findings and policy or practice, both formally through the report, and informally through frequent reminders and updates. In short, the investigator should make it very difficult for a decision maker to ignore the findings of a good assessment study.

Conclusion

We argue in Chapter One that there are plenty of reasons why higher education should take assessment seriously. External pressure is mounting, and tough questions are being asked. What does one get out of a college education? How do we know? Why is the cost of an education rising faster than the cost of living? Why do underrepresented groups drop out at higher rates than others? The demand for answers to these questions are driving efforts by states to mandate assessments, and by regional accreditation associations to require criteria for assessment-oriented outcomes.

Similar questions are being asked of student affairs. Are we delivering what we promised, and are we doing so in a cost-effective, high-quality way? Do our services and programs provide access to underrepresented groups, and are our campus environments free from bigotry, discrimination, and prejudice? Do our services, programs, and facilities contribute to student learning. And there is the ultimate question: Do we really need student affairs at all? The reality is that in recent years, student affairs departments have borne the brunt of budget cuts, disproportionate to other parts of higher education. As a consequence, the very survival of student affairs is at stake.

A comprehensive assessment program can play a critical role in demonstrating the importance and effectiveness of student affairs. It can also help us to deal with issues of quality, access and equity, accountability, and affordability, as well as to play an important role in strategic planning, policy development, and decision making, and respond to important political pressures. Further, a comprehensive assessment program can help us relate our efforts to student learning in general, and the academic success of students in particular. In short, assessment in student affairs is no longer a "luxury" that is done only after all other priorities have been taken care of. Assessment is now a necessity that demands our highest priority.

We understand that student affairs staff are busy. In our combined fifty-five years of experience in student affairs administration, we have encountered many daily problems that have threatened to short-circuit assessment efforts. Nonetheless we have a firm belief that through assessment, we can demonstrate our worth and effectiveness to ourselves, our institutions, our society, and most of all to the students we educate and serve. We owe them nothing less.

Appendix

This selected annotated review, admittedly incomplete, is designed to provide the reader with information about instruments that may have use in assessing student services, programs, and facilities. The reader should contact the publishers of these instruments to gather further information and review their purposes, content, and psychometric integrity before using them.

A very good additional source for annotated assessment instruments and other assessment publications is the Clearinghouse for Higher Education Assessment Instruments (College of Education, University of Tennessee, 212 Claxton Education Building, Knoxville, TN 37996–3400).

Major National Publishers of Assessment Instruments

There are several national publishers of assessment instruments whom the reader may contact for a complete listing and description of their published instruments. They include the following.

ACT Evaluation/Survey Services
2201 North Dodge Street
P.O. Box 168
Iowa City, IA 52243

ETS Institutional Research Program for Higher Education
Educational Testing Service
Princeton, NJ 08541–0001

Noel Levitz Centers
2101 ACT Circle
Iowa City, IA 52245–9581

NCHEMS
1540 Thirtieth Street
P.O. Drawer P
Boulder, CO 80302

Office of Assessment Services
1819 Andy Holt Avenue
University of Tennessee
Knoxville, TN 37996–4350

Psychological Corporation
Order Service Center
P.O. Box 839954
San Antonio, TX 78283–3954

Western Psychological Services
12031 Wilshire Boulevard
Los Angeles, CA 90025–1251

Assessment Instrument Annotations

Academic Advising

Academic Advising Inventory
The purpose is to measure students' perceptions of advising programs along five dimensions: developmental-prescriptive advising,
activity categories, student satisfaction with advising, demographic
information, and locally generated items.

Student Development Associates
110 Crestwood Drive
Athens, GA 30605

College Student Inventory
The purpose is to provide advisers with information on students'
principal attitudes.

Noel Levitz Centers
2101 ACT Circle
Iowa City, IA 52245–9581

Survey of Academic Advising

The purpose is to determine student impressions of an institution's academic advising services. Sections include background information, advising information, academic advising needs, impressions of your adviser, additional advising information, additional local questions, and comments and suggestions.

ACT Evaluation/Survey Services
2201 North Dodge Street
P.O. Box 168
Iowa City, IA 52243

Adult Students

Adult Learner Needs Assessment Survey

The purpose is to explore the perceived educational and personal needs of adult students enrolled at the institution, as well as of prospective adult students in the community. Sections include background information, educational plans and preferences, personal and educational needs, additional local questions, and comments and suggestions.

ACT Evaluation/Survey Services
2201 North Dodge Street
P.O. Box 168
Iowa City, IA 52243

Alumni Surveys

ACT Alumni Outcomes Survey

The purpose is to obtain student satisfaction feedback and self-reported perceptions of growth in many areas considered important by accrediting commissions and other external agencies.

ACT Evaluation/Survey Services
2201 North Dodge Street
P.O. Box 168
Iowa City, IA 52243

ACT Alumni Survey

The purpose is to help the institution evaluate the impact that college had on graduates in both two- and four-year institutions. Sections include background information, continuing education, educational experiences, employment history, additional local questions, current mailing addresses, and comments and suggestions.

ACT Evaluation/Survey Services
2201 North Dodge Street
P.O. Box 168
Iowa City, IA 52243

Alumni Survey, University of Tennessee

The purpose is to survey alumni about their undergraduate experiences, including overall satisfaction, involvement in activities, impact of education, and programs related to major. This also collects employment and background information.

Learning Research Center
University of Tennessee
Knoxville, TN 37996–3400

Comprehensive Alumni Assessment Survey (CAAS)

The purpose is to gather information about alumni, with or without local questions.

NCHEMS
1540 Thirtieth Street
P.O. Drawer P
Boulder, CO 80302

Long-Term Alumni Questionnaire

The purpose is to survey alumni who have been away from the institution more than four years.

NCHEMS
1540 Thirtieth Street
P.O. Drawer P
Boulder, CO 80302

Recent Alumni Questionnaire

The purpose is to survey alumni who have been away from the institution four years or less.

NCHEMS
1540 Thirtieth Street
P.O. Drawer P
Boulder, CO 80302

Career Services, Planning, and Placement

Career Decision Scale

The purpose is to assess the level of the student's career indecision and barriers which prevent career decisions.

Marathon Consulting and Press
P.O. Box 09189
Columbus, OH 43209–0189

Career Development Inventory

The purpose is to assess career development and career maturity based on Duper's theoretical model of career development.

Consulting Psychologists Press, Inc.
3803 East Bayshore Road
P.O. Box 10096
Palo Alto, CA 94303–0096

Cognitive Development

College Outcome Measures Program

The purpose is to measure general education outcomes in three process areas (oral and written communication, problem solving, and values clarification) and three content areas (functioning within social institutions, using science and technology, and using the arts).

ACT Evaluation/Survey Services
2201 North Dodge Street
P.O. Box 168
Iowa City, IA 52243

Measure of Epistemological Reflection

The purpose is to measure six domains of intellectual development, including decision making; role of learner; role of instructor; role of peers; evaluation; and the nature of truth, knowledge, and reality.

American Counseling Association
5999 Stevenson Avenue
Alexandria, VA 22304

Parker Cognitive Development Inventory

The purpose is to yield an objectively scored measure of the sequential and hierarchical cognitive development positions of Perry's theory of cognitive development.

HITECH Press
P.O. Box 2341
Iowa City, IA 52244–2341

Reflective Judgment Interview

The purpose is to assess the seven stages of reflective judgment in the reflective judgment model described by Kitchener and King.

Department of College Student Personnel
330 Education Building
Bowling Green State University
Bowling Green, OH 43403–0249

Watson-Glaser Critical Thinking Appraisal

The purpose is to measure critical thinking dimensions, including inference, recognition of assumptions, deduction, interpretation, and evaluation of arguments.

Psychological Corporation
Order Service Center
P.O. Box 839954
San Antonio, TX 78283–3954

Development and Involvement

Attitude Toward College Inventory

The purpose is to look at student integration, persistence, and retention.

Ernest Pascarella
National Center on Postsecondary Teaching,
    Learning, and Assessment
College of Education, M/C 147
P.O. Box 4348
Chicago, IL 60608–4348

College Adjustment Scales

The purpose is to assess how well students are (on the average) at adjusting to the demands of college and university life. Subscales include depression, anxiety, suicidal ideation, effects of substance abuse, self-esteem problems, interpersonal problems, family problems, academic problems, and career choice problems.

Psychological Assessment Resources, Inc.
P.O. Box 998
Odessa, FL 33556–0998

College Student Experiences Questionnaire (CSEQ)/
Community College Student Experiences Questionnaire (CCSEQ)

The purpose of each instrument is to measure the effort students put into becoming involved with the opportunities and services provided by the institution. Sections include background information, college activities, conversations, reading/writing, opinions about college, the college environment, estimation of gains, and local items.

Center for Postsecondary Research and Planning
201 North Rose Avenue
Bloomington, IN 47405–1006

Extracurricular Involvement Inventory

The purpose is to measure student involvement in the extracurriculum.

Ernest Pascarella
National Center on Postsecondary Teaching,
    Learning, and Assessment
College of Education M/C 147
P.O. Box 4348
Chicago, IL 60608–4348

Iowa Test of Student Development

The purpose is to measure Chickering's vectors of student development.

Albert B. Hood
HITECH Press
P.O. Box 2341
Iowa City, IA 52244–2341

Student Development Task and Lifestyle Inventory

The purpose is to measure Chickering's first three vectors of student development. Subscales include educational involvement, career planning, lifestyle planning, life management, cultural participation, peer relationships, tolerance, emotional autonomy, academic autonomy, and salubrious lifestyles.

Student Development Associates
110 Crestwood Drive
Athens, GA 30605

Student Survey

The purpose is to measure student involvement in the college environment.

Educational Testing Service
Princeton, NJ 08541–0001

The Activity Inventory

The purpose is to measure and evaluate student involvement in a variety of extracurricular activities and to determine the effect that such involvement has on the overall student development.

ACT Evaluation/Survey Services
2201 North Dodge Street
P.O. Box 168
Iowa City, IA 52243

Disabled Students

Disabled Student Survey

The purpose is to measure disabled students' sense of inclusion in the campus environment.

Sue Koeger, Director
Office for Students with Disabilities
University of Minnesota
16 Johnston Hall
101 Pleasant Street S.E.
Minneapolis, MN 55455

Dropout Surveys

Former Student Questionnaire

The purpose is to survey dropout students to determine their reasons for leaving and their reactions to the institution.

NCHEMS
1540 Thirtieth Street
P.O. Drawer P
Boulder, CO 80302

The Student Experience

The purpose is to measure opinions of students who dropped out, including the reasons for dropping out, the dropout process, educational outcomes, student relations, peer relations, classroom experiences, future plans, and background information.

Learning Research Center
University of Tennessee
Knoxville, TN 37996–3400

Withdrawing/Nonreturning Student Survey

The purpose is to determine the reasons students leave an institution prior to completing a degree. Sections include background information, reasons for leaving college, college services and characteristics, additional local items, and comments and suggestions. Long and short forms are available.

ACT Evaluation/Survey Services
2201 North Dodge Street
P.O. Box 168
Iowa City, IA 52243

Drug and Alcohol Surveys

Core Drug and Alcohol Survey

The purpose is to collect information on student attitudes about and knowledge and use of alcohol and drugs.

Cheryl Presley
Southern Illinois University
Carbondale, IL 62901

Institutional Commitment to the Elimination of Alcohol and Other Substance Abuse

The purpose is to self-assess institutional policy, programs, enforcement, and assessment. Available in a faculty/staff form and a student form.

Network of Colleges and Universities Committed
    to the Elimination of Drug and Alcohol Abuse
U.S. Department of Education
555 New Jersey Avenue N.W.
Washington, DC 20208–5524

UCLA Drug Abuse Questionnaire

The purpose is to measure students' knowledge of drug abuse and attitudes toward drug abuse and drug addicts.

ERIC Document Reproduction Service
3900 Wheeler Avenue
Alexandria, VA 22304

Employer and Recruiter Surveys

Employer Survey

The purpose is to survey employers for ratings of job preparation and performance of graduates, as well as comments on skills needed by future graduates. Sections include employer assessment of the value of the graduate's holding of a position, job performance of the graduate, and satisfaction with the graduate.

Office of Assessment Services
University of Tennessee
Knoxville, TN 37996–4350

Recruiter Evaluation Survey

The purpose is to measure placement service recruiters' assessment of placement services.

Bob Greenberg
Career Services
University of Tennessee
Knoxville, TN 37996–4010

Environmental Assessment

Environmental Assessment Inventory

The purpose is to provide college counseling center staff with systematic and continuous data about the campus environment, trends in the environment, and impact on students.

Robert Conyne
340 Tangeman University Center, ML No. 46
University of Cincinnati
Cincinnati, OH 45221

Involving Colleges Interview Protocol

The purpose is to assess student perceptions of campus climate, including mission and philosophy, campus culture, campus environment, policies and practices, and institutional agents.

Center for Postsecondary Research and Planning
201 North Rose Avenue
Bloomington, IN 47405-1006

First-Year and Entering Student Assessment Instruments

Annual Survey of American College Freshmen

The purpose is to survey students' attitudes and values at the beginning of their first year.

Cooperative Institutional Research Program
Graduate School of Education
University of California
405 Hilgard Avenue
Los Angeles, CA 90024

Educational Planning Survey

The purpose is to collect information about entering students' backgrounds, high school academic and out-of-class experiences, expectations about college, educational and occupational plans, and reasons for attending college.

Division of Undergraduate Studies
Pennsylvania State University
102 Grange Building
University Park, PA 16802

Entering-Student Questionnaire

The purpose is to gain information from entering students at both two- and four-year institutions.

NCHEMS
1540 Thirtieth Street
P.O. Drawer P
Boulder, CO 80302

Entering Student Survey

The purpose is to collect information related to entering students' plans, goals, and impressions. Sections include background information, educational plans and preferences, college impressions, additional local questions, and comments and suggestions.

ACT Evaluation/Survey Services
2201 North Dodge Street
P.O. Box 168
Iowa City, IA 52243

Learning and Study Strategies Inventory (LASSI)

The purpose is to measure students' strengths and weaknesses in ten areas causally related to academic success: attitude, motivation, time management, anxiety, concentration, information processing, selecting main ideas, study aids, self-testing, and test strategies.

H & H Publishing Company
1231 Kapp Drive
Clearwater, FL 34625

Student Adaptation to College Questionnaire

The purpose is to measure students' adjustment to college, based on the assumption that the college experience places demands on students and requires various coping responses. Sections include academic adjustment, social adjustment, personal-emotional adjustment, and goal commitment and institutional attachment.

Western Psychological Services
12031 Wilshire Boulevard
Los Angeles, CA 90025–1251

Student Reactions to College

The purpose is to measure students' reactions to college, primarily during the first year. Assesses four major areas of student life: process of instruction, program planning, administrative affairs, and out-of-class activities.

Nancy Beck
Educational Testing Service
College and University Programs
Princeton, NJ 08541–0001

Student Satisfaction: The Freshman Experience

The purpose is to measure first-year students' satisfaction with all aspects of the university.

Office of Assessment Services
1819 Andy Holt Avenue
University of Tennessee
Knoxville, TN 37996–4350

Survey of Postsecondary Plans

The purpose is to survey entering students on career and academic plans and goals.

ACT Evaluation/Survey Services
2201 North Dodge Street
P.O. Box 168
Iowa City, IA 52243

Health Services and Health Education Instruments

Patient Evaluation Forms

The purpose is to evaluate doctors, receptionists and reception area, laboratory, nurses, and other aspects of health care environments.

Fred Young, Director
Student Health Services
1800 Andy Holt Avenue
University of Tennessee
Knoxville, TN 37996–2800

Student Health Services Student Survey

The purpose is to assess various aspects and functions of student health services.

Pat Tschop, Planning and Assessment
University of Kentucky
206 Gillis Building
Lexington, KY 40506–0033

Testwell Wellness Inventory, College Version

This is a software program whose purpose is to measure physical, emotional, social, intellectual, occupational, and spiritual development.

National Wellness Institute, Inc.
1045 Clark Street, Suite 210
Stevens Point, WI 54481–2962

Moral Development

Defining Issues Test

The purpose is to measure how students respond to a series of moral dilemma stories and classify their responses into one of the theoretical stages of Kohlberg's theory of moral reasoning.

Center for the Study of Ethical Development
University of Minnesota
141 Burton Hall
178 Pillsbury Drive S.E.
Minneapolis, MN 55445

Needs Assessment Instruments

College Student Needs Assessment Survey

The purpose is to assist college personnel in assessing the educational and personal needs of college students. Sections include background information, career and life goals, educational and personal needs, additional local questions, and comments and suggestions.

ACT Evaluation/Survey Services
2201 North Dodge Street
P.O. Box 168
Iowa City, IA 52243

Multicultural Awareness and Attitudes

Campus Diversity Survey

The purpose is to assess the perceptions of undergraduate students on issues of campus diversity, environments, experiences, and attitudes and actions, including race, sex, disability, and sexual orientation.

Eric Scouten, Research Projects Coordinator
University of Minnesota
110 Morrill Hall
100 Church Street S.E.
Minneapolis, MN 55455–0110

Campus Opinion Survey

The purpose is to focus on individual sightings of discriminatory behavior and emotional reactions to those sightings.

National Institute Against Prejudice and Violence
University of Maryland
31 South Greene Street
Baltimore, MD 21201

Minority Student Survey

The purpose is to collect information about the experiences, goals, and perceptions of African American students.

Roseann R. Hogan
Planning and Assessment
University of Kentucky
206A Gillis Building
Lexington, KY 40506–0033

Multifactor Racial Attitude Inventory (Form C-8)

The purpose is to measure different aspects of attitudes toward blacks. Subscales include integration-segregation policy, acceptance in close personal relationships, African American inferiority, ease in interracial contacts, derogatory beliefs, local autonomy, private rights, acceptance in status-superior relationships, gradualism, interracial marriage, and approaches to African American progress, militancy, and superiority.

Tests in Microfiche
Educational Testing Service
Princeton, NJ 08541–0001

Residence Hall Instruments

University Residence Environmental Scales

The purpose is to assess the social climates of student living groups, including involvement, emotional support, independence, traditional social orientation, competition, academic achievement, order and organization, intellectuality, social influence, and innovation. There are two versions: an expected social climate form for students who are entering residence halls and a form for current residents.

Consulting Psychologists Press
577 College Avenue
Palo Alto, CA 94306

Satisfaction Instruments

ACT Student Opinion Survey

The purpose is to explore perceptions of enrolled students in both two- and four-year institutions. Sections include background information, college services, college environment, additional local questions, and comments and suggestions.

ACT Evaluation/Survey Services
2201 North Dodge Street
P.O. Box 168
Iowa City, IA 52243

College Assessment Program Surveys (CAPS)

The purpose is to assess a person's personal incentives, opportunities in college to fulfill personal incentives, and perceptions of the culture of the institution. Sections include personal incentives, spirituality, self-esteem, college activities, institution culture, satisfaction, commitment to college, common college concerns, and college resources.

MetriTech, Inc.
111 North Market Street
Champaign, IL 61820

College Descriptive Index

The purpose is to measure student satisfaction with the college experience.

Tests in Microfiche
Educational Testing Service
Princeton, NJ 08541–0001

College Interest Inventory

The purpose is to measure student interest in college curricular areas.

Psychological Development Center
7057 West 130th Street
Parma, OH 44130

Institutional Goals Inventory

The purpose is to measure students' perceptions of institutional goals, including outcome goals (academic development, intellectual orientation, individual personal development, humanism/ altruism, cultural/aesthetic awareness, traditional religiousness, vocational preparation, advanced training, research, meeting local needs, public service, social egalitarianism, and social criticism/ activism). Process goals include freedom, democratic governance, community, intellectual/aesthetic environment, innovation, off-campus learning, and accountability/efficiency.

Educational Testing Service
Princeton, NJ 08541–0001

Student Reactions to College (SRC)

The purpose is to assess major areas of student life: instruction and classroom experience, counseling/advising, administrative regulations, class scheduling/registration, student activities, studying, faculty contact, student goals and planning, daily living, and library/bookstore.

Educational Testing Service
Princeton, NJ 08541–0001

Student Satisfaction: The Freshman Experience

The purpose is to measure student satisfaction with all aspects of the university.

Office of Assessment Services
1819 Andy Holt Avenue
University of Tennessee
Knoxville, TN 37996–4350

Student Satisfaction Survey

The purpose is to measure student satisfaction with campus climate, instructional effectiveness, academic advising effectiveness, and student centeredness. Versions are available for four-year institutions and community, junior, and technical colleges.

Noel Levitz Centers
2101 ACT Circle
Iowa City, IA 52245–9581

Student Satisfaction with University Programs and Services

The purpose is to measure undergraduate satisfaction with general university programs and services, programs related to major, and classroom experiences. Also provides background information on users.

Learning Research Center
212 Claxton Education Building
University of Tennessee
Knoxville, TN 37996–3400

Values Instruments

Annual Survey of American College Freshmen

The purpose is to survey students' attitudes and values at the beginning of their first year. Sections include biographical and background information, financial college, high school activities, self-ratings of abilities factors in the decision to attend college, parents' background, social values, college choice factors, high school academic preparation, probable college major, life goals, and college expectations. Versions are also available for the end of the first year and the end of the senior year.

Cooperative Institutional Research Program
Graduate School of Education
University of California
405 Hilgard Avenue
Los Angeles, CA 90024

Survey of Values

The purpose is to measure certain critical values, including practical-mindedness, achievement, variety, decisiveness, orderliness, and goal orientation.

Science Research Associates
1 Lincoln Center
Suite 1200
Oakbrook Terrace, IL 60181

References

American College Personnel Association. *A Statement of Ethical Principles and Standards*. Alexandria, Va.: American College Personnel Association, 1989.

American College Personnel Association. *The Student Learning Imperative: Implications for Student Affairs*. Alexandria, Va.: American College Personnel Association, 1994.

Andreas, R. E. "Program Planning." In M. J. Barr and Associates, *The Handbook of Student Affairs Administration*. San Francisco: Jossey-Bass, 1993.

Asher, B. T. "A Chief Student Affairs Officer's Perspective." In J. H. Schuh (ed.), *Enhancing Relationships with the Student Press*. New Directions for Student Services, no. 33. San Francisco: Jossey-Bass, 1986.

Astin, A. W. *Assessment for Excellence*. New York: Macmillan, 1991.

Astin, A. W. "The Impact of Dormitory Living on Students." *Educational Record*, 1973, *54*, 204–210.

Astin, A. W. *What Matters in College: Four Critical Years Revisited*. San Francisco: Jossey-Bass, 1993.

Astin, A. W., Korn, W. S., and Berz, E. R. *The American College Freshman: National Norms for Fall, 1990*. Los Angeles: Higher Education Research Institute, University of California, 1991.

Astin, A. W., and Solmon, L. C. "Are Reputational Ratings Needed to Measure Quality?" *Change Magazine*, 1981, *13*(7), 14–19.

Attinasi, L. C., and Nora, A. "Diverse Students and Complex Issues: A Case for Multiple Methods in College Student Research." In F. K. Stage (ed.), *Diverse Methods for Research and Assessment of College Students*. Alexandria, Va.: American College Personnel Association, 1992.

Aulepp, L., and Delworth, U. *Training Manual for an Ecosystem Model*. Boulder, Colo.: Western Interstate Commission for Higher Education, 1976.

Baird, L. L. "The College Environment Revisited: A Review of Research and Theory." In J. C. Smart (ed.), *Higher Education: Handbook of Theory and Research*, Vol. 4. New York: Agathon, 1988.

Baldridge, L. "Parent Survey." *WSU Child Development Center News*, Dec. 1993, pp. 5–14.

Baldridge, V. J. "Strategic Planning in Higher Education: Does the Emperor Have Any Clothes?" In V. J. Baldridge (ed.), *Dynamics of Organizational Change in Education*. Berkeley, Calif.: McCutchan, 1983.

Banning, J. H. "Creating a Climate for Successful Student Development: The Campus Ecology Manager Role." In U. Delworth, G. R. Hanson, and Associates, *Student Services: A Handbook for the Profession*. (2nd ed.) San Francisco: Jossey-Bass, 1989.

Banta, T. W. (ed.). *Implementing Outcomes Assessment: Promise and Perils*. New Directions for Institutional Research, no. 59. San Francisco: Jossey-Bass, 1988.

Banta, T. W., and Associates. *Making a Difference: Outcomes of a Decade of Assessment in Higher Education*. San Francisco: Jossey Bass, 1993.

Barrow, J., Cox, P., Sepich, R., and Spivak, R. "Student Needs Assessment Surveys: Do They Predict Student Use of Services?" *Journal of College Student Development*, 1989, *30*(1), 77–82.

Becker, H. S. "What Do They Really Learn at College?" In K. A. Feldman (ed.), *College and Student: Selected Readings in the Social Psychology of Higher Education*. New York: Pergamon, 1972.

Bellow, P. J., Morrisey, G. L., and Acomb, B. L. *The Executive Guide to Strategic Planning*. San Francisco: Jossey-Bass, 1987.

Best, J. W., and Kahn, J. V. *Research in Education*. Englewood Cliffs, N.J.: Prentice Hall, 1986.

Betz, E. L., Menne, J. W., Starr, A. M., and Klingensmith, J. E. "A Dimensional Analysis of College Student Satisfaction." *Measurement and Evaluation in Guidance*, 1971, *4*(2), 99–106.

Bloland, P. A., Stamatakos, L. C., and Rogers, R. R. *Reform in Student Affairs*. Greensboro, N.C.: ERIC Counseling and Student Services Clearinghouse, 1994.

Bogdan, R. C., and Biklen, S. K. *Qualitative Research for Education*. (2nd ed.) Boston: Allyn & Bacon, 1992.

Bogue, E. G., and Saunders, R. L. *The Evidence for Quality: Strengthening the Tests of Academic and Administrative Effectiveness*. San Francisco: Jossey-Bass, 1992.

Bolton, C. D., and Kammeyer, K.C.W. "Campus Cultures, Role Orientations, and Social Types." In K. A. Feldman (ed.), *College and Student: Selected Readings in the Social Psychology of Higher Education*. New York: Pergamon, 1972.

Borg, W. R., Gall, J. P., and Gall, M. D. *Applying Educational Research: A Practical Guide*. (3rd ed.) White Plains, N.Y.: Longman, 1993.

Borg, W. R., and Gall, M. D. *Educational Research: An Introduction*. (5th ed.) White Plains, N.Y.: Longman, 1989.

Boyer, E. L. *College: The Undergraduate Experience in America.* Report of the Carnegie Foundation for the Advancement of Teaching. New York: HarperCollins, 1987.

Bowering, D. J. (ed.). "Editor's Notes." In *Secondary Analysis of Available Data Bases.* New Directions for Program Evaluation, no. 22. San Francisco: Jossey-Bass, 1984.

Brodigan, D. L. "Focus Group Interviews: Applications for Institutional Research." *AIR Professional File*, 1992, *43*.

Brown, R. D. "Key Issues in Evaluating Student Affairs Programs." In G. D. Kuh (ed.), *Evaluation in Student Affairs.* Alexandria, Va.: American College Personnel Association, 1979.

Brown, R. D., and Podolske, D. L. "A Political Model for Program Evaluation." In M. J. Barr and Associates, *A Handbook of Student Affairs Administration.* San Francisco: Jossey-Bass, 1993a.

Brown, R. D., and Podolske, D. L. "Strengthening Programs Through Evaluation and Research." In R. B. Winston, Jr., S. Anchors, and Associates, *Student Housing and Residential Life: A Handbook for Professionals Committed to Student Development Goals.* San Francisco: Jossey-Bass, 1993b.

Bryan, W. A., Winston, R. B., Jr., and Miller, T. K. (eds.). *Using Professional Standards in Student Affairs.* New Directions for Student Services, no. 53. San Francisco: Jossey-Bass, 1991.

Bryson, J. M. *Strategic Planning for Public and Nonprofit Organizations: A Guide to Strengthening and Sustaining Organizational Achievement.* San Francisco: Jossey-Bass, 1988.

Bushnell, J. H. "Student Culture at Vassar." In R. N. Sanford (ed.), *The American College: A Psychological and Social Interpretation of the Higher Learning.* New York: Wiley, 1962.

Cage, M. C. "To Shield Academic Programs from Cuts, Many Colleges Pare Student Services." *Chronicle of Higher Education,* Nov. 18, 1992, A25–A26.

Camp, R. *Benchmarking: The Search for Industry Best Practices That Lead to Superior Performance.* Rochester, N.Y.: Xerox, 1989.

Canon, H. J. "Guiding Standards and Principles." In U. Delworth, G. R. Hanson, and Associates, *Student Services: A Handbook for the Profession.* (2nd ed.) San Francisco: Jossey-Bass, 1989.

Canon, H. J. "Maintaining High Ethical Standards." In M. J. Barr and Associates, *The Handbook of Student Affairs Administration.* San Francisco: Jossey-Bass, 1993.

Capezio, R., and Morehouse, D. *Total Quality Management: The Road of Continuous Improvement.* Shawnee Mission, Kans.: National Press Publications, 1992.

Carnaghi, J. E. "Focus Groups: Teachable and Educational Moments for All Involved." In F. K. Stage (ed.), *Diverse Methods for Research and Assessment of College Students.* Alexandria, Va.: American College Personnel Association, 1992.

Chaffee, E. E., and Tierney, W. G. *Collegiate Culture and Leadership.* New York: American Council on Education/Macmillan, 1988.

Chickering, A. W. *Commuting Versus Resident Students: Overcoming Educational Inequities of Living Off Campus.* San Francisco: Jossey-Bass, 1974.

Chickering, A. W., and Gamson, Z. "Seven Principles for Good Practice in Undergraduate Education." *Wingspread Journal,* 1987, *9*(2), 1.

Chickering, A. W., and Reisser, L. *Education and Identity.* (2nd ed.) San Francisco: Jossey-Bass, 1993.

Clark, B. R., and Trow, M. "The Organizational Context." In T. M. Newcomb and E. K. Wilson (eds.), *College Peer Groups: Problems and Prospects for Research.* Hawthorne, N.Y.: Aldine de Gruyter, 1966.

Coleman, J. S. "Peer Cultures and Education in Modern Society." In T. M. Newcomb and E. K. Wilson (eds.), *College Peer Groups: Problems and Prospects for Research.* Hawthorne, N.Y.: Aldine de Gruyter, 1966.

Cook, T. T., and Shadish, W. R. "Program Evaluation: The Worldly Science." *Annual Review in Psychology,* 1986, *37,* 193–232.

Cornesky, R., McCool, S., Byrnes, L., and Weber, R. *Implementing Total Quality Management in Higher Education.* Newbury Park, Calif.: Sage, 1991.

Council for the Advancement of Standards in Higher Education. *CAS Standards and Guidelines for Student Services/Development Programs.* Iowa City, Iowa: Council for the Advancement of Standards in Higher Education, 1986.

Crosson, F. *The Philosophy of Accreditation.* Washington, D.C.: Council on Postsecondary Accreditation, 1988.

Crowson, R. L. "Qualitative Research Methods in Higher Education." In J. C. Smart (ed.), *Higher Education: Handbook of Theory and Research,* Vol. 3. New York: Agathon, 1987.

De Coster, D. A., and Mable, P. "Residence Education: Purpose and Process." In D. A. De Coster and P. Mable (eds.), *Student Development and Education in College Residence Halls.* Alexandria, Va.: American College Personnel Association, 1974.

De Coster, D. A., and Mable, P. "Residence Education: Purpose and Process." In D. A. De Coster and P. Mable (eds.), *Personal Education and Community Development in College Residence Halls.* Alexandria, Va.: American College Personnel Association, 1980.

Dean Evans and Associates. *Event Management System.* Maplewood, Colo.: Dean Evans and Associates, 1994.

Deming, W. E. *Out of Crisis.* Cambridge: Massachusetts Institute of Technology Center for Advanced Engineering, 1986.

Dey, E. L. "College Impact and Student Liberalism Revisited: The Effect of Student Peers." Paper presented at the annual meeting of the Association for the Study of Higher Education, St. Louis, Mo., Nov. 1988.

Dillard, J. M. "Caribbean, Black and White College Students' Perceived Satisfaction at a Predominantly White University in the Southwest." *Psychological Reports,* 1989, *65,* 1053–1054.

Dobbert, M. L. *Ethnographic Research: Theory and Application for Modern Schools and Societies.* New York: Praeger, 1982.

Eisner, E. W. "Educational Connoisseurship and Criticism: Their Form and Functions in Educational Evaluation." In D. M. Fetterman (ed.), *Qualitative Approaches to Evaluation in Education: The Silent Revolution.* New York: Praeger, 1988.

Eisner, E. W., and Peshkin, A. "Introduction." In E. W. Eisner and A. Peshkin (eds.), *Qualitative Inquiry in Education: The Continuing Debate.* New York: Columbia University Teachers College, 1990.

El-Khawas, E. "Accreditation: Self-Regulation." In K. E. Young, C. C. Chambers, H. R. Kells, and Associates. *Understanding Accreditation: Contemporary Perspectives on Issues and Practices in Evaluating Educational Quality.* San Francisco: Jossey-Bass, 1983.

Ely, M., and others. *Doing Qualitative Research: Circles Within Circles.* London: Falmer, 1991.

Erlandson, D. A., Harris, E. L., Skipper, B. L., and Allen, S. D. *Doing Naturalistic Inquiry: A Guide to Methods.* Newbury Park, Calif.: Sage, 1993.

Erwin, T. D. *Assessing Student Learning and Development: A Guide to the Principles, Goals, and Methods of Determining College Outcomes.* San Francisco: Jossey-Bass, 1991.

Evans, N. J. "Needs Assessment Methodology: A Comparison of Results." *Journal of College Student Personnel,* 1985, *26*(2), 107–114.

Ewell, P. T. (ed.). *Assessing Educational Outcomes.* New Directions for Institutional Research, no. 47. San Francisco: Jossey-Bass, 1985.

Ewell, P. T. "Establishing a Campus-Based Assessment Program." In D. F. Halpern (ed.), *Student Outcomes Assessment: What Institutions Stand to Gain.* New Directions for Higher Education, no. 59. San Francisco: Jossey-Bass, 1987.

Ewell, P. T. "Implementing Assessment: Some Organizational Issues." In T. W. Banta (ed.), *Implementing Outcomes Assessments: Promise and Perils.* New Directions for Institutional Research, no. 59. San Francisco: Jossey-Bass, 1988.

Fairbrook, P. "Food Services and Programs." In R. B. Winston, Jr., S. Anchors, and Associates, *Student Housing and Residential Life: A Handbook for Professionals Committed to Student Development Goals.* San Francisco: Jossey-Bass, 1993.

Fetterman, D. M. *Ethnography: Step by Step.* Applied Social Research Methods, no. 17. Newbury Park, Calif.: Sage, 1989.

Gilbert, T. F. *Human Competence: Engineering Worthy Performance.* New York: McGraw-Hill, 1978.

Glesne, C., and Peshkin, A. *Becoming Qualitative Researchers: An Introduction.* White Plains, N.Y.: Longman, 1992.

Goetz, J. P., and Le Compte, M. D. *Ethnography and Qualitative Design in Educational Research.* San Diego, Calif.: Academic Press, 1984.

Gottlieb, D., and Hodgkins, B. "College Student Subcultures." In K. Yamamoto (ed.), *The College Student and His Culture: An Analysis.* Boston: Houghton-Mifflin, 1968.

Grose, R. F., Lauroesch, W., and Schiltz, M. E. "Commentary of the Draft Code of Ethics." In M. E. Schiltz (ed.), *Ethics and Standards in Institutional Research.* New Directions for Institutional Research, no. 73. San Francisco: Jossey-Bass, 1992.

Guba, E. G., and Lincoln, Y. S. *Effective Evaluation: Improving the Usefulness of Evaluation Results Through Responsive and Naturalistic Approaches.* San Francisco: Jossey-Bass, 1981.

Guba, E. G., and Lincoln, Y. S. *Fourth-Generation Evaluation.* Newbury Park, Calif.: Sage, 1989.

Hanson, G. R. (ed.). *Measuring Student Development.* New Directions for Student Services, no. 20. San Francisco: Jossey-Bass, 1982.

Hedlund, D., and Jones, J. "Effect of Student Personnel Services on Completion Rates in Two-Year Colleges." *Journal of College Student Personnel,* 1970, *11,* 196–199.

Hinkle, D. E., Wiersma, W., and Jurs, S. G. *Applied Statistics for the Behavioral Sciences.* (3rd ed.) Boston: Houghton Mifflin, 1994.

Hogan, T. J. "TQM, Higher Education, and Student Affairs: Opportunities and Questions." *Insights,* 1992, *3*(1), 15–19.

Holland, D. C., and Eisenhart, M. A. *Educated in Romance: Women, Achievement, and College Culture.* Chicago: University of Chicago Press, 1990.

Horowitz, H. L. *Campus Life: Undergraduate Cultures from the End of the Eighteenth Century to the Present.* New York: Knopf, 1987.

House, E. R. *Professional Evaluation.* Newbury Park, Calif.: Sage, 1993.

Howe, N., and Strauss, W. "The New Generation Gap." *Atlantic Monthly,* Nov. 1992.

Huebner, L. A. "Ethics of Intentional Campus Design." Paper presented at the Second Annual Campus Ecology Symposium, Pingree Park, Colo., June 1984.

Huebner, L. A. "Interaction of Student and Campus." In U. Delworth, G. R. Hanson, and Associates, *Student Services: A Handbook for the Profession.* (2nd ed.) San Francisco: Jossey-Bass, 1989.

Huebner, L. A., and Lawson, J. M. "Understanding and Assessing College Environments." In D. G. Creamer (ed.), *College Student Development: Theory and Practice for the 1990s.* Alexandria, Va.: American College Personnel Association, 1990.

Huebner, L. A., and others. "Stress Management Through an Ecosystem Model in a School of Medicine." In L. A. Huebner (ed.), *Redesigning Campus Environments.* New Directions for Student Services, no. 8. San Francisco: Jossey-Bass, 1979.

Hughes, E. C., Becker, H. S., and Geer, B. "Student Culture and Academic Effort." In R. N. Sanford (ed.), *The American College: A Psychological and Social Interpretation of the Higher Learning.* New York: Wiley, 1962.

Hurst, J. C., and Jacobson, J. K. "Theories Underlying Students' Needs for Programs." In M. J. Barr, L. A. Keating, and Associates, *Developing Effective Student Services Programs: Systematic Approaches for Practitioners.* San Francisco: Jossey-Bass, 1985.

Hurst, J. C., and Ragle, J. D. "Application of the Ecosystem Perspective to a Dean of Students Office." In L. A. Huebner (ed.), *Redesigning Campus Environments.* New Directions for Student Services, no. 8. San Francisco: Jossey-Bass, 1979.

Hutchings, P., and others. "Principles of Good Practice for Assessing Student Learning." *Assessment Update,* 1993, *5*(1), 6–7.

Jacobi, M., Astin, A. W., and Ayala, F., Jr. *College Student Outcomes Assessment: A Talent Development Perspective.* ASHE-ERIC Higher Education report no. 7. Washington, D.C.: Association for the Study of Higher Education, 1987.

Jacoby, B. "Today's Students: Diverse Needs Require Comprehensive Responses." In T. K. Miller and R. B. Winston, Jr. (eds.), *Administration and Leadership in Student Affairs.* (2nd ed.) Muncie, Ind.: Accelerated Development, 1991.

Johnson, J. C. *Selecting Ethnographic Informants.* Qualitative Research Methods, no. 22. Newbury Park, Calif.: Sage, 1990.

Joughin, L. *Academic Freedom and Tenure.* Madison: University of Wisconsin Press, 1969.

Katchadourian, H. A., and Boli, J. *Careerism and Intellectualism Among College Students: Patterns of Academic and Career Choice in the Undergraduate Years.* San Francisco: Jossey-Bass, 1985.

Kelly, E. F., Pascarella, E. T., Terenzini, P. T., and Chapman, D. "The Development and Use of the Adjective Rating Scale: A Measure of Attitudes

Toward Courses and Programs." *Journal of Selected Abstracts in Science,* 1978, *8,* 19–20.

Kennedy, G. E. "Differences Among College Students' Perceptions of Family Satisfaction." *Perceptual and Motor Skills,* 1989, *68*(1), 129–130.

Kerlinger, F. N. *Foundations of Behavioral Research.* Fort Worth, Tex.: Holt, Rinehart and Winston, 1986.

Kitchener, K. S. "Ethical Principles and Ethical Decisions in Student Affairs." In H. J. Canon and R. D. Brown (eds.), *Applied Ethics in Student Affairs.* New Directions for Student Services, no. 38. San Francisco: Jossey-Bass, 1985.

Krueger, D. W. "Total Quality Management." In T. W. Banta (ed.), *Making a Difference: Outcomes of a Decade of Assessment in Higher Education.* San Francisco: Jossey-Bass, 1993.

Kuh, G. D. "Purposes and Principles of Needs Assessment in Student Affairs." *Journal of College Student Personnel,* 1982, *23*(3), 202–209.

Kuh, G. D. "Assessing Student Cultures." In W. G. Tierney (ed.), *Assessing Academic Climates and Cultures.* New Directions for Institutional Research, no. 68. San Francisco: Jossey-Bass, 1990.

Kuh, G. D. *Environmental Influences on Alcohol Use by College Students.* Washington, D.C.: Office of Educational Research and Improvement, 1991.

Kuh, G. D. "Assessing Campus Environments." In M. J. Barr and Associates, *The Handbook of Student Affairs Administration.* San Francisco: Jossey-Bass, 1993a.

Kuh, G. D. "In Their Own Words: What Students Learn Outside the Classroom." *American Educational Research Journal,* 1993b, *30*(2), 277–304.

Kuh, G. D. "Indices of Quality in Student Culture Research." Paper presented at the annual meeting of the American Educational Research Association, New Orleans, Apr. 1994.

Kuh, G. D., and Hall, J. "Cultural Perspectives in Student Affairs." In G. D. Kuh (ed.), *Cultural Perspectives in Student Affairs Work.* Lanham, Md.: University Press of America & American College Personnel Association, 1993.

Kuh, G. D., Schuh, J. H., Whitt, E. J., and Associates. *Involving Colleges: Successful Approaches to Fostering Student Learning and Personal Development Outside the Classroom.* San Francisco: Jossey-Bass, 1991.

Kuh, G. D., and Whitt, E. J. *The Invisible Tapestry: Culture in American Colleges and Universities.* ASHE-ERIC Higher Education report no. 1. Washington, D.C.: Association for the Study of Higher Education, 1988.

Layder, D. *New Strategies in Social Research.* Cambridge, Mass.: Polity, 1993.

Leafgren, F. "Wellness as a Comprehensive Student Development Approach." In R. B. Winston, Jr., S. Anchors, and Associates, *Student*

Housing and Residential Life: A Handbook for Professionals Committed to Student Development Goals. San Francisco: Jossey-Bass, 1993.

Leemon, T. A. *The Rites of Passage in a Student Culture.* New York: Teachers College Press, 1972.

Lenning, O. T. "Use of Noncognitive Measures in Assessment." In T. W. Banta (ed.), *Implementing Outcomes Assessments: Promise and Perils.* New Directions for Institutional Research, no. 59. San Francisco: Jossey-Bass, 1988.

Lenning, O. T., and MacAleenan, A. C. "Needs Assessment in Student Affairs." In G. D. Kuh (ed.), *Evaluation in Student Affairs.* Alexandria, Va.: American College Personnel Association, 1979.

Lewin, K. *Principles of Topological Psychology.* (F. Heider and G. M. Heider, trans.) New York: McGraw-Hill, 1936.

Lincoln, Y. S. "Presentation by Louis B. Smith." In E. W. Eisner and A. Peshkin (eds.), *Qualitative Inquiry in Education: The Continuing Debate.* New York: Columbia University Teachers College, 1990.

Lincoln, Y. S., and Guba, E. G. *Naturalistic Inquiry.* Newbury Park, Calif.: Sage, 1985.

Love, P. G., and others. "Student Culture." In G. D. Kuh (ed.), *Cultural Perspectives in Student Affairs Work.* Lanham, Md.: University Press of America & American College Personnel Association, 1993.

Lyons, J. W. "An Eclipse of the Usual: The Evergreen State College." In G. D. Kuh and J. H. Schuh (eds.), *The Role and Contribution of Student Affairs in Involving Colleges.* Washington, D.C.: National Association of Student Personnel Administrators, 1991.

Lyons, J. W. "The Importance of Institutional Mission." In M. J. Barr and Associates, *The Handbook of Student Affairs Administration.* San Francisco: Jossey-Bass, 1993.

Mable, P., and Miller, T. K. "Standards for Professional Practice." In T. K. Miller, R. B. Winston, Jr., and W. R. Mendenhall (eds.), *Administration and Leadership in Student Affairs: Actualizing Student Development in Higher Education.* Muncie, Ind.: Accelerated Development, 1983.

Mable, P., and Miller, T. K. "Standards of Professional Practice." In T. K. Miller, R. B. Winston, Jr., and Associates, *Administration and Leadership in Student Affairs: Actualizing Student Development in Higher Education.* (2nd ed.) Muncie, Ind.: Accelerated Development, 1991.

McMillan, J. H. "Conceptualizing and Assessing College Student Values." Paper presented at the annual meeting of the American Educational Research Association, San Francisco, Mar. 1989.

Magolda, P. "A Quest for Community: An Ethnographic Study of a Residential College." Unpublished doctoral dissertation, Indiana University, 1994.

Magrath, C. P., and Magrath, D. S. "A Presidential Perspective." In J. H. Schuh (ed.), *Enhancing Relationships with the Student Press*. New Directions for Student Services, no. 33. San Francisco: Jossey-Bass, 1986.

Manning, K. "The Ethnographic Interview." In F. K. Stage (ed.), *Diverse Methods for Research and Assessment of College Students*. Alexandria, Va.: American College Personnel Association, 1992.

Marchese, T. J. "Assessment's Next Five Years." *Association of Institutional Research Newsletter,* Fall-Winter 1990, 1–4. (Special supplement)

Marshall, C., and Rossman, G. B. *Designing Qualitative Research*. Newbury Park, Calif.: Sage, 1989.

Martin, J. *Cultures in Organizations: Three Perspectives*. New York: Oxford University Press, 1992.

Marton, F. "Phenomenography: Exploring Different Conceptions." In D. M. Fetterman (ed.), *Qualitative Approaches to Evaluation in Education: The Silent Revolution*. New York: Praeger, 1988.

Mayhew, L. B., Ford, P. J., and Hubbard, D. L. *The Quest for Quality: The Challenge for Undergraduate Education in the 1990s*. San Francisco: Jossey-Bass, 1990.

Meredith, G. M. "Student-Based Indicators of Campus Satisfaction as an Outcome of Higher Education." *Psychological Reports,* 1985, *56*(2), 597–598.

Merriam, S. B. *Case Study Research in Education: A Qualitative Approach*. San Francisco: Jossey-Bass, 1988.

Miles, M. B., and Huberman, A. M. "Drawing Valid Meaning from Qualitative Data: Toward a Shared Craft." In D. M. Fetterman (ed.), *Qualitative Approaches to Evaluation in Education: The Silent Scientific Revolution*. New York: Praeger, 1988.

Miles, M. M. "Qualitative Data as an Attractive Nuisance: The Problems of Analysis." *Administrative Science Quarterly,* 1979, *24*, 590–601.

Miller, T. K. "Professional Standards: Whither Thou Goest?" *Journal of College Student Personnel,* 1984, *25*(5), 412–416.

Miller, T. K., Carpenter, D. S., Saunders, S., and Thompson, M. J. "Developmental Programming: An Action Planning Model." In F. B. Newton and K. L. Ender (eds.), *Student Development Practices: Strategies for Making a Difference*. Springfield, Ill.: Thomas, 1980.

Miller, T. K., Thomas, W. L., Looney, S. C., and Yerian, J. *CAS Self-Assessment Guides*. Iowa City, Iowa: Council for the Advancement of Standards for Higher Education, 1988.

Moffatt, M. *Coming of Age in New Jersey: College and American Culture*. New Brunswick, N.J.: Rutgers University Press, 1988.

Morgan, D. L. *Focus Groups as Qualitative Research*. Qualitative Research Methods, no. 16. Newbury Park, Calif.: Sage, 1988.

Morgan, G. *Images of Organization.* Newbury Park, Calif.: Sage, 1986.

National Association of Student Personnel Administrators. *A Perspective on Student Affairs.* Washington, D.C.: National Association of Student Personnel Administrators, 1987.

National Association of Student Personnel Administrators. "Standards of Professional Practice." In *NASPA Member Handbook.* Washington, D.C.: National Association of Student Personnel Administrators, 1992–1993.

National Association of Student Personnel Administrators. "Standards of Professional Practice." In *NASPA Member Handbook.* Washington, D.C.: National Association of Student Personnel Administrators, 1993–1994.

National Commission for the Protection of Human Subjects of Biomedical and Behavioral Research. *Ethical Principles and Guidelines for the Protection of Human Subjects Research.* Washington, D.C.: U.S. Department of Health and Human Services, 1979.

National Institute of Education. *Involvement in Learning: Realizing the Potential of American Higher Education.* Washington, D.C.: U.S. Department of Education, 1984.

Newcomb, T. M. "Student Peer-Group Influence." In R. N. Sanford (ed.), *The American College: A Psychological and Social Interpretation of the Higher Learning.* New York: Wiley, 1962.

Newcomb, T. M. "The General Nature of Peer Group Influence." In T. M. Newcomb and E. K. Wilson (eds.), *College Peer Groups: Problems and Prospects for Research.* Hawthorne, N.Y.: Aldine de Gruyter, 1966.

Noel Levitz. *Student Satisfaction Inventory.* Iowa City, Iowa: Noel Levitz, 1994.

Pace, C. R. *Measuring Outcomes of College.* San Francisco: Jossey-Bass, 1979.

Pace, C. R. *CSEQ: Test Manual and Norms.* Los Angeles: Center for the Study of Evaluation, Graduate School of Education, University of California, 1987.

Pascarella, E. T. "Student-Faculty Informal Contact and College Outcomes." *Review of Educational Research,* 1980, *50,* 545–595.

Pascarella, E. T., and Terenzini, P. T. *How College Affects Students: Findings and Insights from Twenty Years of Research.* San Francisco: Jossey-Bass, 1991.

Patton, M. Q. *Qualitative Evaluation and Research Methods.* (2nd ed.) Newbury Park, Calif.: Sage, 1990.

Paul, S. C. "Understanding Student-Environment Interaction." In W. H. Morrill and J. C. Hurst with E. R. Oetting (eds.), *Dimensions of Intervention for Student Development.* New York: Wiley, 1980.

Pfaffenberger, B. *Microcomputer Applications in Qualitative Research.* Newbury Park, Calif.: Sage, 1988.

Rhoads, R. A. "The Brothers of Alpha Beta: An Ethnography of Fraternity Oppression of Women." Unpublished master's thesis. Pennsylvania State University Graduate School, 1992.

Riker, H. C., and De Coster, D. A. "The Educational Role in Student Housing." *Journal of College and University Student Housing*, 1971, *1*(1), 3–7.

Robertson, J. A. "Black Student Satisfaction in the Deep South." *Journal of College Student Personnel*, 1980, *21*(6), 510–513.

Rodgers, R. F. "An Integration of Campus and Student Development: The Olentangy Project." In D. G. Creamer (ed.), *College Student Development: Theory and Practice for the 1990s*. Alexandria, Va.: American College Personnel Association, 1990.

Rodriguez, R. G. "The Ethical Analysis Protocol." In M. E. Schiltz (ed.), *Ethics and Standards in Institutional Research*. New Directions for Institutional Research, no. 73. San Francisco: Jossey-Bass, 1992.

Rossett, A. "Needs Assessment: Forerunner to Successful HRD Programs." In J. W. Pfeiffer (ed.), *The 1990 Annual: Developing Human Resources*. San Diego: University Associates, 1990.

Rossman, J. E., and El-Khawas, E. *Thinking About Assessment: Perspectives for Presidents and Chief Academic Officers*. Washington, D.C.: American Council on Education & American Association for Higher Education, 1987.

Russell, R. V. "Validating Results with Nonreactive Measures." In F. K. Stage (ed.), *Diverse Methods for Research and Assessment of College Students*. Alexandria, Va.: American College Personnel Association, 1992.

Russell, R. V., and Stage, F. K. "Triangulation: Intersecting Assessment and Research Methods." In F. K. Stage (ed.), *Diverse Methods for Research and Assessment of College Students*. Alexandria, Va.: American College Personnel Association, 1992.

Schein, E. H. *Organizational Culture and Leadership*. (2nd ed.) San Francisco: Jossey-Bass, 1992.

Schlossberg, N. K., Lynch, A. Q., and Chickering, A. W. *Improving Higher Education Environments for Adults: Responsive Programs and Services from Entry to Departure*. San Francisco: Jossey-Bass, 1991.

Schuh, J. H. "Implementing the Ecosystem Model: Phase II." *Journal of College and University Student Housing*, 1978, *8*(2), 6–8.

Schuh, J. H. "Assessment and Redesign in Residence Halls." In L. A. Huebner (ed.), *Redesigning Campus Environments*. New Directions for Student Services, no. 8. San Francisco: Jossey-Bass, 1979.

Schuh, J. H. "Streamlining the Ecosystems Approach to Residence Hall Environmental Assessment." *NASPA Journal*, 1990, *27*(3), 185–191.

Schuh, J. H. "Foreword." In F. K. Stage (ed.), *Diverse Methods for Research and Assessment of College Students.* Alexandria, Va.: American College Personnel Association, 1992.

Schuh, J. H. "Fiscal Pressures on Student Affairs." In M. J. Barr and Associates, *The Handbook of Student Affairs Administration.* San Francisco: Jossey-Bass, 1993a.

Schuh, J. H. *Report of Selected Plans of Entering Students at Wichita State University.* Wichita, Kans.: Office of Student Life and Services, Wichita State University, 1993b.

Schuh, J. H. (ed.). *Enhancing Relationships with the Student Press.* New Directions for Student Services, no. 33. San Francisco: Jossey-Bass, 1986.

Schuh, J. H., and Allan, M. R. "Implementing the Ecosystem Model." *Journal of College Student Personnel,* 1978, *19*(2), 119–122.

Schuh, J. H., and Kuh, G. D. "Evaluating the Quality of Collegiate Environments." *Journal of College Admissions,* 1991, *130*, 17–21.

Schuh, J. H., Triponey, V. L., Heim, L. L., and Nishimura, K. "Student Involvement in Historically Black Greek Letter Organizations." *NASPA Journal,* 1992, *29*(4), 274–282.

Schuh, J. H., and Veltman, G. C. "Application of an Ecosystem Model to an Office of Handicapped Services." *Journal of College Student Development,* 1991, *32*(3), 236–240.

Schuh, J. H., and Whitt, E. J. *Longwood College Case Report.* Unpublished manuscript, Farmville, Va., 1990.

Scriven, M. "The Methodology of Evaluation." In R. W. Tyler, R. M. Gagne, and M. Scriven (eds.), *Perspectives on Curriculum Evaluation.* AERA Monograph Series on Curriculum Evaluation, no. 1. Chicago: Rand McNally, 1967.

Selltiz, C., Jahoda, M., Deutsch, M., and Cook, S. W. *Research Methods in Social Relations.* Fort Worth, Texas: Holt, Rinehart and Winston, 1962.

Sherr, L. A., and Teeter, D. J. *Total Quality Management in Higher Education.* New Directions for Institutional Research, no. 71. San Francisco: Jossey-Bass, 1991.

Shulman, L. S. "Disciplines of Inquiry in Education: An Overview." In R. Jaeger (ed.), *Complementary Methods for Research in Education.* Washington, D.C.: American Educational Research Association, 1988.

Siddons, P. "The Frustrations and Rewards of College Journalism." In J. H. Schuh (ed.), *Enhancing Relationships with the Student Press.* New Directions for Student Services, no. 33. San Francisco: Jossey-Bass, 1986.

Silverman, W. H., and others. "Measuring Member Satisfaction with the Church." *Journal of Applied Psychology,* 1983, *68*(4), 664–677.

Smith, L. F. "Ethics in Qualitative Field Research: An Individual Perspective." In E. W. Eisner and A. Peshkin (eds.), *Qualitative Inquiry in Education.* New York: Teachers College Press, 1990.

Smith, N. "Mining Metaphors for Methods of Practice." In D. M. Fetterman (ed.), *Qualitative Approaches to Evaluation in Education: The Silent Revolution.* New York: Praeger, 1988.

Southern Association of Colleges and Schools. *Manual for Accreditation: Commission on Colleges.* Atlanta: Southern Association of Colleges and Schools, 1987.

Southern Association of Colleges and Schools. *Criteria for Accreditation: Commission on Colleges.* (8th ed.) Atlanta: Southern Association of Colleges and Schools, 1992.

Spendolini, M. J. *The Benchmarking Book.* New York: American Management Association, 1992.

Spradley, J. P. *The Ethnographic Interview.* Fort Worth, Tex.: Holt, Rinehart and Winston, 1979.

Stage, F. K. "The Case for Flexibility in Research and Assessment of College Students." In F. K. Stage (ed.), *Diverse Methods for Research and Assessment of College Students.* Alexandria, Va.: American College Personnel Association, 1992.

Stern, G. G. *People in Context.* New York: Wiley, 1970.

Strange, C. C. "Managing College Environments: Theory and Practice." In T. K. Miller and R. B. Winston, Jr. (eds.), *Administration and Leadership in Student Affairs.* Muncie, Ind.: Accelerated Development, 1991.

Stufflebeam, D. L., McCormick, C. H., Brinkerhoff, R. O., and Nelson, C. O. *Conducting Educational Needs Assessment.* Norwell, Mass.: Wolters Kluwer, 1985.

Suskie, L. A. *Questionnaire Survey Research: What Works.* Tallahassee, Fla.: Association for Institutional Research, 1992.

Teeter, D. J., and Lozier, G. G. (eds.). *Pursuit of Quality in Higher Education: Case Studies in Total Quality Management.* New Directions for Institutional Research, no. 78. San Francisco: Jossey-Bass, 1993.

Terenzini, P. T. "Assessment with Open Eyes: Pitfalls in Studying Student Outcomes." *Journal of Higher Education,* 1989, *60*(6), 644–664.

Terenzini, P. T., and Pascarella, E. T. "The Relation of Students' Precollege Characteristics and Freshman-Year Experience to Voluntary Attrition." *Research in Higher Education,* 1978, *9,* 347–366.

Thelin, J. R. "Student Cultures." In B. R. Clark (ed.), *Encyclopaedia of Higher Education.* Oxford: Pergamon, 1992.

Thomas, J. "Needs Assessment: Avoiding the 'Hammer' Approach." In J. W. Pfeiffer and L. D. Goodstein (eds.), *The 1984 Annual: Developing Human Resources.* San Diego, Calif.: University Associates, 1984.

Thrash, P. (ed.). Accreditation [Special issue]. *Journal of Higher Education,* 1979, *50*(2).

Tinto, V. "Dropout from Higher Education: A Theoretical Synthesis of Recent Research." *Review of Educational Research,* 1975, *45,* 89–125.

Tinto, V. *Leaving College: Rethinking the Causes and Cures of Student Attrition.* Chicago: University of Chicago Press, 1987.

Treadway, D. M. "Use of Campuswide Ecosystem Surveys to Monitor a Changing Institution." In L. A. Huebner (ed.), *Redesigning Campus Environments.* New Directions for Student Services, no. 8. San Francisco: Jossey-Bass, 1979.

U.S. Department of Health and Human Services. *Protection of Human Subjects, Title 45: Code of Federal Regulations, Part 46.* Washington, D.C.: U.S. Government Printing Office, 1991.

Upcraft, M. L. "Residence Halls and Student Activities." In L. Noel, R. Levitz, D. Saluri, and Associates, *Increasing Student Retention: Effective Programs and Practices for Reducing the Dropout Rate.* San Francisco: Jossey-Bass, 1985.

Upcraft, M. L. "Teaching and Today's College Student." In M. E. Wiemer and R. Menges (eds.), *Better Teaching and Learning in College: Toward More Scholarly Practice.* San Francisco: Jossey-Bass, 1996.

Upcraft, M. L. (ed.). *Orienting Students to College.* San Francisco: Jossey-Bass, 1984.

Van Maanen, J. "Managing Education Better: Some Thoughts on the Management of Student Cultures in American Colleges and Universities." Paper presented at the 27th Annual Forum, Association for Institutional Research, Kansas City, May 1987.

Van Maanen, J. *Tales of the Field: On Writing Ethnography.* Chicago: University of Chicago Press, 1988.

Wallace, W. L. *Student Culture: Social Structure and Continuity in a Liberal Arts College.* Hawthorne, N.Y.: Aldine de Gruyter, 1966.

Weidman, J. C. "Undergraduate Socialization: A Conceptual Approach." In J. C. Smart (ed.), *Higher Education: Handbook of Theory and Research,* Vol. 5. New York: Agathon, 1989.

Wesley, A. L., and Abston, N., Jr. "Black College Students' Satisfaction at Two Predominantly White Universities in the Deep South." *Psychological Reports,* 1983, *53,* 222.

Western Interstate Commission for Higher Education. *The Ecosystem Model: Designing Campus Environments.* Boulder, Colo.: Western Interstate Commission for Higher Education, 1973.

Whitaker, U. *Assessment Learning: Standards, Principles, and Procedures.* Philadelphia: Council for Adult and Experiential Learning, 1989.

Whitt, E. J. "Artful Science: A Primer on Qualitative Research Methods." *Journal of College Student Development,* 1991, *32*(5), 406–415.

Whitt, E. J. "Document Analysis." In F. K. Stage (ed.), *Diverse Methods for Research and Assessment of College Students.* Alexandria, Va.: American College Personnel Association, 1992a.

Whitt, E. J. "A Room of Her Own: A Study of Women's Colleges." Paper presented at the annual meeting of the American Educational Research Association, San Francisco, Apr. 1992b.

Whitt, E. J. "Making the Familiar Strange: Discovering Culture. In G. D. Kuh (ed.), *Cultural Perspectives in Student Affairs Work.* Lanham, Md.: University Press of America & American College Personnel Association, 1993.

Whitt, E. J. "Encouraging Adult Student Involvement." *NASPA Journal,* 1994a, *31*(4), 309–318.

Whitt, E. J. "I Can Be Anything! Student Leadership in Three Women's Colleges." *Journal of College Student Development,* 1994b, *35*(3), 198–207.

Whitt, E. J., and Kuh, G. D. "The Use of Qualitative Methods in a Team Approach to Multiple Institution Studies." *Review of Higher Education,* 1991, *14,* 317–337.

Whitt, E. J., and Nuss, E. M. "Connecting Residence Halls to the Curriculum." In C. C. Schroeder, P. Mable, and Associates, *Realizing the Educational Potential of College Residence Halls.* San Francisco: Jossey-Bass, 1994.

Wichita State University Office of Academic Affairs. *Wichita State University Handbook for Faculty.* Wichita, Kans.: Wichita State University Office of Academic Affairs, 1988.

Wingspread Group on Higher Education. *An American Imperative: Higher Expectations for Higher Education.* Johnson Foundation, 1993.

Winston, R. B. Jr., and Miller, T. K. "A Model for Assessing Developmental Outcomes Related to Student Affairs Programs and Services." *NASPA Journal,* 1994, *32*(1).

Winston, R. B., Jr., and Saunders, S. A. "Ethical Professional Practice in Student Affairs." In T. K. Miller and R. B. Winston, Jr. (ed.), *Administration and Leadership in Student Affairs.* Muncie, Ind.: Accelerated Development, 1991.

Wolcott, H. F. "How to Look like an Anthropologist Without Really Being One." *Practicing Anthropology,* 1980, *3*(2), 56–59.

Wolcott, H. F. *Writing Up Qualitative Research.* Qualitative Research Methods, no. 20. Newbury Park, Calif.: Sage, 1990.

Worthen, B. R., and Sanders, J. R. *Educational Evaluation: Alternative Approaches and Practical Guidelines.* White Plains, N.Y.: Longman, 1987.

Yerian, J. M., and Miller, T. K. *Putting the CAS Standards to Work*. Washington, D.C.: Council for the Advancement of Standards in Higher Education, 1988.

Young, K. E., Chambers, C. C., Kells, H. R., and Associates. *Understanding Accreditation: Contemporary Perspectives on Issues and Practices in Evaluating Educational Quality*. San Francisco: Jossey-Bass, 1983.

Zeithaml, V. A., Parasuraman, A., and Berry, L. L. *Delivering Quality Services: Balancing Customer Perceptions and Expectations*. New York: Free Press, 1990.

Index

A

Abston, N., Jr., 161
Academic advising instruments, 326–327
Academic Advising Inventory, 326
Academic freedom, and ethical issues, 309
Academic mission, and assessment, 10
Accountability, assessment needed for, 5–7
Accreditation: assessment needed for, 5, 7; associations for, 261–262; defined, 260–261; and outcomes assessment, 224; and peer review, 264–265; and standards, 260–267
Accreditation Association for Ambulatory Health Care, 224, 262
ACHA, 270
Acomb, B. L., 242
ACT Alumni Outcomes Survey, 327
ACT Alumni Survey, 328
ACT Student Opinion Survey, 341
Activities Index, 229
Activity Inventory, 332–333
Adjective Rating Scale, 228–229
Adult Learner Needs Assessment Survey, 327
Affordability, assessment needed for, 13–14
Allan, M. R., 179
Allen, S. D., 196, 201
Alumni instruments, 327–329
Ambiguity, in culture assessments, 199–200

American Association of Higher Education Assessment Forum, 22
American College Personnel Association, 10–11, 313
American College Testing (ACT) Evaluation/Survey Services, 119, 325, 327, 328, 329, 333, 334, 337, 338, 339, 341
American Counseling Association, 330
American Psychological Association, 262
Analysis concept, 93. See also Data analysis
Andreas, R. E., 131
Annual Survey of American College Freshmen, 336, 344
Asher, B. T., 154
Assessment: analysis of need for, 3–31; background on, 3–5; with benchmarking, 240–251; of campus environments, 166–188; challenges of, 273–323; comprehensive model of, 27–30, 315–322; conclusions on, 30–31, 322–323; context for, 1–109; and crises, 3–4, 144; definitions in, 16–22; dimensions of, 111–272; ethical standards for, 290–314; in higher education, 5–7; issues in, 32–51, 316; longitudinal, 220–222; negotiating agreement for, 306–307, 308; ongoing, 318–319; of outcomes, 217–239; principles of, 22–24, 316–322; process issues for, 25–26; with professional standards, 252–272; purpose of, 17, 220;

qualitative methods for, 52–83; quantitative methods for, 84–109; rationale for, 7–16; recommendations on, 315–323; reporting results of, 275–289; of student cultures, 189–216; of student needs, 126–147; of student satisfaction, 148–165; summary on, 51; tracking client use of, 113–125

Astin, A. W., 6, 14, 16, 17, 18, 44, 153, 160–161, 166, 194, 218–224, 226, 227, 232, 233, 239, 265, 278, 286

Attinasi, L. C., 201

Attitude Toward College Inventory, 331

Aulepp, L., 173, 179, 184, 187, 188

Autonomy, respecting, 291–292, 300, 303–304

Ayala, F., Jr., 14, 278, 286

B

Baird, L. L., 201

Baldridge, L., 188

Baldridge, V. J., 14

Banning, J. H., 167

Banta, T. W., 17, 218

Barrow, J., 133, 146–147

Beck, N., 338

Becker, H. S., 191

Behavior: engineering, 175–177; formula for, 168–170; repertory of, 175–176

Bellow, P. J., 242

Benchmarking: aspects of, 240–251; conclusion on, 251; definition and types of, 241–242; keys to, 250–251; steps in, 243–250; uses of, 242–243

Benefit to others, ethics of, 293

Berry, L. L., 157–158

Berz, E. R., 44

Best, J. W., 94, 95

Betz, E. L., 162

Biklen, S. K., 53, 54, 62n, 69, 76, 300, 303, 305, 306, 309

Bivariate analyses, in quantitative methods, 101–105

Bloland, P. A., 11

Bogdan, R. C., 53, 54, 62n, 69, 76, 300, 303, 305, 306, 309

Bogue, E. G., 148–149, 266, 267

Boli, J., 193, 194, 195, 216

Bolton, C. D., 192, 194

Borg, W. R., 20, 21, 61, 85, 87–88, 94, 98, 311

Bowering, D. J., 69

Bowling Green State University, Department of College Student Personnel at, 330

Boyer, E. L., 5

Brinkerhoff, R. O., 127, 143

Brodigan, D. L., 207, 208

Brown, R. D., 20, 25, 135, 143, 146, 162

Bryan, W. A., 253, 263, 269–270

Bryson, J. M., 268, 269

Byrnes, L., 7

C

Cage, M. C., 9

California at Los Angeles, University of (UCLA), instruments from, 334–335, 336, 344

Camp, R., 243

Campus Diversity Survey, 183, 340

Campus Opinion Survey, 183, 340

Canon, H. J., 291, 292, 293–294, 309

Capezio, R., 243

Career Decision Scale, 329

Career Development Inventory, 329

Career planning and placement: databases for, 119–120; instruments on, 329

Carnaghi, J. E., 63, 135, 208

Carnegie Foundation for the Advancement of Teaching, 5

Carpenter, D. S., 269

Case study. See Qualitative methods

Center for Postsecondary Research and Planning, 331

Central Iowa Associates, 342

Certification, and professional standards, 265–267

Chaffee, E. E., 198
Chambers, C. C., 260
Chapman, D., 228
Chickering, A. W., 132, 151, 222, 332
Cincinnati, University of, instrument from, 335
Clark, B. R., 194
Clearinghouse for Higher Education Assessment Instruments, 325
Code of Federal Regulations, Title 45 of, 124
Cognitive development instruments, 329–330
Coleman, J. S., 192, 193
College Adjustment Scales, 331
College Assessment Program Surveys, 341–342
College Board Student Outcomes Information Services, 119
College Characteristics Index, 201
College Descriptive Index, 342
College Experiences Study, 208
College Interest Inventory, 342
College Outcome Measures Program, 329
College Student Experiences Questionnaire, 161, 201, 331
College Student Inventory, 326
College Student Needs Assessment Survey, 339
College Student Satisfaction Questionnaire, 161–162, 342
Commission on Higher Education, 7
Community College Student Experiences Questionnaire, 331
Comprehensive Alumni Assessment Survey, 328
Computers: for data analysis, 106–107; for tracking client use, 122–123
Confidentiality: in benchmarking, 249; ethics of, 295, 296–297, 300, 305; and reporting results, 277–278; in tracking client use, 123–124
Connoisseurship and criticism, as qualitative method, 82
Consulting Psychologists Press, 329, 341

Context: for assessment, 1–109; and professional standards, 252–272; for student culture, 197
Conyne, R., 335
Cook, S. W., 96
Cook, T. T., 275
Cooperative Institutional Research Project, 44, 119, 226, 336, 344
Core Drug and Alcohol Survey, 334
Cornesky, R., 7
Corrazini, 173
Correlation coefficent concept, 95–96
Council for the Advancement of Standards for Student Services/Development Programs, 30
Council for the Advancement of Standards (CAS) in Higher Education, 13, 252, 253–260, 263, 267, 270, 271
Council on Rehabilitation Education, 264
Cox, P., 133
Crisis orientation, and assessment, 3–4, 144
Criterion measures, and professional standards, 256–257, 263–264
Crosson, F., 262
Crowson, R. L., 81
Culture: assessing, 189–216; characteristics of, 191–194; in comprehensive model, 29; conclusion on, 216; defined, 190; guidelines for assessing, 195–200; levels of, 190, 192–193; methods for, 197–198, 200–210; perspectives of, 189–191, 196, 200; reasons for studying, 194–195; respect for, 196–197; sample assessment of, 210–216

D

Data: access and ownership for, 306; accuracy of secondary, 311–312; organizing, 77–78; in qualitative and quantitative methods, 55, 62; reducing, 76, 231; sources of, for culture assessment, 205–206. *See also* Recording data

Data analysis: in benchmarking, 249; challenges of, 78–79; for culture assessment, 207–209, 212–215; issues of, 48–49; for needs assessment, 140–141; for outcomes assessment, 235–237; in qualitative and quantitative methods, 59–60, 62, 75–79, 106–108

Data collection: in benchmarking, 247–249; for culture assessment, 207–209, 212–215; for environmental assessment, 186; ethical issues of, 292–293; issues in, 40–43; for outcomes assessment, 234–235; in qualitative methods, 63–70; in quantitative methods, 106; for self-study, 257–258; for tracking client use, 120–122. See also Investigators

Databases: for career services, 119–120; institutional, 117–118, 155–156; in student affairs, 118–120

Dean Evans and Associates, 122

DeCoster, D. A., 131

Defining Issues Test, 339

Delworth, U., 173, 179, 184, 187, 188

Deming, W. E., 7, 29, 30, 151

Deutsch, M., 96

Dillard, J. M., 161

Disabled Student Survey, 183, 333

Dobbert, M. L., 293, 296–297, 306–307

Document review: for culture assessment, 206, 209; ethics of, 300; for needs assessment, 135; as qualitative method, 69–70, 80

Dropouts, instruments on, 333–334

Drugs and alcohol, instruments on, 334–335

E

Ecomapping, for environmental assessment, 173–174

Ecosystem model, for environmental assessment, 170–173, 179–188

Educational Planning Survey, 336

Educational Testing Service (ETS), 325, 332, 338, 341, 342, 343

Effectiveness concept, 18

Eisner, E. W., 53, 82

El-Khawas, E., 20, 85

Ely, M., 209

Employer Survey, 335

Entering-Student Questionnaire, 336

Entering Student Survey, 337

Environment: in comprehensive model, 29; dimension of, 220–222, 223–224, 227–228

Environmental assessment: application of, 179–188; aspects of, 166–188; background on, 166–167; conclusion on, 188; defined, 167; ecosystem model for, 170–173, 179–188; elements common in, 177–179; instruments on, 183–184, 335–336; methods for, 182–185; models for, 170–177; multiple perspective model for, 174–175; as ongoing process, 178–179; participant-oriented, 179; and person-environment interaction, 167–170, 173, 175–178; purpose of, 167; settings for, 179–180; steps in, 171–172, 173–175, 180–188

Environmental Assessment Inventory, 183, 335

Erlandson, D. A., 196, 201, 204, 207, 210

Erwin, T. D., 21, 25, 161, 163, 195, 218, 280, 295

Ethical issues: aspects of, 290–314; codes for, 313; conclusion on, 313–314; defined, 291; elements in, 295–296; of evaluator effects, 310–311; and fallacies, 312–313; in field-based research, 296–298; in needs assessment, 131; principles for, 291–294, 321; in research, 294–298; and role conflicts, 307, 309; and subjects, 298–305; in tracking, 123–124

Ethnography. See Qualitative methods

Evaluation: of benchmarking, 250; defined, 18–19; for environmental

assessment, 186–188; formative and summative, 19–20; issues of, 26–27, 50; for needs assessment, 141–142; of outcomes assessment, 238; principle for, 321–322; and quantitative methods, 108–109; and reporting results, 286–288; of self-study, 260
Evans, N. J., 132, 135
Evergreen State College, culture at, 192
Ewell, P. T., 17, 18–19, 218
Extracurricular Involvement Inventory, 331–332

F

Fairbrook, P., 157
Faithfulness, ethics of, 294, 309
Fetterman, D. M., 81, 208, 209
Focus groups: for culture assessment, 207–208; in qualitative methods, 74–75; on satisfaction, 157
Food services, and satisfaction, 156–157
Former Student Questionnaire, 333
Funding. See Resources

G

Gall, J. P., 61, 311
Gall, M. D., 20, 21, 61, 85, 87–88, 94, 98, 311
Gamson, Z., 151
Geer, B., 191
Gilbert, T. F., 175–177
Goetz, J. P., 207
Gottlieb, D., 192
Greenberg, B., 335
Grose, R. F., 311
Guba, E. G., 76, 81, 199, 200, 201, 206, 207, 208, 209, 210, 298, 299, 304

H

H & H Publishing Company, 337
Hall, J., 190, 193
Hanson, G. R., 25

Harm, and ethical issues, 292–293, 298–299
Harris, E. L., 196, 201
Health services and education instruments, 338–339
Hedlund, D., 9
Hierarchical setwise regression, for outcomes assessment, 232–234, 235–237
Higher education, assessment needed in, 5–7
HITECH Press, 330, 332
Hinkle, D. E., 85, 94, 95–96, 98, 236
Hodgkins, B., 192
Hogan, R. R., 340
Hogan, T. J., 150
Honesty, ethics of, 297, 303, 304, 309–310
Hood, A. B., 332
Horowitz, H. L., 192, 194
House, E. R., 312–313
Howe, N., 102
Huberman, A. M., 76, 78
Huebner, L. A., 167, 168–169, 173, 174, 177, 179, 300
Hughes, E. C., 191
Hurst, J. C., 179
Hutchings, P., 17, 22

I

Implementation. See Evaluation; Policy decisions
Indiana University, instrument from, 336
Informed consent: for culture assessment, 199; ethics of, 295, 299–300, 301–303; in tracking client use, 123–124
Input-environment-outcome (I-E-O) model, 218–222, 226–228, 232, 239
Inputs, dimension of, 219–220, 224, 226–227
Institutional Commitment to the Elimination of Alcohol and Other Substance Abuse, 334

Institutional Goals Inventory, 342–343
Institutions: and benchmarking, 240–251; comparability of, 30, 245–247, 250–251; culture of, 189–216; environments of, 166–188
Instruments: annotations on, 326–344; for environmental assessment, 183–184, 335–336; guidelines for, 44–45; issues in choosing, 43–47; for needs assessment, 139–140, 339; norms for, 43–44; for outcomes assessment, 228–229; publishers of, 325–326; for qualitative methods, 46–47, 59, 62; for quantitative methods, 43–46, 59, 62, 90–93; on satisfaction, 161–162, 341–344
Interaction effects, 236–237
International Association of Counseling Services (IACS), 224, 262, 270
Interviews: for culture assessment, 207–209; data analysis for, 77; with focus groups, 74–75; issues of, 46–47; for needs assessment, 135, 139–140; as qualitative method, 63–69, 79–80; questions for, 64–69; role and responsibility for, 70–73; types of, 63–64
Investigators: for culture assessment, 204–205, 211–212; effects of, 310–311; and ethical issues, 290–314; issues of, 47; for needs assessment, 139; neutrality of, 58–59, 71; reporting by, 275–289; respondent relationship with, 59, 62; role and responsibility of, 58–59, 70–73; and role conflicts, 307, 309
Involvement: in benchmarking, 244–245, 250; instruments on, 331–333; and reporting results, 278–279
Involving College Audit Protocol, 208–209 Involving Colleges Interview Protocol, 336
Iowa Test of Student Development, 332

J

Jacobi, M., 14, 278, 286
Jacoby, B., 127

Jahoda, M., 96
Johnson, J. C., 207
Jones, J., 9
Joughin, L., 309
Jurs, S. G., 85, 94, 95–96, 98, 236
Justice, as ethical issue, 293–294, 297–298

K

Kahn, J. V., 94, 95
Kammeyer, K.C.W., 192, 194
Katchadourian, H. A., 193, 194, 195, 216
Kells, H. R., 260
Kelly, E. F., 228
Kennedy, G. E., 160
Kentucky, University of, instruments from, 339, 340
Kerlinger, F. N., 85, 93–94, 98
Kitchener, K. S., 291–295, 298, 303, 330
Klingensmith, J. E., 162
Koeger, S., 333
Korn, W. S., 44
Krueger, D. W., 150
Kuh, G. D., 81, 127, 129, 130n, 131, 145, 149, 190, 191, 192, 193, 194, 196, 197, 198, 199, 200, 201, 203, 204, 205, 206, 208, 209, 211, 336

L

Lauroesch, W., 311
Lawson, J. M., 167, 168–169, 177
Layder, D., 54
Leafgren, F., 156
Learning and Study Strategies Inventory, 337
LeCompte, M. D., 207
Leemon, T. A., 194
Lenning, O. T., 17, 127
Lewin, K., 167–170, 171, 177, 269
Licensure, and professional standards, 265–267
Lincoln, Y. S., 76, 81, 199, 200, 201, 206, 207, 208, 209, 210, 298, 299, 304
Long-Term Alumni Questionnaire, 328

Looney, S. C., 255
Love, P. G., 192, 195, 197, 203
Lozier, G. G., 7
Lyons, J. W., 149, 181, 192

M

Mable, P., 131, 253
MacAleenan, A. C., 127
McCool, S., 7
McCormick, C. H., 127, 143
McMillan, J. H., 201, 202, 208
Magolda, P., 194
Magrath, C. P., 154
Magrath, D. S., 154
Manning, K., 63, 208
Marathon Consulting and Press, 329
Marchese, T. J., 5
Marshall, C., 290
Martin, J., 200
Marton, F., 82–83
Maryland, University of, National Institute Against Prejudice and Violence at, 340
Maslow, A., 131
Massachusetts at Amherst, University of, Project Pulse at, 42
Measure of Epistemological Reflection, 330
Measurement scales, types of, 90–93. *See also* Instruments
Menne, J. W., 162
Meredith, G. M., 160
Merriam, S. B., 81, 209
Metaphors, in qualitative methods, 76, 82
Methods: for culture assessments, 197–198, 200–210; for environmental assessment, 182–185; issues in choosing, 35–36; for needs assessment, 138–139; principles for, 319–320; in quantitative methods, 86–87
MetriTech, 342
Miles, M. B., 76, 78
Miller, T. K., 30, 225, 252, 253, 255, 263, 269
Minnesota, University of, 340: Center for the Study of Ethical Development at, 339; Office for Students with Disabilities at, 333
Minority Student Survey, 340
Mission: academic, 10; and environmental assessment, 181; and satisfaction, 149–150, 163–164
Moffatt, M., 70, 194
Moral development instrument, 339
Morehouse, D., 243
Morgan, D. L., 207, 208
Morgan, G., 191, 201
Morrisey, G. L., 242
Multicultural awareness instruments, 340–341
Multifactor Racial Attitude Inventory, 340–341

N

National Association of Student Personnel Administrators, 10, 131, 313
National Center for Higher Education Management Systems (NCHEMS), 119, 326, 328, 329, 333, 336
National Center on Postsecondary Teaching, Learning, and Assessment, 331, 332
National Commission for the Protection of Human Subjects of Biomedical and Behavioral Research, 296
National Institute Against Prejudice and Violence, 340
National Institute of Education, 5
National Institutes of Health, 124
National Wellness Institute, 339
Naturalistic methods. *See* Qualitative methods
Needs assessment: aspects of, 126–147; in comprehensive model, 28–29; conclusion on, 147; in coordination issues, 145–146; defined, 126–128; functions of, 127; instruments on, 139–140, 339; issues and problems in, 142–147; methods for, 138–139; process of, 136–142; purposes of, 128–131; routine, 144–145; and

student wants, 127; techniques for, 132–136, 146; theory-based, 131–132

Negotiated agreements, ethical issues of, 306–307, 308

Nelson, C. O., 127, 143

Network of Colleges and Universities Committed to the Elimination of Drug and Alcohol Abuse, 334

Neutrality by investigators, 58–59, 71

Newcomb, T. M., 194

Newspapers, student: and needs assessment, 135; and satisfaction, 154–155

Noel Levitz Centers, 162, 325, 326, 343

Nora, A., 201

Nuss, E. M., 193

O

Observation: for culture assessment, 206, 209; ethics of, 299–300; for needs assessment, 135; as qualitative method, 70, 80

Office for Protection from Research Risks, 124

O'Neill, T., 16

Organizations, membership in student, and satisfaction, 153–154

Outcomes, dimension of, 222, 223–224, 226

Outcomes assessment: aspects of, 217–239; background on, 217–218; in comprehensive model, 29–30; conclusion on, 238–239; incomplete models for, 223–224; instruments for, 228–229; model of, 218–222; steps in, 224–238

P

Pace, C. R., 160, 161, 163

Parasuraman, A., 157–158

Parker Cognitive Development Inventory, 330

Participation. See Tracking client use

Pascarella, E. T., 8, 222, 225, 228, 232, 237, 331, 332

Patient Evaluation Forms, 338

Patton, M. Q., 21, 35–36, 39, 40, 46, 53, 55, 56–57, 58–59, 61, 63–64, 66, 67, 68, 71, 78, 85, 208, 210, 298–299, 305, 306, 309, 310–311

Paul, S. C., 173, 174–175, 177

Peer review, and accreditation, 264–265

Pennsylvania State University: Division of Undergraduate Studies at, 336; Integrated Student Information System (ISIS) at, 118

Perry, W., 330

Person-environment interaction, and environmental assessment, 167–170, 173, 175–178

Personnel, principle of, 317–318

Peshkin, A., 53

Pfaffenberger, B., 77

Phenomenography, as qualitative method, 82–83

Pilot testing: for qualitative methods, 42–43; of questionnaires, 134

Planning: for culture assessment, 203–204, 211–212, 214; for environmental assessment, 180–181; strategic, 14, 268–269

Podolske, D. L., 20, 25, 135, 143, 146

Policy decisions: assessment needed for, 15; from benchmarking, 249–250; from outcomes assessment, 237–238; principle for, 321–322; from quantitative methods, 108; from self-study, 259–260

Political evaluation: assessment needed for, 15–16; defined, 20; and environmental assessment, 178; and needs assessment, 143–144; and reporting results, 275, 284–285

Population definition: in environmental assessment, 182; issues in, 33–35; for needs assessment, 138, 146–147; for outcomes assessment, 229; in quantitative methods, 87–90

Presley, C., 334

Problem definition: in benchmarking, 243; in culture assessment,

202; in environmental assessment, 181; issues in, 32–33; in needs assessment, 136–138; in outcomes assessment, 225; in quantitative methods, 86; for self-study, 259

Professional associations, standards of, 252–272

Program: review of, and professional standards, 267–268; and satisfaction, 154

Psychological Assessment Resources, 331

Psychological Corporation, 326, 330

Psychological Development Center, 342

Purpose clarification: in benchmarking, 244; in culture assessment, 202–203; and environmental assessment, 181–182; issues in, 33; for needs assessment, 138; in outcomes assessment, 225–226; principle of, 310–317; for quantitative methods, 86; and reporting results, 276–277

Q

Qualitative methods: advantages and disadvantages of, 60–61, 62; aspects of, 52–83; background on, 52; choosing, 35–36; concepts key to, 54–55, 62; conclusion on, 83; for culture assessments, 201; data in, 55, 62; defined, 21, 53–54; document review in, 69–70, 80; examples of, 79–81; features of, 53–54; focus groups in, 74–75, 157, 207–208; instruments for, 46–47, 59, 62; interviews as, 63–69, 79–80; metaphors in, 76, 82; for needs assessment, 138–139; observations as, 70, 80, 135, 206, 209, 299–300; other, 82–83; quantitative methods compared with, 54–62; researcher role in, 58–59; rigor ensured for, 81; sampling issues for, 39–40; on satisfaction, 162–163; for self-study, 258

Quality: assessment needed for, 12–13; defined, 148–149; and ethical issues, 295; and reporting results, 279–285; and total quality management, 6–7, 28–29, 30, 150–151

Quantitative methods: advantages and disadvantages of, 60–61, 62; approaches in, 86–87; aspects of, 84–109; background on, 885; choosing, 35–36; concepts key to, 54–55, 62; conclusion on, 109; for culture assessments, 201; data in, 55, 62; defined, 20–21, 53, 85; for environmental assessment, 183; and evaluation, 108–109; instruments for, 43–46, 59, 62, 90–93; qualitative methods compared with, 54–62; researcher role in, 58–59; sampling issues for, 37–39; for satisfaction, 160–162; for self-study, 258; statistical analyses in, 93–106; steps in, 85–109

Questionnaires: for environmental assessment, 184–185, 186; guidelines for, 41–42, 133–134; for needs assessment, 132, 133–134, 140

Questions: kinds of, 64–66; for probes and follow-up, 68–69; sequencing of, 66; wording of, 66–68

R

Ragle, J. D., 179

Randolph-Macon Woman's College, culture at, 191

Recent Alumni Questionnaire, 329

Recording data: for environmental assessment, 186; in interviews, 73; issues of, 48; for needs assessment, 140; for outcomes assessment, 235; for quantitative methods, 106

Recruiter Evaluation Survey, 335

Reflective Judgment Interview, 330

Reporting results: accuracy in, 295, 309–310; aspects of, 275–289; audience for, 280–281; background on, 275–276; components in, 282–284;

conclusion on, 288–289; controversial, 284–285; of culture assessment, 209–210, 214, 215–216; dissemination of, 285–286; and evaluation, 286–288; format for, 281–282; issues of, 49–50; for needs assessment, 141; principle for, 320–321; and readability, 284; rules for, 276–286

Reputational rankings and ratings, 265

Research: defined, 21; ethical issues in, 294–298

Residence halls instrument, 341

Resources: for culture assessments, 199; principle of, 320

Respect: for autonomy, 291–292, 300, 303–304; for culture, 196–197

Responsibility, ethics of, 297

Results. *See* Reporting results

Rhoads, R. A., 194

Riker, H. C., 131

Robertson, J. A., 161

Rodgers, R. F., 131

Rodriguez, R. G., 299, 305, 307

Rogers, R. R., 11

Rossett, A., 126–127, 133, 134, 136

Rossman, G. B., 290

Rossman, J. E., 20, 85

Russell, R. V., 70, 198, 299–300

Rutgers University: culture at, 194; observation at, 70

S

Sample error concept, 37, 88–89

Sampling: for culture assessment, 206–207; for environmental assessment, 183; issues in, 36–40; for outcomes assessment, 229; in qualitative and quantitative methods, 55–58, 62; size of, 88–90; types of, 56–57, 87–88

Sanders, J. R., 54, 62n

Satisfaction: active measures of, 157–163, 164; assessing, 148–165; blending methods for, 164–165; in comprehensive model, 29; con-

clusion on, 165; defined, 148–149; instruments on, 161–162, 341–344; measuring, 149–163; principles for, 163–165; static measures of, 151–157, 164

Saunders, R. L., 148–149, 266, 267

Saunders, S. A., 269, 291, 292, 293, 294

Schein, E. H., 190–191, 198, 199

Schiltz, M. E., 311

Schuh, J. H., 6, 52, 77, 129, 149, 151, 152, 154, 179, 180, 191, 198

Science Research Associates, 344

Scouten, E., 340

Scriven, M., 19

Secret shoppers, for satisfaction, 158–160

Self-studies, and professional standards, 254, 255–260, 271

Selltiz, C., 96

Sepich, R., 133

Service utilization. *See* Tracking client use

Shadish, W. R., 275

Sherr, L. A., 7

Shulman, L. S., 36, 56, 85

Siddons, P., 154

Silverman, W. H., 160

Skipper, B. L., 196, 201

Smith, L. F., 294–295, 298, 305

Smith, N., 82

Socialization, and student culture, 192, 193–194

Solmon, L. C., 265

Southern Association of Colleges and Schools (SACS), 263–264

Southern Illinois University, instrument from, 334

Spending patterns, and satisfaction, 152–153

Spendolini, M. J., 241, 242, 243, 246, 247–248, 249

Spivak, R., 133

Spradley, J. P., 208

Stage, F. K., 52, 53, 198

Stamatakos, L. C., 11

Standards: and accreditation, 260–267; applying, 269–271; aspects of, 252–272; background on, 252–253; for certification and licensure, 265–267; in comprehensive model, 30; conclusion on, 271–272; ethical, 290–314; models of, 253–260, 267–269; and self-assessment, 254, 255–260, 271; steps in, 255–260

Stanford University, connoisseurship and criticism at, 82

Starr, A. M., 162

States: assessment mandated by, 5; professional standards in, 270–271

Statistical Analysis System, 107, 235

Statistical Package for the Social Sciences, 107, 235

Statistics: bivariate analyses types of, 101–105; inferential, 98, 100; multiple regression for, 106; multivariate analyses for, 106; for outcomes assessment, 229–234; in quantitative methods, 93–106; significance of, 100; types of measures in, 94–95

Stepwise regression, for outcomes assessment, 230–232

Stern, G. G., 229

Strange, C. C., 167, 169–170

Strategic planning: assessment needed for, 14; and professional standards, 268–269

Strauss, W., 192

Student Adaptation to College Questionnaire, 337

Student affairs: assessment context in, 1–109; assessment dimensions in, 111–272; challenges in, 273–323; databases in, 118–120; instruments for, 325–344; need for assessment in, 3–31; purpose of, 12; survival of, 7–12

Student development: and assessment, 10–11; instruments on, 331–333; and needs assessment, 132

Student Development Associates, 326, 332

Student Development Outcome Assessment Model, 225

Student Development Task and Lifestyle Inventory, 332

Student Experience, 333

Student Health Services Student Survey, 338–339

Student Reactions to College, 337–338, 343

Student Satisfaction: The Freshman Experience, 338, 343

Student Satisfaction Inventory, 162

Student Satisfaction Survey, 343

Student Satisfaction with University Programs and Services, 343–344

Student services, and assessment, 11. See also Tracking client use

Student Survey, 332

Students: adult, 327; cultures of, 189–216; disabled, 183, 333; environment in interaction with, 177–178; instruments on, 336–338; and needs assessment, 126–147; satisfaction of, 148–165; tracking use by, 113–125; wants of, 127

Stufflebeam, D. L., 127, 128, 129, 136, 143

Subjects of research: and ethical issues, 298–305; relationship with, 59, 62

Survey of Academic Advising, 327

Survey of Postsecondary Plans, 338

Survey of Values, 344

Suskie, L. A., 37, 38, 41, 42, 44, 84–85, 89, 90, 96, 97n, 98, 99n, 102n, 103–104, 280–282, 284–285

T

Teeter, D. J., 7

Telephone survey issues, 42

Tennessee, University of: Career Services at, 335; clearinghouse at, 325; Learning Research Center at, 328, 333, 344; Office of Assessment Services at, 326, 335, 338, 343; Student Health Services at, 338

Terenzini, P. T., 5, 8, 17, 25, 84, 217, 222, 225, 228, 237
Testwell Wellness Inventory, 339
Themes and patterns, in data analysis, 76–77
Thomas, J., 145, 146
Thomas, W. L., 255
Thompson, M. J., 269
Thrash, P., 260
Tierney, W. G., 198
Timing, principle of, 317
Tinto, V., 228, 232
Total quality management: and assessment, 6–7, 28–29, 30; and satisfaction, 150–151. *See also* Benchmarking; Quality
Tracking client use: aspects of, 28, 113–125; computers for, 122–123; conclusion on, 125; confidentiality and consent for, 123–124; data collection for, 120–122; databases for, 117–120; of educational programs, 121; of facilities, 121–122; information needed for, 115–116; issues in, 124; reasons for, 113–115; and satisfaction, 152, 155–156; of student contacts, 120–121
Treadway, D. M., 179
Trow, M., 194
Trustworthiness, for rigor, 81
Tschop, P., 339

U
UCLA Drug Abuse Questionnaire, 334–335
U.S. Department of Education, 334
U.S. Department of Health and Human Services, 293
University Residence Environmental Scales, 183, 341
Upcraft, M. L., 6, 9, 84, 217, 222

V
Values: institutional, and standards, 272; instruments on, 344

Van Maanen, J., 189, 193, 194, 196, 197, 198, 203, 209, 210
Variance estimate concept, 233
Veltman, G. C., 179, 180

W
Wallace, W. L., 193, 194
Watson-Glaser Critical Thinking Appraisal, 330
Weber, R., 7
Weidman, J. C., 193, 194, 195
Wesley, A. L., 161
Western Interstate Commission for Higher Education (WICHE), 170–173, 179, 188
Western Psychological Services, 326, 337
Whitt, E. J., 69–70, 81, 129, 135, 149, 189, 190, 191, 193, 194, 196, 197, 198, 199, 200, 201, 203, 204, 205, 206, 207, 208, 209, 314
Wichita State University: and ethical issues, 292; observation at, 135; and persistence, 151
Wiersma, W., 85, 94, 95–96, 98, 236
Wingspread Group in Higher Education, 6
Winston, R. B., Jr., 225, 253, 263, 269–270, 291, 292, 293, 294
Withdrawing/Nonreturning Student Survey, 334
Wolcott, H. F., 53, 210
Worthen, B. R., 54, 62n

Y
Yerian, J. M., 255
Young, F., 338
Young, K. E., 260, 261

Z
Zeithamel, V. A., 157–158